Understanding
Narrative Inquiry

This book is dedicated to my parents, who taught me to become a better educator; my daughter, Eunje, who taught me to become a better person; and my former research participants, then high school students, Matto, Kevin, and Michelle, who taught me to become a better researcher.

Understanding Narrative Inquiry

The Crafting and Analysis of Stories as Research

Jeong-Hee Kim

Kansas State University

Los Angeles | London | New Delhi
Singapore | Washington DC | Boston

SAGE was founded in 1965 by Sara Miller McCune to support the dissemination of usable knowledge by publishing innovative and high-quality research and teaching content. Today, we publish more than 750 journals, including those of more than 300 learned societies, more than 800 new books per year, and a growing range of library products including archives, data, case studies, reports, conference highlights, and video. SAGE remains majority-owned by our founder, and after Sara's lifetime will become owned by a charitable trust that secures our continued independence.

Los Angeles | London | Washington DC | New Delhi | Singapore | Boston

Praise for *Understanding Narrative Inquiry*

"This is a thorough and inclusive book that can serve as an excellent introduction to narrative forms of qualitative research in the fields of education, medicine, psychology, and legal studies. But **Understanding Narrative Inquiry** *may also serve to extend the knowledge of researchers and practitioners in those fields who are already familiar with this rapidly maturing inquiry approach. Extremely well researched and referenced, it deftly addresses sophisticated theoretical and philosophical underpinnings of narrative research, including the rationales and justifications for engaging in both storytelling and the analysis of stories. And it also explores a wide variety of helpful strategies for interviewing, fieldwork, and writing. But just as importantly, it grounds and humanizes its sophisticated scholarship through an inviting, conversational style replete with personal anecdotes, while its many concrete examples of research practice in action further enhances its usefulness. A remarkable achievement."*

—Tom Barone, *Professor Emeritus, Arizona State University*

"This is an outstanding text on narrative inquiry. Kim offers the historical and philosophical context for narrative research, ample methodological instruction, and robust examples, making this a truly comprehensive text. I am particularly impressed with her attention to the different genres of narrative including arts-based and visual-based. This is a must-read for anyone interested in narrative research."

—Patricia Leavy, *PhD, independent scholar and author of* Method Meets Art: Arts-Based Research Practice

"Jeong-Hee Kim masterfully positions readers to enter the storied fabric of human life through the medium of narrative inquiry. Readers across all disciplines and interests will find themselves locating and articulating the textured significances of stories as research. Philosophical/theoretical connections substantively frame and permeate the text with readers importantly gaining context, language, and capacities to design and undertake fitting narrative inquiries. The concrete examples depicting a cross section of genres and the inclusion of a glossary make this comprehensive text an invaluable resource for all interested in crafting and analysis of research through narrative inquiry."

—Margaret Macintyre Latta, *Professor and Director, Centre for Mindful Engagement and Graduate Programs, Faculty of Education, University of British Columbia Okanagan, Canada*

"This text offers novice and practicing scholars of narrative inquiry provocative philosophical and methodological insights. The text is beautifully written and draws on art, music, religion, philosophy, and literature to inform researchers' understandings."

—Mary Louise Gomez, *University of Wisconsin–Madison*

"The author's use of a conversational tone—as if she is talking directly to her students—while guiding the reader through complex theoretical material is noteworthy, as are the expertly designed 'Questions for Reflection' and the 'Activities' sections at the end of each chapter. This text will be of interest to anyone teaching Qualitative Research Methods looking for ways to engage their graduate students."

—Thalia M. Mulvihill, *Ball State University*

SAGE

Los Angeles | London | New Delhi
Singapore | Washington DC | Boston

FOR INFORMATION:

SAGE Publications, Inc.
2455 Teller Road
Thousand Oaks, California 91320
E-mail: order@sagepub.com

SAGE Publications Ltd.
1 Oliver's Yard
55 City Road
London EC1Y 1SP
United Kingdom

SAGE Publications India Pvt. Ltd.
B 1/I 1 Mohan Cooperative Industrial Area
Mathura Road, New Delhi 110 044
India

SAGE Publications Asia-Pacific Pte. Ltd.
3 Church Street
#10-04 Samsung Hub
Singapore 049483

Acquisitions Editor: Helen Salmon
Editorial Assistant: Anna Villarruel
Production Editor: David C. Felts
Copy Editor: Kristin Bergstad
Typesetter: C&M Digitals (P) Ltd.
Proofreader: Sally Jaskold
Indexer: Kathy Paparchontis
Cover Designer: Anupama Krishnan
Cover Image: Tom Parish
Marketing Manager: Nicole Elliott

Printed in the United States of America.

Library of Congress Cataloging-in-Publication Data

Kim, Jeong-Hee

Understanding narrative inquiry: the crafting and analysis of stories as research/Jeong-Hee Kim.

pages cm
Includes bibliographical references and index.

ISBN 978-1-4522-8278-7 (pbk.: alk. paper)

1. Narrative inquiry (Research method) I. Title.

H61.295.K56 2015
001.4'33—dc23   2014049296

This book is printed on acid-free paper.

15 16 17 18 19 10 9 8 7 6 5 4 3 2 1

Brief Contents

Detailed Contents

About the Author

Jeong-Hee Kim is associate professor in the Department of Curriculum and Instruction at Kansas State University. Kim is an experienced narrative inquirer whose research centers on a phenomenological understanding of the stories of school people as a way to inform the areas of curriculum studies and teacher education. She has received two awards—Outstanding Narrative Research Article in 2007 and Outstanding Narrative Theory Article in 2009—from the Narrative Research (Special Interest Group) at the American Educational Research Association (AERA). She has also received the Faculty Excellence in Research/Creative Activities Award from the College of Education at Kansas State University in 2011. Her recent publications can be found in the *Journal of Curriculum Studies, International Journal of Qualitative Studies in Education*, and *Educational Philosophy and Theory*. She currently teaches graduate courses on curriculum theory, narrative inquiry, and action research in education.

Preface

After summer break was over, I went to visit my colleague in her office to chat. Her office was usually rather dark and plain, except for the many interesting books ensconced in wall-long bookshelves. But on this day, it felt unusually bright and welcoming. I assumed she must have added better lighting, and that proved to be the case. She had a new, cozy-looking desk lamp. In the middle of our chat, however, something else caught my attention. Hanging on the wall to my left was a patchwork quilt, which I didn't remember seeing previously. It was a beautiful artwork, about three-and-a-half feet by four feet, in shades of purple. I had to exclaim, "What a beautiful quilt this is!" My colleague brightened with a wide smile and said proudly, "Yes, it's beautiful, isn't it? My aunt made it for my birthday." I don't have any hand-craft skills whatsoever, so I was amazed by the fact that my colleague's aunt had made such an incredible thing by hand. So many pieces of cloth in rectangles, triangles, and other shapes and colors were deliberately put together to create a divergent but convergent whole. I asked, "How did she do that?" "Well, it's her hobby. She collects various pieces of clothing that used to be worn by her kids, grandkids, and other family members. She cuts them into different shapes and sews them together in her own design. It is painstaking work that takes hours and hours. I know; it's amazing."

"So, each individual piece holds a personal memory and meaning? And this entire quilt has hidden stories?"

"Pretty much. My aunt said this patchwork quilt has even some pieces of clothing I wore when I was a young child as well as pieces from garments worn by my cousins, nephews, and nieces. So, this quilt is really precious to me." My colleague's right hand was over her heart, seemingly to emphasize the quilt's meaning to her, as we looked into each other's eyes in silence.

I had never viewed a patchwork quilt as a collection of stories. I would have never guessed that each piece of cloth in this superb quilt had a story to tell, and it could evoke fond memories for the people who lived those stories.

I returned to my office and sat in front of my laptop, which has been my close friend for quite some time now. I drank one more sip of coffee that was already cold. I needed to write this Preface by Monday; but I'd been haunted by "writer's block" for the last few days.

Suddenly, my fingers were eager to move on the keyboard. As I typed, inspired by the beautiful quilt I had just seen, I began to understand that this book has become a metaphoric quilt.

I welcome you to the world of my quilt. Each chapter, each section, each paragraph, and even each sentence in this book, has personal meanings and memories in relation to narrative inquiry. I drew upon the work of wonderful scholars, philosophers, and theorists who have shaped my thinking and the thinking of others. I used my previous writings from my own research and teaching. I shared my personal stories, good and bad, in hopes these will help you tease out your own personal stories. More important, I incorporated my former and current students' stories, which may resonate with you. Many parts of this book convey aspects of myself, my relationship with others, and their relationships with me, all of which have impacted my journey of becoming. I hope reading this book will become part of your journey of becoming as well.

Metaphorically speaking, each narrative inquiry is a quilt made out of pieces of personal and social stories that may be collected from any walk of life. The quilt is a reflection of a part of the world in which we live. Methodologically speaking, narrative inquiry is an interdisciplinary, qualitative research that pursues a narrative way of knowing by exploring the narratives or stories of participants. It includes but is not limited to autobiography, autoethnography, biography, life history, oral history, life story, personal narrative, performance narrative, and arts-based narrative (e.g., poetry, novel, fiction, short stories, or creative nonfiction, photographs, visual narrative, and more). It has become an increasingly influential research methodology in humanities and social science research fields such as anthropology, psychology, sociology, philosophy, literature, education, medicine, and law, to name a few. It is easier than ever to find a friend or a colleague who conducts narrative inquiry. Clearly, narrative inquiry is flourishing; it is everywhere (see Connelly & Clandinin, 1990; Chase, 2005; Denzin, 2005). With the burgeoning interest in narrative inquiry, there have been a slew of book publications as well as journal articles on narrative inquiry. Noticing this driving trend, a pioneer of narrative Jerome Bruner (2002) asked a rhetorical question, "Do we need another book on narrative?" (p. 1).

Indeed. Do we need another book on narrative? Perhaps.

Susan Chase states that narrative inquiry is still "a field in the making" (2005, p. 651). I concur, and also feel that narrative inquiry should continue to be a field in the making, questioning and (re)defining itself. There are many researchers and graduate students learning to be narrative researchers, who find narrative inquiry rich but complicated, approachable but elusive, and well defined but still perplexing. Courses on narrative inquiry are offered seldom or not at all in many institutions, and instructors of those courses tend not to have extensive training in narrative inquiry, but they are learning on the job, as Josselson and Lieblich (2003) noted. On the surface, we celebrate narrative inquiry's seeming popularity; in reality, however, a lot of us still feel that we are living on academic archipelagos in our own departments, colleges, and universities, as Mishler expressed in an interview with Clandinin and Murpy, "people [narrative inquirers] are still reporting that they feel like outsiders in their department of psychology or sociology or whatever" (Clandinin & Murphy, 2007, p. 641). There is a noticeable gap in academic culture here; hence, there is a need for another book on narrative inquiry—in fact, not just one, but many more, to make narrative inquiry a more rigorous research practice.

Books are often written by experts who claim to have authoritative knowledge about the topic of their books. That is not the case for this book. In a recent TED Talk, Stuart Firestein, biology professor at Columbia University, argued that what drives science is "not knowing," that is, ignorance. Firestein says not knowing or ignorance is about puzzling over difficult questions, unsettled problems, and further, what remains to be done. Hence, it is this state of ignorance that drives the advancement of science.

Similarly, what drove me to write this book was my own pursuit of not knowing, that is, my own puzzles and quandaries related to narrative inquiry over many years of working and teaching as a narrative inquirer. People ask me what narrative inquiry is and, ironically, I find this simple question difficult to answer because (a) there are so many narrative researchers in different disciplines who have adopted narrative theory and method in different ways; (b) the narrative field is changing and evolving; and (c) narrative inquiry attempts to embrace diversity in methods, avoiding association with only one of the many currently in use. As a narrative inquirer and teacher of a course on narrative inquiry, I had more questions than answers. So, I wanted to explore some of the confounding issues of the why, how, and what of narrative inquiry, and at the same time illuminate the current state of the field of narrative inquiry across disciplines. If you have picked up this book because you don't know much about narrative inquiry and have many questions about it, then, you're in the right place! We can pursue together the unknowns, puzzles, and questions related to narrative inquiry, spurred on by our "ignorance" and not knowing.

Therefore, this book is not a "boilerplate" of what narrative inquiry is, or a "quick guide" to how to conduct narrative inquiry. It is quite comprehensive in nature, intended to expose you to the entire narrative inquiry process, possibly embracing both the breadth and depth of narrative inquiry. There are philosophical, theoretical, and artistic aspects, which may seem at first to have little to do with narrative inquiry, but which are placed strategically to function as "speed bumps" (Weis & Fine, 2000) to help you slow down, pause, and take the time to think and reflect, using your imagination and creativity. Further, I intend this book to provide a "zone" or a major confluence where different narrative "currents" meet, exchange ideas, learn from each other, share questions and curiosities, all of which will eventually lead to enhancing the field of narrative inquiry. Although this book will provide you with hands-on, down-to-earth tactics you can use for your research, I am hoping that it will go beyond that. Ultimately, I want this book to be your inspiration, something that triggers your imagination and creativity, which will take you to a place you have never dreamed of reaching with your research.

As more and more researchers become interested in narrative research, there is a need for us to develop it as a more rigorous research methodology, with firm underpinnings of theoretical, philosophical, social, and practical considerations. This book is an effort to meet such a need. It will address the challenges and questions that are typically brought to the forefront in narrative inquiry courses and introductory/advanced qualitative research methods courses. Therefore, this book is primarily geared toward students and novice researchers who aspire to be quality researchers, and quality narrative researchers in particular. In addition, experienced researchers who have intellectual curiosity about both a theory of narrative and its methodology as a form of inquiry are welcome to join us.

Now I'll give you a brief peek at the inside of the book. Each chapter has the following pedagogical features to help your understanding: It begins with a list of chapter topics, questions to consider, and an introductory narrative, all of which are aimed to orient you to the main ideas of the chapter. Each chapter concludes with reflective questions, activities, and a list of resources that you can use to deepen your knowledge. Please note that you don't need to read the book from Chapter 1 to the end in a linear fashion. Although the chapters are logically connected to each other, each chapter is independent enough to stand on its own; you can enter any chapter any time depending on the stage of your research. If you have any comments or questions about the book, direct them to me at jhkim@ksu.edu. I'm happy to hear your feedback.

Chapter 1, Locating Narrative Inquiry in the Interdisciplinary Context

In this chapter, we first locate qualitative research against the enduring backdrop of Positivism, which leads to the discussion of narrative inquiry along with the concepts of narrative and story. We see how different disciplines have established narrative inquiry in their fields, opening the door for the synergy of interdisciplinarity and responding to criticisms of narrative inquiry. The chapter concludes with a story that will help us to think about what it means to be a narrative inquirer.

Chapter 2, Philosophical/Theoretical Underpinnings of Narrative Inquiry

You will find this chapter much longer than the other chapters. There are many important grand theories, but I could hardly "catch" them all in this limited space. So, I have chosen the theories that I've used for my work and those in which I've had keen interests. The purpose is to introduce you to the theoretical/philosophical underpinnings of narrative inquiry and help you become theorizers and philosophers of narrative inquiry. Because I have seen many students struggle with their interpretive paradigms, I want to provide you with a basis for understanding some of the most important philosophical/theoretical paradigms. It is my hope that you will delve farther into your choice of theory on your own, going beyond the resources provided here. In this chapter, I first discuss the role of theory, and then address macro-level theories that are used as interpretive paradigms and meso-level theories that are used as methodological paradigms. The relationship each theory has with narrative inquiry is also discussed.

Chapter 3, Narrative Research Design: Engaging in Aesthetic Play

This chapter is to help you engage in aesthetic play with your narrative research design. You will learn about the value of interacting with your research ideas playfully and seriously at the same time as you design your research project. After all, designing anything is an aesthetic experience. Research design is not an exception. To be able to design your research, you will need to equip yourself with foundational knowledge about research design. More important, you will need to nourish your imaginative vision with intellectual curiosity, flexibility, openness, and attunement to your research. This chapter is a helpmate that will inspire you to have an aesthetic experience through your research. We discuss basic elements of qualitative research design as well as particular elements of narrative inquiry design.

Chapter 4, Narrative Research Genres: Mediating Stories Into Being

In continuation of narrative research design, this chapter is to help you explore different narrative research genres or narrative forms you can employ for the kinds of stories you would like to tell. Acting as an imaginary "midwife" who mediates stories into being, you will consider a genre or multiple genres in which your research will be represented, whether it is autobiographical, biographical, or arts-based. This chapter aims to provide you with possible narrative research genres that you can choose from, in conjunction with ways to honor our storytellers' own dignity and integrity.

Chapter 5, Narrative Data Collection Methods: Excavating Stories

This chapter takes you to the world of data collection methods that you can use to excavate stories. It not only provides you with down-to-earth logistics and skills that you may be familiar with in collecting qualitative research data but also inspires you with creative ideas to uncover stories that are silently tucked in every corner of human life. This chapter will help you turn your research toolbox to a cabinet of curiosities.

Chapter 6, Narrative Data Analysis and Interpretation: "Flirting" With Data

In the world of research, *flirting* is not a "bad" word, borrowing the term from the field of psychoanalysis. It asks you to undo your commitment to what you already know. Flirting with your narrative data in the process of analysis and interpretation will allow you to dwell on what is perplexing, rendering surprises and serendipities in relation to your research findings. This chapter introduces you to different methods of narrative data analysis and interpretation. You will learn that sorting and sifting through your data for analysis and interpretation is like undergoing a symbolic rite of passage to your researcher-hood.

Chapter 7, Narrative Coda: Theorizing Narrative Meaning

Narrative coda is what comes after the story, which contributes to fulfilling the inquiry aspect of narrative research. For example, we may be good at telling a story but not very good at developing the story's linkage to a broader social context. Hence, this chapter is to help you theorize the meaning of stories, understanding how a story transfigures the commonplace. It offers ways to (un)finalize your research, answering the question of "so what" and learning to become a Scheherazade, who keeps the stories going.

Chapter 8, Critical Issues in Narrative Inquiry: Looking Into a Kaleidoscope

In this chapter, we will address some critical issues in narrative inquiry that require us to employ an imaginary kaleidoscope through which we embrace unexpected patterns and changes. The metaphor of a kaleidoscope is meant to broaden our ways of thinking and understanding, so that we can push the boundaries of narrative inquiry and become the most thoughtful and ethical researchers we can be.

Chapter 9, Examples of Narrative Inquiry: Theory Into Practice

This chapter provides you with several narrative inquiry examples to give you an opportunity to see how theories of narrative inquiry outlined in this book can be used in research practice. You can use this opportunity to practice, question, adapt, and create a narrative inquiry format that may best suit the purpose of your narrative research. I provide an excerpted example of each narrative genre, following general information about the article. After each excerpt, a few questions are suggested to help guide a discussion.

Chapter 10, Epilogue

This chapter is my personal letter to you, which aims to bring you home from our journey together.

Acknowledgments

This book would not have come to fruition without the support of family, friends, colleagues, artists, and students.

First of all, I thank my editor, Helen Salmon, for her enduring support and insights. Helen was the lynchpin of this project; this book would not have been possible without her vision. I also thank Anna Villarruel, Helen's assistant, who was always prompt and precise. In addition, many thanks go to Kristin Bergstad, copyeditor, and David Felts, production editor, who provided relentless editing help on the manuscript. I am indebted to the reviewers of my book, Timothy G. Davies, Colorado State University; Mary Louise Gomez, University of Wisconsin-Madison; Thalia M. Mulvihill, Ball State University; and other anonymous reviewers. Their expertise and constructive feedback strengthened the book in many ways. My heartfelt thanks go to Marjorie Hancock and Linda Duke, my dear friends and mentors, who read my draft chapters and gave me thorough editorial feedback. Their time and expertise were invaluable to this project. I sincerely thank the artists that inspired me throughout the writing process. Joan Backes, Jim Richardson, Richard Ross, and Tom Parish, who generously gave me permission to use their outstanding artwork. I also thank the Beach Museum of Kansas State University for hosting such amazing artists and exhibitions, which became the main source of my creativity and imagination. I am deeply grateful to my friends Linda Duke, Marrin Robinson, Rosemary Talab, and Barbara Veltri, for our weekly hikes, walks, and talks, which kept me sane during challenging times. I thank my department and college for their continuous support for my research. In particular, I am grateful to Dean Debbie Mercer for her genuine caring and support; two department chairs, Gail Shroyer and Todd Goodson, for their professional support and encouragement; Paul Burden for his valuable tips for book proposal writing; Mary Hammel, Art DeGroat, and Rusty Earl for their technological support; and my wonderful colleagues for their collegiality and moral support. I am deeply grateful to all of my brilliant students, but in particular, Jodie, Kevin, Art, Jess, Steve, Chance, and Ron, whose thinking and writing were always thought-provoking, and who kindly gave me permission to use their class assignments. I also want to thank those who helped shape my research and teaching: Tom Barone, my dissertation advisor, mentor, and teacher of narrative inquiry, whose writings and thinking became the foundation of my research; Margaret Macintyre Latta, my informal mentor and friend, whose scholarly work broadened my horizon; and my former research participants, especially Kevin, Matto, and Michelle, whose life experiences taught me so much about being a researcher.

Finally, I cannot thank my family enough for their endless love, which has sustained me during the long, lonely journey of writing. My late father; my mother, who has thankfully recovered from a serious illness; my daughter, Eunje, who taught me to be a better mother; and my family, Sookhee, Bonghee, Dale, Abby, Seungbyn, Kwibin, and Kwanbin, who always believed in me. I am forever grateful.

CHAPTER TOPICS

CHAPTER 1

Locating Narrative Inquiry in the Interdisciplinary Context

QUESTIONS TO CONSIDER

- Why narrative inquiry?
- What is narrative inquiry?
- What makes narrative inquiry distinct from other qualitative research?
- What makes a narrative inquirer a narrative inquirer?

INTRODUCTION

I first learned **narrative inquiry** from the course offered by my dissertation advisor and mentor, Tom Barone. I was immediately drawn to narrative inquiry by its approachability, artistic quality, and non-pedantic nature that values stories of laypeople. It seemed to me that narrative inquiry was a perfect hybrid of research and art (literary art in particular) that could satisfy my inclination for literature. It was "highly seductive" (Munro Hendry, 2007, p. 488) indeed! By the end of that semester, I found myself falling in love with narrative inquiry and decided to use it for my dissertation research although I did not have my dissertation topic yet.

It seems that the author has blindly fallen in love with narrative inquiry even before collecting data, and tries to legitimate its usefulness.

This was a critique I received from one of the anonymous reviewers of Spencer Foundation grant proposal draft that drew upon my dissertation research. When I read this harsh review, I felt quite embarrassed, with my face secretly blushing no end. How did the reviewer detect my "blind" love for narrative inquiry? How could the reviewer sound so disdainful of my love for it? How did the reviewer know I was "trying to legitimate its usefulness" even before collecting data? My romance with narrative inquiry encountered such unprecedented embarrassment, but not to the extent that I wanted to run away. In fact, the to-the-point, direct critique ended up being a bitter medicine that provided an opportunity to see my "reality": an immature understanding of my partner, narrative inquiry. I should have known what Amia Lieblich advised: to be a "good" narrative scholar requires "maturity and experience and sensitivity to people and to one's self, which takes years to develop" (Clandinin & Murphy, 2007, p. 642). I concur. It takes years to develop the maturity and experience that are required to be a good narrative researcher. I had to work at it. I am still working at it.

My journey to becoming a better narrative inquirer continues. As a self-claimed romanticist, I first started by questioning my romance with narrative inquiry. As Munro Hendry (2007) questioned her relationship to narrative by being suspicious of the power of narrative because she felt she had "gotten stuck" in particular narratives (p. 488), it was now my turn to be deeply engaged in questioning my own relationship to narrative. So, what is narrative inquiry? Do I know "my partner" well enough? What was it about narrative inquiry that was so fascinating to me? Didn't I secretly think it was an "easy" methodology that concerns "just telling stories" (Clandinin, Pushor, & Orr, 2007, p. 21)? With a pang of guilty conscience, I had to find ways to elevate my "puppy love" to a mature one to avoid future harsh critiques.

I imagine that some of you are also apprehensive about your "love affair" (or lack thereof) with narrative inquiry. I want you to come along as I dig deeper into narrative inquiry in a quest for what it means to be a narrative inquirer. The purpose of this chapter, therefore, is to take you to a world of narrative inquiry that is conceptually "demanding and complex," although "the rewards are potentially great" (Andrews, Squire, & Tamboukou, 2011, p. 16). We will explore some fundamental issues that will help us know narrative inquiry better. We will first locate qualitative research against the enduring backdrop of Positivism, which will lead to a discussion about narrative inquiry along with the concepts of narrative and story. And we will see how different disciplines have established narrative inquiry in their fields, opening the door for the synergy of interdisciplinarity and, in the process, responding effectively to criticism. The chapter concludes with a story that will help us to think about what it means to be a narrative inquirer.

Scientific Research and Qualitative Research in Tandem

In the first half of the nineteenth century when the scientific movement, industrialism, and technological development rose in Western society, Positivism emerged to give an account of the triumphs of science and technology. It was Auguste Comte who first expressed the three principal doctrines of Positivism: first, empirical science is the only source of positive knowledge about the world; second, human pursuits of mysticism, superstition, and metaphysics are pseudo-knowledge and prevent the development of scientific knowledge; and third, scientific knowledge and technical control no longer exclusively belong to natural sciences, but are pervasive in political and moral arenas as well. By the late nineteenth century, this philosophical doctrine of Positivism had become prevalent as a way to apply the achievements of science and technology to the well-being of humankind. Since then, Positivist epistemology had become built into the academy, where scientific and quantitative research has been the main research paradigm (Schön, 1983).

We all know that Positivism is still alive and well in academia. In fact, many U.S. government policy statements allude to the long-term marriage between positivistic knowledge and power that Lyotard (1979/1984) insightfully questioned. The French postmodern philosopher Jean-François Lyotard points out that in the scientific, positivistic age, the current status of scientific knowledge gives way to the prevailing powers more than ever before, revealing that "knowledge and power are simply two sides of the same question: Who decides what knowledge is, and who knows what needs to be decided?" (p. 9). For Lyotard, the question of knowledge and power is a question of government, which then takes the form of grand narrative. Consider, for example, the American government's grand narrative in education, the No Child Left Behind (NCLB) Act of 2001. It used the phrase *scientifically based research* 111 times (Barone, 2007), calling explicitly for the use of scientific research that involves hard, measurable, and quantifiable data. Further, the National Research Council (2002) published the report *Scientific Research in Education,* calling for evidence-based education research that uses "rigorous, systematic and objective procedures to obtain valid knowledge" (Maxwell, 2004, p. 3). In this positivistic epistemology, human conditions that are the focus of research are viewed as value-neutral, fixed, stable, predictable, and generalizable enough that those prescribed solutions can be applied universally to every human situation. Such adherence to positivistic thinking demonstrates "good, ol' boy" thinking, or "déjà vu all over again" (Lather, 2008, p. 362), making us feel that "the art of storytelling is coming to an end" (Benjamin, 1969, p. 83).

Yet in spite of the prevalence of this grand narrative, researchers have become increasingly aware of the flaws and limitations of applying solely scientific knowledge to the understanding of human phenomena fraught with complexity, uncertainty, uniqueness, instability, ambiguity, and value-conflict. Schön (1983) uses a road metaphor to point out how positivistic professionals walk on the "high, hard ground" where rigor or relevance is equivalent to scientifically based research seeking technical solutions. These positivists, according to Schön, tend to be inattentive to uncertain, unique, and unstable phenomena, discarding them as messy and trivial data. On the other hand, there are those who choose the "swampy lowlands" and carefully engage in messy but crucially important problems, focusing on "experience, trial and error, intuition, and muddling through" (p. 43). They resist confining their research to a narrowly defined, scientific experiment that provides quick fixes as they understand that addressing the problems of human concern is like walking in a "swamp." This metaphor of "walking on the swampy lowlands" (p. 43) is further supported by Dewey (1934/1980) who posits that human beings excel in complexity and minuteness of differentiations because:

> There are more opportunities for resistance and tension, more drafts upon experimentation and invention, and therefore more novelty in action, greater range and depth of insight and increase of poignancy in feeling. As an organism increases in complexity, the rhythms of struggle and consummation in its relation to its environment are varied and prolonged. (p. 23)

The limitations of scientific knowledge seem obvious, then; to rely solely on scientific research to understand the complexity of human life seems like asking Siri on my iPhone to cry for me when I get lost on the road. Luckily, the research community has experienced a paradigm shift (Kuhn, 1962) that has given greater recognition to qualitative research as researchers acknowledge that complex human concerns cannot be understood by testable observation, general principles, and standardized knowledge. Conducting qualitative research is like walking in the swamp, not an easy path, but one that explores the complex issues of what it means to be human. A number of scholars now recognize that both scientific research and qualitative research should exist in tandem and be valued without privileging one over the other.

In the first edition of *Handbook of Qualitative Research,* the editors, Norman Denzin and Yvonna Lincoln (1994), define qualitative research as:

> multimethod in focus, involving an interpretive naturalistic approach to its subject matter . . . qualitative researchers study things in their natural settings attempting to make sense of, or interpret, phenomena in terms of the meanings people bring to them. (p. 2)

Qualitative research informed by different interpretative paradigms uses words rather than numbers in its analyses and focuses on understanding human action through interpretation rather than prediction and control. It does not reduce research results to certainty and measurable objectivity. Rather, it involves an interpretive, naturalistic approach to research phenomena, making sense of the meaning that people bring to them (Denzin & Lincoln, 2011). In their recent fourth edition of the *Handbook of Qualitative Research* (2011), Denzin and Lincoln further situate qualitative research within eight historical moments, which overlap and exist simultaneously in the present:

1. The Traditional (1900–1950)

2. The Modernist or Golden Age (1950–1970)

3. Blurred Genres (1970–1986)

4. The Crisis of Representation (1986–1990)

5. The postmodern, a Period of Experimental and New Ethnographies (1990–1995)

6. Postexperimental Inquiry (1995–2000)

7. The Methodologically Contested Present (2000–2010)

8. The Future (2010–)

For Denzin and Lincoln (2011), the future (which is now) is concerned with moral and critical discourse about democracy, globalization, and justice, confronting the grand narrative associated with evidence-based scientific research. They posit that any definition of qualitative research *must* work within these complex eight historical moments where qualitative research goes through reflexive, complicated developmental processes. Where, then, does narrative inquiry belong in these historical moments? Denzin and Lincoln place it in the fifth moment (1990–1995), sixth moment (1995–2000), and on, as they consider that the postmodern and postexperimental moments "were defined in part by a concern for literary and rhetorical tropes and the narrative turn, a concern for storytelling, for compositing ethnographies in new ways" (p. 3).

Narrative Inquiry

The beginning of the narrative turn, however, was signaled even before the fifth moment, with two issues of the journal *Critical Inquiry* published in 1980 and 1981, which became a book titled *On Narrative* (1981). Thomas Mitchell, editor of *Critical Inquiry*, declared, "The study of narrative is no longer the province of literary specialists or folklorists borrowing their terms from psychology and linguistics but has now become a positive source of insight for all the branches of human and natural science" (p. ix). The book has an interdisciplinary collection of essays written by important thinkers in literary theory, philosophy, anthropology, psychology, theology, and art history, which indicates just how narrative has become the focal point of research in social, human, and even natural sciences.

As you see, building on the tenets of qualitative research including frameworks, research methods, approaches, and strategies, narrative inquiry has become a field of its own with its distinctive nature and significance (Bruner, 2002; Clandinin, 2007; Pinnegar & Daynes, 2007). Using narrative as a phenomenon to understand multidimensional meanings of society, culture, human actions, and life, it attempts to access participants' life experiences and engage in a process of storytelling (Leavy, 2009). Polkinghorne (1988) believes that working with stories holds significant promise for qualitative researchers because stories are particularly suited as a linguistic form in which human experience can be expressed. Narrative inquiry utilizes interdisciplinary interpretive lenses with theoretically, philosophically diverse approaches and methods, all revolving around the narratives and stories of research participants.

Since narrative and story are the center of gravity around which the apparatus of narrative inquiry revolves, an in-depth look at the concepts of narrative and story seems worthwhile. In general, they are used interchangeably, one acting as a synonym for the other (McQuillan, 2000). However, difficulties in doing narrative research might arise due to different opinions about conceptually subtle delineations of "story," "narrative," "narrative inquiry," "narrative analysis," and so on (Verhesschen, 2003). For instance, we say "storytelling" not "narrative telling," "narrative inquiry" not "story inquiry." Further, "narratology" is an official term for the study of narratives, but I have encountered hardly any literature on "storytology" or "storyology" (the study of stories). How, then, are narrative and story the same and how are they different?[1]

What Is Narrative?

First of all, etymologically speaking, the word *narrative* is from Latin *narrat-* "related," "told"), *narrare* ("to tell"), or late Latin *narrativus* ("telling a story"), all of which are akin to Latin *gnārus* ("knowing"), derived from the ancient Sanskrit *gnâ* ("to know"). Thus, a **narrative** is a form of knowledge that catches the two sides of narrative, telling as well as knowing (McQuillan, 2000). A narrator, then, could mean one who knows and tells. As we noted, the importance of narrative in human life has long been recognized, from Aristotle, known as the first great analyst of narrative (Boyd, 2009), to the contemporary philosophers and theorists. As Benedetto Croce, Italian theorist and philosopher, puts it, "Where there is no narrative, there is no history" (cited in Altman, 2008, p. 1). As such, narrative is one of the few human endeavors that is widely spread as a basic aspect of human life and an essential strategy of human expression.

Genealogically, the most common and oldest form of narrative is known to be myth (*mythos* in Greek means "story"), which is transmitted from one generation to the next. Myth is available in most every culture, and has a sacred ritual function that is used to maintain each culture's origins and heroic ancestors, including Greek, Biblical, Native American, Celtic, Persian, Asian, and Incan, just to name a few. According to Kearney (2002), mythic narrative can be divided into two main branches: *historical* and *fictional*. Historical narrative depicts the reality of past events or what actually happened, which leads to the genre of biography. Fictional narrative, on the other hand, focuses on the redescription of events in relation to "beauty, goodness or nobility" (p. 9), with rhetorical devices such as metaphor, allegory, or others, used to embellish the events, which leads to literary genres of narrative and is discussed in Chapter 4.

Our understanding of what narrative is has been propelled by the study of narratives, or narratology (a term coined by philosopher and literary theorist Tzvetan Todorov), which addresses narrative theories. Narratology is a sophisticated area of study that is "international and interdisciplinary in its origins, scope, and pursuits and, in many of its achievements, both subtle and rigorous" (Herrnstein Smith, 1981, p. 209). Early narrative theorists such as Todorov, Roland Barthes, and Gérard Genette established narratology, mainly structuralist narratology, following Saussure's distinction between *la langue* (signifying language system and its principles) and *la parole* (individual utterances produced based on the language system). They privileged the language system or semiotic principles (*la langue*) over the individual narratives (*la parole*). Their main concern was to examine universal structural units that they believed exist independently of individual differences, producing specific narrative texts that can be used as a model for theory building. Thus, they focused on a description of structural analysis of narrative, suggesting that a narrative is a "complex structure that can be analyzed into hierarchical levels . . . of its syntactic, its morphological, or its phonological representation" (Herman, 2005, p. 29).

However, as structuralist linguistics began to be criticized for its deficiencies in the domain of linguistic theory itself, the limitations of structuralist narratology also came to the surface (see Chapter 2 for more details on structuralism and poststructuralism). For example, Fludernik (2005) points out that the problems with this early structuralist narratology lie in the difficult relationship between theory and practice, which begs the critical question, "So what?—What's the use of all the subcategories for the understanding of texts?" (p. 39). In addition, the studies of narrative, influenced by the rise of poststructuralism and cultural studies, began to diverge into a series of subdisciplines of narrative theory. Moving away from the structuralist account, narrative theory became integrated into other disciplines such as the psychoanalytic narrative approach, feminist narratology, and cultural studies–oriented narrative theory, extending to philosophy, linguistics, cultural studies, education, and even the empirical sciences (Fludernik, 2005).

We are also indebted to philosophy for the importance of narrative. Lyotard (1979/1984) posits the importance of narrative as a way of knowing in his seminal book, *The Postmodern Condition*. He claims that there is a preeminence of narrative in the formulation of traditional knowledge. Taking Plato's allegory of the cave as an example of "how and why men yearn for narratives and fail to recognize knowledge" (p. 29), he argues positivistic scientific knowledge cannot be formulated without resorting to narrative knowledge. According to Lyotard, traditional, scientific knowledge:

> [c]annot know and make known that it is the true knowledge without resorting to the other, narrative, kind of knowledge, which from its point of view is no knowledge at all. Without such recourse it would be in the position of presupposing its own validity and would be stooping to what it condemns: begging the question, proceeding on prejudice. (p. 29)

Thus, for Lyotard, narrative is "the quintessential form of customary knowledge, in more ways than one" (1979/1984, p. 19). Then, it makes sense when Hendry (2010) suggests that all inquiry, scientific or non-scientific, quantitative or qualitative, positivist or interpretive, is narrative because all inquiry involves a meaning-making process and uses narrative for it.

Narrative is everywhere, as "we dream in narrative, day-dream in narrative, remember, anticipate, hope, despair, believe, doubt, plan, revise, criticize, construct, gossip, learn, hate and love by narrative" (Hardy, cited in MacIntyre, 2007, p. 211). Barthes (1982) also sums up the ubiquity of narrative in all cultures:

> Narrative is present in myth, legend, fable, tale, novella, epic, history, tragedy, drama, comedy, mime, painting . . . , cinema, comics, news item, conversation. Moreover, under this almost infinite diversity of forms, narrative is present in every age, in every place, in every society; it begins with the very history of mankind and there nowhere is nor has been a people without narrative. All classes, all human groups, have their narratives, enjoyment of which is very often shared by men with different even opposing, cultural backgrounds. Caring nothing for the division between good and bad literature, narrative is international, transhistorical, transcultural: it is simply there, like life itself. (pp. 251–252)

I find the statement, "Narrative is international, transhistorical, transcultural" to be powerful. It seems that narrative is in a time machine that transcends time and space. Similarly, MacIntyre (2007) believes that human actions are enacted in narratives as we all live out narratives in our lives. Each of us is at the center of constant action all our lives. Hence, narrative is "not the work of poets, dramatists, and novelists reflecting upon events which had no narrative order before one was imposed by the singer or writer; narrative form is neither a disguise nor decoration" (p. 211). What MacIntyre contends is that we are the authors of our lives (Holquist, 2011), which we share with others. MacIntyre emphasizes this social dimension (sharing with others) when he says, "I am part of [others' stories], as they are part of mine. The narrative of any life is part of an interlocking set of narratives" (p. 218). Because we understand our own lives in terms of the narratives that we live out and share, narrative is appropriate for understanding the actions of others. For MacIntyre, therefore, "the unity of a human life is the unity of a narrative quest" (p. 219), which is one of the pursuits of narrative inquiry.

What Is Story?

How, then, do we distinguish narrative from story, or story from narrative? Although these two terms are used interchangeably, as mentioned, many literary theorists agree that a narrative is a recounting of events that are organized in a temporal sequence, and this linear organization of events makes up a story (Abbott, 2002; Cohan & Shires, 1988). Thus a **story** is a detailed organization of narrative events arranged in a (story) structure based on time although the events are not necessarily in chronological order. This is what we mean when we say stories (not narratives) have a beginning, middle, and end, which become, in Ricoeur's phrase, "models for the redescription of the world" (cited in Bruner, 1986, p. 7). In this sense, a story has a connotation of a "full" description of lived experience, whereas a narrative has a connotation of a "partial" description of lived experience. Therefore, story is clearly a higher category than narrative as the latter constitutes the former; and they are deeply intertwined. Stories, just like narratives, are always subject to interpretation; that is, stories as we know them begin as interpretations (Kermode, 1981). Narratives constitute stories, and stories rely on narratives.

Robinson and Hawpe (1986) point out that a story straddles the line between uniqueness and universality. It has the particularity of an event because it is told in a contextualized account. It also resembles other stories to varying degrees because it is built upon a generic set of story structure and relationships. The propositions of story are delineated in Table 1.1.

Table 1.1 Propositions of Story

- Stories are everywhere.
- Not only do we tell stories, but stories tell us: If stories are everywhere, we are also in stories.
- The telling of a story is always bound up with power, property, and domination.
- Stories are multiple: There is always more than one story.
- Stories always have something to tell us about stories themselves: They always involve self-reflexive and metafictional dimensions.

(Bennett & Royle, cited in McQuillan, 2000, p. 3)

As we can understand from the propositions of story, telling stories is the primary way we express what we know and who we are. We tell stories about particular people and their unique experiences, and those stories tell us. By way of storytelling, we allow stories to travel from person to person, letting the meaning of story become larger than an individual experience or an individual life. Such storytelling provides inspiration, entertainment, and new frames of reference to both tellers and listeners (Shuman, 2005); this has been pervasive in human history, as seen in the ancient myths, fables, and parables. We human beings are, indeed, a "story-telling animal" (MacIntyre, 2007, p. 216). Storytelling is "active, organic, responsive, reactive; it is here and now (Jackson, 2007, p. 9) and it improves our social cognition and the conceptions of our own lives beyond the here and now (Boyd, 2009; Martin, 1986), reflecting power relationships and domination. Walter Benjamin (1969) offers an insightful view of storytelling[2]:

> The storytelling that thrives for a long time in the milieu of work—the rural, the maritime, and the urban—is itself an artisan form of communication, as it were. It does not aim to convey the pure essence of the thing, like information of a report. It sinks the thing into the life of the storyteller, in order to bring it out of him again. Thus the traces of the storyteller cling to the story the way the handprints of the potter cling to the clay vessel. (p. 91)

This view of storytelling as an "artisan form of communication," not as reporting, is significant because it justifies the functions of storytelling. Table 1.2 provides five functions of storytelling that Kearney (2002) discusses extensively drawing upon Aristotle's Poetics: Plot (*mythos*), Re-creation (*mimesis*), Release (*catharsis*), Wisdom (*phronesis*), and Ethics (*ethos*). I find his discussion informative and insightful, as it has many implications for the work we do as narrative inquirers.

Table 1.2   Functions of Storytelling

1. *Plot (Mythos)*: *Mythos* is a way of making our lives into life-stories. It gives a specific grammar to this life of action by transposing it into (1) a telling; (2) a fable or fantasy; and (3) a crafted structure. Through these three transpositions, mythos becomes poiesis that has beginning, middle, and end.

2. *Re-creation (Mimesis)*: *Mimesis* is a pathway to the disclosure of the inherent "universals" of existence that make up human truth. It is not a mere imitation but an active remaking of the real world in light of its potential truths, interweaving past, present, and future.

3. *Release (Catharsis)*: *Catharsis* has the power to change us by transporting us to other times and places where we can experience things otherwise. It provides the power of empathy vicariously experienced through narrative imagination and ethical sensitivity that helps us to understand what it is like to be in someone else's shoes.

4. *Wisdom (Phronesis)*: *Phronesis*, a form of practical wisdom, provides knowledge about the world learned from stories. It is prudence that is capable of respecting the particularity of situations as well as the universality of values in human actions.

5. *Ethics (Ethos)*: *Ethos* is an ethical role of storytelling. Storytelling shares the ethic of a common world with others since the act of storytelling involves the audience.

(Adapted from Kearney, 2002)

Narrative Inquiry in Different Disciplines

Now that we have some clarifications about narrative, stories, and storytelling that are the center of gravity around which narrative inquiry revolves, I'd like us to look into how narrative inquiry has developed into a rigorous research methodology. We will see how it satisfies the stringent research community, and how it has been established in different disciplines. We are indebted to Jerome Bruner as one of the main contributors who established narrative inquiry as a legitimate form of generating knowledge in social science research. Bruner (1986) postulates that human beings utilize two modes of thought or two ways of knowing in understanding truth and reality: *paradigmatic mode* and *narrative mode*. According to Bruner, the two modes are not reducible to one another although they can be complementary, used as means for convincing each other. However, they differ radically in their procedures for verification: The paradigmatic mode establishes formal and empirical proof by creating well-formed arguments while the narrative mode establishes verisimilitude by creating good stories that are lifelike. Let me elaborate.

The paradigmatic mode of thinking, or scientific thinking, influenced by Positivism (as discussed earlier) is pervasive in quantitative research because it relies on theory, scientific analysis, logic, empirical evidence, and discovery guided by a reasoned hypothesis. It is concerned with general categories and general principles in an effort to fit particular, individual details into a larger pattern and to minimize ambiguity but discern universal truths that can be empirically tested. Its primary goal is to promote certainty by seeking a definite answer, or objective truth, linking the particular to the general and reducing it to rules and generalities that are applicable to and replicable in other situations (Polkinghorne, 1995). Thus, the paradigmatic mode seeks to "transcend the particular by higher and higher reaching for abstraction" (Bruner, 1986, p. 13). The product of this mode is generalizations of rules and principles, which are context-free, value-free, usually abstract, reproducible, and testable only by further formal scientific activity.

The narrative mode of thinking, on the other hand, typically considered less important than the paradigmatic in the academy, uses stories to understand the meaning of human actions and experiences, the changes and challenges of life events, and the differences and complexity of people's actions. It strives to put events into the stories of experience in order to locate the experience in time and place. It incorporates the feelings, goals, perceptions, and values of the people whom we want to understand, and thus also leads to ambiguity and complexity. In so doing, it provides explanatory knowledge of human experiences, which allows the portrayal of rich nuances of meaning in emplotted stories. These nuances and ambiguities cannot be expressed or tolerated in the paradigmatic mode of knowledge with its insistence on definitions, statements of fact, and generalized rules (Polkinghorne, 1995).

The paradigmatic mode is rigid, eliminating ambiguity and uncertainty while the narrative mode is flexible, open to multiple interpretations. The former is concerned with generalities of causes, categories, and principles by focusing on reducing particularities to fit into a larger pattern. The latter is concerned with particularities, analogies, and metaphors that go beyond the facts and rules, and that provide open invitations to different reactions, feelings, and interpretations for the reader (Spence, 1986). The establishment of the narrative mode of knowing as parallel with and complementary to the paradigmatic, scientific mode has legitimized and justified the use of stories in research, hence narrative inquiry as a research methodology.

Van Manen (1990) suggests the significance of using story in human, social science research, further validating narrative inquiry, as shown in Table 1.3.

In the following, we will now look into how various disciplines have pursued narrative inquiry to inform their fields. From many possibilities, I have selected only four areas for discussion: psychology, law, medicine, and education. I hope you will find commonalities among them as well as differences across the disciplines. Most important, I hope you will notice how each discipline has responded to the positivistic view of research, valuing narrative as the core of the human research, which in turn brings all the disciplines together with one commitment: to improve the human condition through narrative.

Table 1.3 Significance of Using Story in Human and Social Science Research

- Story provides us with *possible human experiences.*
- Story enables us to experience life situations, feelings, emotions, and events *that we would not normally experience.*
- Story allows us to broaden the horizons of our normal existential landscape by creating *possible worlds.*
- Story tends to appeal to us and involve us *in a personal way.*
- Story is an artistic device that lets us turn back to *life as lived,* whether fictional or real.
- Story evokes the quality of vividness in *detailing unique and particular aspects of a life* that could be my life or your life.
- Great stories *transcend the particularity of their plots* and protagonists, etc., which makes them subject to thematic analysis and criticism.

(Adapted from van Manen 1990, p. 70, italics in original)

Narrative Inquiry in Psychology: "Psychology Is Narrative"

Sarbin (1986) claims that narrative psychology is a viable alternative to the positivist paradigm as it leads to a more profound understanding of the human condition than the scientific examination of the authoritarian, mechanistic perspective that is prevalent in the traditional psychology. In fact, Sarbin proclaims, "psychology is narrative" (p. 8). This shift makes clear that "story making, storytelling and story comprehension are fundamental conceptions for a revived psychology" (p. vii), which reveals the storied nature of human action. Thus, the movement to stress the narrative in psychology and psychoanalysis became pervasive in the early 1980s as leading psychologists such as Schafer (1981), Spence (1982, 1986), and Sarbin (1986) examined the practice of psychoanalysis from a narrativist viewpoint. For example, using a root metaphor, Sarbin (1986) considers the narrative an organizing principle for human action as human beings think, perceive, imagine, and make moral choices based on narrative structures. Sarbin states:

> The narrative is a way of organizing episodes, actions, and accounts of actions; it is an achievement that brings together mundane facts and fantastic creations; time and place are incorporated. The narrative allows for the inclusion of actors' reasons for their acts, as well as the causes of happening. (p. 9)

The narrative tradition in psychoanalysis is by some traced to Freud (see Spence, 1982; Schafer, 1981; Steele, 1986). Spence posits that it was Freud who "made us aware of the persuasive power of a coherent narrative" (Spence, 1982, p. 21). Steele (1986) also acknowledges, "Freud is a builder of narratives which he uses to make sense of people's lives" (p. 257). Gergen and Gergen (1986) contend that there are progressive and regressive narratives in the three major developmental theories in psychology: Skinnerian behavioral learning theories, Piagetian cognitive learning theory, and Freudian psychoanalytic theory.

They particularly elaborate how Freud's psychoanalytic theory offers two competing narratives, progressive and regressive in character, as it acknowledges that the normal person's social adaptation presents the progressive narrative while disclosing the psychic burden of the past experience (regressive narrative).

Similarly, drawing upon Freud's narrative tradition, Spence (1982) distinguishes narrative truth from historical truth. The former, narrative truth, is what the patient says to the psychoanalyst; and the latter, historical truth is what actually happened, an account of the way things were. Sometimes, narrative truth, is confused with historical truth. Spence, for example, notes, "What is effective for a given patient in a particular hour (the narrative truth of an interpretation) may be mistakenly attributed to its historical foundations" (p. 27). Spence's point is that because narrative truth works so well within the clinical setting heavily influenced by Freud's success with the narrative tradition, psychoanalysts have a tendency to rely on narrative truth without considering historical truth, which might be different from the narrative truth. Thus, psychoanalysts should not rely completely on what a particular patient tells at a particular time and place in order to come to a conclusion. This is why it becomes particularly important to recognize the difference between narrative and historical truth. As we recognize the particular virtues of the narrative truth as well as its limitations, we can be in a better position to build more lasting theories of narrative psychology.

In sum, narrative psychology emphasizes the importance of narrative in psychology that has had an influence on the way the psychologists listen to patients, the way the patients tell their stories, the way psychoanalytic research is conducted, and the way psychologists observe their patients. For example, psychoanalysis (e.g., Schafer, 1981, 1992) not only relies on patients' storytelling but methodologically utilizes dialogue and narrative for clinical purposes. According to Fludernik (2005), such uses of narrative in therapy practice and in the theorization of the therapeutic process are what makes narrative research effective in an interdisciplinary manner, methodologically and theoretically.

Narrative Inquiry in Law: Promoting Counter-Stories

The relationship between narrative and law is ancient, and narrative has played a crucial role in the legal field for a long time (Winter, 1989). If you take a moment to visualize a court scene, you will picture witnesses and defendants telling stories, while prosecutors, lawyers, and judges produce narratives of legitimation and justification to convince juries. Despite this early, close relationship between narrative and law, it was not until the early 1980s that much interest in narrative in legal scholarship took hold, thus giving rise to conferences and publications on legal narrative. The legal community also became more diverse as it began to admit women and people of color to the field (see Scheppele, 1989).

Cover (1983) points out that in the normative world we live in, the rules and principles of justice, the formal institutions of the law, are important, and narrative plays an important part in such a world. Cover elaborates:

No set of legal institutions or prescriptions exists apart from the narratives that locate it and give it meaning. . . . Once understood in the context of the narratives that give it meaning, law becomes not merely a system of rules to be observed, but a world in which to live. (p. 4)

For Cover (1983), therefore, narratives are the codes that relate the normative system to our social constructions of reality and to our visions of what the world might be or should be. Hence, a legal story told before a court of law, involves a comparison of what actually happened with what should or should not have happened in relation to precedents (just like Spence's notions of historical vs. narrative truth), which will allow us to envision what the world should be. Thus, appropriate precedents become templates for guiding an attorney in organizing a story of the present case.

In his little book that I cherish, Bruner (2002) talks about how narrative tradition connects the three areas of law, literature, and life. He discusses how literature has found its way into the law field, leading to a new and respectable genre of legal scholarship, Law and Literature. Bruner states that there is an "odd kinship" (p. 61) of literary and legal narratives in that literature looks to the possible, exploiting the semblance of reality, while law looks to the actual record of the past. However, the two share the medium of narrative, "a form that keeps perpetually in play the uneasy alliance between the historically established and the imaginatively possible" (p. 62). Thus, he argues that there is always a question of the dialectic (opposing stories) between the comfort of the familiar past and the allure of the possible, as narratives change to "reflect the spirit of their times" (p. 58). Therefore, narrative is, according to Bruner, "the medium par excellence for depicting, even caricaturing, human plights" (p. 60) and storytelling is "a way to give the law back to the people" (p. 60).

Opposing stories, or counter-stories, are called for by Delgado as "a way to give the law back to the people." Delgado, in his letter to editors of *Michigan Law Review,* makes a convincing case as to why legal scholarship needs to pay attention to narratives. (Later, Delgado founded critical race theory with Derrick Bell, which we shall discuss in Chapter 2.) In the letter, Delgado writes, "We believe that stories, parables, chronicles, and narratives are potent devices for analyzing mindset and ideology—the bundle of presuppositions, received wisdoms, and shared understandings against a background of which legal discourse takes place" (Delgado, 1988, cited in Scheppele, 1989, p. 2075). Delgado's letter led to a special issue on Legal Storytelling for *Michigan Law Review* the following year. In his contribution to the special issue, Delgado (1989) examined the use of stories in exploring the struggle for racial reform and proposed counter-hegemonic storytelling to sensitize the human conscience to prevailing social and legal stories that have been shaped by the dominant group's ideology.

Delgado (1989) believes that counter-stories function to question complacency regarding mainstream ideas and the status quo. That is, they are the means by which groups contest the dominant ideology and the assumptions that support it. As counter-stories are the concrete particulars of the experience of individuals or groups that conventional legal reasoning excludes, they can open new windows into reality, help us construct a new world, and imagine possibilities for life other than the ones we lived. Delgado further suggests that in order for counter-stories to be effective, they must be or must appear to be "noncoercive," meaning that counter-stories should:

> [i]nvite the reader to suspend judgment, listen for their point or message, and then decide what measure of truth they contain. They are insinuative, not frontal; they offer a respite from the linear, coercive discourse that characterizes much legal writing. (p. 2415)

Although much of narrative inquiry in legal practice takes the form of counter-stories, we should understand that counter-stories are not easily accepted by the law. In fact, Brooks (2005) cautions how the law can be entangled with narrative and may react to it with unease and suspicion, resulting in the neglect of narrative as a legal category. Courts tend to cling to the controlling view that there is only one true version of a story and only one right way to tell it. Such a positivistic view of narrative in the legal system, however, is "possibly an act of repression, an effort to keep the narrativity of the law out of sight" (p. 415). Courts can deny the differences and disagreements that inevitably exist in a pluralistic society. The first step for legal storytellers, then, is to realize that the presence of different, competing versions of a story is itself an important feature of the dispute at hand that courts are being called upon to resolve (Scheppele, 1989).

In summary, despite the traditional legal court's challenges to oppositional narrative, or counter-storytelling, narrative inquiry in law has made "an undeniable impact in legal-scholarly debates, if not necessarily in the practice of law" (Brooks, 2005, p. 416). As we have seen, the field of law has become more conscious of its storytelling functions and its procedures more open to challenges to traditional procedures. Hence, "The Narratology in the courtroom? Yes, it is very much needed there" (p. 426).

Narrative Inquiry in Medicine: Developing Narrative Competence

Medicine has always been a storied enterprise (Peterkin, 2011) and has never been without narrative concerns (Charon, 2006). Hunter (1986, 1989), for example, emphasized the significant role of medical anecdotes and case stories in training physicians by stating, "Medicine is filled with stories. Indeed, among the scientific disciplines, medicine can be characterized by its dependence on narrative" (1986, p. 620). Hunter argued how patients' stories have an important epistemological function that builds up medical knowledge, directing us to areas needing research attention. She proposed that medicine is a form of casuistry that is essentially case-based knowledge and practice, hence, the "narrative construction of illness is a principal way of knowing" (1989, p. 193).

In recent years, the need to humanize medicine has increasingly been recognized among medical practitioners, and narrative is gaining its momentum in the field of medicine as a result (Bury, 2001; Charon, 2006; Charon & DasGupta, 2011). In the United Kingdom, for example, narrative-based medicine, in which doctors are asked to write, read, and share texts about their clinical encounters, has gained popularity, offering meaningful approaches to understanding and improving the doctor-patient relationship (Peterkin, 2011). In North America, narrative medicine with a more humanizing philosophy of care has also emerged as an alternative. This practice recognizes the importance of narrative knowledge in working with patients, while incorporating the knowledge and practice of the social and human science field (Charon, 2006). Thus, narrative medicine is an effort to combine the humanities and medicine, and is specifically defined as "medicine practiced with the narrative competence to recognize, absorb, interpret, and be moved by the stories of illness" informed by contemporary narratology (Charon, 2006, p. vii).

Linking medicine with the humanities was popularized by Robert Coles, psychiatrist and professor at Harvard Medical School. His penchant for storytelling as a way to promote understanding, empathy, and moral imagination in the doctor-patient relationship is well evidenced in his autobiographical work, *The Call of Stories* (1989). In it, he probes his own teaching practices in which he used the established literary canon to link medicine and humanities, and urges his medical students to pay attention to their patients' stories and to find meaning in them.

Narrative medicine also developed with the work of anthropologists in the mid- and late 1980s who began to examine narrative in medicine and its relationship to illness and healing in the context of biomedical care (Mattingly, 2007). Drawing upon narrative theory from multiple disciplines such as sociology, linguistics, literary theory, philosophy, and psychology, narrative medicine focuses on the meaning-making aspects of illness and healing, rendering the "illness narrative" (Kleinman, 1988). Since the early 1980s, Cheryl Mattingly (2007), an anthropologist, has undertaken ethnographic studies of occupational therapists and other health professionals such as physical speech therapists, rehabilitation aides, oncologists, surgeons, nurses, and so on. In her study of occupational therapists, for example, Mattingly (1998a) examined how narrative was an important vehicle for therapy, which allowed therapists to deal with human agency, complex social relationships, emotions, cultural differences, and other matters that challenge the dominant medical discourse.

Similarly, Drummond's (2012) narrative study in medicine on a resident's experience with a young dying patient discusses how narrative medicine requires practitioners' moral judgment. For example, through narratives, the resident Nick and his fellow residents considered the dying patient with drug addiction a victimizer, not an innocent victim. They suspected that the dying patient could be a potential abuser of the medical system, trying to fool the resident into the role of "dealer" (p. 139) who could supply drugs for the patient. Using the embedded narratives in a medical case discussion, Drummond shows how the residents began to play the role of adjudicators of "who deserves care" rather than the role of "deliverers of care" (p. 140). Drummond finds that narratives play a role in not only moving the discussion from clinical reasoning to narrative reasoning, but also to moral reasoning about who deserves (or does not deserve) medical care. Thus, Drummond urges medical researchers to interrupt the dominant narratives in the medical field that call for an objectivity/neutrality and to learn to value practitioners' moral judgment through narrative.

The field of narrative medicine is currently striving to take into consideration the whole person of a patient as a practical undertaking (Charon, 2006). According to Charon, what is currently missing in the field, however, is an acknowledgment of narrative competence as fundamental skills that need to be required of medical professionals. These narrative competence skills that are lacking include "how to systematically adopt others' points of view; how to recognize and honor the particular along with the universal; how to identify the meaning of individuals' words, silences, and behaviors" (p. 10). Charon further notes:

> A medicine practiced with narrative competence will more ably recognize patients and diseases, convey knowledge and regard, join humbly with colleagues, and accompany patients and their families through the ordeals of illness. These capacities will lead to more humane, more ethical, and perhaps more effective care. (p. vii)

Therefore, Charon argues that health professionals like doctors, nurses, and social workers need to be equipped with narrative competence for their medical practice. She suggests that narrative competencies could allow them to better serve the sick with carefully thought-out, respectful care attuned to the needs of individual patients. She proposes narrative competence as a basic skill needed by health professionals to fulfill their responsibilities.

In order to equip medical students with such narrative competence, some medical schools and residency training programs have developed humanities-based courses. They aim to help medical students develop empathy, trustworthiness, awareness, and sensitivity toward patients. In so doing, they also explicitly recognize the art of medicine even while upholding the importance of technical knowledge and skills (Reilly, Ring, & Duke, 2005). For example, the College of Physicians and Surgeons, Columbia University's School of Medicine in New York, and the Occupational Science Department at the University of Southern California's School of Medicine, just to name a few, have been working to find ways to train health professionals to approach, elicit, interpret, and act on their patients' stories, and to use stories to better understand dimensions of human experience as opposed to the persistent fact and number focus of conventional medicine (Charon & DasGupta, 2011). As Mattingly (1998b) argues, narrative medicine or clinical storytelling is becoming one way in which "clinical practice exceeds the bounds of its own ideology" (p. 274).

The most recent reaffirmation of the efforts of these narrative scholars in medicine, health, and bioethics seems to come in the birth of a journal, entitled *Narrative Inquiry in Bioethics,* published by the Johns Hopkins University Press. In its inaugural issue (2011, Volume 1.1), the editors recognize how narratives and personal stories can inform bioethics discourse concerning healthcare, health policy, and health research. They point out that research in this area has been plagued with instances of dehumanizing treatment of patients, not to mention the fact that their needs have been ignored or poorly met. Hence, the goal of this journal is to "rehumanize ethical decision-making" (DuBois, Iltis, & Anderson, 2011, p. v) while promoting empathy and the fair and just treatment of human beings through narrative inquiry.

It is particularly encouraging and enlightening to see that fields like medicine whose research methods traditionally excluded the narrative mode of knowing, heavily relying on the paradigmatic mode, are paying attention to narratives and personal stories. Research shows that the field of medicine has benefited in many ways from the development of narrative medicine. In brief, narrative medicine, as a way of (re)humanizing the field, helps medical practitioners develop narrative competence, in enabling them to act upon their empathy, trust, and sensitivity.

Narrative Inquiry in Education: Exploring the Lived Experience

Narrative inquiry is an influential research methodology in education, gaining popularity as the "theory/practice/reflection cycle of inquiry" (Smith, 2008, p. 65). In studying the lived experiences of teachers and students (Casey, 1993; Clandinin & Connelly, 2000; Clandinin et al., 2007; Goodson, 1995), narrative researchers in education have strived to honor teaching and learning as complex and developmental in nature, seeking connections and continuous engagement in reflection and deliberation (Kim & Macintyre Latta, 2010). As teacher education programs put more emphasis on what it means to be a reflective practitioner (Schön, 1983), teachers' stories of their personal and professional experiences along with stories of young children (e.g., Kohl, 1967; Kozol, 1991; Paley, 1986) have become key devices in understanding the complex nature of a classroom.

It is Connelly and Clandinin (1990) who first used the term *narrative inquiry* in the educational research field in an article published in *Educational Researcher*. With the view that education is the construction and reconstruction of personal and social stories of teachers and learners, Connelly and Clandinin argue that narrative inquiry embodies theoretical ideas about educational experience as lived and told stories. The main claim for the use of narrative in educational research is that narrative is a way of organizing human experience, since humans lead storied lives individually and socially. Using Dewey's theory of experience as the conceptual and imaginative backdrop, Connelly and Clandinin posit that the study of narrative is "the study of the ways humans experience the world" (p. 2). Experience is the starting point and the key term for narrative inquiry. Connelly and Clandinin (2006) later offered a more elaborate definition of narrative inquiry where story is used as a portal through which a person enters the world and by which their experience of the world is interpreted and made personally meaningful. They state:

> Viewed this way, narrative is the phenomenon studied in inquiry. Narrative inquiry, the study of experience as story, then, is first and foremost a way of thinking about experience. Narrative inquiry as a methodology entails a view of the phenomenon. To use narrative inquiry methodology is to adopt a particular narrative view of experience as phenomena under study. (p. 477)

Considering the continuity and wholeness of an individual's life experience as their research problem, Clandinin and Connelly (2000) believe that education and educational studies are a form of experience since "education is a development within, by, and for experience" (Dewey, 1938/1997, p. 28), which will be discussed more in depth in Chapter 2.

There has been a series of narrative turns (see Pinnegar & Daynes, 2007) that reaffirms narrative research as a legitimate way of knowing that shapes our conceptions and understandings about the world around us, as we saw in Bruner's work (Bruner, 1986, 1994). These narrative turns in educational research come to challenge traditional paradigmatic epistemological paradigms that view the very nature of knowledge as objective and definite (Munro, 1998), and to problematize the unitary way of knowing (Polkinghorne, 1988). In using narrative, educational researchers intend to interrogate the nature of the dominant curricular stories through which humans have shaped their understandings of education and schooling within the paradigmatic perspective. In so doing, narrative educational researchers purport to bring the lived experiences of teachers and students to the forefront as a way to reshape the views on education (Casey, 1993; Connelly & Clandinin, 1990; Goodson, 1992; Kim, 2010b; Munro, 1998; Sparkes, 1994). In a true sense, the telling of the story is the construction of a life (Hatch & Wisniewski, 1995). This storying is, thus, believed to have the potential for advancing educational research in representing the lived experience of schooling (Goodson, 1995, 2000; Goodson & Gill, 2011).

Narrative inquiry in education is grounded in educational philosophy. For instance, Dunne (2005), a contemporary educational philosopher, emphasizes the importance of stories in education research, drawing upon Aristotle, who long ago suggested that stories can instruct and move us precisely because they reveal universal themes in their depiction of particular cases and characters. From Dunne's perspective, stories are critical in education research because stories in a particular setting are capable of illuminating other settings through their epiphanic power (hence, *catharsis*). Therefore, according to Dunne (2003), research into teaching is best served by narrative modes of inquiry since "to understand a teacher's practice (on her own part or on the part of an observer) is to find an illuminating story (or stories) to tell of what she has been involved in with her students" (p. 367). Thus, education researchers realize that they need to be good storytellers and listeners to make sense of what goes on in schools and engage in dialogues among students, parents, practitioners, researchers, and policy makers. In so doing, they seek to view the lives of others and their own lives as a whole into which the fragmented parts of narratives can be integrated and embodied (MacIntyre & Dunne, 2002).

The popularity of narrative inquiry in education has extended beyond research methodology. Narrative inquiry is now used as a curricular and pedagogical strategy in the field of teacher education (Conle, 2003; Coulter, Michael, & Poynor, 2007); as an intentional reflexive process of teachers interrogating their own teaching and learning (Lyons & LaBoskey, 2002); as a medium for professional development for pre-service and in-service teachers (Conle, 2000a); and as an inquiry into the interrelationships between literacy, pedagogy, and multiculturalism (see Clark & Medina, 2000; Grinberg, 2002; Phillion, He, & Connelly, 2005). Through this burgeoning of publications in recent years, narrative inquiry has made a transformative impact in education and contributed to the advancement of education research methods and methodology, curriculum, teaching and learning, and teacher education.

Some Cautionary Tales About Narrative Inquiry

By juxtaposing narrative inquiry at work in different disciplines (e.g., psychology, law, medicine, and education), we can see the ways thinkers in each discipline have turned to narrative and stories to better inform their fields after realizing the limitations of positivistic inquiry. Although we looked at only four areas here, there are many other disciplines that pursue narrative inquiry, e.g., anthropology, sociology, history, and philosophy, just to name a few. Narrative research is now being used in economics (Rodrik, 2011; Romer & Romer, 2010) and business (Dennings, 2005). Narrative sociology has been developed to understand sociohistorical and sociopolitical realities (Gotham & Staples, 1996). Narrative inquiry in and about organizations was also established in the early 1990s (Boje, 1991; Czarniawska, 1997, 2007).

These disciplines share a deep understanding of the importance of narrative, story, and storytelling, while each discipline has its unique understandings and approaches to narrative inquiry. The commonalities and the variegations of narrative inquiry that we see in different disciplines are harbingers of the "maturation of the field of narrative research, one that refuses a tight set of methodological and definitional prescriptions, but that is still being tilled by members of a community of discourse who sense a certain degree of professional affinity" (Barone, 2010, p. 149).

With this good news, you might feel ready to join me on the journey of narrative inquiry. No, not yet. Before you are comfortably ensconced in your seat, I'd like to point out some cautionary tales that have been issued by established narrative inquirers, so that you don't "blindly" fall in love with narrative inquiry, as I did. I want to take you back to my journey to become a better narrative inquirer, which I mentioned in the beginning of this chapter.

I shared with you that the beginning of that journey started with the questioning of my romance with narrative inquiry, not in order to discard it but to get to know it better. To do that, I had to be pragmatic, neither too ideal nor too romantic; I had to think about my reality, such as getting a job after graduation. I started posing questions to myself: Would I be able to get a job with my background in narrative methodology, not in quantitative research? Would I be able to publish my narrative work? I started feeling torn to realize that my partner (narrative inquiry) might not be that great after all if it didn't get me the job I wanted. To make these doubts worse, as I was digging deeper into narrative inquiry, I was encountering some serious concerns and even some warning signs to novice narrative researchers, raised by prominent names. Basically, those concerns from different disciplines—albeit somewhat old but still true today—point to the fact that it could be a risky business for a fledgling researcher to be involved with narrative inquiry, as we live in the age when the positivistic view of world dominates the discourse on research. Sarbin (1986), for example, states:

> Some critics are skeptical about the use of the narrative as a model for thought and action as they think storytelling is related to immaturity and playfulness associated with fiction, fantasy, and pretending. But this world view places a high value on positivism, technology, and realism and a low value on imagination. (p. 12)

Casey (1995) also adds:

> However much we may be convinced of the compelling nature of narrative, we must move beyond such statements of inevitability to explain the extraordinary self-conscious fascination with story telling that prevails at present. (p. 212)

Munro's (1998) concern is more specific. She posits that the neglect of the inquiry aspect in narrative inquiry would allow narrative research to "romanticize the individual and thus reify notions of a unitary subject/hero" (p. 12), resulting in narrative inquiry being subject to be criticized as a "form of narcissism or navel gazing" (p. 12). Conle (2000b) echoes this concern by pointing out how some narrative researchers are "so taken up by the process, enjoying the doing of it, that they are not much interested in characterizing its inquiry quality abstractly" (p. 190), which causes the doubts of critics of narrative work. Barone (2007) also speaks of "narrative overload" (p. 463), which may result in a pointless and futile cacophony of individual interests. This concern of "narrative overload" reflects the skepticism (even antagonism) that some critics have with regards to narrative inquiry: How can anyone's story be just as worthy as anyone else's? And, how is storytelling research?

Narrative inquiry also confronts methodological challenges due to the difficulty of presenting a complex, layered, and dynamic reality (Elbaz-Luwisch, 2007) and the lack of any single widely accepted narrative research method at present (Webster & Mertova, 2007). Moreover, publishing narrative work in refereed journals has not been easy, as acknowledged by narrative researchers (see Conle, 2000b). An influential narrative researcher in psychology, Amia Lieblich, in an interview with Clandinin and Murphy, shares her concern about the political context of narrative inquiry:

> I would be very careful in advising people to go only in their narrative or qualitative way. I would make it very clear that with all the richness and the real complexity that one can touch with this matter, there are also many, many risks and dangers involved in pursuing this manner of research. (Clandinin & Murphy, 2007, p. 640)

Elliot Mishler joins Lieblich, saying, "And I know that this, it's not easy, and if you're a young person trying to get promoted or get tenure you're kind of caught in this" (Clandinin & Murphy, 2007, p. 645).

Narrative Inquiry as the Synergy of Interdisciplinarity

These warnings are real. However, they are not meant to scare you away. Rather, my aim is to help you realize that narrative inquiry is not "the" research methodology, as I once believed it to be. I hope that these cautionary tales will inspire you to work diligently to be a narrative researcher who has enough confidence and competence to avoid pitfalls and respond effectively to criticisms. One of the reasons why it is important for us to know what is going on in other disciplines in terms of narrative inquiry as sketched earlier is that this information can help us share, borrow, and adapt new ideas from each other. This sharing will cement solidarity in the narrative research community while giving indispensable support to incoming narrative researchers. Each discipline offers its unique approach to narrative inquiry (variegations) while sharing narrative inquiry's commonalities. Adopting and integrating those differences and commonalities into our own work will enrich and enhance our research practice, further developing the synergy of interdisciplinarity in narrative inquiry.

We should use the term **interdisciplinarity** with care, however, because there is an assumption that interdisciplinarity is by nature superficial due to an attempt to know too much or a tendency to not know enough (Friedman, 1998; Kincheloe & Berry, 2004). Each discipline is governed by a general set of rules and categories that guides the pursuit of knowledge (Allen & Kitch, 1998). They don't usually leave room or build capacity for a conversation with other fields. However, isn't it true that human phenomena always overlap numerous disciplines? Therefore, to be able to understand the human experience through narrative inquiry, we cannot solely rely on disciplinary knowledge because "the traditional disciplines have become particularly adept at providing partial knowledge about isolated segments of the cosmos. Such knowledge, of course, is profoundly inadequate when directed toward the solution of ill-defined social, psychological, and educational problems" (Kincheloe & Berry, 2004, p. 71).

Hence, what we as narrative inquirers need to strive for is to have a deep understanding of our own discipline first and find ways to broaden our field by reaching out to other disciplines. The success and productiveness of interdisciplinarity depends on the researcher's rigorous understanding of his/her own disciplinary field (Friedman, 1998). Lyon (1992) contends that interdisciplinarity fundamentally involves "giving up territory" in favor of convergence of diverse fields, which I interpret as a call to avoid becoming territorial in order to be truly interdisciplinary. Friedman (1998) also posits that interdisciplinarity resists the policing effects of disciplinary regulation; it not only promotes a collaborative process where people from different disciplines interact but also encourages an individual researcher to travel away from his/her home discipline. The goal is for the researcher to bring back new knowledge and have it synthesized and integrated into the researcher's home discipline. This integration is what makes interdisciplinarity distinct from multidisciplinarity in which scholars from various disciplinary backgrounds collaborate but little integration occurs (Klein, 1990).

While reading about narrative inquiry in different disciplines, you have probably noticed how narrative inquiry becomes the confluence where unlikely fields meet, creating a synergy of interdisciplinarity. One great example was Robert Coles, who trained to be a child psychiatrist in medical school, and later taught a literature course in a medical education program. He called for stories whether the story was from the literature or from the patients.

We are narrative inquirers who come from many different disciplines. We converge into and diverge from narrative inquiry. We understand that narrative inquiry has a deep root in the way we humans think, live, and act, as narrative is a basic meaning-making process. Narrative inquiry begins with a story that maybe quite ordinary and from any walk of life, which requires us to be interdisciplinary as we examine it. Successful narrative inquirers are interdisciplinarians even while they pursue rigorous standards in their home disciplines.

Learning to Be a Storyteller in the Interdisciplinary Context

As we learn to be storytellers of the ordinary from all walks of life, I think a small story by Tolstoy may fit here. In his essay "Why Do Men Stupefy Themselves?," first published in Russian in 1890, Leo Tolstoy (1998) talks about how life begins with tiny, unnoticeable changes. He recounts the story of the painter Brüllof, who was correcting a pupil's work. The pupil, amazed, said, "Here, you only changed it a tiny bit, but it is entirely changed." Brüllof replied: "Art begins where scarcely begins." About this anecdote, Tolstoy concludes:

> This observation is strikingly true, not in relation to art alone, but to all of life. It may be said that a true life begins where "scarcely" begins—where the scarcely perceptible, almost infinitely small, changes take place. The true life is produced . . . where the scarcely differentiated changes occur. (p. 150)

We know that narrative research begins where a true life begins. But we might have not noticed that a true life begins where "scarcely" begins—very tiny little aspects of life that are most important but unnoticeable because of their simplicity and familiarity. We might have overlooked such a story that seemed trivial but in fact might give an important clue to understanding the subject of our study. Narrative inquiry, although it does not deny that great events are important, presumes the importance of the everyday, the ordinary, the quotidian stories that have frequently gone unnoticed. In so doing, narrative inquiry extends our understanding of human phenomena as a way of "honoring the sacredness of our humanity" (Munro Hendry, 2007, p. 496). And honoring the sacredness of our humanity would begin with true life where scarcely begins.

Therefore, upon learning to be a narrative inquirer who pays attention to quotidian stories, we are also learning to be a storyteller. According to Benjamin (1969), the storyteller "has counsel like the sage" (p. 108) who uses his or her life like "the wick of a candle" (p. 108). Hence, the storyteller is the person "who could let the wick of his life be consumed completely by the gentle flame of his story. This is the basis of the incomparable aura about the storyteller" (pp. 108–109). To this beautiful remark, I would like to add that the gentle flame of our story could merge into a collective flame with the flames of others' stories. This collective flame could shine through the dark corners of our lives. This, I think, is the power of narrative research and storytelling.

Conclusion: A Falling Apple

In this chapter, we looked at how we have come to understand narrative inquiry as it is. The topics included narrative as a way of knowing, understanding the notion of narrative and story, some concerns regarding narrative inquiry, and narrative inquiry in varied disciplines, for example, psychology, law, medicine, and education, creating the synergy of interdisciplinarity.

Now, before we move on to the next chapter, I want you to take a look at the picture of a sculpture (see Image 1.1).

Marcuslim at en.wikipedia.com

Image 1.1 Salvador Dali, *Homage to Newton* (1985). Signed and numbered cast no. 5/8. Bronze with dark patina.

This sculpture, *Homage to Newton,* is one of the eight original sculptures that the leading figure of Surrealism, Salvador Dali, produced in 1985. What do you notice? Yes, the open area of Newton's head and torso, and a falling apple courtesy of a thin chain. In the seventeenth century, Sir Isaac Newton (1643–1727), British physicist, mathematician, philosopher, and astronomer (was he an interdisciplinarian or what?) discovered his famous law of gravity when an apple fell on his head. Why would Dali make Newton's head and torso open? The Salvador Dali Society explains that the open area of Newton's head and torso was Dali's way of symbolizing Newton's open-mindedness (open head) and open heartedness (open torso) as two qualities necessary for any great human discovery (http://www.dali.com/gallery/detail/Sculptures/Singles/Homage + to + Newton + EA).

In addition to Newton's open head and torso, I think about the symbol of a falling apple as well. For me, the falling apple is a taken-for-granted aspect of life that is most important but unnoticed because of its simplicity and familiarity, which is what Leo Tolstoy speaks of: "[T]rue life begins where 'scarcely' begins." For Newton, his theory of gravity began where scarcely began, like a falling apple. For narrative inquirers or storytellers, research should begin with the hardly noticed, like a falling apple, or a story of an ordinary person. We narrative inquirers should approach it with an open heart and open mind to be able to understand the meaning of a falling apple. This way, we become the wick of a candle.

QUESTIONS FOR REFLECTION

- What is your story of becoming a narrative inquirer? That is, why are you interested in learning to be a narrative inquirer?
- How are narratives and stories different from each other?
- What are the functions of stories and storytelling?
- How do you think narrative inquiry has enhanced research in your discipline?
- How do you think narrative inquiry is perceived by your committee members?
- What is your understanding of interdisciplinarity?

ACTIVITIES

1. Find or meet a person who is not in your discipline. Exchange research ideas with each other and see what you can learn from each other.

2. Bring a story (6 to 7 minutes long) that you think is interesting and share it in class. Try to experience what it is like to tell a story and to listen to a story.

3. Share with each other a good storyteller you admire and explain what makes the person a good storyteller.

NOTES

1. The effort to distinguish the difference between narrative and story is not to pigeonhole one from the other but to understand the subtle nuances between them. The discussions of both narrative and story contribute to the rigor of narrative inquiry.
2. The notion of storytelling as an art leads to storytelling as performance, which is discussed in Chapter 8.

CHAPTER TOPICS

- The Role of Theory
- Philosophical/Theoretical/ Interpretive Paradigm
- Theory and Narrative Inquiry
- Critical Theory
  - *The Origin of Critical Theory*
  - *Reproduction in Critical Theory*
  - *From Reproduction to Resistance in Critical Theory*
  - *Reconceptualization of Critical Theory and Narrative Inquiry*
- Critical Race Theory
  - *History of Critical Race Theory*
  - *Characteristics of Critical Race Theory*
  - *Branches of Critical Race Theory*
  - *The Future of Critical Race Theory*
  - *Critical Race Theory and Narrative Inquiry*
- Feminist Theory
  - *Liberal Feminist Theory*
  - *Critical Feminist Theory*
  - *Intersectionality in Feminist Theory*
- Phenomenology
  - *Methods of Phenomenological Knowledge*
  - *Hermeneutical Phenomenology*
  - *Resurgence of Phenomenology and Narrative Inquiry*

- Poststructuralism/Postmodernism/ Deconstruction
  - *After Structuralism*
  - *Nietzschean Influences on Poststructuralism*
  - *Gilles Deleuze (1925–1995): Rhizomatic Thinking*
  - *Rhizomatic Thinking and Narrative Inquiry*
  - *Michel Foucault (1926–1984): An Analysis of Power Relations*
  - *Foucauldian Approach and Narrative Inquiry*
  - *Jacques Derrida (1930–2004): Deconstruction for Justice*
  - *Poststructuralism and Narrative Inquiry*
- Dewey's Theory of Experience
- Bakhtin's Theory of Novelness
  - *Epic Versus Novel*
  - *Polyphony*
  - *Chronotpe*
  - *Carnival*
- Conclusion: No Theory Used as a Procrustean Bed

CHAPTER 2

Philosophical/ Theoretical Underpinnings of Narrative Inquiry

QUESTIONS TO CONSIDER

- What is the role of theories?
- Why do I need a theory to understand a story?
- Which theory can I use for my interpretive paradigm?

INTRODUCTION

As I write this chapter on philosophical/theoretical underpinnings of narrative inquiry, I think of some of my students who ask, "Why do I have to take a theory course?" "How does theory/philosophy help me write my dissertation on strategies for struggling readers?" Since they are well equipped with their discipline-specific or content-specific theories (micro-level theory), these students feel that they don't need another theory to study. Some of them simply scoff at the word "theory" because they believe theory belongs to the realm of more sophisticated research that has nothing to do with practice, hence the word "theory" feels intimidating to them. They are not interested in overarching philosophical ideas that could serve as their orientation to the world, worldview, or interpretive paradigm. Understandably, these students question the use of theory, believing that theory is given too much prestige for establishing academic legitimacy (Thomas, 1997). In fact, some of them feel that reading about "big T" Theories is like "walking into a karate ring clad in a rusty suit of heavy armor borrowed from some long-dead knight's exotic wardrobe" (Rajagopalan, 1998, p. 336). Theory seems esoteric, extinct, and antique, as most of the grand theories are dead people's knowledge, anyway. Students feel that they need good stories, not theories.

Understood.

Then, I also think of some of my students who have multiple epiphanies as they learn about these big T Theories. They jump up and down with a sudden leap of understanding about the phenomena they couldn't articulate before without a theory. After gaining some understanding of theory, they feel that they have the "language" to explain why certain things happen in the way they do. Once they have that understanding, there is no stopping them. Their quest for uncertainty begins. They realize that, as thinkers, they are not only what they know but also what they don't know. They suddenly start "doing" philosophy, questioning what they have known as truth, and risking displacement from the familiar place they have known for years. According to Foucault (1984),

> The displacement and transformation of frameworks of thinking, the changing of received values and all the work that has been done to think otherwise, to do something else, to become other than what one is—that, too, is philosophy . . . it is a way of interrogating ourselves. (p. 329)

Hence, students who start doing philosophy begin to interrogate themselves as researchers as they transform their framework of thinking and challenge ideas they have taken for granted. As a result, their discussions become deeper, more engaging, and more complex. These students experience a turning point. And, I want you to be one of these students.

The purpose of this chapter, hence, is to introduce you to some of the theoretical/philosophical underpinnings of narrative inquiry and help you to become theorizers and philosophers of narrative inquiry. In this chapter, I first discuss the role of theory, and then the relationship between theory and narrative inquiry, followed by macro-level and meso-level theories that can be used for narrative inquiry.

The Role of Theory

There is a widely held view that theory is anything but practice, which implies a simple theory-practice continuum or the either-or dichotomy. That is, theory is at one end of the continuum and practice is at the other, and the continuum is tilted placing one into a higher position than the other (e.g., some people might value theory more than practice or vice versa). There is a centrifugal force in the theory-practice continuum (see Figure 2.1).

This centrifugal force in the theory-practice continuum evokes anti-theory sentiments among practitioners. In lieu of this view, Thomas (1997) calls for a need for an anti-theory movement. He argues that theory has been an "instrument for reinforcing an existing set of practices and methods in education" (p. 76) rather than a vehicle for enhancing the practice. He further criticizes that although strong anti-theoretical strands have emerged in postmodern thought, researchers (referring to educational researchers) continue to adhere to theory that works to stabilize the status quo, "a hermetic set of rules, procedures, and methods" (p. 76). Before we quickly discard Thomas's anti-theory argument, let's consider it a sign of widespread overreliance on theory, a tendency to give theory an absolute, authoritarian role that discourages new observations and understandings. In fact, Rajagopalan (1998)[1] points out that we tend to naïvely believe that once a theory is formulated in a rigorous fashion, we can "apply" the theory to any practice automatically, making the application entirely unproblematic, in ways analogous to a computer program for automatic piloting. We inadvertently believe that theory, once applied, will work in any practice setting.

In the interview with Foucault (Foucault & Deleuze, 1977), Deleuze provides an insight into the role of theory. Deleuze states that theory is always local and related to a limited field. Thus, the moment a theory is applied in another sphere, it begins to encounter obstacles, walls, and blockages, which require it to be redirected or related to another type of discourse. Hence, Deleuze proposes a new relationship between theory and practice where "practice is a set of relays from one theoretical point to another, and theory is a relay from one practice to another. No theory can develop without eventually encountering a wall, and practice is necessary for

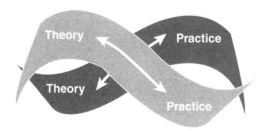

Figure 2.1 Centrifugal Force in Theory-Practice Continuum

piercing this wall" (p. 206). What Deleuze suggests is that theory may derive a kind of practice, and practice may instantiate a particular theory. Deleuze further states:

> A theory is exactly like a box of tools. It has nothing to do with a signifier. It must be useful. It must function. If no one uses it, beginning with the theoretician himself (who then ceases to be a theoretician), then the theory is worthless or the moment is inappropriate. (p. 208)

A literary theorist, Iser, concurs that theories are "first and foremost intellectual tools" (2006, p. 5) that are used for mapping out or piecing together observed phenomena in an effort to discern meaning. They are not to predict or discover laws or general principles (as in natural sciences), rather, they are the intellectual tools that we use to achieve understanding, to investigate meaning and function, and to address the question of "why" (Iser, 2006).

Hence, we cannot bestow onto theory authoritarian or totalizing power. Rather, we have to recognize that there is a strong interlocking relationship between theory and practice; they interlock just like gears, with our personal experience serving as a lubricant (see Figure 2.2). This view beckons an act of *theorizing* on our part. Here, Foucault offers an insight: "Each time I have attempted to do theoretical work, it has been on the basis of elements from my experience—always in relation to processes that I saw taking place around me" (cited in Rajchman, 1985, p. 35). Foucault is telling us that theory requires our experiences derived from practice, and our experiences require theorizing through which we make sense of our lives, experiences, and

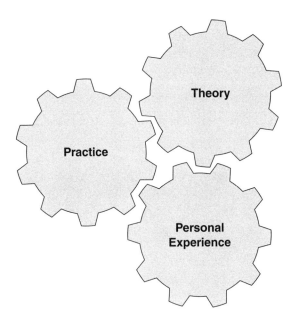

Figure 2.2 Interlocking Relationships Among Theory, Practice, and Personal Experience

practices. Theorizing is an intellectual activity that links lived experience to scholarship and practice. According to van Manen (1990), theorizing is the "intentional act of attaching ourselves to the world, to become more fully part of it, or better, to *become* the world" (p. 5, italics in original). Thus, learning theories is not enough. We will need to engage in *theorizing*, knowing how to utilize theory to understand and to become fully a part of the world for the purpose of improving it. This way, theory can be useful.

Philosophical/Theoretical/Interpretive Paradigm

Denzin and Lincoln (2011) declare, "All qualitative researchers are philosophers" (p. 12). I wholeheartedly agree with this statement. Qualitative researchers, and narrative inquirers in particular, cannot be just technicians who possess skills and knowledge about how to conduct research. Being in the qualitative research field is like "walking swampy lowland" that is full of dilemmas, challenges, complexities, and puzzles; hence, qualitative researchers inevitably engage in philosophy because they have to challenge what they have already known as truth. As Foucault notes above, when we do philosophy, we become displaced and transformed by a framework of thinking differently from the formerly accepted values. We become other than what we have been by interrogating ourselves. Hence, we are, in a sense, always in the way of becoming. Merleau-Ponty (1962/2007) confirms this view in his statement, "Philosophy is not the reflection of a pre-existing truth, but, like art, the act of bringing truth into being" (p. xxiii). Philosophy is not about perpetuating the pre-existing truth; rather, it is a creation of truth like an act of art. Hence, when we qualitative researchers attempt to theorize our understanding as an intellectual activity to link lived experience to scholarship and practice, we also philosophize to bring into being truth that might challenge the premise of absolute truth. In this sense, theorizing becomes philosophizing, rendering all qualitative researchers philosophers.

Let's further consider Denzin and Lincoln's remark that all qualitative researchers are philosophers. Qualitative researchers are guided by highly abstract principles, which include a combination of the researcher's beliefs about ontology (questions about being and reality), epistemology (questions about knowledge), and methodology (questions about the methods of obtaining knowledge). Denzin and Lincoln (2011) term these beliefs a "paradigm" or "interpretive framework" (p. 13) that functions to shape how the qualitative researcher sees the research phenomena and interprets them. Hence, qualitative researchers operate within one or more interpretive (or theoretical) paradigm(s) (frameworks), which is the second phase in their description of the research process.[2] Denzin and Lincoln state:

> all research is interpretive, guided by a set of beliefs and feelings about the world and how it should be understood and studied. . . . Each interpretive paradigm makes particular demands on the researcher, including the questions that are asked and the interpretations that are brought to them. (p. 13)

Similarly, Creswell (2007) discusses how the research design process in qualitative research begins with philosophical assumptions that researchers have and how researchers employ interpretive and theoretical frameworks to further shape their research. He states, "Good research requires making these assumptions, paradigms, and frameworks explicit in the writing of a study, and, at a minimum, to be aware that they influence the conduct of inquiry" (p. 15).

In my view, when qualitative researchers employ philosophical, theoretical frameworks or paradigms to shape their studies, they engage theory at the macro level. Social and human science theories that work at the macro level, the so called big T theories, include critical theory, critical race theory, feminist theory, phenomenology, poststructuralism, postmodernism, and more. They are used by qualitative researchers from a range of disciplines, and they are the main topics of this chapter.

It is also important for you to know theories that are specifically related to your chosen research methodology, whether it is narrative inquiry, case study, grounded theory, or ethnography. I would put these theories in the **meso level**, by which I mean the level of methodology and methods. I would say that reading this book is one way to work on your understanding of theories of narrative inquiry methodology (*meso level*). In this chapter, I have included discussions of Dewey's theory of experience and Bakhtin's theory of novelness because I find them particularly useful for narrative inquiry.

In addition, you will need to be aware of many other theories that are specific to your content area. For example, my students in education need to know some theories in teaching and learning or theories in reading because these are related to their particular research topics. I would place these theories in the **micro level**, which I view as functioning at the disciplinary level (see Figure 2.3).

To be able to justify your worldview, choices of your methodology, and research topics, I encourage you to be well versed in theories at the macro, meso, and micro level. The more articulate you are at all the levels, the more effective you will be as a narrative inquirer.

- Macro-level theory (interpretive paradigm): Holistic level for all qualitative research
- Meso-level theory (methodological paradigm): Methodological and methodical level for the specific qualitative research methodology, e.g., narrative inquiry[3]
- Micro-level theory (disciplinary paradigm): Disciplinary level for the individual content and topic area

Theory and Narrative Inquiry

The distinction of these levels of theory is not fixed, but it is something we want to think about as part of our research design and process. Clarity on this point can save us from confusion. A few years ago, I received an interesting comment from a blind reviewer on my proposal that was submitted to the Narrative Research Special Interest Group of AERA. The proposal was about a narrative inquiry in which phenomenology was employed as a theoretical framework (**macro-level theory, interpretive paradigm**). The reviewer made a moderate harangue on my

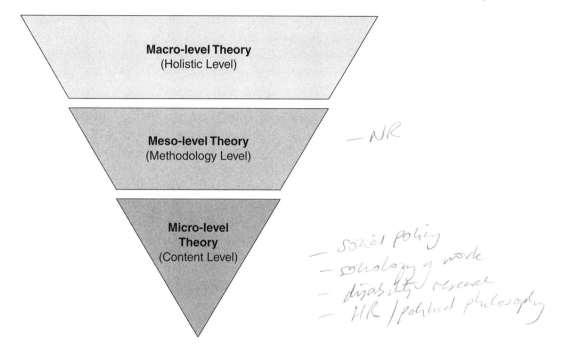

Figure 2.3 Levels of Theory

theoretical discussion, saying that the author (me) did an extensive review on phenomenology as a theoretical framework, but narrative inquiry work didn't need phenomenology to tell us what to do because narrative inquiry had established its own theoretical framework within the methodology. I agreed with the unknown reviewer that narrative inquiry has been established as a rigorous methodology (**meso-level theory, methodological paradigm**), but I was also puzzled by the reviewer's dismissal of a macro-level theory.

Although many of us understand that it is theory that helps us to understand, analyze, and evaluate stories (Bal, 1997), lack of theory in narrative inquiry, which is often translated as "lack of academic rigor," has been pointed out as one of narrative inquiry's drawbacks by both positivists and narrative researchers (see Behar-Horenstein & Morgan, 1995; Brinthaupt & Lipka, 1992; Clandinin & Connelly, 2000; Conle, 2000; Phillips, 1994). In my previous effort to strengthen my "romance" with narrative inquiry, I have posited that the lack of "narratology" in narrative inquiry is a weakness that invites this criticism (see Kim, 2008). For example, I pointed out:

- Clandinin and Connelly (2000), who acknowledge the academic concern that "narrative inquiry is not theoretical enough" (p. 42);
- Behar-Horenstein and Morgan (1995), who argue that stories in narrative inquiry do not seem to offer political or theoretical foundations that can help us create new understandings, despite the emergent power of narrative inquiry;

- Brinthaupt and Lipka (1992), who discuss difficulties in integrating theoretical perspectives into narrative research; and
- Hollingsworth and Dybdahl (2007), who point out how many narrative inquiry works have failed to make transparent the methodological and theoretical frameworks behind their conclusions.

There is a strong disagreement across the social sciences about the role of theory in narrative inquiry (Josselson & Lieblich, 2003). Traditionally, theory is associated with authority, which may lead some to feel that the story is overshadowed and perhaps devalued by the authority of theory. My emphasis on the articulation of the three levels of theory is not a subscription to the authority of theory that devalues stories. As noted above, theories are intellectual tools to help us better understand the meaning of stories. Rorty (1991) offers more insight into this issue between theory and narrative:

> Earlier I said that theorists like Heidegger saw narrative as always a second-best. . . . Novelists like Orwell and Dickens are inclined to see theory as always a second-best, never more than a reminder for a particular purpose, the purpose of telling a story better. I suggest that the history of social change in the modern West shows that the latter conception of the relation between narrative and theory is the more fruitful. (p. 80)

For Rorty, stories are more paramount than theory as theory serves as a medium to fulfill the purpose of telling a story better. The point here is that stories are not devoid of theory; the meaning of a story can be elucidated by theory in ways that matter. Hence, theory needs to be conceived as a medium or "a box of tools" as Deleuze points out above, with which we make sense of the world full of stories.

Josselson and Lieblich (2003) provide valuable advice about theoretical framework:

> The theoretical part of the background section of the proposal must open the inquiry, not narrow and focus it. By stating the boundaries of the theoretical/conceptual field within which the student intends to work, it outlines in a general way the student's erudition and frame of mind. It provides orienting (but not operational) definitions of key terms that enclose the investigation. In what theoretical language does the student think, with what concepts, what lenses? To which theorists is the student likely to turn to move phenomenological description to more abstract, conceptual ground? Or perhaps the student intends to challenge or extend a particular theoretical position by analyzing cases that question or enlarge theoretical assumptions, or to try to enrich a theory by parsing in more detail than is customary particular instances that the theory addresses. (p. 263)

I like the fact that Josselson and Lieblich advise us to have theoretical discussion open the inquiry, not narrow it. In particular, it seems to me that their questions, "In what theoretical language does the student think [micro-level of discipline] . . . with what concepts [meso-level of methodology] . . . what lenses [macro-level of interpretive paradigm]?" encompass the three levels of theory. We should use theories to construct the meanings of stories with conscious attention to the three levels of theory. But this is not to say that theory is more important than story. As Rorty pointed out, it is stories that will help us stay attuned to the ever-changing understandings of our humanness.

Below, I will first discuss some macro-level theories (interpretive framework) that have shaped our intellectual understanding in the social and human sciences for the last century: critical theory, critical race theory, feminist theory, phenomenology, and poststructuralism. And then I will discuss some meso-level theories that I find pertinent to narrative inquiry: Dewey's theory of experience and Bakhtin's theory of novelness. These brief overviews probably will not satisfy your insatiable desire to learn about them. However, I will be delighted if the short discussions of these theories "tease" your curiosity and send you to the original sources. A deep understanding of these key theories will serve as our orientation to the world or to the research phenomena that we seek to understand.

Critical Theory

Kincheloe and McLaren (2011) recently reconceptualized critical theory, incorporating "post-discourses" of the twentieth century. They state that critical theory is a term that is often evoked and frequently misunderstood. I concur. I have some doctoral students who are turned off by what they perceive to be the very nature of critical theory, which is to disrupt and challenge the status quo. They fear the possibility of critical theory producing "undeniably dangerous knowledge" (p. 286). They mistakenly believe that critical theory is a Marxist idea, which they also erroneously equalize to be a "communist" idea. Behind this resistance among students to understand critical theory as an intellectual property, there seems to be a benign assumption that there is nothing wrong with society as it is, or that society is much better than before (we have our first Black president, after all); so, to these students, the idea of working for social change is an extreme "leftist" idea. To make matters worse, assigned readings of critical theory, they lament, are too difficult to understand, with lots of jargon and authoritative language. Their minds are simply closed to this theory. I do sympathize with their difficulties in understanding the readings. I remember my days as a doctoral student when I was in panic and in dire need of help with readings by Bourdieu and Habermas in a doctoral seminar on critical theory. Because I couldn't understand what these critical theorists were saying, I went to see my professor (Dr. Donald Blumenfeld-Jones) during his office hours so many times. I am still grateful to him for his patience; he helped me understand critical theory well enough that I ended up using critical theory as the theoretical framework for my narrative dissertation.

The Origin of Critical Theory

Critical theory originated from the Frankfurt School connected to the Institute of Social Research at the University of Frankfurt in Germany. More specifically, in 1937, the *Journal of the Institute for Social Research* published an essay by Max Horkheimer, titled "Traditional and

Critical Theory." From that moment, critical theory has been designated as a school of thought (Ingram & Simon-Ingram, 1992). Theorists such as Max Horkheimer, Theodor Adorno, Jürgen Habermas, and Herbert Marcuse are the ones who created critical theory by initiating a conversation regarding the German tradition of philosophical and social thought, especially that of Marx, Kant, Hegel, and Weber. These early critical theorists, whose perspectives were shaped by postwar Germany's economic depression in the early 1930s, focused on analyzing the forms of domination and injustice, while reinterpreting Marxist orthodoxy (Kincheloe & McLaren, 2011). Critical theory was then introduced to the American intellectual community in the 1960s, after the early critical theorists fled to the United States to escape Nazi persecution and found their academic home in America, albeit temporarily. Thanks to their work, critical theory gained a wider acceptance in the 1970s and 1980s in the United States.

What, then, is critical theory? About what is it concerned? In a nutshell, critical theory, considered a socio-cultural and political theory, examines relationships of domination and subordination that create social inequality in society, focusing on notions of distribution, production, and reproduction. For critical theorists, the ability to look at the contradictions inherent in a society is a starting point to develop forms of social inquiry that interrogate "what is in reality" and "what should be." Thus, the rationale behind critical theory is to support the idea that action should be grounded, as Marcuse stated, "in compassion, [and] in our sense of the sufferings of others" (cited in Giroux, 2001. p. 9). Scholars view critical theory as a method of understanding forms of power and domination. However, the premise of critical theory is its moral imperative and its emphasis on the need for both individual empowerment and social transformation. That is, it emphasizes the need to develop critical consciousness in people as well as the need to change society (Weiler, 1988).

When I taught a Curriculum Theory class a year ago, one of the course topics was critical theory. I asked students to come up with their own working definitions of critical theory after a couple of weeks of "grueling" readings and heated discussions on it. Although we "struggled" together to understand the content, we loved the challenges and I was proud of them for being able to come up with these wonderful definitions. Here are a few unedited versions:

- Critical theory exposes sociological inconsistencies and injustices in an effort to discuss, debate, and take actions to materialize social improvements.
- Critical theory is a transformative endeavor that challenges oppression, confronts injustice, and brings privilege and inequality into question; it strives to empower individuals.
- Critical theory seeks to counter hegemony to confront injustice in socially and historically rooted power relations.

I think that these definitions capture the core of critical theory. Coming up with our own definitions of the theory was a good exercise, and I think all of us were less intimidated by the theory after that.

Now, let's look at two major subcategories of critical theory: reproduction and resistance. Although the discussion here centers around the school as a main social institution, you can replace the school context with other social institutions, such as governments, communities, churches, prisons, hospitals, and more, to understand similar social problems through a critical theory lens.

Reproduction in Critical Theory

Critical theory became an intellectual tool with which educational researchers could explain and analyze how schools function to maintain the existing social order. Hence one important notion of critical theory is reproduction or correspondence theory where the school is viewed as a sub-system of the larger society. It concerns how the sorting and selecting of students through school procedures mimics social expectations that hard work and talent determine attainment (Spring, 1989). American sociologist Talcott Parsons (1959) investigates the role of schools in serving the interests of society and maintaining social order and stability. Parsons contends that schools must legitimatize the ideology that inequalities in social stratification are to be expected; therefore, these inequalities that yield different consequences in students' educational achievements should be acceptable.

The notion of achievement here maintains that those who do well in school ought to be highly rewarded, therefore, different rewards based on different levels of achievement should be considered to be fair. Such an ideology positions subsequent differences in occupational or social class outcomes as fair, thus discouraging resentment by "the losers" in the competition, and conflict is thereby avoided (e.g., if you fail, it's your fault). Reproduction theory explains how the school functions to promote this whole process of achievement as fair while inculcating in students the societal values that sustain a common American culture (Parsons, 1959).

Building on Parsons's proposition, one of the most informative works that examines how schools reproduce the existing social structure is Marxist economists Samuel Bowles and Herbert Gintis's (1976) influential book, *Schooling in Capitalist America,* where they theorize that schools are capitalist agencies of social, economic, cultural, and bureaucratic reproduction. They draw attention to the tacit norms of school life and how schools reproduce class positions. They coin the term "correspondence thesis" to describe the relationship between school norms and capitalist structures of inequality. That is, the educational system functions as a way to channel youth into the economic system that is equivalent to their social class identifications. The correspondence thesis can be seen in the following processes:

- Students from different social classes are subject to different school experiences in terms of the curriculum, teachers' expectations of them, types of schoolwork, and treatment by teachers.
- Hidden curricula and tracking systems assign students into specific coursework that matches their social classes while simultaneously conditioning them to accept social inequality.
- While students in high-class communities are trained with the drive to achieve and distinguish themselves, those in working-class schools rehearse behaviors such as obedience or following directions, appropriate for low-skill, low-autonomy work (Anyon, 1980; Bowles & Gintis, 1976; Lareau, 1989).

To my delight, one of my graduate students, Art, has become interested in critical theory after learning of reproduction theory. Art, who is studying the lived experience of military students in higher education, became elated after realizing how critical theory could serve to illuminate his research topic. Before learning critical theory, he told me, he was not able to understand why many military students struggle and lag behind in university courses. In fact, he confessed that he had assumed a blaming-the-victim ideology (Valencia, 1997) in which he believed it was the military students' lack of will and motivation that prevented them from being successful in challenging university courses. However, critical theory, according to Art, helped him understand why military students, most of whom come from families of low socio-economic status (SES), were not well prepared for college. It was not necessarily because of their lack of effort, as he used to believe, but because of the school system that stereotyped them as "non-college-material" and thus neglected to provide them with the necessary information and knowledge required for going to college. Through the critical theory perspective, Art was able to see the ways in which many schools reproduced the existing social order, ensuring that students from low SES background remained at the bottom rung of the society. Art was turning into a critical theorist.

From Reproduction to Resistance in Critical Theory

Reproduction theory, however, could not explain why there were oppositions in each social institution. It tended to discard oppositional behavior as "deviate," "disruptive," and "defiant," hence it was reductionistic and simplistic (Giroux, 2001). In the early 1980s, critical theorists such as Paul Willis, Paulo Freire, Michael Apple, Jean Anyon, Henry Giroux, and Peter McLaren criticized the deterministic view of the reproductive function of schooling (e.g., humans cannot do anything to change the system) and concluded that reproduction theory was helpful but not complete by itself; hence, they offered the notion of "resistance" that challenges the oppressive nature of education.

This notion of resistance emerged in the past several decades from neo-Marxist examinations of power struggles to explain various student behaviors occurring in schools. These behaviors indicate the existence of tensions and conflicts between school, students, and the wider society to which students belong (Alpert, 1991; Lindquist, 1994). Critical theorists sought to understand the degree to which students' resistant behavior was associated with their struggle against domination (Knight Abowitz, 2000).

In my ethnographic, narrative inquiry at an alternative high school in Arizona, I first sought to see how the alternative school was functioning to reproduce the existing social structure in conjunction with the correspondence theory. On the surface, the school was a perfect example of the correspondence theory at work. However, on a deeper level, I observed that students were not mere passive agents who just conformed to rules regardless of how unrealistic the rules were. There were always conflicts and tensions that were created by the students, who were called "unruly." But to me, their "unruly" behavior was too significant to ignore because what they had to say about their school experience was often insightful! I could not explain this phenomenon with reproduction theory. I had to turn to resistance theory. **Resistance theory** helped me understand the behavior of Michelle, a fifteen-year-old ninth grader, in a different light. The following is a description of Michelle that I wrote at the time:

> Michelle appeared to be stubborn, outspoken, and unruly. She was also smart and articulate, and had a strong sense of self. She was a typical student at Borderlands Alternative High School (pseudonym) who frequently showed acts of resistance enduring the consequences of being "kicked out" of the classroom. During an interview with her, she told me that patience was the virtue that she had never learned, therefore she was not going to be patient with teachers, especially those who did not make sense to her. (Kim, 2010a, p. 261)

Michelle also said:

> I am goofy. I don't care what others think about me. But at school, I get into trouble because of that. Teachers don't like my personality. Ms. Hardy said to me the other day, "I don't like your personality. You need to stop acting out. You need to change your personality. Then, your school life will be a lot easier." I was really upset. Why do I have to change my personality? I don't care if she likes it or not. I have my own opinions unlike other kids. But teachers think I'm acting out, disruptive, unruly, and rude. Because I like to speak up, I get kicked out of the classroom all the time. (Kim, 2010a, p. 272)

Without the concept of resistance, I would have discarded Michelle as someone who was simply acting out, playing victim of the school's ideology. However, using critical theory's notion of resistance as a tool, I was able to understand how Michelle's resistance signified a "struggle for identity (self-definition)" or "identity politics" (Miron & Lauria, 1995, p. 30), working as a communicative act to affirm her agency and self-empowerment. This interpretation led me to raise questions about teachers who could not embrace Michelle's human agency as a pedagogical act. In studying students' resistance, I was able to discuss how resistance theory could be used as "a theoretical and pedagogical medium with which teachers and students interrogate together to create an equitable school environment, transcending conflicts and tensions and moving beyond zero-tolerance policies" (Kim, 2010a, p. 274).

Hence, although schools work to reproduce the existing social class to maintain the status quo, they can become sites of resistance and democratic possibility through collaborative efforts among teachers and students to work within a pedagogical framework. Giroux, for example, views schools as venues of hope, where forms of knowledge, values, and social relations are taught for the purpose of educating young people for critical empowerment rather than subjugation (Giroux, 1983a, 1983b, 2001). Students who have been traditionally voiceless in schools can be empowered to critically examine how society has functioned to thwart their aspirations and goals. Giroux reconfirms the political nature of education and a pedagogy that can work for social change, which has come to be termed critical pedagogy. In critical pedagogy, teachers link critical teaching and learning to the experiences and stories that students bring to the classroom.

Giroux posits that through critical pedagogy, the space of schooling can become a site of contestation, resistance, possibility, and hope. Critical pedagogy, critical theory's "sibling tradition" (Peters, 2005, p. 36), is both a field of study and a set of practices. It aims to transform education and pedagogy as part of the project of radical democracy. Freire's work, *Pedagogy of the Oppressed* (1997), strongly influenced by critical theory, became the foundation of critical pedagogy. Freire worked to raise consciousness and eradicate oppression and the culture of domination through praxis in which critical pedagogy is enacted. However, as the popularity of critical theory waned in the twenty-first century, critical pedagogy also became "domesticated, disoriented, or dogmatized" (Gur-Ze'ev, 2005, p. 7), and for some, critical pedagogy is "in crisis" (Tubbs, 2005, p. 240).

Reconceptualization of Critical Theory and Narrative Inquiry

Critical theory started losing its popularity as it was critiqued and overhauled by the "post-discourses," such as postmodernism, poststructualism, and critical feminism of the twentieth century (Kincheloe & McLaren, 2011). Peters (2005), for example, laments how critical theory has become commodified with lack of historical depth and with misunderstanding and argues that critical theory's main intention is left out in the analysis of power and domination. Thus, he suggests we need to return to the origins of critical philosophy to better understand critical theory.

Peters (2005) considers Thomas McCarthy a thinker who has offered a series of important reflections on the current status of critical theory. So, I looked up McCarthy's (2001) work in which he points out:

- Critical theory has exclusively focused on culture rather than on economics.
    - → We need to get back in touch with the Marxist roots focusing on the role of economic patterns of inequality.

- Critical theory has been too confident about its reach in the idea of emancipation represented as self-consciousness, self-determination, and self-realization.
    - → We need to recognize its limit.

- Critical theory has been too closely tied to academic work and distanced from the lived forms of oppression as they are experienced by groups in the population.
    - → We need to get back to the lives of people who suffer from class and economic oppression.

Now I know why I have not heard much "buzz" about critical theory in recent years, although I was well aware of the feminist theorist Elizabeth Ellsworth's work that points out how critical theory is mainly the work of white males who overlook gender oppression (see Ellsworth, 1989). Critical theory doesn't seem popular any more at conference presentations, where I hear more frequently about "post" theories. It seems that critical theory is in dire need of reconceptualization and revitalization as voiced in McCarthy (2001):

> Feminist theory, race theory, gay and lesbian studies, postcolonial studies and the like have recently been better at this [the progressive social movement] than critical social theory—though they too have had their problems with too much distance from the lived forms of oppression they theorize. The Marxian tradition has been tied primarily to class politics, and in many industrialized countries, that form of politics has waned. In any case, new forms of politics have arisen and there is a need constantly to develop critical theory so as to articulate the concerns of new social movements. (p. 428)

It is Kincheloe and McLaren (2011) who have responded seriously to this call to develop a critical theory that can "articulate the concerns of new social movements." They have reconceptualized critical theory to incorporate the twenty-first century's social movements and to be concerned with "issues of power and justice and the ways that the economy, matters of race, class, and gender, ideologies, discourses, education, religion, and other social institutions, and cultural dynamics interact to construct a social system" (p. 299). They suggest that this reconceptualized critical theory be used as a map or a guide to the social sphere rather than a determining factor for how we see the world. Thus, a reconceptualized critical theory is emergent as critical social inquiry that turns to critical philosophy based on reflexivity (Peters, 2005), diverging to multiple types of critical theory such as Deleuzian, Foucauldian, or Derridean critical theory, and critical feminist theory (Marshall, 2005).

So, what does the reconceptualized critical theory have to do with narrative inquiry? I want to reiterate what McCarthy told us above: "too much distance from the lived forms of oppression they theorize." We need to make an effort to remove the distance between theorizing and reality. Theory devoid of lived experience would be like an empty tin can that just makes noise. Hence, we need to get to the narratives and stories of people whose reality resides in homelessness, unemployment, minimum wage, lack of health care, not to mention lack of food. We know that stories of the "lived forms of oppression" abound, engendered by class politics in an age of abundance.

Critical Race Theory

Critical race theory (CRT) is becoming increasingly "popular" among graduate students. When Professor Gloria Ladson-Billings was invited as keynote speaker for the inauguration of the Distinguished Lecture Series that our college launched in the fall of 2013, we, both the faculty and students, were elated. After the lecture, one student wrote to me, "Wow, I feel like I was in the presence of a rock star today! It is such a cool feeling to be so near someone who is so influential and has made such huge contributions to the field of education and CRT." This was pretty much what all of us felt. But unlike the stereotypical "rock star," Dr. Ladson-Billings is an intellectual who is down-to-earth, caring, and attentive with a brilliant sense of humor. Most of all, she is a captivating storyteller.

CRT, developed in the United States in the 1970s, focuses on race. Although it draws upon critical theory (Solórzano & Yosso, 2001), CRT is a theoretical construct that explains racial issues that many critical theorists could not address appropriately (Hylton, 2012). For example, Gloria Ladson-Billings and William Tate (1995), who have brought CRT to the field of education, posit that although theoretical analyses of gender and class were well established by feminists and critical theorists, race remained under-theorized until the birth of CRT. The significance of race, they argue, cannot be explained with theories of gender or class. Thus, researchers who focus on the impact of race and racism use CRT as their theoretical framework. In CRT, race is placed at the center of research analysis with respect to how minority groups, such as African Americans, American Indians, Chicanos/Chicanas, Asian Americans, and others, experience racial oppression within normative standards of whiteness.

History of Critical Race Theory

The birth of CRT is extremely important because until the creation of CRT, race was used merely as a categorical variable rather than as a theoretical lens to explain social conditions, despite the ground-breaking work of such scholars as DuBois (1906/1990) and Woodson (1933/1990) (Tate, 1997). Historically, critical race theory can be viewed as both an outgrowth of and an entity separate from American critical legal studies (CLS) scholarship. As we observed in Chapter 1, CLS evolved to challenge the traditional legal scholarship (which focused on one master narrative serving the then-dominant ideology) in civil rights litigation in the United States (Delgado, 1995; Ladson-Billings, 1998; Taylor, 2009). Although the civil rights movement and other social movements in the 1960s and 1970s contributed to social improvement, there was a backlash against progressive racial reforms in schooling, hiring, and housing, which prevented a steady racial reform. Frustrated by the backlash from conservatives and by traditional civil rights theories and methods that failed to bring about change, a group of legal scholars, including Derrick Bell, Richard Delgado, Charles Lawrence, Patricia Williams, and Kimberlé Crenshaw, began to interrogate the role of law and attempted to conceive a new approach to CLS. They focused on the ways in which law could transform racial discrimination and make a difference in the concrete lives of people of color affected by law (Crenshaw, 1988). These early critical legal scholars eventually organized the first workshop in 1989 in Madison, Wisconsin, where they agreed on the name, *critical race theory*, and produced a program for its future scholarship (Taylor, 2009). Particularly, Derrick Bell's work as a civil rights lawyer and academic (law faculty of Harvard University) was at the forefront of the CRT scholarship (for more details about how CLS and CRT movements have departed from each other, see Tate, 1997).

To be able to better understand CRT, an understanding of a concept of race might be in order, for which we will turn to sociologist Howard Winant in particular, whose work centers around the issues of race and racism. Winant (2000) defines race as a "concept that signifies and symbolizes sociopolitical conflicts and interests in reference to different types of human bodies" (p. 172). That is, although the concept of race references the physical, morphological features of humans, racial categorization is known to be a social and historical process. Winant (2007) articulates extensively how the concept of race has persisted as a significant theme in twenty-first-century research and scholarship in such social and human sciences as sociology, anthropology, and education, to name just a few. For example, not long ago, the American Sociological Association (ASA) reiterated the importance of conducting social scientific research on race in response to a politically conservative movement to eliminate racial classification in state agencies such as schools, health institutions, prisons, and elsewhere (see American Sociological Association, 2003). Race, in fact, has been a global issue since World War II despite controversy over the meaning and significance of race (Ladson-Billings, 2012; Winant, 2000).

In CRT scholarship, the terms "White" and "Black" are not meant to signal individuals or even group identity. Rather, they indicate "a particular political and legal structure rooted in the ideology of White European supremacy and the global impact of colonialism" (Taylor, 2009, p. 4), evidenced in conceptual categories of race that are implied in our discourses. For example, notions of "conceptual whiteness" represent high achievers, middle classness, high intelligence, and beauty; and those of "conceptual blackness" denote gangs, low achievers, laziness, welfare recipients, and the underclass. In these conceptual categories, albeit fluid and shifting, whiteness becomes the norm while blackness is marginalized and de-legitimated (Ladson-Billings, 1998), resulting in racism. Racism is defined as "a system of ignorance, exploitation, and power used to oppress African-Americans, Latinos, Asians, Pacific Americans, American Indians and other people on the basis of ethnicity, culture, mannerisms, and color" (Marable, 1992, p. 5). CRT makes it possible for us to analyze racism, racial relations, implicit/explicit understandings, and consequences for such arbitrary conceptualizations. Thus, it is an "important intellectual and social tool for deconstruction, reconstruction, and construction: deconstruction of oppressive structures and discourses, reconstruction of human agency, and construction of equitable and socially just relations of power" (Ladson-Billings, 1998, p. 9).

Characteristics of Critical Race Theory

CRT scholarship is fundamentally grounded in the distinctive experiences of people of color while challenging taken-for-granted ideas about accepting the experiences of Whites as the norm. Hence, CRT scholars share two overarching aims (see Ladson-Billings, 1998; Villenas & Deyhle, 1999):

- To understand how white supremacy and its subordination of people of color have been created and maintained in the United States;
- To be committed to social justice by working toward eliminating racial oppression as part of the larger goal of eradicating all forms of oppression.

To reach these aims, CRT scholars question the concepts of White privilege, colorblindness, and the very terms *race* and *racism*. In particular, they problematize colorblindness that seems to be positioned as an ideal in the dominant discourse (Dixson & Rousseau, 2005). Colorblindness assumes a universal or a standard way of being, which is usually grounded in the cultural values and norms of the dominant culture. In a society that is both culturally diverse and racist, colorblindness, according to Thompson (1998), is a "willed ignorance of color that, although well intended, insists on assimilating the experience of people of color to that of Whites" (p. 524). Hence, in the colorblindness mindset, pretending not to notice "color" is construed as a particularly virtuous act that reflects a fair and impartial stance. For example, I hear many teachers say, "I don't see color in my students." This "not seeing color" might unwittingly imply anything but a neutral stance, which, as a result, serves as a highly political stance that could advantage White middle-class males and females, who benefit from the present racial, gendered, and socio-economic hierarchies (Thompson, 1998).

Given these overarching aims and problems to address, CRT scholars have provided some basic tenets of CRT, as listed in Table 2.1.

Table 2.1   Tenets of CRT

1. CRT recognizes that racism is endemic to American life, deeply ingrained legally, culturally, socially, and psychologically.

2. CRT challenges the dominant ideologies such as White privilege, race neutrality, objectivity, colorblindness, and meritocracy.

3. CRT attends to Derrick Bell's theory of *interest convergence,* which contends that racial equality has been gained only when the interests of people of color promote those of Whites.

4. CRT insists on a contextual/historical analysis of race and racism not in order to dwell on the past, but to move beyond it.

5. CRT appreciates the experiential knowledge of people of color as legitimate, valid, and critical to interrogate race and racism.

6. CRT relies on stories and counter-stories of the lived experiences of people of color as a way to communicate the realities of the oppressed.

7. CRT is inter/trans/cross-disciplinary, drawing upon other disciplines and epistemologies to provide a more complete analysis of racial inequalities.

8. CRT focuses on race and racism for a critical race analysis but includes their intersection with other forms of subordination such as gender and class discrimination.

(Delgado, 1995; Ladson-Billings, 1998; Matsuda, Lawrence, Delgado, & Crenshaw, 1993; Solórzano, 1997; Solórzano & Yosso, 2009; Tate, 1997; Taylor, 2009)

Branches of Critical Race Theory

I would be remiss if I didn't mention branches of CRT that are emerging. As you might have noticed, the early critical race theorists focused on revealing the oppressed experience of Black people. However, critical scholars of late have expanded their interests to the experiences of people of color other than Blacks. They have created offshoots of critical legal studies and critical race theory such as LatCrit, AsianCrit, TribalCrit, WhiteCrit, and FemCrit theories, using critical social science and scholarship from Black studies, Latino/a studies, Asian American studies, and feminist studies (see Solórzano & Yosso, 2001). These emerging theories have broadened the discussion of race and racism from the Black/White binary discourse to one that includes other races and ethnicities. Although they share the tenets of CRT, each theory has developed its own "theorizing space" as in Anzaldúa's (1990) insightful statement: "it is *vital* that we occupy theorizing space, that we not allow white men and women solely to occupy it. By bringing in our own approaches and methodologies, we transform that theorizing space" (p. xxv, emphasis in original). However, it is important to note that although each branch of CRT occupies its own theorizing space, the branches are not mutually exclusive or in contention with one another. In other words, they do not compete to measure one form of oppression against another (Yosso, 2005). Rather, the importance of these offshoot theories resides in the fact that they mutually inform by recognizing each other's blind spots.

I provide some resources for those who might be interested in the branches of CRT at the end of this chapter.

The Future of Critical Race Theory

Before we get into the discussion of how CRT can be used in narrative inquiry, I'd like to point out two important issues that deserve close attention as we move toward enhancing the theory: One is the growing interest in CRT among scholars outside the United States, rendering CRT global and transnational; and the other is the changing direction of CRT following Delgado's (2003) thought-provoking analysis of recent trends in CRT. I will elaborate.

First, CRT is becoming transnational. Although CRT had its birthplace in the United States, it is now a global phenomenon, taking on an international dimension (Hylton, 2012; Ladson-Billings, 2012). For example, just recently, British CRT scholars Namita Chakrabarty, Lorna Roberts, and John Preston (2012) edited a special issue on CRT in England (see *Race Ethnicity and Education,* Vol. 15, January 2012). The editors observe that CRT in England is still in its infancy and has encountered some negative critiques by Marxist scholars (e.g., M. Cole & Maisuria, 2007) that racial oppression in the United States is different from British racial oppression, hence American CRT cannot be applied in the British context. Notwithstanding, CRT has become established as a robust approach to social theorizing in the UK (Hylton, 2012) where Gillborn (2011) has called it *BritCrit.* Hylton posits that achieving racial justice through intersecting politics of race is a global challenge (not just an American challenge). Thus it is not surprising that CRT is becoming transnational, applied in the UK and elsewhere, which, it seems to me, opens the door for scholars in different countries to create a region-specific CRT that fits their own historical and social contexts.

Second, a number of CRT theorists today express frustration at the fact that CRT analysis has come to focus on the textual analysis of "race" in academic discourse without much activism against racism (M. Cole & Maisuria, 2007). Delgado (2003), for example, laments that "Critical Race Theory, after a promising beginning, began to focus almost exclusively on discourse at the expense of power, history, and similar material determinants of minority-group fortunes" (p. 122). Doesn't this sound familiar with the concern raised in critical theory, which we just read, regarding a distance between academic discourse and lived forms of oppression? Delgado's concern is that while in its early years CRT was dominated by the writing of the racial realists (activists) such as Derrick Bell, many contemporary CRT scholars work almost entirely in the realm of discourse adopting "idealist" approaches. In other words, CRT theorists tend to write about race intellectually and academically (i.e., only in discourse) without much action or political activism for change. Hence, Delgado suggests we need to combine two ways to think about race rather than focusing on one or the other. That is, "*race*" (referring to the word itself in academic discourse in quotation marks) and *race* (referring to the real-world phenomenon without quotation marks) should be taken into consideration. Either alone is not complete.

To me, this is where the importance of narrative inquiry comes in.

Critical Race Theory and Narrative Inquiry

People are moved by stories more than by legal theories.

—Derrick Bell

One of my students, Chance, wrote the following in his weekly assignment, one that I call the Epiphany of Learning assignment. This assignment was written after reading Ladson-Billings's (1998) thought-provoking article "Just What Is Critical Race Theory and What's It Doing in a Nice Field Like Education?"

One final area of confusion I'm still stuck on with Critical Race Theory is the idea of story-telling. Realizing it is often stated as central to the theory (Ladson-Billings, 1998, p. 8), I have not yet developed a sophisticated understanding of the rationale for utilizing story-telling. I understand that the story-telling that occurs is meant to share voices previously not heard or not represented in history books and curriculum that caters to majority and privileged groups. But what I'm failing to grasp is the rationale for utilizing story-telling as a key component of the theory, when it seems to be a very easy means to reach a skewed conclusion. Further, who gets to tell the story in this process? Are the researchers presenting exact stories from "members in the out groups" (1998, p. 15), or are those stories presented through the lens of the researcher, thus constructing a new reality? (Chance's Weekly Epiphany of Learning assignment, Week Two)

Admittedly, Chance raises honest and thoughtful questions that you might also have asked while reading about CRT. How could storytelling be utilized as a key component of the theory? Who gets to tell the story in this process? Here was my lame response to these thought-provoking questions: "Great questions! Why don't you take my narrative inquiry class next fall?" This wasn't just evasion on my part, however. I thought Chance was asking exactly the kind of questions that all narrative inquirers should grapple with and I didn't think there was any one right answer to give at the moment. But then, wasn't there any narrative work I could show him as an example?

One great example of CRT in narrative inquiry comes from Harvard Law professor Derrick Bell's *And We Are Not Saved* (1987). As mentioned above, Bell was one of the influential founders of CRT. His book explores human racial plights through imagination in ten "metaphorical tales, or chronicles" (p. 6) in which two fictional narrators, a courageous and talented Black civil rights attorney, Geneva Crenshaw, and her unnamed male colleague and friend, who serves as overall narrator. In these chronicles, Bell engages in counter-storytelling to "challenge the accepted view of how Blacks gain, or might gain, from civil rights laws and policies" (pp. xi–xii), thus displaying the tenets of CRT.

In the book, Bell does not provide any conclusion that might have been easily "skewed," as my student Chance feared. Rather than providing one conclusion, Bell lets readers come to their own conclusions through compelling stories. Bell writes fictional stories using two imagined narrators. Why fictional stories? Bell justifies his choice of fictional narrative genre (see Chapter 4 for narrative genres) by quoting Professor Kimberlé Crenshaw:

> Allegory offers a method of discourse that allows us to critique legal norms in an ironically contextualized way. Through the allegory, we can discuss legal doctrine in a way that does not replicate the abstractions of legal discourse. It provides therefore a more rich, engaging, and suggestive way of reaching the truth. (p. 7)

Indeed, each Chronicle works as an allegory or metaphor that helps us imagine real-life situations and works as a "method of discourse" that is rich, engaging, and suggestive to reach truth and justice. According to Bell, "the Chronicles employ stories that are not true to explore situations that are real enough but, in their many and contradictory dimensions, defy understanding" (p. 7). Hence, using these contradictory dimensions, Bell doesn't intend to suggest solutions that might come from understanding; rather, he invites us to engage in problem finding, which is what a great storyteller does, as Bruner (2002) points out.

Feminist Theory

Feminist theory has a very personal resonance for me. At the age of 23, right after college, I became a teacher and got married in the same year. The following year, my daughter was born, and I continued to teach after two months of maternity leave. Gender oppression by the man who was then my husband became very evident around that time, as he kept nudging me to quit the teaching job I loved. His belief was that it was the woman who needed to stay home to raise a child. If we had both been working, I might have accepted his wishes. The woman in me who had been socialized from birth to accept sexist thoughts and patriarchy as the norm, controlled my conscience, whispering to me to obey him. However, it seemed to me that our situation at that particular time, in which he had lost his job just a year prior, was more of a survival issue than a gender issue. It didn't make sense to me that he would force me to quit teaching to raise our daughter when he could raise our child himself because he was unemployed. I believed that I needed to be the one who "brought home the bacon" and he should be the "househusband" caring for our daughter. But, alas, he wouldn't accept this atypical gender role that went against his patriarchal belief. He began to threaten that he would file for a divorce if I didn't quit. This psychological and emotional gender oppression in our household went on for more than a year until he finally announced to me that he could not love the woman who was not obedient to her husband, and therefore, he had to go to the court to file a divorce. That was the end of my marriage. After my divorce in the early 1990s, when society in my home country of Korea was still hostile toward divorced women (though usually behind their backs), I suffered inside from shame and a guilty conscience for a long time. These feelings persisted even when I started living in the United States. It was not until I was exposed to feminist theory in graduate school, reading bell hooks's *Teaching to Transgress* (1994), that I finally felt vindicated in my defiance of the man I was supposed to obey. The theory simply empowered me. Now, whenever I discuss feminism and feminist theory, this personal story of mine still haunts me with mixed feelings. It also serves to remind me of the oppressive patriarchy, gender inequality, and sexism still experienced by so many other women in the world today.

In my teaching these days, however, I have a sense that students do not take feminist theory seriously because it seems out of date to them. Sexism? What are we talking about? We are living in the twenty-first century when it's possible we might soon have Hillary Clinton as the first female president in U.S. history! This is what some students think, although we all know, admit it or not, that the most obvious thing working against her candidacy is her gender. "I don't think you've lived long enough," is Clinton's remark, responding to assertions that feminism is old-fashioned or out of date (Clinton, 2014).

As gender oppression or sexism is an ongoing global issue for women, while patriarchy is still alive and well throughout the world on many levels and in many ways, feminism and feminist theory are particularly pertinent to the time in which we're living. Through patriarchy, men continue to control politics and the economy while women are disadvantaged and exploited in a variety of ways (Weiler, 2001). Even though masses of women have entered the workforce and gained access to higher education and high-paying professions, most women throughout the world continue to perform the majority of domestic household chores, while men continue to hold the most powerful political and economic positions worldwide. Moreover, the threat to abortion legislation and the questioning of maternity rights, among other things, are indicative of a "war against women" (B. Cole, 2009, p. 564). Such situations of patriarchy, the unequal ways people are treated due to their gender and sexuality, and the meanings we construct or that are constructed by the prevailing value system that assigns gender roles, are the subjects of feminist analysis and critique. bell hooks (2000) defines feminism as a "movement to end sexism, sexist exploitation, and oppression" (p. 1). It is an effort to eradicate gender injustice, which started as the women's liberation movement, later known as "feminism," during the 1960s and 1970s. According to Mitchell (1971), the women's liberation movement was the "most public revolutionary movement ever to have existed" (p. 13). It is, however, unfortunate that many people tend to have a misconception of feminism as work by women against men, a misunderstanding promoted in the patriarchal mass media. According to hooks (2000), a lot of people consider feminism anti-male, an "angry" response to male domination, seeking to be equal to men. She posits that we are all participants in perpetuating sexism until we let go of sexist thoughts and actions and replace them with feminist thoughts and actions to end patriarchy. Feminist theories, then, address the question of women's subordination to men, including how it arises, how and why it is perpetuated, and how it might be changed. Hence, they serve a dual purpose, as "guides to understanding gender inequality and as guides to action" (Acker, 1987, p. 421). Like critical theory, feminist theory has sub-theories: liberal feminist theory and critical feminist theory.

Liberal Feminist Theory

We'll begin with the work of liberal feminist theory, as most women today are enjoying the harvests of its work, beginning with the achievement of women's suffrage. Speaking of women's suffrage, I am proud of the city of Manhattan, Kansas, a conservative Midwest town, because it has a middle school named after Susan B. Anthony, founder of the National Woman Suffrage Association. I do not know how the legacy of Anthony's work is maintained and passed on to students there, but that would make an interesting research topic.

The main aim of liberal feminism is to secure equal opportunities for the sexes. It is focused on (1) equal opportunities; (2) socialization of gender identity and sex stereotyping; and (3) sex discrimination (Acker, 1987). Equal opportunities rhetoric is the sine qua non of liberal feminist perspective. Equal means the same, which implies that separate educational provision for girls has usually meant inferior facilities and restricted features. Even so, equal, comparable facilities may still produce unequal outcomes. But the discourse of equal opportunity, however flawed, is the language of central governments and quasi-governmental agencies in the English-speaking world, including Britain, the United States, and Australia. According to Acker, socialization, sex roles, and sex stereotypes are a second major concern of liberal feminists. Proponents of this theory interrogate how girls are socialized by the family, the school, and the media to accept traditional sex roles and sex stereotypes; as a result, their futures are limited unnecessarily to stereotyped occupational and family roles that disadvantage females. Hence, they examine sexual bias and gender stereotyping in curricular materials, classroom interaction, and/or official and unofficial policies of schools. A third concern of liberal feminists is the notion of discrimination, examining the ways that sexism and gender discrimination are enacted in schools and addressing sexual stratification and sexual inequality.

Liberal feminist theory has been extremely important in documenting gender discrimination and the analysis of specific sexist texts and practices. By gathering and disseminating such documented information and evidence, liberal feminists work to alter socialization practices; educate teachers, children, and parents to change attitudes; and provide teachers with ideas for combating sexism. Liberal feminism's greatest political achievement in the United States is Title IX of the 1972 Education Amendment that prohibits the granting of federal funds to any public educational institution that practices sexual discrimination (Tyack & Hansot, 1990). Similarly, in Britain, the Equal Opportunities Commission (EOC) has been created to put informal pressure on schools and education authorities (Acker, 1987).

Critical Feminist Theory

Some feminists are not happy with liberal feminism on the grounds that it does not help us with an understanding of why there are still unequal social relationships between girls and boys or men and women within capitalist society. They complain that liberal feminism does not explain the various, subtle forms of men's power and privilege that work together and that cause the constraints and suffering that many women experience at home, in the workplace, and in society (Weiler, 1988, 2001; Pinar, Reynolds, Slattery, & Taubman, 2008). Hence, they call for a critical or radical feminist theory.

To be exact, critical feminist theory is a confluence of critical theory and feminist theory, as it is concerned with the production and reproduction of gender privilege under a system of patriarchy, in parallel with critical theory's production and reproduction of class structure, if you recall. However, critical feminist theorists realize that traditional critical theory is inadequate to reveal the nature of women's experience and oppression because it focuses on class issues. Critical feminist theory provides two approaches: feminist reproduction theory and feminist resistance theory, utilizing critical theory's notion of reproduction and that of resistance, while placing gender oppression at the center of the theory.

Feminist reproduction theory is concerned with the ways in which schools function to reproduce gender divisions and oppression through sexist texts and discriminatory practices. The major focus of this approach is "on the connection between sexist practices in the school and women's oppression in society as a whole" (Weiler, 1988, p. 31). Since these theorists are concerned with the role of schooling in the reproduction of existing gendered hierarchy and gender inequality, their analyses focus on the way schools work to prepare girls to accept their gendered roles, for example, directing girls to home economics courses, and their status as low-paid or unpaid workers. However, this theory fails to acknowledge human beings as agents who are able to contest the ideological messages schools implicitly or explicitly send to them. Human agency, the ability to determine one's own action, is unexamined by feminist reproduction.

In response to these limitations of feminist reproduction, practitioners of feminist resistance theory examine girls' and women's lived experiences in schools from the perspective of resistance and cultural production theories (Brown & Gilligan, 1992; Robinson & Kennington, 2002;

Robinson & Ward, 1991). For feminist resistance theory, directly influenced by neo-Marxist critical theory, resistance is an important concept in looking at the lives of girls and women in schools, because it highlights their ability as human agents to make meaning and to act in social situations as well as to be acted upon.

Intersectionality in Feminist Theory

Our discussions of liberal feminist theory and critical feminist theory so far provide a brief explanation of how feminism and feminist theory have developed in the academy. Currently, feminist scholars and students in all the different disciplines embrace the popularity of **intersectionality**, advancing feminist theory to a more complex and sophisticated field of study. According to Davis (2008), intersectionality—"the interaction of multiple identities and experiences of exclusion and subordination" (p. 67)—is becoming a "buzzword," creating a successful phenomenon within contemporary feminist scholarship throughout the United States and Europe. In fact, McCall (2005) sees intersectionality as one of the most important feminist contributions to women's studies and related fields in understanding different experiences of women. To defy the criticism of feminism that feminist theory speaks universally for all women, feminist researchers are acutely aware that it is almost impossible to use gender as a single analytical category; they must attend to multiple identities and subjective experiences of subordination, hence, intersectionality is an inevitable concept.

Intersectionality is defined as the "interaction between gender, race, and other categories of difference in individual lives, social practices, institutional arrangements, and cultural ideologies and the outcomes of these interactions in terms of power" (Davis, 2008, p. 68). Davis traces the origin of the concept of intersectionality to Kimberlé Crenshaw, whose name is familiar to us from critical race theory, and who addressed the fact that the lived experiences and struggles of Black women had fallen through the cracks between feminist and anti-racist discourse. Realizing that neither feminist theory focusing on female experience nor critical race theory focusing on racial experience could fully explore the experiences of Black women, Crenshaw (1989) urged theorists to take both gender and race into consideration and address in their analyses how they intersect to shape the multiple dimensions of Black women's experiences.

Similarly, another critical race theorist and feminist, Patricia Hill Collins (1986), coined the term Black Feminist Thought to refer to Black women's outsider-within status vis-à-vis sociology. Her main idea is that Black feminist scholars have been marginalized in intellectual discourse; but they may be one of many distinct groups of marginal intellectuals whose standpoints promise to enrich contemporary sociological discourse (Collins, 1986). Collins defines three key themes in Black Feminist Thought (BFT). First, BFT is produced by Black women, focusing on the meaning of self-definition and self-valuation; second, there is attention to the interlocking nature of race, gender, and class oppression in the work of Black feminists; and third, BFT involves efforts to redefine and explain the importance of Black women's culture (Collins, 1986). As I see it, then, the future might bring Asian Feminist Thought, Native American Feminist Thought, Latina Feminist Thought, and more. Anyone?

Intersectionality in feminist theory does not end in a combination with race and class. It integrates other intellectual thoughts and disciplines. For example, Judith Butler, an American philosopher and feminist who has been influential in academic feminism and queer theory, advances feminist theory drawing upon postmodernism/poststructuralism and the work of French philosopher and feminist Julia Kristeva, in her seminal book, *Gender Trouble* (Butler, 1990). Butler interrogates and theorizes women's individual subjectivity, subversion of identity, problematizing feminism that values women's group identity as and for women and moving toward performative feminist theory. Butler (1992) further employs poststructural feminist theory for analysis of taken-for-granted ideas about gender, sex, materiality, violence, rape, and the like.

As you see, intersectionality has advanced feminist theory and has been the subject of debates by feminist scholars and students alike from all different disciplines. Intersectionality places the issue of difference and diversity at its center. It is a fitting concept in the age of post-modernism and poststructuralism in understanding the effects of race, class, gender, and sexuality on women's identities, experiences, and struggles and in exploring how categories of race, class, and gender are intertwined and mutually influential. Thus, it is now common to ask questions like how race is "gendered" and how gender is "racialized," and how both are linked to social class in shaping the experiences of women's struggles (Davis, 2008). For example, Davis contends that it is unimaginable that gender studies would focus only on gender. She further informs that feminist journals are likely to reject articles that have not given sufficient attention to race, class, and other differences, along with gender. Thus, any scholar who neglects difference would run the risk of having her or his work viewed as "theoretically misguided, politically irrelevant, or simply fantastical" (p. 68). Then, it is clear that the concept of intersectionality should be utilized not only in feminist theory but also in other areas of contemporary intellectual thought.

Before we move on to the discussion of phenomenology, I would like to share with you a narrative by Jessica, a feminist doctoral student who taught undergraduate physics before becoming a full-time graduate student. This narrative comes from her weekly Epiphany of Learning assignment submitted in my curriculum theory class:

I really get riled up when I read extremely negative and chauvinistic comments posted to online news sources when they publish stories that highlight female achievements in non-traditional female roles. For instance, a few months ago, a story was published about the achievements of physicist and astronaut Sally Ride, the first American woman in space. There was such a disproportionate number of disgraceful public comments made about her sexual orientation and her ability to make sandwiches for the men aboard the spacecraft with her. I was so appalled! If it were an article about the first American man in space, I am sure I would have found far fewer— perhaps no—negative reactions to the story. Another thing I noticed was how it appeared to be a bandwagon affect of insulting remarks. People kept feeding off one another and the words became more and more hurtful. This type of groupthink can become a dangerous thing and if transferred to physical rather than verbal action, women stand to suffer severe bodily harm such as gang rape. We have seen this happen in teenaged crowds and bullying in schools. More must be done to address the proper treatment and respect of women and all "unmasculine" humans to include people with mental or physical disabilities and homosexual and transgender men. (Jessica's Weekly Epiphany of Learning assignment, Week Seven)

I share her narrative here because through her observation of online media, Jessica was able to penetrate all the critical issues of the contemporary feminist theory, which includes gender stereotyping, gender role, female body, harassment, violence, rape, sexual orientation, gender identity, and transgender. She problematizes the "gaze" that appeared in *disgraceful public comments,* and contests "the place and authority of the masculine position" (Butler, 1990, p. vii), calling for *proper treatment and respect of all "unmasculine" humans.* It seems to me that Jessica's narrative is particularly insightful as she points to the problems that arise from the meanings we have traditionally given to the division of human beings into male and female, our attitudes that are associated with biological and hormonal differences that we understand to be sexual, and increasing violence toward women.

For an example of narrative inquiry that uses feminist theory as theoretical framework, see Chapter 6, the section on Analysis in Biographical Narrative Inquiry.

Phenomenology

My doctoral student Jodie and I met the other day to discuss her narrative data analysis for her dissertation research. Jodie's dissertation research is a narrative inquiry into the lived experience of physical education (PE) teachers with an interpretative framework of phenomenology. She had just come back from a conference, the ICNAP (Interdisciplinary Coalition of North American Phenomenologists), which was held in St. Louis, Missouri.

I was proud of her for her intellectual investment in learning phenomenology beyond her class reading. When I asked her about her conference experience, her face lit up immediately:

Jodie: (in her usual convivial voice) Oh my gosh, it was SO phenomenal, I mean, phenomenological, I should say! Some of the things that they were talking about were way over my head, you know? I was like, huh? My head hurt so much, but I learned so much! I kept jotting down notes so that I wouldn't forget!

Me: (I was cracking up) So, what did you learn?

Jodie: (she looked at her scribbled notes and said) Oh my gosh, I hope I can remember what I wrote here!

And then, she delved into her notes and shared her learning with me as much as she could. She shared how researchers in different disciplines were using phenomenology to understand the lifeworld, health, well-being, narratives, and more. Listening to her, I was further convinced of the close kinship between phenomenology and narrative inquiry.

Phenomenology[4] was a philosophical movement that arose in Germany before World War I, and occupied a unique place in twentieth-century philosophy. Founded by Edmund Husserl, whose dictum was "to return to the things themselves," it was further developed by Heidegger, Merleau-Ponty, Gadamer, Sartre, and others. According to Gadamer (1975/2006), phenomenology wants to "bring the phenomena to expression" (p. 131), and it was regarded by Husserl as the only way of elevating philosophy to the status of a rigorous science (Gadamer, 1975/2006; Merleau-Ponty, 1962/2007). Hence, phenomenology has had a significant impact in the history of modern Western philosophy (Peters, 2009b), and its impact has extended beyond philosophy to fields such as education, psychology, sociology, anthropology, politics, linguistics, architecture, feminist studies, and environmental studies. In addition, as I learned from Jodie, there are also "applied phenomenologies" in the studies of commodification, social media, and kinesthetic empathy, to name just a few.

Phenomenology is a philosophy that "cannot define its scope" (Merleau-Ponty, 1962/2007, p. viii) very easily, as Husserl himself had contradictions in his own philosophy. It has long remained "a problem to be solved and a hope to be realized" (p. ix). Even so, according to Merleau-Ponty,[5] there is still a need to understand the significance of this philosophy. Hence, Merleau-Ponty attempts to capture general characteristics of phenomenology, as shown in Table 2.2.

Methods of Phenomenological Knowledge

According to Merleau-Ponty, phenomenology is accessible "only through a phenomenological method" (p. viii), hence we need to understand the method of gaining phenomenological knowledge with the "celebrated phenomenological themes" (p. viii) used when engaging in phenomenology. The "celebrated phenomenological themes" we will discuss here include *subjectivity, intersubjectivity, phenomenological reduction, bracketing (epoche),* and *intentionality.*

Table 2.2   Characteristics of Phenomenology

- It is "the study of essences" (p. vii): the essence of perception, the essence of consciousness, the essence of lifeworld (Lebenswelt), or the essence of experience of everyday life.
- It is a philosophy that "puts essences back into existence" (p. vii) as it attempts to understand a phenomenon from any starting point other than its facticity.
- It is a "transcendental philosophy which places in abeyance the assertions arising out of the natural attitude" (p. vii) in order to better understand the world filled with phenomena because "the world is always 'already there' before reflection begins" (p. vii).
- It attempts to provide "a direct description of our experience as it is, without taking account of its psychological origin and the causal explanations which the scientist, the historian or the sociologist may be able to provide" (p. vii).
- It "can be practiced and identified as a manner or style of thinking" (p. viii).

(Adapted from Merleau-Ponty, 1962/2007)

Subjectivity

In phenomenology, knowledge begins with *subjectivity,* and this *subjectivity* is the epistemological starting point in phenomenology (Levering, 2006). Any ordinary human being is regarded as the epistemological subject who gives meaning to the world (the object), claiming his or her own subjectivity. *Subjectivity,* hence, means giving personal meaning to a phenomenon, acknowledging that each human individual has his or her own outlook on reality shaped by his or her own experience. Phenomenologists believe that the subject, "I," is at the center of the object (the world, or the experience) because "I" is the one who knows the world while giving meaning to it. Hence, "All my knowledge of the world, even my scientific knowledge is gained from my own particular point of view" (Merleau-Ponty, 1962/2007, p. ix), and "I cannot conceive myself as nothing but a bit of the world, a mere object of biological, psychological or sociological investigation" (p. ix). In addition, "I am the absolute source, my existence does not stem from my antecedents from my physical and social environment" (p. ix). This subjectivity, first-person knowledge, is the beginning of phenomenology. Hence, phenomenology is also defined as "the study of conscious experience as lived, as experienced from the first-person point of view" (Smith & Thomasson, 2005, p. 1). But does this subjectivity mean that phenomenology relies on introspection, which is a "way of being a spectator on our inner states of mind" (Thomasson, 2005, p. 116)? According to Thomasson (2005), it is often thought that phenomenological knowledge must be based in the introspection of our mental states, but Husserl was against such introspectionist views of first-person knowledge and developed the method of *phenomenological reduction* as a source of knowledge of our own "consciousness" or "active meaning-giving operation" (Merleau-Ponty, 1962/2007, p. xii). In other words, for Husserl, first-person knowledge is based on awareness directed toward the world, "outer observation of the world, rather than a direct inner observation of one's own experiences" (Thomasson, 2005, p. 116).

Phenomenological Reduction

Hence, Husserl's method of *phenomenological reduction,* known as his "greatest discovery" (Moran, 2000, p. 12), refers to a way of acquiring knowledge based in nonjudgmental, outer-awareness of the world. For example, when I try to understand a phenomenon represented in lived experience, I have to withhold my claim, commitment, or prior knowledge regarding its real existence and nature. When we engage in phenomenological reduction, we say how a phenomenon *looks* to us rather than *claiming what a phenomenon is.* Therefore, in order to get back to things themselves, we must endeavor to withhold not only our personal judgment or claim but also set aside scientific concepts, including "the causal explanations which the scientist, the historian or the sociologist may be able to provide" (Merleau-Ponty, 1962/2007, p. vii). In order to engage in phenomenological reduction, therefore, we must "bracket the assumption that our judgments are true, our experiences veridical" (Thomasson, 2005, p. 124), and this bracketing is the basic method of phenomenological reduction.

Bracketing, [ ], also called *epoché,* a Greek term meaning "to refrain from judgment" (Moustakas, 1994, p. 33), is a strategy we must adopt during the process of phenomenological reduction in order to acquire phenomenological knowledge about the essence of the lived experience (a phenomenon). By this process, we can encounter even the familiar as something strange, wondrous, and unfamiliar to us. It is Husserl's belief that through the method of phenomenological reduction with a strategy of bracketing (epoché), the subjective "I" can arrive at the essence of a phenomenon, and every phenomenon has its own consciousness (or intentionality, see below). This is where phenomenological reduction renders "transcendental idealism" (Merleau-Ponty, 1962/2007, p. xii), which treats the essence of a phenomenon as an "indivisible unity of value" (p. xii). This essence of a phenomenon, an "indivisible unity of value," can be shared by my subjectivity and others' subjectivity without a problem, which gives way to the notion of intersubjectivity in which different perspectives blend. *Intersubjectivity* refers to a "communication" (p. xii) between my consciousness (my act of giving meaning) and your consciousness (your act of giving meaning), and we are not going to have any problem in our communication about the essence of a phenomenon because we both understand that it has the same meaning or truth ("indivisible unity of value") since we both have acquired it through our own phenomenological reduction process—well, at least in theory.

However, this is easier said than done! Can we really arrive at the essence of a phenomenon, an indivisible unity of value without any influence from our own preconceived ideas? More specifically, can you and I arrive at the same meaning or truth of the phenomenon that we try to understand through our own phenomenological reduction? Husserl understood this conundrum and pointed out the impossibility of a complete reduction; and this is why "Husserl is constantly re-examining the possibility of the reduction" (p. xv). Since we are always influenced by our reflections on the world we are trying to seize, this reduction or bracketing becomes a never-ending process. Hence, the phenomenologist is:

> a perpetual beginner, which means that he takes for granted nothing that men, learned or otherwise, believe they know. It means also that philosophy itself must not take itself for granted, in so far as it may have managed to say something true; that it is an ever-renewed experiment in making its own beginning; that it consists wholly in the description of this beginning. (p. xv)

Therefore, we need to continuously check, like a "perpetual beginner," whether our understanding of the essence of a phenomenon is tainted by our own preconceptions.

Intentionality

Then, so what? What are we supposed to do with an understanding of the essence of a phenomenon? Merleau-Ponty carefully reminds us that understanding the essence is not the end, but a means by which we understand our involvement in the world, for "our effective involvement in the world is precisely what has to be understood" (p. xvi). One of the aims of phenomenological understanding is to "take in the total *intention,* not only what these things are for representation . . . but the unique mode of existing expressed in the properties of the pebble, the glass or the piece of wax, in all the events of a revolution, in all the thoughts of a philosopher" (p. xx, italics my emphasis). Merleau-Ponty explains that this notion of *intentionality,* known as another main discovery of phenomenology, is phenomenological comprehension that is distinguished from the traditional scientific way of knowing in which knowledge is confined to true, immutable natures. In phenomenological understanding, however, an understanding of the essence serves as a means to help us understand its intentionality of why the properties of the world (or phenomena) have such a unique mode of existing, expressed in distinct patterns. For example, if a phenomenon that we want to study is a certain event, we first have to understand the essence of the event, and then we need to understand its intentionality, a "formula which sums up some unique manner of behavior towards others" (p. xx). To do this, we must seek to understand from "all different angles and all levels simultaneously" (p. xxi), such as ideology, politics, science, religion, economics, or psychology, because every phenomenon has meaning or *intentionality.*

Hermeneutical Phenomenology

Then, understanding intentionality involves knowing more than the "what" of a phenomenon (description) and requires an understanding of the "why" of the description, thus an interpretation. Building upon Husserl's phenomenology, Heidegger, who studied with Husserl, developed hermeneutical (interpretive) phenomenology. In fact, Merleau-Ponty posits that there is a distinction between Husserl's and Heidegger's phenomenology, although Heidegger's phenomenology has sprung from Husserl's. What, then, is the distinction?

For Husserl, phenomenology is "a matter of describing, not of explaining or analyzing" (p. ix) (hence, it is a descriptive phenomenology), but for Martin Heidegger (1889–1976), phenomenology is not only descriptive but also hermeneutical and interpretive because there are many hidden aspects in phenomena that need to be uncovered and interpreted (Heidegger, 1962/2008). Hence, according to Heidegger, phenomenology takes the form of interpretive inquiry, rendering a hermeneutical phenomenology. Hermeneutical phenomenology offers "insight not just by exhibiting what is already self-evident in awareness, but by drawing out, eliciting, evoking, uncovering what lies hidden or buried in and around whatever manifests itself openly in the world" (Carman, 2008, p. xviii). This act of digging up, uncovering, and interpreting is called "hermeneutical excavation and elucidation" (Carman, 2008, p. xviii).

To go a bit further in comparing Husserl and Heidegger, Husserl's phenomenology is epistemological in that his aim is to reveal truth and knowledge that surpasses or transcends our assumptions about human experience through the description of the essence of the experience, while Heidegger's interpretive phenomenology is ontological as he aims to understand being itself. In his seminal book, *Being and Time* (1962/2008), Heidegger pursued the question of being and time by undertaking a phenomenology of human understanding. According to Heidegger, "phenomenology is our way of access to what is to be the theme of ontology, and it is our way of giving it demonstrative precision. *Only as phenomenology, is ontology possible*" (p. 60, italics in original). So, for Heidegger, ontology and phenomenology are inseparable from each other as philosophical disciplines.

Hence, phenomenology can be descriptive and interpretive, epistemological and ontological. The phenomenological world is:

> the sense that is revealed where the paths of my various experiences intersect, and also where my own and other people's intersect and engage each other like gears. It is thus inseparable from subjectivity and intersubjectivity, which find their unity when I either take up my past experiences in those of the present, or other people's in my own. (Merleau-Ponty, 1962/2007, p. xxii)

In this sense, the main task of a phenomenologist is, just like art, to reveal the mystery of the world and of human experiences with attention, wonder, awareness, and intention to seize the meaning of the world and to let the meaning come into being (Merleau-Ponty, 1962/2007). Therefore, a phenomenological inquiry is an artistic endeavor, a creative attempt to capture a certain phenomenon of life in a way that is holistic, evocative, powerful, unique, and sensitive (van Manen, 1990).

Resurgence of Phenomenology and Narrative Inquiry

Despite its philosophical importance, phenomenology was neglected and remained vague for a while, giving way to deconstruction, poststructuralism, and postmodernism (Pinar & Reynolds, 1991). We have experienced the rise of poststructuralism and deconstruction, intellectual thoughts that contest phenomenology asserting that it is impossible to get to the essence of experience; and that the meaning of reality is created by the discourse and the language, which needs to be deconstructed. The decline of phenomenology is vividly described by David Jardine, a contemporary curriculum theorist: "phenomenology got out of hand and climbed down below the severed head when Husserl wasn't looking" (Jardine, 1992, p. 129).

We are in luck, however. Currently, there is a resurgence of interest in phenomenology as a philosophy and as a research movement. It has become an increasingly important tool for understanding the twenty-first century's dynamic, ambiguous, and complicated phenomena (Dall'Alba, 2009). Dall'Alba argues that phenomenology explores the phenomena under study as a way of inquiring; hence it can offer deeper insights into what it means to live and what it means to be human in such a complex society. For example, educational researchers had a special symposium on phenomenology at the European Conference in Educational Research held in Geneva in 2006. Papers presented at the conference were later published in a special issue of *Educational Philosophy and Theory* (see Dall'Alba, 2009), using phenomenology in combination with other research approaches, such as feminist scholarship. This intellectual amalgam of phenomenology and other scholarships characterizes contemporary phenomenology, whereby phenomenology is "enriched by other research approaches while also making a substantial contribution to them" (p. 7).

Personally, I owe phenomenology; it has enhanced my work as I strive to embody its main ideas in my teaching and researching. In teaching, for example, I try to understand the essence of my students' lived experience from their perspectives. As for research, I conducted a narrative inquiry into a student's lived experience from a phenomenological perspective (Kim, 2012). In this study, phenomenology allowed me to "bracket" my own value judgment on a student who used to be a gang member, engaged in violence. It also helped me honor the student Matto as he was, bringing the meaning of his lived experience to the fore (see Chapter 4).

Poststructuralism/Postmodernism/Deconstruction

Poststructuralism was clearly a French movement, as the main thinkers of poststructuralism are French philosophers: Foucault, Deleuze, Derrida, Lacan, Guattari, Kristeva, Lyotard, and Baudrillard, to name a few. According to Poster (1989), however, poststructuralism as a theory (as opposed to the actual movement), was an "American practice" (p. 6) in which Americans adopted the ideas of Foucault, Derrida, and the rest as poststructuralist theory. Today, it is not just an American practice. Poststructuralism has deeply penetrated academic discourse in many countries over the past two decades. Increasingly, scholars and researchers, including fledgling doctoral students who do not follow the epistemology of positivism, adopt poststructuralism as their overarching worldview or philosophical/theoretical framework. It certainly informs narrative researchers who cast doubt on classical notions of truth, reality, meaning, and knowledge, who seek to interrogate power relations appearing in narratives and stories, and who attend to the ramifications of multiple truths in an effort to reject the meta-narrative or the universal truth.

In my doctoral seminar, Curriculum Theory, when it was time to discuss poststructuralism/postmodernism/deconstruction,[6] we moaned and groaned together in seeking to understand poststructuralism; after all, even Foucault said he didn't know what it was! The more we read, the more confused we were. We found the concepts and definitions of poststructuralism complex, complicated, and hard to pin down. We wanted to identify one concrete, crisp, totalizing definition or concept of poststructuralism although we were told that the identification of poststructuralism was not possible without taking its multiplicities into account. Poststructuralism constitutes multiple formations of thought, multiple sources of ideas, multiple thinkers, and their influences in multiple disciplines (Peters, 1998). In fact, Peters contended that poststructuralism cannot simply be reduced to "a set of shared assumptions, a method, or a body of theory" (p. 2). I suddenly found myself being a cheerleader to help my students keep interested in poststructuralism despite these complexities. Interestingly, however, these complexities actually freed us from the fear of not knowing and became an impetus to explore poststructuralism with open minds. I hope you will join me in an exploration of poststructuralism with inquisitiveness.

After Structuralism

In his first edition on structuralism, Sturrock (1986) posits the "post" in "post-structuralism" in terms of "coming after and of seeking to extend structuralism in its rightful direction" (p. 137). Sturrock views poststructuralism as a critique of structuralism that turns some of structuralism's arguments against itself and points to some inconsistencies in its method. Therefore, to better understand the poststructuralism that came after structuralism, it will be helpful if we look at what structuralism is and how it is criticized by poststructuralists. According to Peters (1998), the genealogy of the poststructuralist movement is bifurcated: one branch is tied to structural linguistics of the 1950s, more precisely Saussure's groundbreaking transformation of linguistics into a systemic theory of language; and the other is related to the Nietzschean influences on French philosophers. Let me explain.

Structuralism, adopted from the Saussurean linguistics perspective, is a method of analysis that privileges structures, systems, or sets of relations (Pinar et al., 2008). It seeks to identify the structures that are believed to be invariant and examine how the underlying structures have shaped individual experiences. For structuralists, individual meanings come from those invariant structures, systems, and sets of relations. It is the structure or the system that defines reality and gives meaning to reality. Hence, structuralism disregards subjectivity (unlike phenomenology); it attempts to stop the influence of subjectivity in meaning making. In that sense, structuralism was an opposition to existentialism and phenomenology. In structuralism, reality and meaning can be found by the invariant structures and human subjectivity is merely the product of such invariant structures.

What is important here is that structuralism turns to language as the medium through which structures reveal themselves. For structuralists, language becomes the field of investigation. Thus, structuralists draw upon Saussurean linguistic theory of *langue* (language) and *parole* (speech), where language is believed to be the system of the signifier (spoken and written word) and the signified (meaning of the word). The relationship between the signifier and the signified, then, is culturally determined; hence, it is arbitrary. Structures and systems are revealed in language and thus language is taken as reality. As Eagleton (2008) points out, within structuralism "reality is not reflected by language but produced by it" (p. 108). Therefore, in structuralism, codes, structures, and systems replace human consciousness, while decentering sovereign consciousness of the subject and rejecting subjectivity as the origin of meaning. Meaning is formed by language, as it is already conditioned, constrained, and delimited in ambient structures.

Nietzschean Influences on Poststructuralism

As mentioned above, poststructuralism is a critique of structuralism. Intellectuals started attacking structuralism, creating a movement in the 1970s. Historically speaking, poststructuralism refers to a cultural, political, and historical movement that rejects structuralism and modernism, both modes of thinking that espouse universal truths and meta-narratives based on reason (Peters, 1998). According to Rabaté (2003), it was François Dosse who noted in his chronicle of French structuralism that the year 1966 marked the end of structuralism, a climax and a turning point. In this year, Foucault's *The Order of Things* was published in France, and at a conference at Johns Hopkins University in the United States, Barthes, Lacan, Derrida, Todorov, and other distinguished scholars from different fields were invited to explain structuralism and its discontents. These watershed events led to the slogans and posters of 1968 that marked the "death of structuralism." Radicals and student critics perceived structuralism as compromised by the discourse of authority and knowledge (Rabaté, 2003).

By the early 1970s, structuralism was seriously criticized by emerging scholars like Derrida, Foucault, and Deleuze. The term *poststructuralism* was coined in the late 1970s in parallel with postmodernism, replacing the term neo-structuralism in French, which never became current in English (Rabaté, 2003). Moving from the era of structuralism, the reign of poststructuralism began as "a style of thought which embraces the deconstructive operations of Derrida, the work of the French historian Michel Foucault, the writings of the French psychoanalyst Jacques Lacan, and of the feminist philosopher and critic Julia Kristeva" (Eagleton, 2008, p. 116).

Where, then, did the poststructuralists find their intellectual sources? To whom did they have recourse? Both Peters (1998) and Schrift (1995) argue that poststructuralists drew from several shared sources, one of which is Nietzsche, although his influence was later eclipsed. They posit that the importance of Nietzsche was prevalent in the thinking of poststructuralists, including Foucault, Deleuze, and others during the 1960s as they turned to Nietzsche as a way to express their dissatisfaction with the theory of the subject in phenomenology. Because there is no one interpretation that constitutes true Nietzscheanism (Foucault, 1983), the relationships of individual poststructuralists to Nietzsche differ greatly (Peters, 1998). However, Nietzsche's general emphases on the critique of truth and the different relations of power and knowledge have become the central problems of the poststructuralists.

Schrift (1995) points out that poststructuralism is not a theory with a uniform set of shared assumptions; rather, it is "a loose association of thinkers" (p. 6) who have developed their own distinctive philosophical lines of thought, but share the common umbrella of poststructuralism. Thus, it is important for us to understand several common characteristics of poststructuralism (see Table 2.3),

Table 2.3   General Characteristics of Poststructuralism

- It attends to questions of language, power, and desire in ways that emphasize the context in which meaning is produced while challenging all universal truth.
- It challenges the assumptions that give rise to binary thinking.
- It acknowledges differences, particularities, fragmentation, instead of claiming universality and unity.
- It questions the humanistic notion of subject, which assumes autonomy and transparent self-consciousness.
- It situates the subject in a complex intersection of social forces and practices present in a discourse.
- It uses forms of discourse analysis and deconstruction as new means of analysis.

(Adapted from Schrift, 1995)

and at the same time, to identify each thinker's unique philosophical thoughts that distinguish them from each other.

Next, I briefly discuss three main poststructuralists: Deleuze, Foucault, and Derrida.[7] But the scope of the discussions here offers less than an introduction to their huge projects. It is my hope that this little taste of each poststructuralist will motivate you to read more about them on your own to inform your research.

Gilles Deleuze (1925–1995): Rhizomatic Thinking

Peters (1998) argues that Deleuze is an originator of French poststructuralism and that Deleuze's Nietzschean critique of Hegel should serve as the conceptual grounding for poststructuralism. In fact, Deleuze drew upon Nietzsche in order to critique and reject Hegel's negative dialectical framework, and established a theoretical framework separate from Hegel (Leach & Boler, 1998). One of Deleuze's (and his collaborator, Guattari's) ultimate goals was to distance themselves from the traditional binary logic where one operates in the object, and the other in the subject. For Deleuze and Guattari (1987), this dichotomous thinking that dominates psychoanalysis, linguistics, structuralism, and even information science, does not provide any better understanding of multiplicity than nature itself. They turn to nature in order to dismantle binary logic as they remark, "Nature doesn't work that way: in nature, roots are taproots with a more multiple, lateral, and circular system of ramification, rather than a dichotomous one. Thought lags behind nature" (p. 5). I particularly love the last statement: "Thought lags behind nature," which seems inspired by Albert Einstein's (1879–1955) remark, "Look deep into nature, and then you will understand everything better." Okay, back to Deleuze and Guattari.

Taking a cue from nature for their intellectual thinking, Deleuze and Guattari have expounded **rhizomatic thinking** that shifts the traditional binary logic of dualism to multiplicity that is circular, multiple, and lateral. They call a system of this kind a *rhizome*. In their seminal book, *A Thousand Plateaus: Capitalism and Schizophrenia,* Deleuze and Guattari (1987) define a rhizome as "a subterranean stem [that] is absolutely different from roots and radicles" (p. 6). They further enumerate more approximate characteristics of the rhizome in nature:

> Bulbs and tubers are rhizomes. Plants with roots or radicles may be rhizomorphic in other respects altogether: the question is whether plant life in its specificity is not entirely rhizomatic. Even some animals are, in their pack form. . . . The rhizome itself assumes very diverse forms, from ramified surface extension in all directions to concretion into bulbs and tubers. (pp. 6–7)

After learning the concept of a rhizome in my curriculum theory class one night, a doctoral student, Ron, had an epiphany. When he got home, he wrote:

> I have an entirely new perspective on my wife's daylilies and her persistent separation of the roots, transplanting, thinning, and fertilizing—She is doing what educational theorists have been doing and are continuing to do. (Ron's class assignment submitted on October 6, 2013)

I truly appreciated Ron's sign of rhizomatic thinking discovered in a quotidian life that he had not noticed before. A rhizome connects any point to any other point; it is composed not of units but of dimensions, or rather directions in motion. It has neither beginning nor end, but always a middle (milieu) from which it grows and which it overspills. It is made of plateaus that are always in the middle, not at the beginning or the end. It is always in the middle, between things, interbeing, *intermezzo* (Deleuze & Guattari, 1987, p. 25). The fabric of the rhizome, therefore, is the conjunction, "and . . . and . . . and . . ." (p. 25). The rhizome is not the object of reproduction, but instead operates by variation, expansion, conquest, rupture, and offshoots (Deleuze & Guattari, 1987).

Based on these characteristics of the rhizome, Deleuze and Guattari postulate the principles of rhizomatic thinking shown in Table 2.4.

Rhizomatic Thinking and Narrative Inquiry

Sermijn, Devlieger, and Loots (2008) use the concept of the rhizome as a metaphor for the narrative construction of selfhood. They describe selfhood as a rhizomatic story with multiple entryways. They assume that there is no single correct point of entry that can lead the researcher to "'the truth' about the selfhood of the participant" (p. 638), unlike the traditional story that has only one entry and exit point (the beginning and the end). They theorize how selfhood as a rhizomatic story has many possible entryways, and how each entryway leads to a temporary rendering of selfhood. They make a point that there is no such thing as a fixed authentic, prediscursive self.

Table 2.4 Principles of Rhizomatic Thinking

- *Principles of connection and heterogeneity*: "Any point of a rhizome can be connected to anything other, and must be. A rhizome ceaselessly establishes connections between semiotic chains, organizations of power, and circumstances relative to the arts, sciences, and social struggles" (p. 7).
- *Principle of multiplicity*: "A rhizome has multiplicity that cannot increase in number without the multiplicity changing in nature. Multiplicities are defined by the outside: by the abstract line, the line of flight[8] or deterritorialization according to which they change in nature and connect with other multiplicities" (p. 9).
- *Principle of a signifying rupture*: "A rhizome may be broken, shattered at a given spot, but it will start up again on one of its old lines, or on new lines. There is a rupture in the rhizome whenever segmentary lines explode into a line of flight, but the line of flight is part of the rhizome. These lines always tie back to one another. That is why one can never posit a dualism or a dichotomy, even in the rudimentary form of the good and the bad" (p. 9).
- *Principle of cartography and decalcomania*: "The rhizome makes a map, and not a tracing. The map is open and connectable in all of its dimensions; it is detachable, reversible, susceptible to constant modification. A map has multiple entryways, as opposed to the tracing, which always comes back to the same" (p. 12).

(Deleuze & Guattari, 1987)

More recently, Loots, Coppens, and Sermijn (2013) demonstrate how rhizomatic thinking can be applied in narrative inquiry by presenting a case study on life narratives in a community in Northern Uganda. They investigate the life stories of parents whose children have been kidnapped. Their narrative analysis from a rhizomatic perspective led to "a visualization of the multitude of polyphony of the different voices" (p. 115),[9] which include voice of pain/suffering; voice of no control; voice of fighting back; voice of being a born again Christian; and evaluative voice. In their study, they posit how a rhizome approach has helped them move in a decentralizing way, allowing "the polyphonic voices emerge and expand in a continuous process of differentiating, connecting, and rupturing, and grow into divergent lines" (p. 121). They suggest that engaging in narrative research from a rhizomatic approach should be encouraged, as it could become "a possible source of inspiration for trying out other ways of doing narrative enquiry" (p. 121).

Michel Foucault (1926–1984): An Analysis of Power Relations

If Deleuze is considered an originator of poststructuralism, I think Foucault is the most popular poststructuralist. Foucault is also connected to Nietzsche by his critique of truth in relation to the problem of self (Mahon, 1992; Peters, 1998). Foucault (1983) noted how his childhood was influenced by the impending war and the political situation of the time. He received his doctorate on the history of madness after working in psychiatric institutions and prisons. Later, he became very involved with a group that supported prisoners' right to speak for themselves and to set up their own active organizations. Foucault believed this type of human rights advocacy to be the proper role of intellectuals (Marshall, 1998).

Foucault did not claim to be a poststructuralist. When asked in an interview how he situated himself within the postmodern current, Foucault (1983) stated, "What are we calling post-modernity? I'm not up to date" (p. 204). And then he continued:

> While I see clearly that behind what was known as structuralism, there was a certain problem broadly speaking, that of the subject and the recasting of the subject—I do not understand what kind of problem is common to the people we call post-modern or post-structuralist. (p. 205)

Then, why do we call Foucault a poststructuralist? It is mainly because of his reservations toward structuralism and phenomenology. Although Foucault recognized the value of structuralism in language analysis, he regarded it as a shallow philosophy that was too close to positivism and dissociated himself from structuralism elsewhere by saying, "I did not want to carry the structuralist enterprise beyond its legitimate limits. And you must admit that I never once used the word 'structure' in *The Order of Things*" (1966/1970) (quoted in Rabaté, 2003, p. 3). What Foucault called for was a history of human subjectivity to serve as a renewed awareness of the types of political domination underpinning it.

What is Foucault's problem, then? Foucault (1983) himself states his main problem has always been "an analysis of the relation between forms of reflexivity—a relation of self to self—and, hence, of relations between forms of reflexivity and the discourse of truth, forms of rationality and effects of knowledge"[10] (p. 203). In doing so, he questions the phenomenological notion of the subject as a free, sovereign consciousness. He further asks, "How is it that the human subject took itself as the object of possible knowledge?" or "At what price can subjects speak the truth about themselves?" (p. 202). Through these questions, Foucault disregards the valorized, free, sovereign subject (that subjectivity which we saw is the starting point in phenomenology). Instead, he seeks a more ambivalent subject constrained in institutional forces while postulating a notion of a subject that is both autonomous and disciplined, and both actively self-forming and passively self-constructed. Thus, one of Foucault's problems has been to explore how human beings are made subjects, hence an *objectification of the subject*. The word *subject* here has two meanings: one, subject to someone else by control and dependence, and the other tied to the individual's own identity by a consciousness or self-knowledge. Both meanings suggest a form of power that subjugates and makes one subject (Schrift, 1995).

I think that the discussion of an objectification of the subject is rather important in understanding Foucault. We can turn to Rabinow (1984) for assistance. According to Rabinow, Foucault has three modes of objectification of the subject, which can be considered the main theme of Foucault's work:

1. *The first mode of objectification of the subject* is what is called "dividing practices," which are used by people in power as techniques of domination exercised mainly on the marginalized. These practices were exemplified in the rise of modern psychiatry and its entry into the hospitals and prisons throughout the nineteenth and twentieth centuries. Through dividing practices, Foucault questioned how the subject was objectified by a process of division from others with efficiency. In this mode of objectification, explained in his *Discipline and Punish* (1979), the human subject is seen as a victim, caught in the processes of objectification and constraint.

2. *The second mode of objectification of the subject* is related to scientific classification that arises from the mode of inquiry that attempts to achieve the status of sciences, which is the main topic of Foucault's *The Order of Things* (1966/1970). Foucault explicated how the discourses of life, labor, and language were structured into disciplines aiming to create universals of human social life. This is where Foucault rejects structuralism and is highly suspicious of claims to universal truths.

3. *The third mode of objectification,* called "subjectification," concerns the way human beings turn themselves into subjects. Through the notion of subjectification, Foucault analyzed how people subjectifed themselves through a variety of "operations on their own bodies, on their own souls, on their own thoughts, on their own conduct" (Rabinow, 1984, p. 11), usually mediated by an external authority figure like a psychoanalyst or a plastic surgeon. As an example, Foucault pointed to a growing obsession with Freudian scientific discourses about sex and sexuality as a key to self-understanding.

These three modes of objectification of the subject are closely related to the issue of power and knowledge, as Foucault suggests that it is a form of power that makes individuals subjects. When Foucault speaks of power, however, he does not attempt to construct a theory of power. Rather, his question about power is a "how" question, not a "what" question, for example, *how* power is exercised rather than what is power (Foucault, 1983). Foucault thus engages in a highly sophisticated analysis of the mechanism of power, focusing not on the subjects of power but on power relations. That is, Foucault's analysis focuses on how different forms of power are exercised and how they come into play in family relations, in an institution, or in an administration. Foucault also acknowledges that power involves a certain kind of knowledge that is located within the deep regimes of discourse and practice. Hence, power and knowledge are intricately intertwined in the way that knowledge of all sorts is entangled in the political dominations and power struggles, described in Foucault's analysis. The legitimacy of knowledge is what constitutes the regime of truth; and it cannot be dissociated from power. Hence, for Foucault, the "will to knowledge" is concomitantly part of the danger and a tool to fight the danger (Rabinow, 1984). Therefore, Foucault advises us to attend to the diverse ways that power is exercised, for it is at least as important to understand "*how* power is exercised as it is to identify *who* exercises it" (Schrift, 1995, p. 41, italics in original). As we can see, the main foci of Foucault's thoughts are knowledge, power, discourse, truth, and the subject/the self, among which Foucault attempts to draw connections (see Table 2.5).

Foucauldian Approach and Narrative Inquiry

A Foucauldian approach to narrative inquiry has been explored by Maria Tamboukou (2013). She understands narrative as embedded in discourse, power, and history, which are the foci of Foucault. She has worked with women's autobiographical or biographical narratives exploring the formation of the female self using Foucault's thought as a research tool along

Table 2.5 Discourse and Power in Foucauldian Analysis

Discourse is a discursive language, spoken or written, in which the social, cultural, and political perspectives of the people involved in it are embedded.

Power is "dominating and imposing its rationality upon the totality of the social body" (Foucault, 1983, p. 207).

To analyze a *discourse* means to investigate how it works in what conditions, how it intersects with the context in which it is spoken or written, and how a particular discourse comes to shape a certain reality. There are multiple *power relations* at work in a discourse in various contexts. There are determining elements in power relations exerting themselves upon one another, which, then, become a field of analysis for poststructuralists.

(Adapted from Foucault, 1983)

with feminist theory (Tamboukou, 2003). Taking women's autobiographical narratives as effects of power/knowledge relations, Tamboukou explains how she has followed a genealogy of conflicting episodes and paradoxes in the discursive constitution of the self in women teachers. She posits that Foucauldian genealogy is "the art of archival research" (2013, p. 88) that requires patience to work meticulously with old documents to discover both significant and "insignificant" details, discourses, and practices that human beings used to make sense of the world. Tamboukou notes, "In navigating the sea of Foucauldian analytics, I have charted a map of genealogical problematics, research strategies and themes emerging from a Foucauldian approach to narratives" (p. 103). Those themes include: narrative modalities of how power operates as a productive force; how apparatuses of power function through narratives and counter-narratives; narratives as technologies of power and as technologies of the self; and who speaks or writes? Using a Foucauldian approach, Tamboukou problematizes and multiplies the meaning of stories while decentering the author.

Jacques Derrida (1930–2004): Deconstruction for Justice

I believe, however, that I was quite explicit about the fact that nothing of what I said had a destructive meaning. Here and there I have used the word deconstruction, which has nothing to do with destruction. That is to say, it is simply a question of (and this is a necessity of criticism in the classical sense of the word) being alert to the implications, to the historical sedimentation of the language we use—and that is not destruction. (Derrida, 1972, p. 271)

Derrida's quote above reflects how deconstruction has often been seen as a form of critical analysis that aims at tearing everything apart, thus destructive, not deconstructive. **Deconstruction**, hence, was misunderstood as "ethically void, politically impotent, and utterly dangerous" (Biesta, 2009, p. 15). In fact, Peters (2009a) reports that when Derrida died in October 2004, American and British readers responded to his death in two opposite ways: There was a group of people who regretted it deeply; and the other celebrated his death as if it were the death of deconstructionism! These polar responses show how Derrida's deconstructionism was largely misunderstood despite his eleven honorary degrees and the 70 books he wrote in his life (Peters, 2009a).

In the field of literary theory, however, Derrida, known to be the most acute critic of structuralism, is regarded as the creator of poststructuralism with his deconstruction of Saussure's theory of meaning (Eagleton, 1983; Sturrock, 2003). Derrida came to prominence in the late 1960s, when he delivered his influential paper "Structure, Sign and Play in the Discourse of the Human Sciences" at Johns Hopkins University in October 1966, the event previously mentioned. This delivery was American scholars' first encounter with deconstruction in the English-speaking world, which made Derrida an important figure of poststructuralism although he preferred to be called a "deconstructionist" (Sturrock, 2003).

Derrida holds an important place in the history of the subject for the invention of the concept of *différance* (Peters, 2009b). The term *différance* means both "'differing" and "deferring" (due to the fact that *différance* and *différence* sound the same in spoken French). Derrida remarks that *différance* refers not only to the "movement that consists of deferring by means of delay, delega-tion, reprieve, referral, detour, postponement, reserving," but also to "the unfolding of differ-ence," of the ontological difference (cited in Peters, 2009b, p. 66). That is, there is always this ontological difference between any logic that pretends truth and reality, and being; and on the other hand, there is also always deferral of the meaning of them. Derrida posts that language does not create meanings, but rather reveals them, which implies that meanings pre-exist their expression. For Derrida, meanings are always formulated in language; thus, we cannot reach outside language: "*Il n'y a pas de hors-texte*" (There is no outside text) (Derrida, 1967, p. 227, cited in Pinar et al., 2008, p. 465). This is where Derrida's deconstruction of text enters.

We should not understand *deconstruction* as something indifferent to everything, a moral nihilism as it is commonly misunderstood (Kearney, 1993). Derrida has insisted that deconstruc-tion "is not an enclosure in nothingness but an openness towards the other . . . deconstruction seeks not to abandon ethics but to resituate and reinscribe its key concepts of the self and other" (cited in Kearney, 1993, p. 31). Thus, for Derrida, deconstruction is an effort to reestablish ethi-cal issues toward the self and other, affirming the other. For this reason, Derrida has claimed that deconstruction is justice (Biesta, 2009) because justice is always directed toward the other, or the relation to the other. To illustrate this, Biesta (2009) quotes Derrida's distinction between justice and the law:

> [The] law as such can be deconstructed and has to be deconstructed. That is the condition of historicity, revolution, morals, ethics, and progress. But justice is not the law. Justice is what gives us the impulse, the drive, or the movement to improve the law, that is, to deconstruct the law. Without a call for justice we would not have any interest in deconstructing the law. (p. 32)

It is in this sense that Derrida argues that deconstruction is justice, "a response to a call" (cited in Biesta, 2009, p. 33). What deconstruction is most concerned about is to do justice to what is excluded; and it does so by constantly subverting its own assertions (Biesta, 2009). To repeat, then: the aim of deconstruction is not to destroy but to do justice to the impossible, to what cannot be foreseen as a possibility, and to what precedes language. This is what drives the critical work of deconstruction (Biesta, 2009). We are now ready to look at the relevance of poststructuralism to narrative inquiry.

Poststructuralism and Narrative Inquiry

Table 2.6 contains an excerpt from the conversation that Foucault had with Deleuze in 1977. In it, they reflect on a period of civil unrest and general strikes that occurred in France in 1968, popularly known as the "events of May." Foucault and Deleuze were mutual admirers. Foucault wrote a number of articles about Deleuze; and Deleuze not only wrote often on Foucault, but also described Foucault as the greatest thinker of our time. I would like to present this conversa-tion to you as a way to think about how we can use the poststructuralists' accounts of power, discourse, representation, and knowledge in narrative inquiry. I find this conversation powerful, as it has a lot of implications for who we are (or who we intend to be) as narrative researchers and intellectuals.

Foucault says the work of intellectuals is not just to awaken our consciousnesses; we should practice theory not from a "safe distance," because theory *is* practice. Theory is local and regional, not totalizing. Deleuze also speaks of the *indignity* of speaking for others. That's a practice of which many of us may feel guilty; we inadvertently tend to engage in "speaking for others" as one dimension of our research. We assume that our research participants don't have their own voice, or they need to be "empowered," hence, they are in need of someone to speak for them. When we tell the stories of others through narrative inquiry, are we trying to speak for/with/of them? What is our disposition toward our participants? How do we negotiate power in this relationship?

Table 2.6 Conversation Between Deleuze and Foucault: Implications for Narrative Inquiry

Foucault: In the most recent upheaval, the intellectual discovered that the masses no longer need him to gain knowledge: they know perfectly well, without illusion; they know far better than he and they are certainly capable of expressing themselves. . . . The intellectual's role is no longer to place himself "somewhat ahead and to the side" in order to express the stifled truth of the collectivity; rather, it is to struggle against the forms of power that transform him into its object and instrument in the sphere of "knowledge," "truth," "consciousness," and "discourse." *In this sense theory does not express, translate, or serve to apply practice: it is practice. But it is local and regional, as you [Deleuze] said, and not totalizing.* This is a struggle against power, a struggle aimed at revealing and undermining power where it is most invisible and insidious. It is not to "awaken consciousness" that we struggle (the masses have been aware for some time that consciousness is a form of knowledge; and consciousness as the basis of subjectivity is a prerogative of the bourgeoisie), but to sap power, to take power; it is an activity conducted alongside those who struggle for power, and not their illumination from a safe distance. A "theory" is the regional system of this struggle.

Deleuze: *A theory does not totalize; it is an instrument for multiplication and it also multiplies itself.* It is in the nature of power to totalize and it is your [Foucault] position, and one I fully agree with, that theory is by nature opposed to power. . . . In my opinion, you were the first—in your books and in the practical sphere—to teach us something absolutely fundamental: *the indignity of speaking for others.*

(Excerpted from Foucault & Deleuze, 1977, pp. 207–208; emphasis added)

Dewey's Theory of Experience[11]

As we discussed in Chapter 1, the focus of narrative inquiry is the human experience presented in narratives and stories. Experience is the starting point. With the narrative mode of thinking (Bruner, 1986), we seek to understand the meaning of human experiences, including the challenges of life events and the complexity of human actions. We seek to expand our knowledge and understanding of what it means to be human through stories of human experiences, for narrative is the primary form that organizes human experience into temporally meaningful stories (Polkinghorne, 1988). Indeed, Clandinin and Connelly (2000) define narrative inquiry as a way of understanding the human experience. Later they further elaborate, "Narrative inquiry, the study of experience as story, then, is first and foremost a way of thinking about experience" (Connelly & Clandinin, 2006, p. 477). Hence, a theory of experience is fundamental to narrative inquiry, and serves as a meso-level theory (methological level).

What, then, do we mean by "experience"? For a **theory of experience**, we draw upon American philosopher John Dewey (1859–1952). In his book, *Experience and Education,* Dewey (1938/1997) posits that experience is not a self-explanatory idea. Rather, the meaning of experience is "part of the problem to be explored" (p. 25). Hence, to be able to better understand narrative inquiry, we want to delve into the meaning of experience. Dewey's theory of experience has implications for the organic connection between narrative inquiry and personal experience since experience in narrative research is an ever-present process. The nature of experience, Dewey (1916/2011) contends, can be understood only by a combination of an active and a passive element. That is, when we experience something, we do something with it (e.g., a child sticking her finger into a flame and having a burned finger: active element); then we suffer or undergo the consequences (e.g., a child undergoing the pain of a burn as a consequence: passive element). Dewey says, "We do something to the thing and then it does something to us in return" (p. 78). This combination of an active and a passive element, that is, a combination of doings and undergoings, is the nature of experience. Therefore, to learn from experience means to "make a backward and forward connection between what we do to things and what we enjoy or suffer from things in consequences" (p. 78).

Dewey calls attention to two principles that he believes are fundamental in the constitution of experience: *the principles of continuity and interaction.* These two principles intercept and are inseparable as they provide the measure of the educative significance and value of an experience in their active union with each other. Let me explain more.

The first principle, *continuity of experience,* also called "experiential continuum" (Dewey, 1938/1997, p. 28) means that every experience builds up from previous experiences and modifies in some way the quality of the experiences that come after. To further illustrate this point, Dewey (1938/1997) cites Tennyson's legendary poem, *Ulysses:*

> Yet all experience is an arch wherethrough
>
> Gleams that untraveled world, whose margin fades
>
> For ever and for ever when I move. (p. 35)

"Yet all experience is an arch." What a beautiful metaphor! The continuity of experience, then, like an arch with fading margins, moves with us as we live our life, opening to our next experience, which helps us glimpse that "untraveled world." Thus, the realm of meaning is not static; it is enlarged by the new experience.

The second principle, *interaction of experience,* is an interplay of objective and internal conditions that form what we call a *situation* (Dewey, 1938/1997, p. 42). Thus, when we say we live in a world, it means that we live in a series of situations where interaction is going on between an individual and objects and/or other persons. Therefore, "all human experience is ultimately social; it involves contact and communication" (p. 38). According to Dewey, an experience is a result of a "transaction taking place between an individual and what, at the time, constitutes his environment." And the environment or situation is "whatever conditions interact with personal needs, desires, purposes, and capacities to create the experience which is had." (p. 44). Thus, as Polkinghorne (1988) posits, experience is a construction made out of the interaction between our organizing cognitive schemes and the impact of the environment on our life.

When we narrative inquirers understand the theory of experience in relation to these two principles of continuity and interaction, we think of our participant's experience in continuity of the past, present, and future, not in a linear but circular or even rhizomatic way. We consider the participant's interaction with his or her situation or environment, which includes the interaction with the researcher. Such experience "signifies active and alert commerce with the world; at its height it signifies complete interpenetration of self and the world of objects and events" (Dewey, 1934/1980, p. 19). Therefore, experience is "art in germ" (p. 19), rendering an aesthetic experience, even in its rudimentary forms, because it fulfills life's struggles, dilemmas, achievements, and transformations.

Dewey (1934/1980) explains that aesthetic experience refers to "experience as appreciative, perceiving, and enjoying, from the consumer's rather than the producer's standpoint" (p. 47), appealing to the consumer's imagination. Imagination, according to Dewey, is "the only gateway" (p. 272) through which meanings can find their way into a present experience. That is, since there is always a gap between the here-and-now of direct interaction and past interactions, whose meaning we are to grasp, we will have to use our imagination to fill the gap, as a "venture into the unknown" (p. 272). Aesthetic experience is imaginative, or has some degree of imaginative quality. Thus, aesthetic experience becomes a mode of knowledge that is merged with nonintellectual elements. In this case, knowledge is "instrumental to the enrichment of immediate experience through the control over action that it exercises" (p. 290). Hence, through narrative inquiry, we should find ways to make the "tangled scenes of life more intelligible in esthetic experience" (p. 290). Aesthetic experience, indeed, is experience par excellence as it reflects the nature of experience in general (Iser, 2006).

Drawing upon Dewey elsewhere (Kim, 2008, 2010b), I suggest that we practice narrative inquiry as an aesthetic inquiry whose purpose is to produce aesthetic experience as a mode of knowledge through captured meanings of the lived experience of participants in their stories. Narrative inquiry as an aesthetic inquiry intends, in turn, to provide aesthetic experience for the reader. Dewey (1934/1980) contends that rigid attachment to convention, coerced submission to such practice, inflexibility, and incoherence lead in the opposite direction from aesthetic experience. When we let imagination come to us without a predetermined set of purposes, we allow "aesthetic experience to tell its own tale"[12] (p. 275), making the aesthetic integral to narrative research. We provide an aesthetic experience for the reader to gain empathic and imaginative understandings, knowledge, and perceptions of the world through a story that has "such reach that gives story its loft beyond the particular, its metaphoric loft" (Bruner, 2002, p. 25). In this way, we enlarge the meaning of experience itself to link together with other experiences that are similar but not exactly the same. It is an arch through which we glimpse the untraveled world as in Tennyson's poem. Narrative inquiry that draws on the metaphorical aspect of experience can work to construct its meanings that in turn illuminate larger wholes.

Recently, some narrative researchers have prioritized experience in narrative inquiry by making a distinction between event-centered narrative and experience-centered narrative. Patterson (2013), for example, posits that although event-centered personal narratives, grounded in the Labovian structural analysis,[13] have their advantages, they tend to short-change experience-centered narratives. Patterson points out, "it makes no sense to treat the complexity and subtlety of the narration of experience as though it should have an orderly, complete structure by reducing it to the one type of text that conforms to the paradigmatic model" (p. 43). Squire (2013)[14] also engages in narrative research that focuses on experience-centered first-person storytelling. This kind of work, Squire states, "often rests on a phenomenological assumption that experience can, through stories, become part of consciousness." (p. 48). According to Squire, experience-centered narrative inquiry aims at understanding through "a hermeneutic approach to analyzing stories" (p. 48), unlike Labov's structural analysis.

Bakhtin's Theory of Novelness

Another meso-level theory potentially useful for narrative inquiry that I want to discuss is **Bakhtinian novelness.** Barone is one of the champions of using Bakhtin in narrative inquiry (see Barone, 2001), along with Tanaka (1997) and Coulter and Smith (2009). I, too, have used Bakhtin in my narrative research (Kim, 2006).

Bakhtin and I, we have a special relationship. In my first semester of doctoral coursework, I took a course on Cultural Studies. On the first day of class, my professor listed several theorists' names on the blackboard, none of which rang the bell for me. We (about seven classmates) were asked to select one theorist to study and on which to make a presentation at the end of the semester. I was hesitant to choose because I didn't know any name there on the list. Finally, when it was my turn to choose, there was one name left and it was Bakhtin! I don't know how I delivered my presentation, but I barely passed. I was like a blind man touching the leg of an elephant and presenting that leg as the elephant. Who would have guessed that I would later use him in my narrative work? Our first connection was total serendipity.

As we narrative inquirers try to understand the lived experiences of our participants and transform this understanding into significant social implications, it is important to allow each of our storytellers to speak for themselves. Bakhtinian theory of novelness might be one idea that can help us understand how this can be done while avoiding the representation of a single, unified point of view.

Mikhail M. Bakhtin (1895–1975) is known as perhaps one of the most influential narrative theorists of the last quarter of the twentieth century. Born in Russia, he was a leading intellectual in the post-Stalinist rethinking of literary studies. Because he had a brother who was associated with a counterrevolutionary organization and living in exile in Britain, Bakhtin was arrested during the mass raids on intellectuals during the early Stalinist years. This forced him to remain silent. However, Bakhtin re-emerged in the 1960s when his work was taken up by structuralists in Paris, and by the early 1970s his work was widely available in translation. By the time of his death he was a sought-after figure in the Soviet Union, and posthumously his fame spread through Europe to the United States in the 1980s (McHale, 2005; Morson & Emerson, 1990).

Bakhtin (1981, 1984, for example) developed a number of global concepts in literary theory over the years that impart the following messages:

- Avoid imposing a fixed plot, conceived as the only one possible.
- Focus on the importance of the everyday, the ordinary, and the quotidian.
- Value a dialogic truth derived from unmerged voices.
- Embrace unfinalizability as essential to our freedom, openness, and creativity.

Bakhtin's theory of novelness, which includes essential concepts such as polyphony, chronotope, and carnival, grounded in his notion of dialogism (as opposed to monologism), represents these messages and has strong implications for narrative inquiry.

The term *novelness* might be confusing to us because it is associated with a novel as a literary genre. Bakhtin makes a distinction between "novels" and "novelness," the former referring to actual examples of the literary genre we recognize as the novel, and the latter referring to major features that all stories share, but that are not confined to novels as such (Holquist, 1994, 2011). Hence, Bakhtin's concept of novelness is not just a theory of the literary genre of the novel. He refers to novelness as the particular features that all stories share, stressing the importance of openness. Novelness, as Bakhtin describes it, allows ideas to grow and change, as exemplified in the work of the Russian novelist Dostoevsky, which Bakhtin uses as a model of his conception of novelness. According to Bakhtin (1984), Dostoevsky allows his work to transcend some boundaries and let the real connection begin where the ordinary plot ends. Isn't this what we want to do with our narrative inquiry, creating the open-endedness of story that connects a participant or a reader to another and one story to another?

Epic Versus Novel

According to Bakhtin (1981), though, all stories are not the same. Depending on what kind of purpose a story has, it becomes either an epic or a novel. In an epic, stories are told with a centripetal force that imposes a monologic (single) unity spoken from one point of view that is "official." That is, the centripetal force of an epic seeks to impose order and unity[15] on a heterogeneous and messy world. Thus, an epic pursues unity that is brought to bear by an "official" force that privileges a singular authoritative point of view that represents only one dominant world or one reality that is orderly and complete (D. Coulter, 1999).

In contrast, a novel, as the term is used by Bakhtin, represents many languages competing for truth from different vantage points. Whereas centripetal force is at work in an epic, centrifugal force, which allows multiple voices to emerge, is at work in the novel. The world of the novel is messy, complex, and incomplete. There is not a sense of formal beginning or closure in a novel; as Bakhtin states, "One may begin the story at almost any moment, and finish at almost any moment" (Bakhtin, 1981, p. 31). This impulse to begin and impulse to end at any moment are found in novels and they are possible only in a world with open-endedness. Hence, for Bakhtin, a novel provides more than plot (unlike the idea of formalist narratologists such as Chatman, Genette, and Todorov), and it cannot be understood merely as a collection of narrative techniques (Morson & Emerson, 1990). In a novel with a centrifugal force, real dialogue is achieved, even if ultimately composed by a single author. Thus the concept of the novel is revolutionary in the sense that:

> The novel is the expression of a Galilean perception of language, one that denies the absolutism of a single and unitary language—that is, that refuses to acknowledge its own language as the sole verbal and semantic center of the ideological world. (Bakhtin, 1981, p. 366)

We should note that Bakhtin is not insisting that his concept of novel is "the" only best genre, replacing epic. Bakhtin makes it clear that even his revolutionary concept of novel must operate in the Galilean conceptual universe where it is also one of many worlds. He states, "A newly born genre never supplants or replaces any already existing genres. Each new genre merely supplements the old ones, merely widens the circle of already existing genres" (p. 271). Hence, we should take his novelness as one of the many ways to enhance, complement, and broaden the field of narrative inquiry.

What, then, is novel? What constitutes novelness? To elaborate his theory of novelness, Bakhtin posits that there are three major features of novelness: *polyphony, chronotope,* and *carnival.* I will explain.

Polyphony

First, *polyphony* refers to "a plurality of independent, unmerged voices and consciousnesses" (p. 6), or simply multiple voices, where no voice enjoys an absolute privilege. That is, in polyphony, different voices including the author's are heard without having one voice privileged over the others. Polyphony requires a situation where the author (or the researcher, metaphorically) does not exercise monologic control, as the researcher's consciousness is nothing but one of many of conscious voices (of participants). The author, instead, lets different consciousnesses (conveyed in each voice) encounter each other as equals and engage in a dialogue. This does not mean that the researcher should not have his or her own view. Polyphony is often criticized as a theory that posits the absence of an authorial point of view, but

Bakhtin explicitly states that the polyphonic author neither lacks nor fails to express his or her ideas and values:

> The consciousness of the creator of a polyphonic novel is constantly and everywhere present in the novel, and is active to the highest degree. But the function of this consciousness and the forms of its activity are different than in the monologic novel: the author's consciousness does not transform others' consciousnesses (that is, the consciousness of the characters) into objects, and does not give them secondhand and finalizing definitions. (pp. 67–68)

Bakhtin lets us know here that what polyphony calls for is not the absence of the researcher's voice, but the position of the researcher in a text, which does not valorize one particular point of view, avoiding "navel gazing." The concept of polyphony reminds us that our role as a narrative researcher is not to pursue one centripetal or final truth; rather, it is to pursue a dialogic sense of truth that is sought through a "plurality of independent, unmerged voices." According to Bakhtin, therefore, dialogic truth is different from "*official* monologism, which pretends to *possess a ready-made truth*" (p. 110, italics in original). Dialogic truth is "born *between people* collectively searching for truth, in the process of their dialogic interaction" (p. 110, italics in original). The concept of dialogic truth provides us with a rationale for co-constructing our narrative inquiry with the participants.

Chronotope

Bakhtin posits that to promote a genuine dialogue or dialogic truth, which is a goal of a novel, polyphony has to be placed within *chronotope* in which "the knots of narrative are tied and untied" (p. 250). Hence, the second feature of novelness is *chronotope,* which means time (*chrono-*) and space (*-tope*) in Greek. More specifically, Bakhtin defines it as "the intrinsic connectedness of temporal and spatial relationships that are artistically expressed in literature" (p. 84). That is, the authenticity of individual experiences of characters (or narrators) in a novel depends on a particular combination of time and space manifested in their narratives. Hence, Bakhtin emphasizes the individual historicity and sociality of experience located in both time and space, rendering chronotope an important concept for understanding our lives as individuals and social beings.

While time is always historical and biographical, space is always social (Morson & Emerson, 1990); therefore, chronotope denotes historical, biographical, and social relations that delimit the parameters of events and lived experiences to be studied. It helps us understand the nature of events and actions as they are "tied and untied" in chronotope. Holquist (1994) surmises that a story of experience must be a chronotope *of* someone *for* someone *about* someone, as "time, as it were, thickens, takes on flesh, becomes artistically visible; likewise, space becomes charged and responsive to the movement of time, plot and history" (Bakhtin, cited in Morson & Emerson, 1990, p. 371). The significance of chronotope is that it allows the lived experiences of our research participants to be illuminated from historical, biographical, spatial, and social perspectives while providing a vicarious experience for the reader.

Carnival

The last concept of the dialogic nature of "novelness" is the concept of *carnival* or "*the carnivalesque.*" Think about a carnival, Mardi Gras in New Orleans and in other countries, for example, where people wear special costumes, masks, and other paraphernalia to enjoy the carnival without revealing who they are. Carnival, according to Bakhtin (1981), is a concept in which everyone is an active participant, openness is celebrated, hierarchy is invisible, and norms are reversed. Bakhtin believes that the novel should play the same role in literature that carnival is alleged to play in the real life of cultures (Morson & Emerson, 1990). For instance, the carnivalesque novel, through "laughter, irony, humor, and elements of self-parody" (Bakhtin, 1981, p. 7), offers an unofficial truth, where the symbols of power and violence are disturbed and counter-narratives are promoted with equal value. One formal and privileged way of life or way of thinking is discarded, but different views and styles are valued by representing the wide range of languages and experiences. Moreover, in the carnivalesque novel, voices of the marginalized or silenced are promoted and respected, acts that are not possible otherwise.

I think that the Bakhtinian novelness of *polyphony, chronotope,* and *carnival* has profound implications for narrative inquiry. Bakhtin says "the novel's roots must ultimately be sought in folklore" (1981, p. 38), which implies that novelness is for, of, and by lay people who traditionally did not have power and privilege, which is also what narrative inquiry is about. Bakhtin's theory of novelness is a meso-level theory that may be useful for our work in narrative inquiry.

Conclusion: No Theory Used as a Procrustean Bed

In this chapter, we have explored macro-level and meso-level theories: critical theory, critical race theory, feminist theory, poststructuralism, theory of experience, and theory of novelness. I've given you brief overviews of these as some of the theories we narrative inquirers can/may adopt during our research journeys. I will ask you to explore micro-level theories that are important in your own disciplines. The point of this chapter is that narrative inquiry cannot exist in a vacuum. In other words, we cannot make sense of the stories told without the help of a theory or the intersection of multiple theories.

As you can see, the theories discussed here are not independent of each other. They inform, expand, and intersect with each other while maintaining their own clear focus/foci. Thus, we find "theory blurring" (as in genre blurring) galore, as we see in feminist postmodernism, post-structuralist critical theory, critical feminist race theory, and more. We should find ways to utilize these theories to inform our own practice, and avoid what C. Wright Mills (1959) called "abstract theorizing," which is the "withdrawal into systematic work on conceptions" (p. 48), devoid of a realistic ground of practice. This abstract theorizing, far from being useful, may become the boundary to inquiry that hampers efforts to bring about changes for the better (Anyon, 1994).

Peters (2005) also laments that some students of social science and the humanities tend to focus on contemporary theorists of "post"-culture, such as Foucault, Derrida, without engaging in the historical depth and tradition of critical philosophy. The lack of depth in understanding of a theory or theories that we adopt for our research might put us in danger of turning theories into mere "academic commodities" (Peters, 2005, p. 43).

I hope that this chapter provides you with some "food for thought" or a "hook" to a certain theory that you find interesting and relevant to your research, and that it inspires you to be more inquisitive and creative in ways that expand and deepen the rigor and vigor of your research.

I have a story tell you before you take a short break from reading this book: The myth of Procrustes.

> Procrustes was a host who adjusted his guests to their bed. Procrustes, whose name means "he who stretches," kept a house by the side of the road where he offered hospitality to passing strangers, who were invited in for a pleasant meal and a night's rest in his very special bed. Procrustes described the bed as having the unique property that its length exactly matched whomsoever lay down upon it. As soon as the guest lay down, Procrustes went to work upon him, stretching him on the rack if he was too short for the bed and chopping off his legs if he was too long. Theseus turned the tables on Procrustes, fatally adjusting him to fit his own bed. (http://www.mythweb.com/teachers/why/basics/procrustes.html)

I tell you this story because I don't want us to be like Procrustes with our theories. Listening to the stories of our research participants, we might attempt to fit their stories into our theories at the risk of missing the "real, important" aspects of the stories. That is, our theories should not function as a Procrustean bed. If we invite research participants to tell us their stories and we only get a partial story that fits the Procrustean bed of our theory, it leads to "chopping off" the rest of the story. Theories should inform or guide us to understand a story but not to diminish our ability to listen. Theories are there to be used, not to dictate to us or shape our stories. We should not be like Procrustes.

QUESTIONS FOR REFLECTION

- What are the roles of theory?
- In what way does each theory (presented here) inform narrative research?
- What is your theoretical/philosophical framework, and how does it mesh with your research topic?

ACTIVITIES

1. Choose a theory or a theorist that you want to delve further into. Become an expert on that theory (or the theorist) and present it to your classmates.

2. Try to write down the main characteristics of each theory and discuss possible intersectionalities among different theories.

SUGGESTED READINGS

LATCRIT RESOURCES

Delgado Bernal, D. (2002). Critical race theory, LatCrit theory, and critical raced gendered epistemologies: Recognizing students of color as holders and creators of knowledge. *Qualitative Inquiry, 8*(1), 105–126.

Hernandez-Truyol, B. (1997). Indivisible identities: Culture clashes, confused constructs and reality checks, symposium: LatCrit theory: Naming and launching a new discourse of critical legal scholarship. *Harvard Latino Law Review, 2,* 199–230.

Iglesias, E. (1997). Foreword: International law, human rights, and LatCrit theory. *University of Miami Inter-American Law Review, 28,* 177–213.

Stefancic, J. (1998). Latino and Latina critical theory: An annotated bibliography. *La Raza Law Journal, 10,* 423–498.

Valdes, F. (1997). Poised at the cusp: LatCrit Theory, outsider jurisprudence and Latina/o self-empowerment. *Harvard Latino Law Review, 1,* 1–59.

TRIBALCRIT RESOURCES

Brayboy, B. M. K. J. (2005). Toward a tribal critical race theory in education. *The Urban Review, 37*(5), 425–446.

Writer, J. H. (2008). Unmasking, exposing, and confronting: Critical race theory, tribal critical race theory and multicultural education. *International Journal of Multicultural Education, 10*(2).

ASIANCRIT RESOURCES

Chang, R. (1993). Toward an Asian American legal scholarship: Critical race theory, post-structuralism, and narrative space. *California Law Review, 81*(5), 1241. Available at http://scholarship.law.berkeley.edu/californialawreview/vol81/iss5/4

Wing, A. K. (2001). USA 2050: Identity, critical race theory, and the Asian century. *Michigan Law Review, 99*(6), 1390–1408.

FemCrit Resources

Berry, T. R. (2010). *Engaged pedagogy and critical race feminism*. Retrieved from http://www.eric.ed.gov/
 PDFS/EJ902670.pdf
Wing, A. K. (Ed.). (1997). *Critical race feminism: A reader.* New York: New York University Press.

On Intersectionality

Burman, E. (2003) From difference to intersectionality: Challenges and resources. *European Journal of
 Psychotherapy, Counseling and Health, 6*(4), 293–308.
Ludwig, A. (2006). Differences between women? Intersecting voices in a female narrative. *European Journal
 of Women's Studies, 13*(3), 245–258.
McCall, L. (2005). The complexity of intersectionality. *Signs, 30*(3), 1771–1800.
Phoenix, A. (2006). Editorial: Intersectionality. *European Journal of Women's Studies, 13*(3), 187–192.
Prins, B. (2006). Narrative accounts of origins: A blind spot in the intersectional approach. *European Journal
 of Women's Studies, 13*(3), 277–290.

On Black Feminist Thought

Collins, P. H. (1990). *Black feminist thought: Knowledge, consciousness and the politics of empowerment.* New
 York, NY: Routledge.
hooks, b. (1994). *Teaching to transgress: Education as the practice of freedom.* New York, NY: Routledge.

On Gender Issues in Other Countries

International Review of Education, Vol. 33, No. 4, 1987; Special issue: Women and education.
International Review of Education, Vol. 55, No. 5/6, 2009; Special issue: Undoing gender.

On Critical Race Feminism

James, J. (1999). *Shadowboxing: Representations of Black feminist politics.* New York, NY: St. Martin's
 Press.
Wing, A. K. (Ed.) (1997). *Critical race feminism: A reader.* New York: New York University Press.
Wing, A, K. (Ed.) (2000). *Global critical race feminism: An international reader.* New York, NY, and London,
 UK: New York University Press.

On Feminist and Narrative Inquiry

Munro, P. (1998). *Subject to fiction: Women teachers' life history narratives and the cultural politics of
 resistance.* Buckingham, UK: Open University Press.

NOTES

1. Please see Rajagopalan (1998) for an elaborated counter-argument to Thomas (1997).
2. Denzin and Lincoln define the five phases of the research process: Phase 1, The researcher as a multicultural subject; Phase 2, Theoretical Paradigms and Perspectives; Phase 3, Research Strategies; Phase 4, Methods of Collection and Analysis; and Phase 5, The Art, Practices, and Politics of Interpretation and Evaluation (see Denzin & Lincoln, 2011, pp. 12–15).
3. Some macro-level theory might work at the meso-level as well. For example, phenomenology can work both as a philosophy (interpretive paradigm) and a method for analysis.
4. Please note that phenomenology is both philosophy and methodology although I focus on phenomenology as an interpretive paradigm here.
5. I mainly draw upon Merleau-Ponty for the discussion of phenomenology here, as he delineated central themes of phenomenology in the preface of his seminal book, *Phenomenology of Perception* (1962/2007).
6. In this section, I use the term *poststructuralism*. Poststructuralism and postmodernism are commonly conflated with each other, and sometimes conflated with deconstruction (Butler, 1992). Butler says, "I don't know about the term 'postmodern,' but if there is a point, and a fine point, to what I perhaps better understand as poststructuralism" (p. 6), which means she prefers the term poststructuralism. But a number of poststructuralists, including Jean-François Lyotard and Jean Baudrillard, have systematically engaged the term postmodernism, while others, such as Michel Foucault, are regarded as poststructuralists.
7. The choice of these poststructural philosophers is an arbitrary one. I am regretful that I am not discussing other important poststructuralists such as Kristeva, Lyotard, Baudrillard, and more.
8. Flight means not only the act of fleeing or eluding but also flowing, leaking, and disappearing into the distance. It has no relation to flying (Deleuze & Guattari, 1987, p. xvi).
9. Polyphony will be discussed later in this chapter.
10. Forms of reflexivity are discussed in Chapter 8, including Foucault's understanding of reflexivity as askēsis (to take care of self).
11. I consider the next two discussions (Dewey's theory of experience and Bakhtin's novelness) *meso-level theories* that are particularly pertinent to the narrative inquiry methodology.
12. This notion is revisited in Chapter 3.
13. The Labovian model is discussed in Chapter 6.
14. Squire's main argument is for the use of socioculturally oriented approaches to narrative while embracing experience-centered narratives.
15. It is not that Bakhtin rejected unity completely. Rather, he rejected the idea of unity as conformity to an underlying structure or an overarching scheme because this kind of unity would oppress true creativity. Bakhtin believed that without some unity, the world would cease to make sense. He attempted to rethink the concept of unity in order to allow for the possibility of genuine creativity to evolve (Morson & Emerson, 1990).

CHAPTER TOPICS

- Engaging in Aesthetic Play
- Standards for Humanities-Oriented Research
- Learning to Think Narratively
- Plowing Before Sowing: On Reviewing the Literature
- Developing "Good" Research Questions
- Imagining the Researcher-Participant Relationship: From "Spy" to "Friend"
- Ethical Issues in Narrative Inquiry
  - *Ethics in Practice or Micro-ethics*
  - *Narrative Ethics in Practice*
- *Developing Phronesis (Ethical Judgment) Through Reflexivity*
- Qualitative Writing or Scientific Writing
- Imagining Narrative Writing as Aesthetic Play
  - *Creation of Virtual Reality/ Verisimilitude*
  - *Fidelity to Told Stories*
  - *Voice of the Narrative Inquirer*
  - *Cultivation of Narrative Imagination*
- Conclusion: Where Your Heart Belongs

©Tom Parish, T. Candon—Root Cellar,
Liberty Township, Geary County, KS 2012

CHAPTER 3

Narrative Research Design

Engaging in Aesthetic Play

QUESTIONS TO CONSIDER

- How shall we approach narrative research design?
- How can we organize our research ideas in a way that they complement each other?
- How can we think narratively throughout the research project?

INTRODUCTION

A thoughtful doctoral student, Bryan, in the Department of Counseling, approached me a while ago. He needed a new committee member to replace one who had just retired. He asked me to be on his committee to help him with his narrative inquiry. I asked him what his research topic was. As a professional counselor, he was seeing some serious problems at the clinic where he worked. In particular, he was concerned that his clients, most of whom were from a lower socio-economic status, were not well served by his clinic. He had a lot of empathy for his clients. So for his research, he wanted to hear their stories to explore how the clients experienced the clinic's service. As I liked his topic, I happily agreed to be on his committee.

Me: So, how are you going to design your narrative inquiry?

Bryan: (surprised) What do you mean by "design"?

Me: Well, a research project is like building a house. You will need to care-
        fully design a house you want to build, using your imagination, right?

Bryan: Right.

Me: Exactly.

Like Bryan, some of you may not conceptualize your research from a design perspective. You may not view yourself as a research designer. This chapter is about narrative research design that will help you imagine your research project holistically, like a designer. Hence, the purpose of this chapter is to provide you with the foundational knowledge you will need to become a narrative research designer. We will first look into the notion of aesthetic play, an artistic meaning-making approach to narrative research design. And then we will discuss fundamental research design elements, required of qualitative research in general and narrative inquiry in particular. I hope this chapter will nourish your imagination and creativity as designers of narrative inquiry.

Engaging in Aesthetic Play

An internationally known American artist, Joan Backes, came to Kansas State University in October, 2013 to install her work, titled *Where the Heart Belongs,* for the outdoor Stolzer Gallery of the Beach Museum of Art. In this particular installation, Backes interrogates the notions of "house" and "home," provoking multiple interpretations and meanings of the open structure (http://beach.k-state.edu/explore/exhibitions/backes.html). Backes invites the viewer to imagine various kinds of human dwellings from the past and present, in pursuit of "*Where the Heart Belongs.*" In a personal conversation with her, she told me that she came up with this particular title after paying a separate visit to Manhattan, Kansas, prior to her installation. Backes emphasized how significant this title is to her, and wanted to reflect it in these three layers of the home structure (see Image 3.1).

I find Backes's work profound, as I begin to question the meaning of "home" that I have taken for granted. The installation awakens my consciousness about the notion of home. Her work is powerful because it makes the familiar strange as a way to bring our senses back to the essence of our lived experience (like Heidegger would do) in relation to our "home." She asks us to embody the meaning of dwelling, belonging, and being.

As I view Backes's installation, I further begin to wonder how the artist came to conceive these structures to explore her quest. What was Backes envisioning when she created this daringly naked structure of the home in three layers? The open, bare bones of the structures, though standing solidly on their own, seem to require a great deal of deliberation and imagination to view an anticipated research project holistically. I start imagining how a researcher can or should think like an artist to design his or her own research project.

Courtesy of Communications and Marketing Photo Services at Kansas State University.

Image 3.1 Joan Backes, *Where the Heart Belongs,* ©2013/14, steel, oak, logs. Large Steel House 13 feet high.

As my imagination begins to focus on design, I attempt to embody the notion of **aesthetic play** that my informal mentor and friend, Margaret Macintyre Latta (2013), posits. In her recent book, *Curricular Conversations: Play Is the (Missing) Thing,* Macintyre Latta theorizes the notion of *aesthetic play,* drawing upon Deweyan ideas of aesthetics, with an aim to "put the reader into play with the play of ideas, concretely negotiating meaning-making as a fundamental encounter between self (subject) and other (world)" (p. xiii). She posits that aesthetic play is a "necessity to awaken the artistic/meaning-making spirit in each of us" (p. 110). As I encounter Backes's artistic world, I feel the notion of aesthetic play beckoning me. I am willing to "enter into play" (p. 14) as my artistic meaning-making spirit is being awakened.

Now, allow me for a moment to indulge myself in my own aesthetic play with Backes's home structures placed in the museum. Standing in front of the naked home structures, I start playing with an idea of imagining the home structure as narrative inquiry. I begin to imagine that my research home is narrative inquiry where my heart belongs. Because the home structure is placed in the neutral space of the museum, I have carte blanche to put the naked home structure wherever I want. Through my imagination, I give my narrative research a context, an environment, landscape, or surroundings, that consist of a theoretical perspective, a research setting, a research field, the world, and all of the above. Hence, I enter another Backes installation of a home structure now placed in a forest (see Image 3.2).

Photo courtesy of the artist.

Image 3.2 Joan Backes, *Berliner Häuser,* ©2011, Douglas Fir. 12 feet 6 inches x 10 feet x 8 feet, approximate dimensions for each house (Permanent Installation, Berlin, Germany).

This home (Image 3.2), made of Douglas fir, sits comfortably in the forest where it seems to belong. I cannot imagine this home placed in New York with skyscrapers. The home and the wooded forest embrace each other, bringing both near to an understanding that comes with being in a relationship with each other. This nearness positions me to attend to the particular contexts and relations, animating more ideas, as I think about my narrative research design. As Dewey (1934/1980) claims, I try to achieve wholeness through seeking connections with surroundings, seeing my research in relation to the world. Furthermore, the open structure of the home in this installation tells me that there is still "room for deliberation," "room for intuition," "room for anticipation," "room for natality," and "room for enlarging realizations" (Macintyre Latta, 2013, pp. 66–70).

Finally, I imagine my completed research project through another Backes installation (see Image 3.3).[1] The skeleton of the home is now filled with the materials gathered from the surroundings. The home, as a fuller being, gives meaning to its surroundings and the surroundings give meaning to the home in return. This home, silently embraced by the equally snow-covered ground, provides me with aesthetic experience of "grace or dignity" (Dewey, 1934/1980, p. 49), allowing it to "tell its own tale" (p. 275). This is where I want to be with my research. I want my research project to tell its own tale with grace or dignity, consisting of harmony, balance, consistency, and integrity.

Photo courtesy of the artist.

Image 3.3   Joan Backes, *Forest House,* ©2010. Odenwald Forest hardwood, 14 feet 6 inches x 12 feet x 9 feet (Permanent Installation, Darmstadt, Germany).

But to get there, I need to attend to my own creative process within the process of designing my research, which is in itself an imaginative vision (Dewey, 1934/1980). Attunement to process that constitutes thinking and attunement to research methods within the process are needed in the making. The making, found within the attunement to processes of narrative inquiry, insists on the researcher's openness to "the perception, selection, and responsiveness to qualities encountered through the making process" (Macintyre Latta, 2013, p. 84). The researcher's attunement to process in a research situation is reflected in the researcher's ability to derive or draw from the data. This "attentive care" (Dewey, 1938/1997, p. 49) devoted to research situations and conditions is required to generate research that is truly meaningful.

While Macintyre Latta (2013) encourages her readers to engage in aesthetic play in curricular practices, I want narrative inquirers to engage in aesthetic play in research practices. I want us to pursue such play seriously "drawing on aesthetic traditions and engagement, including experimentation, multisensory attentiveness, and non-linear as well as linear ways of thinking and acting" (p. 3). Is it then possible to play seriously? I mean, how can we take narrative inquiry design playfully and seriously at the same time? Macintyre Latta quotes John Dewey to answer this question:

To be playful and serious at the same time is possible, and it defines the ideal mental condition. Absence of dogmatism and prejudice, presence of intellectual curiosity and flexibility, are manifest in the free play of the mind upon a topic. To give the mind this free play is not to encourage toying with a subject, but is to be interested in the unfolding of the subject on its own account, apart from its subservience to a preconceived belief or habitual aim. Mental play is open-mindedness, faith in the power of thought to preserve its own integrity without external supports and arbitrary restrictions. (p. xii)

How eloquent! To be playful and serious is the ideal mental condition where there is no dogmatism but intellectual curiosity and flexibility. Borrowing Macintyre Latta's idea of aesthetic play in curricular practices, I posit that when we work on our narrative research design, we should engage in aesthetic play in the following ways:

- We interact with our research ideas, playfully and seriously at the same time, negotiating the meaning-making process as we encounter each of those ideas, and bringing nearness that reveals reciprocity, connectedness, and coherence.
- We embody intellectual curiosity, flexibility, open-mindedness, and attunement to the research processes, allowing room for deliberation, intuition, and anticipation (remember Dali's sculpture, *Homage to Newton,* in Chapter 1).
- We let our research unfold in a way that preserves its own integrity and let it tell its own tale, without being subservient to preconceived beliefs and arbitrary research restrictions.

Standards for Humanities-Oriented Research

To be playful and serious at the same time with our narrative research design, I want to first bring our attention to research standards for humanities-oriented research because we cannot be just "playful" without seriously knowing the standards for quality research. In 2009, the Council of the American Educational Research Association (AERA) adopted seven standards for any research that involves the human including "arts-based and narrative research" (p. 482).[2] Humanities-oriented research has the general purpose of exploring and understanding various human phenomena. Hence, humanities-oriented researchers, and narrative researchers in particular, seek to identify troubling human conditions that are introduced in the stories of the ordinary people. It is critical that we understand these standards for humanities-oriented research as we conduct our research to generate ideas and theories that advance human well-being.

Table 3.1 lists seven standards, which include the significance, conceptualization, research design, substantiation, coherence, quality of communication, and ethics of your research. Take a moment to read and imagine how you are going to address the questions raised in each standard. When you formulate your research ideas, you can use these standards and questions as overall guides (not as the "gold" standard that you must adhere to) while you engage in aesthetic play with your research ideas in the design process.

Table 3.1 Seven Standards for Humanities-oriented Research

1. Significance of Research
   o Is your research topic timely and significant in the ways it addresses an issue that needs attention, fills a gap in current knowledge, and makes a scholarly contribution to advance your field?

2. Conceptualization
   o Do you clearly conceptualize your inquiry based on the scholarly literature and state explicitly the scope and limits of your inquiry that aligns with your perspective and the aims of your inquiry?

3. Research Design (Methodology and Methods)
   o Is your research design well planned and executed in an adequate, credible, and flexible manner to accomplish the aims of your inquiry?

4. Substantiation
   o Do you establish your knowledge claims, arguments, descriptions, and interpretations using evidence from your research data and other relevant scholarly literature?

5. Coherence
   o Is your research internally and externally coherent? That is, do the various research design elements including methods, data, arguments, warrants, and literature review mesh with your research topic and aims in light of the cultural, social, and political context?

6. Quality of Communication (Clarity)
   o Does the structure of your research text including the title of your research, headings, and subheadings clearly convey your intention and facilitate readers' understanding of your research?

7. Ethics
   o Do you adhere to integrity of scholarship and IRB (Institutional Review Board) approval with respect to informed consent, confidentiality agreements, and data protection plans?
   o Do you discuss your possible bias, your perspective, or any potential conflicts of interests that could influence the analysis (such as sponsorship or funding)?
   o Do you make it clear how participants' perspectives were respected and honored?

(Adapted from AERA, 2009)

Learning to Think Narratively

As part of aesthetic play of narrative inquiry design, we narrative inquirers need to learn to think narratively while embracing the big picture of the research standards. Connelly and Clandinin (2006) posit that to become a narrative inquirer means more than learning appropriate techniques of data collection or understanding the research standards. They contend that although narrative inquiry shares some commonalities with other qualitative inquiry, such as phenomenology, case study, or ethnography, what is crucial to the design of a narrative inquiry is to learn to think narratively. They suggest the following considerations[3] that would help us to learn to think narratively.

(1) *Imagining a lifespace:* Designing a narrative inquiry involves "an act of imagination" (p. 481). We have to imagine the lifespace where our research will take place, where our participants live, where the lived experiences exist. Thus, to design a narrative inquiry is to "plan to be self-consciously aware of everything happening within that space" (p. 481) (see Image 3.1 again).

(2) *Living and telling as starting points for collecting field texts:* Thinking narratively involves imagining the life as lived in the past (telling) and living the life under study as it unfolds (living). Most narrative inquiry begins with (story)telling whether the story is biographical or autobiographical. *Telling* is collected through interviews, personal journals, photographs, artifacts, conversations, and so on, and *living* is acquired through living in the research field through observations or/and participant observations. Thus, narrative inquiry involves all four actions: *living, telling, retelling, and reliving* (Clandinin & Connelly, 2000; Connelly & Clandinin, 2006) (see Image 3.2 again).

(3) *Defining and balancing the commonplaces (temporality, sociality, and place):* As we imagine a lifespace, we need to take into consideration the commonplaces of narrative inquiry.

   o *Temporality:* Narrative inquiry acknowledges that an event or a person is in temporal transition. Therefore, an event or a person is described in relation to a past and a present, projecting a future if possible.
   o *Sociality:* Narrative inquiry is concerned with both personal and social conditions of the participant and/or the inquirer. Sociality prevents a narrative inquiry from focusing mostly on a person's thoughts and feelings or focusing mostly on social conditions that are depersonalized.
   o *Place:* Narrative inquiry needs to acknowledge the aspects of place and place's impact on the study, for example, school, home, community, or environment. A narrative inquirer needs to think through the impact of each place (see Image 3.3 again).

(4) *Investment of the self in the inquiry:* As we design a narrative inquiry, we need to invest ourselves as part of the inquiry, collecting data living in the field. In doing so, we may find ourselves intimately intertwined with the lives of our participants, which would influence data collection, our relationship with the participants, and the research texts (Connelly & Clandinin, 2006).

Plowing Before Sowing: On Reviewing the Literature

Now, we are getting into your own focus area: reviewing the literature of your own field. Some of you might be wondering whether a literature review is a part of research design. I, along with others, would say that a good research design begins with a good literature review. Reviewing the literature for your research is like a farmer plowing the soil to prepare for the planting of seeds. I present you another image. This time, imagine the farmer in Image 3.4. In order to have a good harvest for the year, the farmer works diligently with the help of horses to plow every single furrow. The seasoned farmer, well poised on his little seat, seems to know what he is doing. The vigor and rigor of his plowing, through which he tries to understand the old ground to prepare the field for planting new seeds, is clearly visible against the backdrop of a clear sky. Without such good plowing before sowing, the farmer would not be able to expect a good harvest for the year. Good plowing is a harbinger of a good harvest. The same logic goes for research. A good literature review is a harbinger of good research. Hence, "a substantive, thorough, sophisticated literature review is a precondition for doing substantive, thorough, sophisticated research" (Boote & Beile, 2005, p. 3).

I view a review of the literature as the work of plowing, an important part of any research design process, just as important as plowing is to farming. We have to imagine the humble "farmer" in us and do the important groundwork as we launch our research. The groundwork means to get to know the field well enough to seed your research idea. It is to help us to ensure that our work doesn't redo something already done by other scholars. Renowned sociologist Howard Becker (1986) points out that social and human sciences are "cumulative enterprises" (p. 140) and none of us invent it all from scratch. We depend on our predecessors. In fact, according to Becker, this mutual dependence and cumulation is what Thomas Kuhn (1970)

©Jim Richardson

Image 3.4 Plowing, Wisconsin.

termed *normal science*. That is, "to do a piece of good work others can use, and thus increase knowledge and understanding" (p. 140) is the goal of normal science. This means that since nothing is original, a good way to prove your new idea is to connect it appropriately to relevant literature. We researchers must be able to say something new while connecting it to what is already been said by others (Becker, 1986). For example, we should be able to create some of our argument based on new data we have collected, so that we can contribute to expanding the literature of our own field, but without knowing the literature well enough, this wouldn't be possible. We are not here to make scholarly revolution singlehandedly. Thus, this is why we need to know the literature well: Knowing the literature that is available to us lets us construct our argument instead of wasting time doing what has already been done.

Hence, we need to be good at reviewing the literature. What is a well-done literature review? Unfortunately, I have read many papers whose literature review section was not well "plowed." Sometimes, it was just a summary of selected publications without synthesizing and interrogating, just "name dropping" of scholars instead of engaging in a deep discussion about the existing research, or using sources that are not credible enough to be conducive to a scholarly work. I think we need to work on learning to become good at plowing.

Being good at reviewing the literature means that we all need to be scholars before becoming researchers (Boote & Beile, 2005), that is, we need to be well versed in the area of our own research interest. We will not be able to perform significant research without being a scholar of our own research field. By understanding the literature, we can identify a gap between what has been done and what should be done. That is, doing a literature review is to figure out the strengths and weaknesses of existing studies and identify what needs to be done to enhance our own field. To fill this gap becomes the purpose of our research, research questions, and a source of our conceptual framework that informs and supports our research. Therefore, the purpose of a literature review is to inform a planned study—"to create a focus, conceptual framework, design, and justification for the study" (Maxwell, 2006, p. 28). A good literature review, thus, becomes the beginning of a solid research design. As Boote and Beile (2005) point out, if we are not "substantive, thorough, or sophisticated" enough with our literature review, we might draw a research design that would shortchange the field rather than enhance it.

However, we don't need to position ourselves as "the one who knows" or the "expert in the field." Rather, we can write a literature review "as a way of knowing" (Lather, 1999, p. 4), or as the process by which we come to our knowing and understanding. A well-done literature review indicates that we are up to date with the current field and we understand our research methodology. It shows our ability to generate new scholarship built upon the existing scholarship and research, which needs to be communicated to a target audience. Thus, the ability to write a sophisticated literature review is a distinctive form of scholarship that requires a broad range of knowledge and skills. In fact, well-done, state-of-the-art literature reviews are "legitimate and publishable scholarly documents" (LeCompte, Klingner, Campbell, & Menk, 2003, p. 124).

We also need to understand that a "thorough" literature review doesn't mean we have to include everything we read. As Maxwell (2006) advises, we need to be selective to discuss relevant works that inform our research purpose, design, and interpretation, not simply those that deal with the topic of our research. Thus, we need to consistently ask ourselves, "Why am I including this study or reference?" (Rudestam & Newton, 2001, p. 59). By justifying the inclusion of certain studies, we make our research logic coherent.

Traditionally, a paper or a dissertation has five sections: Introduction, Literature Review, Methodology, Results, and Conclusions. However, in narrative inquiry, a literature review does not always follow the introduction. Some narrative researchers start with stories and put the literature review at the end of their paper (see, for example, Clough, 2002). Narrative researchers do not necessarily isolate the literature review in the second chapter. In addition, this traditional format (where the literature review section appears in the second chapter) gives the wrong impression that a review of the literature involves the literature in your content area only. This explains why I have seen many dissertations that are strong in the content area literature review, while being weak in the areas of theory and methodology. However, I want you to note that the topics of a literature review should include the literature in your theoretical and methodological frameworks, in addition to your content area. Our knowledge in these areas should be reflected in our writing. Hence, it would be critical to be well versed in all areas of the literature including your specific content, theory, methodology, and methods that you use for your research. What is important to remember is that a literature review is like plowing before planting, an effort to produce fruitful research results.

Before moving on to our next topic, let's take a look at Table 3.2. It provides a summary of essential tasks of a literature review.

Table 3.2 Essential Tasks of a Literature Review

1. To distinguish what has been done in the field from what needs to be done;
2. To discover important variables relevant to the topic;
3. To synthesize and gain a new perspective on the literature;
4. To identify relationships between ideas and practices;
5. To establish the context of the topic or problem;
6. To rationalize the significance of the problem;
7. To acquire and enhance the subject vocabulary;
8. To understand the structure of the subject;
9. To relate ideas and theory to applications;
10. To identify the main methodologies and research techniques that have been used; and
11. To place the research in a historical context to show familiarity with state-of-the-art developments.

(Excerpted from Hart, 1999, p. 27)

Developing "Good" Research Questions

As you conduct your literature review, your research interest will become a more informed intellectual curiosity. After finding a gap between what has been done and what needs to be done, for example, you will know more clearly what it is that you want or need to explore, which will constitute your research purpose. Once you are clear about the purpose of your research, you can turn the purpose (which is usually a statement) into potential research questions. Of course, I don't mean to suggest that you will have research questions only after a literature review, but that your research questions will be more informed ones after a literature review.

Developing research questions is extremely important as they give shape and direction to your study. Research questions work as a guide of inquiry to explore your research agenda. I find that coming up with "good" research questions is not as easy as it sounds, however. It requires much deliberation. What I mean by "good" research questions is they are good because they mesh with the overall research design, including the theoretical and methodological frameworks, helping you accomplish your research purpose. Agee (2009) posits that although good research questions do not guarantee good research, poorly conceived questions will likely create problems that would threaten the rigor of your study. So, it is necessary to write, review, and rewrite research questions and spend considerable time developing good research questions (Daiute & Fine, 2003).

Bryan, whom I introduced you to at the beginning of this chapter, was in the process of revising his research questions for his dissertation proposal when he e-mailed me about them while I was on my sabbatical. He began to realize that there was much more involved in creating research questions in narrative inquiry. I think Bryan's e-mail message presents a good discussion point for us here:

> Dr. Kim, I hope that this message finds you well. Thank you for your comments on my previous research questions. Is this a more appropriate overarching research question?:
>
> How have adult voluntary clients from the low socioeconomic status experienced the counseling service at a community mental health center?
>
> Also, I think that three sub-research questions that make sense to me are:
>
> 1) Are we treating clients who have missed their scheduled appointments, and who appear to have dropped out of their treatment prematurely, with dignity?
>
> 2) What problems seem to exist in terms of how we are engaging with these clients and building therapeutic alliances with them?
>
> 3) Is there a way to better serve these adults, outpatient community mental health center clients, particularly those of low socio-economic status? If their experiences are not ideal, what should those experiences be like?

Does this seem a bit clearer? Please let me know what your thoughts are, and thank you so much for your time.

Sincerely,
Bryan

   As we discussed, research questions usually evolve from the literature review because you might find a gap in the existing literature, but in Bryan's case, his research questions arose from his practice as a clinical counselor for the last 20 years or so, which I think is truly valuable. In fact, many practitioners who are pursuing a higher degree like Bryan would have research questions derived from their practices. To me, Bryan represents a "reflective practitioner" in Donald Schön's sense (1983), as reflected in his proposed research questions.

   Whether your research questions are derived from the literature or your own personal and practical experience, they can be succinct, to the point, and at the same time open enough to invite discoveries, explorations, surprises, and more questions. In fact, qualitative research questions are exploratory, and emerge over time. Rogers (2003) notes that research questions usually become clear only after one has been involved in a research project for a considerable period. They may become even clearer during data analyses. In general, qualitative research questions are posed to uncover the perspectives of an individual, a group, or different groups, with relatively small numbers of participants, focusing on the particularities of the local with the "thick description" of human interactions in that context (Geertz, 1973). So, a good research question would be focused enough to reflect a *particular* situation with a *particular* person or group that is a primary research topic. Hence, in constructing your research questions for your narrative inquiry, you should first consider: *Whose* stories about *what* event in *which* particular context am I going to research?

   Maxwell (2005) cautions that questions should not be too broad and should not lack reference to a specific context. But, starting with a question that is too focused can lead to tunnel vision, which will inhibit a researcher's ability to understand and analyze data properly. Agee (2009) thus posits that a single overarching question is supposed to indicate the basic goals of the study and it can give direction for the research design and data collection methods along with sub-questions. It is also important not to load up a question with multiple sub-questions (Agee, 2009).

   To take Bryan's research questions as an example, he created an overarching question to guide his inquiry process, followed by three sub-questions that narrow the broader focus of the overarching question. Bryan was able to define his specific research context (community mental health center) and his participants (voluntary clients from low socioeconomic statuses). However, I found Bryan's research questions in need of revisions for the following reasons:

- His questions seem to be too narrow in general, which might lead to tunnel vision, only focusing on the participants' experience of the counseling sessions without considering their overarching life experiences.

- The questions are not conducive to producing stories, hence do not reflect his research methodology, narrative inquiry.
- The use of yes-no questions should be avoided as they do not encourage exploration and discovery.
- Multiple questions are loaded in one question.

Bryan and I exchanged a few more emails and agreed on the revised questions showed in the right-hand column of Table 3.3.

With the revised questions, Bryan broadened the scope of his research to include an exploration of the life stories of his participants to discover which lived experiences shaped who they were. These revised research questions will allow Bryan to investigate his clients' life experiences in a descriptive way (overarching question); in doing so, he can explore major life events that led his clients to seek out the mental health service (sub-question 1); he can explore his clients' stories about the experience of the community mental health center (sub-question 2);

Table 3.3 Revising Research Questions (Bryan's Case)

Draft Questions	Revised Questions
Overarching Question *How have adult voluntary clients from the low socioeconomic status experienced the counseling service at a community mental health center?*	*What are the life stories of adult voluntary clients from low socioeconomic status who experienced the counseling sessions at a community mental health center?*
Sub-question 1 *Are we treating clients who have missed their scheduled appointments, and who appear to have dropped out of their treatment prematurely, with dignity?*	*What kinds of lived experiences have led these clients to seek out the services of the community mental health center?*
Sub-question 2 *What problems seem to exist in terms of how we are engaging with these clients and building therapeutic alliances with them?*	*What do these clients' stories reveal about the practice of the community mental health center?*
Sub-question 3 *Is there a way to better serve these adults, outpatient community mental health center clients, particularly those of low socio-economic status? If their experiences are not ideal, what should those experiences be like?*	*What can the counselors at the community mental health center learn from the clients' stories in order to improve their practice?*

and he can find ways to improve the practice through the clients' stories (sub-question 3). But I am sure Bryan will further refine the questions during his research process.

Josselson and Lieblich (2003) say that a research question in narrative inquiry must be clearly stated, "not as one that can be answered, but as one that calls for exploration" (p. 265). So, the research questions usually have a "How" or a "What kinds of" that prompts exploration or discovery rather than a simple answer. They can describe (the what), explore the process (the how), and discover the meanings and intentions (the why) of the lived experience of the humans, reflected in stories. They are not meant to be fixed or unchangeable throughout the research process. This is particularly true as more recent qualitative inquiry, and narrative research in particular, has moved toward involving the researcher and participants in the process of inquiry (e.g., Maxwell, 2005; Pinnegar & Daynes, 2007). New questions might evolve as we witness the lives and perspectives of others unfolding. It is therefore not surprising that good research questions are refined in all stages of a reflexive and interactive inquiry journey. Wrestling with our questions through reflection and imagination will ultimately help us to become better narrative inquirers. Narrative research questions, hence, are used not just as destinations that need to be reached (or answered) but also as guiding points in the inquiry process that allow unexpected but meaningful results and conclusions to emerge. Since narrative research deals with participants' stories, the stories will be read, felt, sensed, and touched by readers, which will yield unexpected research outcomes that may have little to do with the proposed research questions. My point is that the research questions in narrative inquiry are not an end goal.

In brief, developing research questions is also a part of the aesthetic play of the narrative research design process. We work with our research ideas, playfully and seriously at the same time, to come up with meaningful research questions that bring us closer to the research phenomena. Research questions are constructed as part of intellectual curiosity, flexibility, open-mindedness, and attunement to research processes, allowing room for deliberation, intuition, and anticipation. Hence, research questions are our guides to let our research unfold in a way that preserves its own integrity and lets it tell its own tale.

Imagining the Researcher-Participant Relationship: From "Spy" to "Friend"

Imagining a possible relationship with our participants is a part of narrative research design (Connelly & Clandinin, 2006). As you design your narrative inquiry, you begin to think narratively, in terms of living, telling, reliving, and retelling, as we discussed earlier. As you imagine the lifespace of your participant, investing yourself in the inquiry, you understand that you will inevitably develop sympathy and empathy and as a result, a close and intimate relationship is possible.

Speaking of the researcher-participant relationship, I have an interesting story to tell. During my fieldwork in August 2003 for my dissertation research, I was confronted by one of the students in Mrs. Emm's classroom where I was doing my observation. Here's the story:

On the second day of my observation in her class, there were two boys, one girl, and one male adult in the classroom. The adult didn't look like a student. When Mrs. Emm was explaining about a writing project that students needed to work on in class, the adult kept reading a magazine as if he had nothing to do with the class. Fifteen minutes later, he stood up abruptly and left the classroom without saying anything. As soon as he left, the class got noisy. "Who's that guy?" Matt asked. "He's a school counselor. He's new," Steven answered. "Why was he here?" Matt asked the teacher. It was obvious that the kids were bothered by the school counselor's presence. Mrs. Emm shrugged her shoulders and said: "I don't know. See, I told you. People like to come to my class to check out and leave. I don't know why. They just do." Then, Chelsea, who was absent on my first day of observation, so didn't know who I was, looked at me and asked honestly. "Are you a spy, too?" Everybody in the classroom looked at me, waiting for my answer. Chelsea's question completely caught me off guard. I was embarrassed for a minute, but managed to answer with a fake smile. "No. I'm a student at ASU. I'm observing your school for my study." (Kim, 2005, pp. 51–52)

"Are you a spy, too?" It was a straightforward question from my participant, demanding her "right to know" as a research participant. I clearly remember how her question lingered in my mind all day long. I was an intruder in their small community, viewed as a spy who would "tell on" them. And the fact that she added the word, "too," meant that any adult (including the school counselor) could be viewed as their "enemy." It was a warning to me. I was at risk of failing my sensitive young participants. I had to do something to earn their trust.

Pinnegar and Daynes (2007) explicate four turns that researchers tend to experience as they turn to narrative inquiry. These include: changes in the relationships of researchers and research participants, kinds of data collected for a study, the focus of the study, and kinds of knowing embraced by the researcher (p. 6). Out of these four turns, they observe that the change in an understanding of the relationship of the researcher to the researched is the most important change that happens among narrative inquirers. That is, the largest realization that narrative researchers experience is how they cannot wholly distance themselves from the researched because the researched is not an "object" of research. As the researcher's view of the research participant changes toward a more relational view, the researcher begins to question the role of the "authoritative" researcher, and to become more responsive and interactive with the research participants. Pinnegar and Daynes (2007) state:

> In this turn toward narrative inquiry, the researcher not only understands that there is a relationship between the humans involved in the inquiry but also who the researcher is and what is researched emerge in the interaction. In this view, the researched and the researcher are seen to exist in time and in a particular context. They bring with them a history and worldview. They are not static but dynamic and growth and learning are part of the research process. Both researcher and researched will learn. (p. 14)

The kind of a relationship that Pinnegar and Daynes speak of is one of the unique features of narrative inquiry, called relational narrative inquiry, where the storyteller (participant) and the storylistener (researcher) are in a dynamic relationship that promotes growth and learning for both (Connelly & Clandinin, 1990). Connelly and Clandinin describe how narrative inquiry becomes shared relational work:

> We found that merely listening, recording, and fostering participant story telling was both impossible (we are, all of us, continually telling stories of our experience, whether or not we speak and write them) and unsatisfying. We learned that, we, too, needed to tell our stories. Scribes we were not; story tellers and story livers we were. And in our storytelling, the stories of our participants merged with our own to create new stories, ones that we have labeled *collaborative stories*. The thing finally written on paper (or, perhaps on film, tape, or canvas), the research paper or book, is a collaborative document; a mutually constructed story created out of the lives of both researcher and participant. (p. 12, italics in original)

In fact, many narrative inquirers in education engage in relational narrative inquiries where the researchers work with teachers, teacher educators, administrators, parents, and students in co-researcher relationships (Clandinin & Murphy, 2009). With the notion of co-researching, it becomes much more difficult to abide by the traditional research notions of distance and objectivity. Narrative inquiry, open-ended, emergent, and evolving, allows narrative inquirers to invite participants to become co-researchers, co-constructors, co-narrators, and co-storytellers. It gives us a possibility to embrace a relational understanding of the roles and interactions of the researcher and the researched. What is critical to remember in this kind of relational understanding, though, according to Pinnegar & Daynes (2007), is to act in integrity and demonstrate trustworthiness, virtuosity, and rigor throughout our research endeavor. We can utilize general qualitative strategies such as member checks, triangulation, and audit trails, which are commonly used to establish trustworthiness.

Similarly, Mahoney (2007) calls for *collaborative storytelling methodology,* where research participants are "narrators, storytellers, and collaborators" (p. 575). He believes that this research collaboration or story co-construction between the researcher and the participants creates opportunities for more democratic ways of knowledge construction between the two parties. However, he also cautions that most of the storytelling collaborators (participants) have little experience with the research process or fieldwork process. The complications and complexities lurking in the process might cause a "failed research/collaboration" (p. 578). Mahoney states, "Blurring the lines between our friendship (private intimate relationship) and our research collaboration (public fieldwork relationship) was a balancing act" (p. 589). Hence, he advises that research collaboration requires reflexive and participatory practice on the researcher's part. To bring out a successful research collaborative relationship, Mahoney suggests some tips to keep in mind:

- Keep a self-reflexive fieldwork journal that works as substantive and methodological records of the research process. We need to make clear not only our own assumptions but how these assumptions frame the nature of the undertaking of our narrative inquiry.
- Keep the researcher's voice and stories of the collaborators alive and vibrant simultaneously.

- Share the methodological considerations, such as narrative-based research and in-depth interviewing, with the research collaborators.

A close relationship between the narrative inquirer and the participant is what makes narrative inquiry a "vulnerable genre" (Behar, 1996, p. 13). Although vulnerability doesn't mean that "anything personal goes" (p. 13), vulnerability becomes a necessary methodological device through which we reveal ourselves as a narrative character along with our participants to better understand the lived experience under study (Tierney, 1998). In brief, to imagine a relationship with our storytellers (or storygivers) requires our moral, ethical, emotional, and intellectual commitment to them in the research design process.

So, going back to my research relationship with my student participants, here's how I emerged from an alleged "spy" researcher to their "friend":

> The question, "Are you a spy too?," made me think critically about my role as a researcher. I had to make sure that the distinction between the researcher and the informants was as minimal as possible. I also had to ensure that there would be mutual trust, friendship, and respect. Here, I remembered what Cusick (1973) stated:
>
>> A participant observer begins by locating himself [sic] by and making himself acceptable to those he wishes to study. While it may not be absolutely necessary for him to adopt their dress and customs, he has to begin by respecting their behavior and accepting them as reasonable human beings. Then, over an extended period of time, he makes himself familiar with their day to day lives, keeps extensive notes and records of their comments and behavioral pattern (p. 4).
>
> Thus, my role as a participant observer became more paramount. I took part in classroom activity, interacting, helping students with schoolwork and sharing their experiences while having lunch with them. A main approach to the fieldwork was "conversation as research" (Kvale, 1996). Conversations of daily life I had with students and the school staff during the break time, lunch hours and in class helped me build informal relationships with each of them, developing a level of comfort to share in what the students normally talk about, which increased the "subjects' level of comfort" (Bogdan & Biklen, 1998, p. 73). In this way, I was able to be friends with students and the school staff. In fact, a ninth grader, T-J, introduced me to her teacher as her friend, and some students invited me to their lunch table. Sometimes we shared our food while complaining together about how "terrible" the school food was. (Kim, 2005, pp. 52–53)

Ethical Issues in Narrative Inquiry

As you can see, the development from a "spy" researcher to a "friend" researcher calls for careful attention to issues of ethical research. According to Zaner (2004), "relationships are the centerpiece for ethics" (p. 84). Unless we are conscious of research ethics, we may fail to conduct a "balancing act" between a research relationship and personal friendship. Or we might just end up taking advantage of our research participants, exploiting their vulnerabilities. Being an ethical researcher is a paramount disposition that cannot be too emphasized.

Ethics deals with moral principles that govern our human behavior. It concerns what it means to act morally as a human in general. We will encounter unexpected ethical dilemmas and moral concerns during the process of conducting research that cannot be explained in your application for an Institutional Review Board's (IRB) approval. It is critical that all researchers implement ethical practice at every level of research from the very beginning of the research design. When dealing with ethical considerations, however, there are "no definitive rules or universal principles that can tell you precisely what to do in every situation or relationship you may encounter, other than the vague and generic 'do no harm'" (Ellis, 2007, p. 5). Isn't that true!

The very first official introduction you may have to ethical research conduct is a training program that your institution's research ethics committee, Institutional Review Board (IRB), might provide. In the United States, the main role of IRBs in universities is to oversee all research activities involving human subjects and is mandated by federal laws and regulations. An IRB does play an important role in providing ethical principles and guidelines that researchers working with human subjects need to abide by. In my institution, Kansas State University, for example, we have six training modules that all researchers and student researchers alike must complete every three years to be eligible to submit a research application for an IRB approval. These modules offer an opportunity to learn basic ethical guidelines to protect "human subjects," such as confidentiality and informed consent.

These six modules, although they provide some ethical guidance for understanding the fundamental ethical issues in general terms, fall short of serving as guides to individual ethical reflection or action, particularly for my students who are learning to be qualitative researchers, and narrative inquirers in particular. The training modules are mainly for biomedical and behavioral research and they include mandated regulations that researchers must follow at the policy level. Hence, they seem to be "the vague and generic 'do no harm' guidelines" as Ellis (2007) points out, and they are not meant to provide guidelines specific enough to help researchers in humanities like narrative inquirers.

So, for the sake of informing my students, I, again, turned to the American Educational Research Association (AERA, 2009) research standards for humanities that we discussed previously as they do have standards for ethics for humanities (see Table 3.4).

Ethics in Practice or Micro-ethics

Wait a minute. My students and I quickly discovered that these AERA ethical standards, just like the six modules of training although slightly more insightful, are merely general guidelines that do not necessarily reach all the "itchy spots" that we encounter while conducting research. Both our institution's IRB and AERA's ethical guidelines are like a generic brand of medicine that does not work for every case. Guillemin and Gillam (2004) call this *procedural ethics,* which addresses ethics in general terms. My students frequently asked me subtle ethical questions that put them in an ethical or moral dilemma. We discovered that these general (read "generic") ethical guidelines are not sufficient for locally arising ethical dilemmas.

Table 3.4   AERA Standards for Ethics

- *Human Consent/Access to Information*: Honor human consent agreements and any other agreements pertaining to gaining access to the research site, and other artifact. It should be explicitly stated that your inquiry was carried out in accordance with IRB (Institutional Review Board) approval.
- *Perspectives and Voice*: It should be clear how participants' perspectives were respected and honored.
- *Bias*: In humanities-oriented research, no research (no researchers) is neutral when it comes to values. Describe any potential conflicts of interests that could influence the analysis (such as sponsorship or funding), and the researcher's perspective should be acknowledged in the research, as appropriate.
- *Evidence/Reasoning*: Describe how evidence was used to make claims or follow the line of reasoning that led to the researcher's conclusions.
- *Funding/Sponsorship:* Indicate any funding or sponsorship if there was any.

(Adapted from AERA, 2009 Standards for Humanities Research)

Speak of the devil. As I write this, literally, here comes an email from my student, Jodie, who is busy collecting her research data in public schools, interviewing physical education teachers. The first line of her email reads, *"I have an ethical research question."* It continues:

> I was at my research school yesterday and at the end of the day both teachers sat me down and said they needed to talk with me. My participant's co-teacher said they had been talking and need to ask me something. His voice was serious and even cracked a little. I was thinking, "Crap, they are going to ask me to leave." I was thinking, "What on earth did I say or do to make them want me to leave?" Well, turns out they would really appreciate any feedback and help I can give them regarding their teaching. Which brings me to my ethical dilemma. Am I allowed to do that? They are helping me out by allowing me to conduct my research there, but would I be overstepping my boundaries as a researcher? I would be lying if I said that I was not flattered and honored to be asked for my opinions. They already allow me to redirect students, help give individual instruction to students, etc. I would appreciate any guidance you have for me.

Jodie's email goes to show how frequently we researchers experience ethical dilemmas while conducting research. And those issues are not written in the IRB training modules or in the AERA guidelines. Guillemin and Gillam (2004) are right when they point out that there is a disjuncture between bioethics (or macroethics, or universal general ethics) and everyday ethics in local research practice. The former comes short of providing guidance to individuals in an ethical dilemma at the local level. According to Guillemin and Gillam, bioethics or macroethics focuses on medically ethical issues, such as euthanasia, cloning, and reproductive technologies and works to provide recommendations for public policy, but it does not address everyday ethics that takes place in every interaction between every doctor and every patient. To make their point,

Guillemin and Gillam use Komesaroff's (1995) term, *micro-ethics,* as a way to think about ethical issues that arise in everyday clinical practice at the local level. Drawing upon Komesaroff's *micro-ethics* from the medical field, Guillemin and Gillam (2004) apply the concept of micro-ethics to qualitative research. They define *micro-ethics* as **ethics in practice**, or everyday ethics, that deal with locally arising ethical issues while conducting qualitative research. They posit that the dimension of *ethics in practice* consists of ethically important moments throughout the research process, hence, it would be naïve to believe that the approval of an IRB would cover all the ethical issues in the practice of research. It is within this dimension of *ethics in practice* that we need to exercise our ethical competence.

Narrative Ethics in Practice

In addition to all the research ethics, macroethics, bioethics, IRB requirements, AERA ethics standards, and ethics in practice, we need an ethics pertinent to narrative inquiry, which I would call *narrative ethics in practice.* Richardson (1990) contends that "narrativizing, like all intentional behavior . . . is a site of moral responsibility" (p. 131). Adams (2008) also argues that "If narratives are tools and if the crafting and sharing of stories involve morals, then a discussion of ethics is a necessary component of narrative inquiry" (p. 177). Narrative research as a site of moral responsibility can begin with a development of ethical relationships with our participants. The essence of narrative inquiry lies in this ethical relationship between the researcher and the participant, for narrative inquiry is relational (Clandinin & Connelly, 2000), as we discussed earlier. In fact, Clandinin and Murphy (2009) note, "Ontological commitment to the relational locates ethical relationships at the heart of narrative inquiry. The ethical stance of narrative inquirers is best characterized by a relational ethics" (p. 600).

Placing a relational ethics at the heart of narrative inquiry, the researcher endeavors to obtain data from "a deeply human, genuine, empathic, and respectful relationship to the participant about significant and meaningful aspects of the participant's life" (Josselson, 2007, p. 539). We need to be transparent about our research interests and purposes so as to make an alliance and a trustworthy relationship with the participant. Good narrative practice, according to Josselson (2007), requires ethical practice that involves the need to respect the dignity and welfare of our participants and intense collaboration with them about the area of the participants' experiences and stories that are of interest to us. In other words, we should honor the "sacredness of our participants' humanity" (Munro Hendry, 2007, p. 496). In so doing, the process of doing narrative inquiry becomes a sacred space where:

> 1) people feel "safe" within it, safe to be and experiment with who they are and who they are becoming; 2) people feel "connected"—perhaps to each other, or a community, or nature, or the world they are constructing on their word processors; 3) people feel passionate about what they are doing, believing that their activity "makes a difference"; and 4) people recognize, honor, and are grateful for the safe communion. (Richardson, cited in Munro Hendry, 2007, p. 496)

This kind of sacred place can be created through *narrative ethics in practice* in which we pay attention to ethical issues arising in the process of listening to and sharing stories with our participants. We create such a sacred place by respecting the dignity of our participants and honoring the sacredness of their humanity as we develop trustworthy relationships with them. Hence, narrative inquiry becomes a site of communion where the researcher and the researched are interconnected in an inquiry, meaningfully informing each other (Munro Hendry, 2007), thus ensuring the integrity of the research itself.

Developing *Phronesis* (Ethical Judgment) Through Reflexivity

Thus far, we have discussed why we need to go beyond the IRB requirements and AERA's ethical standards, and raise critical awareness of *narrative ethics in practice* as a way to think about ethical issues that arise in every respect of narrative research at the local level in order to honor our participants' humanity and dignity. How, then, do we go about addressing narrative ethics in practice? How can we become wise decision makers when encountering moral dilemmas? I do not have prescribed guidelines about "how to" implement such narrative ethics in practice. This is because, first of all, ethics is not a set of procedures, but "decisions or judgments about respectful, beneficent, and just relationships" (Rallis & Rossman, 2010, p. 496), and second, ethics "does not amount simply to a logical working out of rules that could then be applied to specific cases" (Zylinska, 2005, p. 36). Each case would present different ethical issues that require different actions and approaches. The "surprise element of any action" toward ethical issues, Zylinska writes, "can never—'perhaps' even *should* never—be mastered" (p. 48). What we can do is to engage in an ethics that "calls for judgment *always anew*" (p. 48) through exercising "permanent vigilance" (p. 48) and a sensitivity to "the contingencies involved in specific, historically situated encounters" (p. 59).

Narrative ethics in practice, as we can see in Jodie's question and in the works of both Rallis and Rossman and of Zylinska, calls for *judgment* as a way to address ethical issues that we encounter in specific, situated cases of our narrative inquiry. Then, perhaps we narrative researchers should work on developing our ethical judgment, or what Aristotle calls *phronesis*. **Phronesis** is what I have been promoting among my students who are mostly practicing teachers. Now, I am promoting *phronesis* development among narrative researchers. Let me elaborate. First, please take a look at my reply to Jodie's question above about the ethical issue that arose in her research situation:

> My sense is why not. Why not help them out if they ask you to help. That way, you're not just "using" them for your research. Your help, offered per their request, would benefit them as well, so that the research relationship becomes reciprocal and relational. Also, you're not there to evaluate the teachers, so your help would not "skew" your research findings. That's my thought. But, you have to use your phronesis to judge your action.

So, on to *phronesis*. "Neo-Aristotelianism" has been revived in the field of education in the last decade, with a focus on *phronesis* (moral, ethical judgment in Greek) that connects educational practice and reflection to praxis (see Kemmis & Smith, 2008; Kristjansson, 2005). In *Nicomachean Ethics* (Aristotle, 1985), Aristotle argues that moral value is one of the virtues that each person has and *phronesis* is a unifying virtue and an essential habit of the mind. He defines *phronesis* as "a state grasping the truth, involving reason, concerned with action about what is good or bad for a human being" (p. 154 [1140b]). For Aristotle, *phronesis* is a moral and intellectual virtue rooted in a natural human capacity "to do the right thing in the right place at the right time in the right way" (MacIntyre, cited in Carr, 2004, p. 62). *Phronesis* is the moral, ethical judgment to act wisely and prudently, which is more than the possession of *episteme* (general content knowledge) or *techne* (skills or techniques). It is the ability to put into action the general knowledge and skills with relevance, appropriateness, or sensitivity to a particular context (Dunne, 2005). Therefore, *phronesis* requires the understanding of specific particulars of a specific time and place while focusing on the question of how to act wisely in a particular situation and finding a helpful course of action on the basis of strengthened awareness (Aristotle, 1985).

Phronesis is deeply related to deliberation that requires reflection, which has to do with "the understanding of specific concrete cases and complex or ambiguous situations" (Kessels & Korthagen, 1996, p. 19). It is not a simple application of research techniques and knowledge, for narrative research situations are complex, ambiguous, and unpredictable. *Phronesis* calls for reflection that is concerned with the particulars of a situation, thus it is a capacity that a narrative inquirer can acquire only through reflection, action, practice, and practical experience of research (Korthagen & Kessels, 1999). Dealing with ambiguities, uncertainties, and unpredictabilities of narrative inquiry requires us to develop *phronesis*. As we design our narrative inquiry, our commitment to *phronesis* is a necessary element for conducting ethical research in confidence.

How, then, do we develop *phronesis?* What is a practical way to improve our *phronesis* that will actually lead to the narrative inquirer's ethical research practice? I would posit that **reflexivity** should play an important role in *phronesis* development. We understand that *phronesis* calls for reflection, but it should go beyond reflection. If reflection takes one step back, reflexivity involves taking two steps back from the research process (Carr, 2004; Jenkins, 1992). The first step back is the reflection of objective observation of the research subject; the next step back is the reflection of the reflection of the observation. Therefore, reflexive researchers do not merely report the "facts" of the research but also take stock of their actions based on *phronesis* and their role in the research process. Researchers place their actions under the same critical scrutiny as the rest of their data, addressing the question of "How do I know what I know?" and/or "How am I being ethical?" rather than merely reporting the findings of the research (Hertz, 1997; Jenkins, 1992).

The concept of reflexivity has increasingly been used as a means to improve the rigor of qualitative research rather than to address an ethical purpose (Guillemin & Gillam, 2004). Generally, reflexivity has been understood as involving the researcher's critical reflection on the research process including what sorts of factors might influence the research planning and findings, and what kind of role the researcher himself or herself plays in the research process. The goal of reflexivity in this sense is to improve the quality and validity of the research and recognize the limitations of the knowledge that is produced, thus leading to more rigorous research and making qualitative research "at least quasi-objective" (Foley, 2002, p. 473). For example, Foley (2002) explicates four types of reflexivity, including confessional, theoretical, textual, and deconstructive, but does not include an ethical dimension.[4] Hence, Guillemin and Gillam (2004) propose that reflexivity is an important medium for ethical research as they state, "reflexivity is a helpful conceptual tool for understanding both the nature of ethics in qualitative research and how ethical practice in research can be achieved" (p. 263). McGraw, Zvonkovic, and Walker (2000) also use reflexivity as part of ethical research. They state that reflexivity is a "process whereby researchers place themselves and their practices under scrutiny, acknowledging the ethical dilemmas that permeate the research process and impinge on the creation of knowledge (p. 68)." Further, Rossman and Rallis (2010) argue that "morally grounded researchers are ethically reflexive practitioners" (p. 380). However, Rallis and Rossman call rigorous ethical reasoning "*caring reflexivity*" (p. 496) where reflexivity alone is not sufficient to guarantee ethical practice. Caring, enacted through relationships that honor the research participants, has to be central to reflexivity, although caring reflexivity does not necessarily result in a more trustworthy study (Rallis & Rossman, 2010) if the researcher is unable to use her phronesis.

Clearly, there is an interlocking connection among ethical issues, *phronesis,* reflexivity, and caring. Ethical issues can be addressed through ethical judgment (*phronesis*), and ethical judgment should be further developed through the enactment of caring reflexivity throughout the research process. A caring reflexive narrative inquirer would exercise her phronesis (ethical judgment) by constantly interrogating the ethical dimensions of research practice, including the interpersonal/intrapersonal aspects of research and the interactions/relationships between researcher and participant. A caring reflexive narrative inquirer would be attuned to her ways of respecting the dignity and integrity of her research participants, paying special attention to everyday narrative ethics in practice while preserving her integrity as the researcher as well. In other words, the more we are reflexive, the more *phronesis* we utilize in everyday ethical situations encountered during research. Narrative inquirers need to be phronetic researchers who navigate the world of narrative research with caring reflexivity.

Qualitative Writing or Scientific Writing

The last issue I want to address in this chapter about narrative research design is writing. Do you think I am being too judgmental if I say that writing is an area that gets the least attention from student researchers, especially as a research design element? Have you ever thought about reading a book on academic writing or taking formal training by taking a writing class? If you have, I commend you for that! But the reality is that we take many research methods classes, probably because they are required, but hardly ever writing classes. A scholarly writing class is not a requirement in many doctoral programs although it may be an elective, sending a hidden message that you have to work on your writing on your own (read "sink or swim").

I have to speak for myself. As a doctoral student, I didn't take any professional training in scholarly writing or take any writing course simply because I thought I didn't need to! It never occurred to me that I needed to take a writing course although some advanced qualitative research courses I took did mention writing. I simply thought that writing courses are for professional writers, but not for researchers. If I had time to take another course, I would take more research courses, or so I thought. I believed that as long as I knew the main structure of a traditional dissertation (Introduction, Literature Review, Methods, Results, and Discussion), I had enough writing skills. Shame on me!

However, there is one book that saved me from total shame. It is Becker's *Writing for Social Scientists* (Becker, 1986), which I read in one of my introductory graduate courses. You know that Becker gave me some inspirations about the importance of a literature review. Again, it was his book that challenged what I knew about scholarly writing. I mean, I used to believe that I should use academic prose with classy vocabulary for scholarly writing to make me sound "smart." I was on my way to academic elitism that was a part of seemingly graduate students' culture, just like the graduate student Becker used as an example. I was one of those students who "knew plain English but didn't want to use it to express their hard-earned knowledge" (p. 41). But he convincingly defied my misconception by stating, "If we write in a classy way, then, we show that we are generally smarter than ordinary people, have finer sensibilities, understand things they don't, and thus should be believed" (p. 34). This is exactly what narrative inquirers are not supposed to do! Becker became the voice of reason for me because he corrected my misunderstanding of what academic writing was about in general. Becker also warned, "Knowing the tips won't solve the problems. None of this will work unless you make it your habitual practice" (p. 165). A lot of us, qualitative researchers and narrative researchers in particular, have not made writing our "habitual practice."

Almost a decade after Becker's book, another sociologist and established qualitative researcher, Laurel Richardson (1994), revealed her secret displeasure with much of qualitative writing. She says, "For 30 years, I have yawned my way through numerous supposedly exemplary qualitative studies. Countless numbers of texts have I abandoned half read, half scanned" (p. 516). Sound familiar? She further points out how "students are trained to observe, listen, question, and participate" (p. 517), yet they are trained to learn writing as "writing up" the research, rather than as a method of discovery. She laments on how qualitative research training validates the mechanistic model of writing, even though that model shuts down the creativity and sensibilities of the individual researcher.

You think this trend has changed? Maybe not. It seems to be a persistent "leech," an ingrained habit that we cannot get rid of. As proof, just recently Helen Sword, a scholar, award-winning teacher, and poet who teaches at the University of Auckland in New Zealand, published *Stylish Academic Writing* (2012). For this book, she examined a data set of one thousand academic articles from across the sciences, social sciences, and humanities, to see what kind of "stylish" writing was employed in academia. She found that professors still believed that "a dull writing style is an academic survival skill" (p. 7). Most of them still believed that was what scientific writing was about, not to mention that's what editors of academic journals wanted. Sword asks, "So why do universities—institutions dedicated to creativity, research innovation, collegial interchange, high standards of excellence, and the education of a diverse and ever-changing population of students—churn out so much uninspiring, cookie-cutter prose?" (p. 6). It was not that writings about academic writing were scarce. Sword initially found more than five hundred entries on academic writing across the disciplines, and narrowed them down to one hundred writing guides published between 2000 and 2010, most of them targeted at graduate students and faculty. Despite the fact that there are so many publications available on writing, a lot of researchers still typically produce and publish boring texts. Pick a peer-reviewed journal in your field and start reading it. Most likely, you will find yourself yawning, like Richardson, at impersonal, rigid, authoritative, jargon-laden, and disengaged work, right? Richardson (1994) writes, "One reason, then, that our texts are boring is that our sense of self is diminished as we are homogenized through professional socialization, through rewards and punishments" (p. 517). I think this insistence on homogenization into what is traditionally considered academic writing, which privileges the omniscient voice of the researcher over individual voices, is one of the reasons why so many qualitative researchers (not to mention quantitative researchers) still insist on the traditional notion of what "scientific writing" should be.

Recently, I have seen an increasing number of doctoral students from the Chemistry or Biology Department in my education courses, that is, teaching methods classes, that have nothing to do with their majors. So I asked them why they were in my class. They said that they were there because they wanted to be better teachers when they got a job in higher education. They added that in their disciplines, they were taught to be good researchers but not teachers, so they tended to struggle in teaching the content as a teaching assistant. Hence, their advisors have begun to send them to the College of Education to prepare them to be better teachers. Likewise, then, we might want to borrow some expertise from the English Department for our research writing. Sword (2012) points out how researchers lack formal training in writing. She states that some academics are lucky enough to become superb writers despite their lack of formal training, but most researchers are not into developing and improving their writing. Perhaps this is a good time for a bunch of us to meet in a writing class in the English Department next semester. If it is a creative writing class, that will be better. Anyone?

I am afraid that I've been preaching to the choir. But hopefully, you've got my point. My point here is that writing is an important part of research design. Depending on what kind of writing you choose, it can shape your research design if you start writing early since "academic writing is a process of making intelligent choices, not of following rigid rules" (Sword, 2012, p. 30). For example, Becker (1986) advises writing early in your research, even before you have all your data, because you can begin cleaning up your thinking sooner. This advice differs from the more common notion that you do your research first and then "write it up." Again, it goes along with what Richardson recommends: Consider writing as a mode of inquiry or a mode of discovery. Writing as a mode of inquiry is a critical element of narrative research design that we need to pay attention to. Bochner (2012), who is a strong advocate of narrative inquiry such as autoethnography and evocative writing (see Chapter 4), postulates that the goal of narrative inquiry is viewed not only as representation but also as *communication*, and asks us to see ourselves not as reporters but as writers (just what Becker and Richardson said). He states:

> If our research is to mean something to our readers—to be acts of meaning—our writing needs to attract, awaken, and arouse them, inviting readers into conversation with the incidents, feelings, contingencies, contradictions, memories, and desires that our research stories depict. The question that arises, then, is: How shall we write about human experiences? (p. 158)

How, indeed, shall we write about human experiences in narrative inquiry? This is a question that all we narrative inquirers need to ask as a research design element. Further, how can we consider narrative writing as a part of the aesthetic play of the research design process? How do we make writing for narrative inquiry distinct from writing for other types of qualitative research in general? Are there certain characteristics of narrative writing? Follow me.

Imagining Narrative Writing as Aesthetic Play

> I am offered a text. This text bores me. It might be said to *prattle* . . . You address yourself to me so that I may read you, but I am nothing to you except this address . . . It can be said that after all you have written this text quite apart from bliss; and this prattling text is then a frigid text, as any demand is frigid until desire, until neurosis forms in it . . . The text you write must prove to me *that it desires me*. This proof exists: it is writing. Writing is the science of the various blisses of language, its Kama Sutra (this science has but one treatise: writing itself). (Barthes, 1975, pp. 4–6, italics in original)

As I type Barthes's quote here, you know, I am getting squirmy as if Barthes is talking directly to me about my writing of this text! I take this particular statement to heart: "The text you write must prove to me *that it desires me*." Barthes connects desire with a Kama Sutra of writing. I look it up. My computer online dictionary says Kama Sutra is an ancient Sanskrit treatise on the art of love and technique. It seems to me that Barthes considers writing an intimate business that desires an audience, an art of love for the audience through one's writing. To me, Barthes calls for an aesthetic play through our narrative writing that invites the reader to join the play. There are many narrative forms available, which is the topic of the next chapter (Chapter 4), but I'd like to think about what might be the elements of writing that *desire* the reader, rather than just *address* the reader, regardless of which narrative genre we select.

Creation of Virtual Reality/Verisimilitude

The first element I want to think about is *virtual reality* or *verisimilitude*, which has a capacity to have the reader vicariously experience the reality of the text. I discuss virtual reality in relation to ambiguity and metaphor. First, virtual reality or verisimilitude is "conceivable experience"

(Bruner, 1986, p. 52) that seems real to the reader at the time of reading even though in fact it is very far from the reader's own reality. Through virtual reality, the reader can realize the text, thus experience vicariously or virtually the event or story that is presented in the text. We can follow literary theorist Iser's logic here. Iser (1974) suggests that our writing should have two poles: the artistic and the esthetic. "The artistic refers to the text created by the author, and the esthetic refers to the realization accomplished by the reader" (p. 274). So, our text (the artistic) will be experienced differently depending on the reader's esthetic realization (not necessarily identical with the reality of the text). To allow our written text to take on its own life, the text has to be realized by the reader. The reader's realization, then, happens when it engages the reader's imagination in the task of reading. Thus, narrative writing that provides the reader with the virtual world of the text should be the field of aesthetic play in which the reader participates in "a game of the imagination" (p. 275) with the writer. When we keep the reader's imagination as busy as our own, we can produce an aesthetic text that provides a virtual reality or verisimilitude that will be realized by our readers. Hence, this virtual reality would make it possible for the reader to "write his/her own virtual text" (Bruner, 1986, p. 26) in which multiple meanings of the story can be realized. This way, our story can become both "readerly" and "writerly," which Barthes called for. Hence, Bruner encourages us to write a text that recruits the reader's imagination, a text that enlists the reader in the "performance of meaning under the guidance of the text" (p. 26). Bruner states, "Like Barthes, I believe that the writer's greatest gift to a reader is to help him [sic] become a writer" (p. 37).

Then, are there ways for us to achieve such virtual reality that can be both "readerly and writerly"? Iser advises that if we provide the whole story to the reader or lay everything out for the reader, then there would be nothing left for the reader to do, that is, the reader's imagination would never enter the text, which would result in the boredom that a lot of us (including Richardson) have often felt while reading qualitative research texts. This boredom may happen due to the lack of *ambiguity* in the text.

Closely related to virtual reality is *ambiguity,* given how important it is to leave room for the reader's imagination in our narrative writing. In fact, I am thinking that it is almost impossible not to have certain ambiguities in our narrative writing. How can we possibly write the stories of self and others precisely when we deal with lived experiences that are fraught with the puzzles and vicissitudes of human actions and intentions? Narrative writing will have some ambiguities, or some gaps that need to be filled in by the reader's imagination (Barone & Eisner, 1997), using the tactic of narrative smoothing (see Chapter 6). We know that traditional researchers have a problem with an ambiguous text, for their goal is to reduce uncertainty, thus eliminating all possible ambiguous statements. On the other hand, certainty is not a goal for narrative researchers, as Bateson, a narrative anthropologist, would argue. She states, "Ambiguity is the warp of life, not something to be eliminated" (Bateson, cited in Clandinin & Connelly, 2000, p. 9). Ambiguities can be achieved by the omission of certain details, an effective way to engage the reader's imagination, rather than laying out every detail cut and dried for the reader. Another way to promote ambiguity and virtual reality is the use of *metaphors.*

Instead of providing every detail to the reader, we can use a *metaphor* to help readers imagine, as metaphors are connotative and suggestive to help us understand one thing in terms of another. We use metaphors as a way of understanding and integrating developmental processes (Santostefano, 1985). Richardson (1994) considers metaphors the backbone of qualitative research writing. Lakoff and Johnson (1980), whose work is a compendium of examples of metaphors in everyday life, argue that all language is deeply metaphorical, embodying our lived experience. They note that we

> seek out personal metaphors to highlight and make coherent our own pasts, our present activities, and our dreams, hopes, and goals as well. A large part of self-understanding is the search for appropriate personal metaphors that make sense of our lives. (p. 232)

When a metaphor is used in our narrative research text, it makes abstract concepts become more accessible and approachable, and allows the reader to bring in different perspectives, resulting in different interpretations of the text. Metaphors are symbolic images through which meanings are implicitly delivered to the reader. Thus they help the reader to re-create and re-interpret the lived experiences of our protagonists based on their own understandings. They are analogous in a way that encourages the reader to use his or her imagination to understand the meaning of the lived experiences created in virtual reality. According to Barone (2000), it is this analogical understanding that makes the reader engage in a meaning-making process from his or her own vantage point.

Fidelity to Told Stories

As we narrative inquirers use literary devices like *metaphor* and *ambiguity* to create *virtual reality,* one thing we have to keep in mind is that our writing should present *fidelity* to what happened to our participant. *Fidelity* is one of the characteristics that distinguishes a story as research from a story that is read for leisure because the term *fidelity* implies something to be trusted. Blumenfeld-Jones (1995) presents *fidelity* as a criterion for evaluating narrative inquiry, linking it to both social science and art. He takes the concept of fidelity from Grumet's statement: "Fidelity rather than truth is the measure of these tales" (cited in Blumenfeld-Jones, 1995, p. 26). Blumenfeld-Jones posits that while truth is what happened in a situation (the truth of the matter), fidelity is what it (what happened) means to the storyteller (fidelity to what happened for that person). Fidelity, according to Blumenfeld-Jones, refers to the bond between the teller and the listener (researcher), which takes place by honoring the told story and preserving the value and dignity of the teller. Acknowledging that the original storyteller is also reconstructing his or her experiences, a narrative inquirer must maintain fidelity both toward the person's story and toward what that person is unable to articulate about the story and its meanings. Blumenfeld-Jones writes, "Narrative inquiry is an artificial endeavor existing within layers of intention and reconstruction. This artificiality brings fidelity and narrative inquiry into the arena of artistic process" (p. 28).

One way to maintain fidelity to and honor the told story by our protagonist is the use of contextualized and vernacular language. The use of vernacular, everyday language within a particular context has the advantage of inviting a broader range of readers, compared to the language of social scientists, which has a tendency to be linear, analytical, and overly technical. A narrative text that has fidelity to our research data depends on the use of vernacular language used by our research participants in a particular context (Barone & Eisner, 1997). Vernacular forms of speech are more likely to be useful in making the text highly accessible to any reader, making accessibility a hallmark of narrative inquiry (Barone, 2000).

Voice of the Narrative Inquirer

Another important element in narrative writing I want to think about is the voice of the researcher. As you compose your narrative inquiry writing someone else's stories, using their vernacular language, you will encounter a dilemma: Where is my voice? Or you would ask, "Am I supposed to hide my voice in order to better represent my participant's voice?" You will struggle to know how to balance between your voice and your participant's voice, all the while attempting to create a research text that *desires* the reader. Most of you were probably trained to avoid *I* and *We* in your research writing, to maintain an objective authorial stance, like "scientists," even though the American Psychological Association publication manual has advocated the use of personal pronouns since 1974 (Sword, 2012). We have been told that researchers who write in a highly subjective, first-person voice "run the risk of sounding unprofessional and self-indulgent to their peers" (Sword, 2012, p. 43). Hence the balance has to be sought by using our phronesis.

The voice of the researcher as part of research design is important as it refers to the researcher's decision about how to be present in the research text (Geertz, 1988). It is a means for representing "the *distinctiveness* of what otherwise is called a 'point-of-view'" (Holquist, 1994, p. 164, italics in original). Therefore, we have to think about how to maintain the balance in the weight of our voice: an overly dominant researcher voice could be accused of the abuse of subjectivity, while a weak researcher voice runs the risk of not thinking through (Clandinin & Connelly, 2000). Deborah Britzman states:

> Voice is meaning that resides in the individual and enables that individual to participate in a community. . . . The struggle for voice begins when a person attempts to communicate meaning to someone else. Finding the words, speaking for oneself, and feeling heard by others are all a part of this process. . . . Voice suggests relationships: the individual's relationship to the meaning of her/his experience and hence, to language, and the individual's relationship to the other, since understanding is a social process. (cited in Connelly & Clandinin, 1990, p. 4)

It is with Britzman's concept of voice that we can establish our voice either implicitly or explicitly, coming from the meaningful relationship we have with our participants. As discussed before, narrative inquiry is a process of collaboration involving mutual storytelling between the researcher and the participants, in which both voices are heard. Thus, we need to consider the multiplicity of voices both for participants and for researchers (see Chapter 2 for a discussion of Bakhtin's polyphony) and consider a research text where we are all characters with multiple plotlines (Clandinin & Connelly, 2000). Thus, we can use our voice as a site that can be reflexively reconfigured via interpretation of multiple subject positions (Pinar, 1997), making the personal social, which encourages our narrative writing to promote *narrative imagination* (Nussbaum, 1998) among readers.

Cultivation of Narrative Imagination

Lastly, as part of narrative writing, I want to think about the notion of **narrative imagination**, a concept that American philosopher Martha Nussbaum posits. As we explore what is entailed in narrative writing, we have so far discussed three major elements: *creation of virtual reality, fidelity to told stories,* and *voice of the narrative inquirer.* All these elements, I would say, are needed in order to cultivate narrative imagination among readers.

In her seminal book *Cultivating Humanity* (1998), Nussbaum argues that becoming an educated citizen means learning more than facts and techniques of reasoning. It means learning "how to be a human being capable of love and imagination" (p. 14). She believes that the role of higher education is to cultivate what she calls *narrative imagination.* Nussbaum posits that narrative imagination is:

> the ability to think what it might be like to be in the shoes of a person different from oneself, to be an intelligent reader of that person's story, and to understand the emotions and wishes and desires that someone so placed might have. (p. 11)

For Nussbaum, *narrative imagination* is a must-have characteristic of a democratic and cultivated world citizen who wants to understand the lives of others beyond his or her local region or group. *Narrative imagination* can be understood as taking the perspective of others consciously and compassionately. It is a process that involves deconstructing and transcending our preconceived ideas and prejudices, which in turn enlarges our empathic understanding. Through education, Nussbaum claims, we should work on cultivating our students' narrative imagination in an effort to educate them for democratic citizenship. Nussbaum maintains that literature can play a central part in developing narrative imagination. That is, by reading literature, we are involved with stories of others (or characters). And stories of others help us perceive "the invisible people of their world—at least a beginning of social justice" (p. 94).

Here, I want us to pay attention to the role of the story that Nussbaum speaks of. She posits that stories about others that we read through literature can help us cultivate narrative imagination that enlarges our empathic understanding.[5] Hence, to me, Nussbaum speaks of the potential role of narrative inquiry as a storytelling methodology in cultivating narrative imagination. If we narrative inquirers write stories that can foster the reader's narrative imagination and promote the reader's empathic understanding, I think we are getting closer to reaching the goal of narrative inquiry.

How, then, do we write a story that promotes the reader's narrative imagination that Nussbaum speaks of? Our story has to be *persuasive.* Our narrative writing should have a *moral persuasiveness* that makes the reader engage in imagination to take the perspective of our protagonists and consider new and different things possible and important. That way, the reader can join in solving human problems that are posed by the research. A persuasive story, according to Barone (2000), is one with the capacity to promote a kind of critical reflection that results in the reconstruction of the reader's value system. Barone notes that the reader can be persuaded by a good story to reconsider the usefulness of alternative meanings presented by the story's characters. Through a persuasive story that encourages the reader's narrative imagination to take the perspective of others, encouraged the reader is to examine her or his own perspectives and values for deficiencies.

In this section, I discussed possible elements for a kind of narrative writing as aesthetic play that *desires* the reader, which include creation of virtual reality/verisimilitude, fidelity to told stories, voice of the narrative inquirer, and cultivation of narrative imagination. There are other ingredients that I have left out here; for example, points of view, authorial distance, narrator reliability, and more (Barone & Eisner, 1997, 2012; Coulter & Smith, 2009). But I think you've got my point. Ruth Behar, again, widely admired narrative inquirer and anthropologist, advises that "Writing must be done with grace, with precision, with an eye for the telling detail, an ear for the insight that comes unexpectedly, with tremendous respect for language . . . and with a love of beauty" (Behar, 1999, p. 477). I couldn't agree more. Narrative writing approached as aesthetic play should evoke the reader's narrative imagination, and the work of narrative writing should start early as in the research design process.

Conclusion: Where Your Heart Belongs

In this chapter, we discussed narrative research design as aesthetic play. When we approach our inquiry design with this understanding, there are no rigid plans that we must stick with. Our research design invites evolvement, unfolding, and discovery in which we allow our narrative inquiry to tell its own tale. With this understanding, I hope you feel that narrative inquiry is *where your heart belongs.*

QUESTIONS FOR REFLECTION

- What issues should be considered when designing your narrative inquiry?
- What is the most significant narrative inquiry design element that you believe you need to work on improving?
- How do you imagine living in your research field and your relationship with your participants?

ACTIVITIES

1. After reading the seven standards of humanities-oriented research, take a look at Table 3.5. Try to fill in the blanks and then write how your research plan meets the standards.

Table 3.5 Understanding Seven Standards for Humanities-Oriented Research (AERA, 2009)

	Definitions	Elements to Consider	Your Research
1. Significance			
2. Methods			
3. Conceptualization			
4. Substantiation			
5. Coherence			
6. Quality of Communication			
7. Ethics			

2. Come up with the purpose of your narrative inquiry and your tentative research questions that fit your narrative research design.

3. Practice writing a short story (fictional, biographical, or autobiographical) in a way that it *desires* the reader. Try to incorporate the elements of narrative writing.

NOTES

1. I do not intend to suggest that Joan Backes created the three installations in a step-by-step, linear fashion. In fact, Image 3.3 is an earlier project than Image 3.1. I use each installation as a visual symbol to illustrate a research design process. I thank her for kindly giving me permission to "play" with her installations.
2. These standards were completed to complement the standards for empirical social science research published in 2006 (AERA, 2009).
3. Connelly and Clandinin (2006) suggest seven considerations that are crucial to the habit of thinking narratively. However, I do not list the last three considerations here, which include researcher-participant relationship, duration of study, and ethical issues, because they are not necessarily unique to narrative inquiry, as they point out. I discuss them separately as a part of research design in general later in this chapter.
4. In this chapter, I focus on reflexivity as an ethical dimension. Reflexivity as a methodological element is discussed in Chapter 8.
5. For more discussions about narrative imagination and empathic understanding underscored by other philosophers such as Mead and Arendt, see von Wright (2002).

CHAPTER TOPICS

- Narrative Inquirer as a Midwife
- Narrative Research Genres
- Autobiographical Narrative Inquiry
  - o *Autobiography*
  - o *Autoethnography*
- Biographical Narrative Inquiry
  - o *Bildungsroman*
  - o *Life Story/Life History*
  - o *Oral History*
- Arts-Based Narrative Inquiry
  - o *The Origin of Genre Blurring*
  - o *Eisner and Barone's Arts-Based Research*

- Literary-Based Narrative Inquiry
  - o *Creative Nonfiction and Short Story*
  - o *Fiction and Novel*
- Visual-Based Narrative Inquiry
  - o *Photographic Narrative*
  - o *Photovoice*
  - o *Archival Photographs*
  - o *Digital Storytelling*
- Conclusion: Blurring Genres

©Tom Parish, T. Candon—Root Cellar,
Liberty Township, Geary County, KS 2012

CHAPTER 4

Narrative Research Genres

Mediating Stories Into Being

QUESTIONS TO CONSIDER

- What narrative research genres are available in narrative inquiry?
- Which narrative genre would interest you most and why?
- Which narrative genre will be most compatible with your research design?

INTRODUCTION

Bryan called me again the other day. This time, he had many ideas. He told me that he had some former clients in mind for his interviews.

Me: What do you want to do with them?

Bryan: (proudly) I want to interview them.

Me: Yes, I know. But I mean, what stories do you want to collect from the interviews?

Bryan: (hesitantly) Well, I want to collect their personal stories about . . . like, what brought them to our counseling center and why they quit coming after the first or second counseling session.

Me: And then?

Bryan: And then . . . I want to see what we can do to keep them coming to the center.

Me: Sounds good. But once stories are collected, how are you going to represent them in your research?

Bryan: What do you mean?

Me: I mean, once stories are collected, you will have to choose a narrative genre in which you retell the stories to the reader. I mean, you could retell the story in a biographical form, which includes oral history or life history, or you could write a *Bildungsroman,* or you could use a literary form, which includes short stories, creative nonfiction, fiction, novel, poetry . . .

Bryan: What? Fiction? *Bildungsroman?* Novel? Is it even possible to write fiction for my dissertation?

Some of you may be wondering how you are going to represent your participant's stories in your work. Just like Bryan, you may not have thought that different narrative research genres are available, including arts-based narratives such as fiction, creative nonfiction, and photographic narratives. This chapter is about narrative research genres (or forms). As you begin to think about your research design, including your research topic, research questions, and literature review, you know (sort of) whose and what kind of stories you would like to tell. Hence, the objective of this chapter is to help you determine ways to represent those stories, focusing on different forms (genres) of narrative research.

Narrative Inquirer as a Midwife

In Chapter 1, we learned that narratives are what make up a story. Narrative inquiry is, then, a storytelling methodology through which we study narratives and stories of experience. Schafer (1981) calls this telling "narrative actions" (p. 31). Through the narrative actions of storytelling, we try to understand human experiences, which in turn helps us to better understand what it means to be human. Then, whose stories are we telling? Our narrative action involves either telling our own stories (autobiographical) or others' stories (biographical), or it could be a combination of both where narrative action takes place in a monologue, dialogue, conversation, discourse, or communication, diachronically and/or synchronically. I would say, then, that narrative research could broadly be characterized as autobiographical or biographical, or both at the same time. Therefore, as part of the narrative research design process, you might first want to think about whether your narrative inquiry is going to be autobiographical or biographical, or both. And then, you might further want to think about the form your final research text will take. This will lead you to a more complex consideration of narrative forms or narrative genres.

Abbott (2002) defines the term *genre* as "a recurrent literary form" (p. 49) that a text belongs to, while a text can combine two or more genres. I would say narrative research genre is a form that a narrative inquiry text can take, which may include autobiography, autoethnography, biographical research, oral history, life story/life history, *Bildungsroman* (a story of personal growth), and arts-based narrative research in which researchers integrate the arts into narrative inquiry, such as literary arts (e.g., short story, fiction, creative nonfiction, poetry, drama, etc.) and visual arts (e.g., photography, video art, painting, drawing, etc.). If we follow Abbott's thinking about a genre, we can also combine two or more genres in our narrative work.

Choosing a narrative inquiry genre involves deciding how to retell (represent) stories that you gather. That is, we, as "researcher-storytellers" (Barone, 2007, p. 468) have to put stories (our data) together in a narrative form that best represents our research data. In that sense, the story represented in narrative inquiry, as Abbott (2002) points out, is "always mediated—by a voice, a style of writing, camera angles, actor's interpretations—so that what we call the story is really something that we construct" (p. 20). Then, one of the narrative inquirer's tasks is to mediate stories into being, grounded in ontological (Chapter 1), epistemological (Chapter 2), and methodological (Chapter 3) understandings. A narrative inquirer takes the role of a midwife to mediate stories into being.

During my own narrative inquiry, I felt as if I were acting as a midwife who was trying to deliver stories conceived by my participants. I needed help from Eileithyia (or Ilithyia), the midwife or the goddess of childbirth and labor pains in Greek mythology. I had to have the spirit of Eileithyia in an effort to bring stories into being in my research text. At the intersection between narrative data analysis and my dissertation text, I wrote:

> In constructing the stories, I, as a researcher, played a role of a "midwife" who tried to carefully deliver a story of my protagonist's while maintaining fidelity, the bond between the protagonist and myself. To use the metaphor of a narrative inquirer as a midwife is an attempt to move away from the position of traditional researchers who are "behind [the] backs [of informants] to point out what they could not see, would not do, and could not have said" (Britzman 1995, cited in Lather, 1997, p. 252). The metaphor of midwife signifies the role of the researcher who will work with "what is in the womb" and collaborate with the informants in delivering "healthy, trustworthy" stories. Of course, I also used my own discretion and imagination, as a midwife would do, in reconstructing the protagonist's reality of what I heard and saw. (Kim, 2005, pp. 57–58)

I positioned myself as a midwife who mediated the demands of research with the meaning of personal stories, while staying away from the traditional position of researcher as authority. Connelly and Clandinin (1990) also note that "the narrative inquirer undertakes this mediation from beginning to end and embodies these dimensions as best as he or she can in the written narrative" (p. 8). As a "midwife" who would mediate evolving dimensions of narrative inquiry, I also wanted to honor the participants, their voices, their feelings, and experiences. To do so, I had to "step back" from my role as a researcher-storylistener, as Clandinin and Connelly (2000) write that narrative inquirers:

> must become fully involved, must "fall in love" with their participants, yet they must also step back and see their own stories in the inquiry, the stories of the participants, as well as the larger landscapes on which they all live. (p. 81)

After leaving the research field and beginning to compose my research text, I had to find ways to remain close to my participants while stepping back from the relationship so that I could see the larger landscape in which my narrative inquiry was situated. Just how to do it was the challenge. It was increasingly complex to go through my narrative data, seek what mattered to my participants, and find their narrative meanings. I had to create a "temporal distance" (Gadamer, 1975/2006, p. 295), a temporary separation between familiarity and strangeness. It was a process that needed "particular kinds of wakefulness" (Clandinin, Pushor, & Orr, 2007, p. 21).

Imagining myself as a metaphorical midwife helped me to bring particular kinds of wakefulness to the stories I was mediating. It required me to use my own *phronesis* (wise, ethical judgment), taking into consideration the three dimensions of narrative inquiry: temporality, the personal and social, and the place (see Chapter 3). Being a research midwife meant that I was in "a relational process" (Clandinin & Murphy, 2009, p. 600) as I mediated stories to come into being through rhythmic movements from field texts to research texts, back and forth. As a responsible story mediator, I had to think about what form the story would or should take to accomplish such a meaningful task. Again, my ethical, moral responsibility needed to take precedence through the exercise of my *phronesis* (see Chapter 3).

The following discussions will acquaint you with different forms of narrative inquiry from which you can choose for your narrative inquiry. Like Bryan, you might be nicely surprised!

Narrative Research Genres

As you think about how to take the role of a metaphoric midwife, someone who will mediate told stories into being in your narrative inquiry, I first want to note that some of you may wonder if it is necessary to identify a narrative form or genre for your narrative inquiry. For example, you are not interested in researching your own story (autoethnography), somebody else's personal identity development story (*Bildungsroman*), someone's entire life story, or oral history. Moreover, you think that you are not innovative enough to write short stories or fiction, not to mention visual-based narrative inquiry. But you're still interested in your participants' stories of lived experiences that do not necessarily belong to one of these genres. If so, you have a legitimate point. In fact, many narrative inquirers do not categorize their work into one of the narrative genres you will learn in this chapter. Hence, I want you to feel comfortable to say that your work is narrative inquiry although you don't identify its specific narrative genre.

Why, then, do I engage in an understanding of narrative research genres? Catherine Riessman (2013) observes that attention to form (genre) is largely missing from narrative papers, and wonders why so few narrative scholars attend to form, given that narrative study originated in drama. I concur. I think that attention to narrative genres is an important step in the research design process, not only because it is a way to make narrative inquiry distinct from traditional qualitative research, but also because it will guide you clearly as to what types of narrative data you will need to collect. Identifying your narrative research genre lets you stay more attuned to the direction of your data collection and writing.

For our discussion, I divide **narrative inquiry genres** to three areas: autobiographical, biographical, and arts-based. For autobiographical narrative research, we have autobiography and autoethnography. For biographical narrative research, we have *Bildungsroman,* life story/life history, and oral history. And for arts-based narrative research, we have literary-based narrative inquiry (creative nonfiction, fiction, novel, poetry, etc.) and visual-based narrative inquiry (photographic narrative, photovoice, archival photographs, digital storytelling, etc.). (See Figure 4.1.)

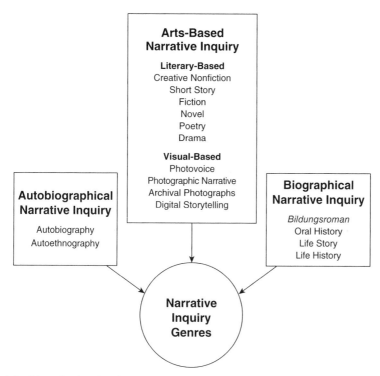

Figure 4.1 Narrative Inquiry Genres

Autobiographical Narrative Inquiry

Maya Angelou, the legendary poet and writer, said, "There is no greater agony than bearing an untold story inside you."

Autobiographical narrative inquiry, which includes autobiography and autoethnography, is an inquiry that takes the researcher himself or herself as the subject of research, using the story of the researcher's self. Some of you might think that it is a bit out of kilter to write a story about yourself as research. You ask, "How could my own personal story be research?" In addition, you think, it would be much easier to "talk about" someone other than yourself. True. Talking about your own story, whether it is glorious or sad, is not easy. In fact, it requires considerable intellectual judgment on your part to avoid being solipsistic, navel gazing, narcissistic, or self-serving. For example, when you read Ronai's (1995) autoethnographic research, which is about her lived experience of child abuse, you weep not because you take a pity on her, but because you realize that it could be anyone's story, perhaps your story, your cousin's story, or your best friend's story. It doesn't remain Ronai's personal story any more. You find yourself revering Ronai for her courage to speak, not for herself but for others, at the expense of her own self. Through the researcher's personal story, you inevitably turn to the broad social problems of child abuse, sexual abuse, and more.

You, too, may have a compelling story to tell. As Angelou said, you may want to share an untold story that you hold inside you, because autobiographical narrative inquiry helps us travel to the self that illuminates a larger social problem. Below, we will look into two types of autobiographical narrative inquiry: autobiography and autoethnography.

Autobiography

Speaking of Maya Angelou, she wrote seven autobiographies. Rumor has it that Angelou didn't want to write any book, especially an autobiography, because she believed herself to be a poet. It was her prominent Random House editor, Robert Loomis, who persuaded her to write her autobiography. Loomis challenged her by saying (cynically) that to write an autobiography as literature would be almost impossible. Angelou took the challenge, and the result was her first autobiography, titled *I Know Why the Caged Bird Sings* (1969), which brought her international fame (D. Smith, 2007). I mention this because we narrative inquirers encounter a similar challenge. The challenge we face is: writing an autobiography as research would be almost impossible. Really? I hope some of you will accept this challenge.

Although some tend to use the terms *autobiography* and *autoethnography* interchangeably, it will be useful to know the differences between the two. Since autoethnography is a blend of autobiography and ethnography (Reed-Danahay, 1997), it seems reasonable to say that autoethnography is a genre that encompasses autobiography. In fact, Ellis, Adams, and Bochner (2011) write that "autoethnography combines characteristics of autobiography and ethnography" (para. 5). Hence, looking first at the characteristics of autobiography would be helpful.

The eighteenth-century philosopher Jean-Jacques Rousseau (1712–1778) wrote one of the most famous autobiographies, *Confessions* (1782). Rousseau provides us a great definition of autobiography. He states:

> I may omit or transpose facts, or make mistakes in dates; but I cannot go wrong about what I have felt, or about what my feelings have led me to do; and these are the chief subjects of my story. The true object of my confessions is to reveal my inner thoughts exactly in all the situations of my life. It is the history of my soul that I have promised to recount, and to write it faithfully I have need of no other memories; it is enough if I enter again into my inner self, as I have done till now. (cited in Gutman, 1988, p. 102)

Rousseau tells us how he used autobiography as a medium for conversing with his self, his soul, and his memory. He reminds us that autobiography is not a chronological, factual story of what happened in one's life, as one might "omit or transpose facts, or make mistakes in dates"; rather, it is a revelation of one's inner thoughts and feelings about "all the situations" of one's life. Hence, autobiography, from Rousseau's perspective, is the history of the writer's soul that the writer is about to recount.

Autobiography in the field of literature is an umbrella term for "diverse kinds of life narratives that engage historically situated practices of self-representation" (S. Smith & Watson, 2005, p. 357). In particular, it is a narrative construction of identity that discusses how a life came to be what it was, or how a self became what it is, written in retrospect (Martin, 1986). It gives rise to the "I," the self, that is neither hypothetical nor fictional. The autobiographer does not always attempt to describe a self that he or she already knows, but rather, intends to discover one that awaits an act of self-recognition that "will draw all of the past together in the 'I' of the present" (Martin, 1986, p. 76).

Smith and Watson (2005), who engage in theorizing autobiography from the perspective of narrative theory, discuss how an "I" is fragmented and provisional, and has multiple referents that are neither stable nor unified. They caution that autobiographers need to be aware that there are tensions and contradictions in representing an "I" to various audiences. That is, it is sometimes hard to tell if one is fiction or autobiography, as reflected in the title *The Autobiography of My Mother (1996),* written by Jamaica Kincaid.

I find Smith and Watson's discussion fascinating here, as they point out the boundary issues that exist between fictional and nonfictional forms in contemporary autobiographical narratives. For example, one of the questions they address is, "What difference does it make if a writer impersonates someone else or appropriates another's experience in an autobiographical hoax?" (p. 358). They suggest that thinking about the autobiographical as a practice and act rather than as a single genre will blur the polarizing boundary between fiction and nonfiction. In that sense, autobiography is no longer regarded as a monologic retrospective narrative documenting the researcher's (or the writer's) lived past. Is there anything we narrative researchers can learn from this? Probably. I see some possibilities in which a narrative inquirer writes a participant's "autobiography" as a nonfictional or fictional account in a dialogic retrospective manner.

Autoethnography

Autoethnography[1] is a form of narrative research that seeks to systematically analyze the researcher's personal experience embedded in a larger social and cultural context. The term *auto* (self) is commonly used in the academy when the researcher engages in critical reflections and interpretations of his or her personal experience. The hybrid term *autoethnography* is rooted in anthropological methodology (ethnography) where the fieldwork was the researcher's own life and the lives of others in which the researcher had an active part. This type of ethnographic experience was called both "ethno-sociology" and "auto-ethnography" in anthropology (Tedlock, 1991). Autoethnography as a genre of narrative inquiry, then, refers to a research form that presents critical self-study or an analysis of the experience of the self (Hughes, Pennington, & Markris, 2012). It is a genre of first-person narrative scholarship (Bochner, 2012) based on the premise that understanding the self is "a precondition and a concomitant condition to the understanding of others" (Pinar, cited in Casey, 1995, p. 217).

Writing an autoethnography is an act of self-representation, but the goal is not to indulge yourself by shining a "spotlight" on your life, but to problematize social and cultural norms and practices in light of your personal experience. To reach that goal, then, the acts of self-representation and self-narration have to be historical, cultural, and political, embodied in one's subjectivity. Thus, as Holman Jones (2005) states, autoethnography works to hold "self and culture together, albeit not in equilibrium or stasis" (p. 764).

Just as qualitative researchers in the human sciences advocated a turn toward narrative inquiry in the 1980s and 1990s, interest in autoethnography in a wide spectrum of disciplines has also increased. The field of communication is a great example, as reflected in Baxter's (1992) statement that "personal narratives are likely to emerge as the distinguishing method of social approaches to personal relationships" (p. 333). Following Baxter, Carolyn Ellis and Arthur Bochner, who are champions of autoethnography, sponsored a project on personal narrative and autoethnography that became the impetus for the proliferation of autoethnographic research (Bochner & Ellis, 1992; Ellis & Bochner, 2000). With a strong conviction that there should be a closer connection between the research text and the personal life of the researcher, Bochner and Ellis created a space in which social science texts could be viewed as stories told by the researcher. They called autoethnographies "ethnographic alternatives" that emphasize subjectivity, self-reflexivity, and emotionality, with the goal of connecting social sciences to humanities through storytelling. They encouraged social scientists to turn an ethnographic eye on themselves and their own lived experiences to interrogate larger issues of society (Bochner, 2012). In so doing, they wanted to present personal, emotional, and visceral narratives as a way to produce meaningful, accessible, and evocative research that would appeal to the readers' capacity to empathize with people. Hence, Ellis (2004) defines *autoethnography* as:

> Research, writing, and method that connect the autobiographical and personal to the cultural and social. This form usually features concrete action, emotion, embodiment, self-consciousness, and introspection . . . [and] claims the conventions of literary writing. (p. xix)

Although reflection is at the heart of autoethnographic storytelling (Bochner, 2012), the autoethnographer goes beyond reflection and makes herself or himself a subject for critical analysis. Researchers acknowledge the fact that personal experience influences the research process (Ellis, Adams, & Bochner, 2011). Thus, as the researcher engages in a critical examination of the act of conducting research of the self in relation to others, a distance has to be created between the researcher himself or herself and the self as a research subject. After selecting personal experiences that are part of the research, the autoethnographer writes about them in retrospect. He or she engages in an analysis of personal experiences to interrogate why his or her story is valid and legitimate as a research subject. Mitch Allen advises on this particular point:

> [An autoethnographer must] look at experience analytically. Otherwise [you're] telling [your] story—and that's nice—but people do that on *Oprah* every day. Why is your story more valid than anyone else's? . . . You have a set of theoretical and methodological tools and a research literature to use. That's your advantage. If you can't frame it around these tools and literature and just

frame it as "my story," then why or how should I privilege your story over anyone else's I see 25 times a day on TV? (as cited in Ellis et al., 2011, para. 8)

Thus, autoethnographers have to distinguish their approach from simply reflective story-telling by

- Comparing and contrasting personal experiences against the existing research
- Analyzing personal experience in light of theories and literature
- Considering ways others may experience similar experiences
- Illustrating facets of cultural experience embedded in personal experience (Ellis, et al., 2011).

In addition, as Foley (2002) notes, autoethnographers should go beyond valorizing notions of emotion, intuition, and aesthetics as their ground of knowing. Autoethnographers should find ways to use personal experience as a critical examination of class, cultural, racial, and gender struggles from historical, social, and political perspective by creating the "space of dialogue, debate, and change" between the researcher and readers (Holman Jones, 2005, p. 764).

Autoethnography, along with autobiography, values ordinary, connotative language over scientific, denotative language, while relying on the literary language of metaphor, irony, parody, and satire (Foley, 2002). These allow researchers to evoke the richness and complexity of everyday life through personal stories. In this sense, both autobiography and autoethnography integrate literary writing into research, allowing this genre to serve as a precursor to arts-based narrative research, which will be discussed later in this chapter. Some characteristics shared by both autobiography and autoethnography are shown in Table 4.1.

Biographical Narrative Inquiry

Unlike autobiography or autoethnography, biographical narrative inquiry tells stories about others. It includes *Bildungsroman,*[2] life story/life history, or oral history, which share common interests in personal accounts in a manner that respects and values what people have to say (Chamberlayne, Bornat, & Wengraf, 2000). Biographical narrative research explores lived experiences and perspectives that people have of their daily lives, including their past, present, and future, focusing on how they make sense of the meanings they give to the stories they tell (Denzin, 1989). Biographical narrative research has claimed its place in academic research for a long time in various disciplines such as literature, history, sociology, anthropology, and education, to name a few (Merrill & West, 2009). It is increasingly popular, as we see various academic disciplines creating research centers and conferences that are dedicated to researching lives and the stories of people's lives. For instance, Merrill and West introduced the Economic and Social Research Council's Teaching and Learning Programme in the United Kingdom, which has welcomed increasing use of biographical approaches in the study of education, higher education, and lifelong learning.

Table 4.1   Shared Characteristics of Autoethnography and Autobiography

- The text is usually written in the first person, making the researcher one of the objects of research.
- The narrative text highlights generalization within a single case extended over time, different from the traditional focus on generalization across cases.
- The story format of autoethnography is akin to forms of writing associated with the novel or fiction, blurring boundaries between social science and literature.
- The story often discloses hidden details of the private life of a vulnerable self, highlighting emotional experience, to challenge the culturally dominant discourse.
- Relationship experiences are portrayed in episodes that dramatize the motion of connected lives across the curve of time, and thus resist the standard writing practice of portraying a relationship as a snapshot.
- Truths are pursued, but they are emotional, dialogic, and collaborative truths rather than literal truths.
- The text is not intended to be received passively, but rather to be encountered actively, conversed with, and appreciated by the reader.

(Adapted from Bochner, 2012, pp. 158–161)

Biographical work focuses on personal narratives with a premise described by C. Wright Mills: "Man is a social and a historical actor who must be understood, if at all, in close and intricate interplay with social and historical structures" (1959, p. 158). Hence, it is important for us to recognize that personal narratives are never simply "personal." They are crucial entry points or portals for examining one's lived experience in relation to historical, social, and cultural contexts (Chase, 2005, 2011; Maynes, Pierce, & Laslett, 2008; Personal Narratives Group, 1989; Xu & Connelly, 2010). The focus on personal narrative in biographical narrative research, therefore, is an effort to place people and their humanity at the core of social and human research. In biographical research, as compared with traditional ethnography, participants are treated as active interpreters of their own life experience rather than as mere reporters of their life stories. The aim of biographical research, then, is to understand how the participants construct and interpret their life experience, appreciating participants' genuine accounts and interpretations, which are largely absent from more traditional qualitative approaches. For this reason, Gubrium and Holstein (1995) call biographical work a "new ethnography" where participants are treated as "ethnographers in their own right" (p. 46). Biographical narrative research underscores how individuals' lives are constructed in combination with their interpretations of the social environments where their experiences are embedded.

However, as we briefly alluded to it in Chapter 1, we do not want to romanticize the role of personal narratives. Indeed, it can be "troubling, disturbing, and even harmful to collectives or individuals" (Juzwik, 2010, p. 376). For example, for some participants, telling their stories of traumatic life experience could be "a way of *re-enacting* the suffering over and over" (p. 376).

Hence, Juzwik cautions that researchers should be careful about the "*unintended consequences of telling stories*" (p. 377, italics in original).

Next, I will discuss *Bildungsroman,* life story/life history, and oral history, respectively, as part of biographical narrative research.

Bildungsroman

Bildungsroman[3] is a German term that is a combination of *Bildung* (formation or education) and *Roman* (a story). It is a story of one's *Bildung* that focuses on one's personal growth and identity development. *Bildungsroman* is close to my heart, as it fits well in the field of education in which there are many stories of students who have turned their lives around despite challenges, furthering their personal growth. It is a pedagogical story that projects the human being's resilience and persistence as well as his or her vulnerability. Hence, *Bildungsroman* would be a good genre for a story about a participant who developed into maturity despite or because of tribulations that were experienced by the participant while growing up. I've been fascinated by the concept of *Bildung,* and have explored it elsewhere (Kim, 2011, 2013). As a former teacher, I was interested in the stories of my students' personal growths. Now, as a teacher educator, I have a conviction to promote the concept of *Bildung* for teachers' professional development.

What, then, is *Bildung?* **Bildung** is not a concept that has clear definitions, although we can loosely define it as "formation, cultivation, and education" (Davey, 2006, p. 37). Philosophers have grappled with a variety of obscure meanings of *Bildung,* as it is a rich and complicated term that has a long history with philosophical roots (see Davey, 2006; Gadamer, 1975/2006; Hardin, 1991). *Bildung* originated in the eighteenth-century idealism of Humboldt and Schiller, who identified *Bildung* as the primary goal of humanity. They believed that it was up to humans to develop to their full potential through active engagement with the world around them (Kontje, 1993). For them, passive ripening is not good enough for human beings. That is, *Bildung* is not an inherent concept that people are born with; rather, each individual can develop personally through education and cultivation (Wahlström, 2010). Thus, *Bildung* designates the human way of developing or cultivating one's capacity or oneself (Gadamer, 1975/2006), and it is an identity-shaping activity, making meaning of one's own person (Mortensen, 2002). It also indicates an action by which a person creates a "self" that is held to be valuable (Schneider, 2010). In short, the concept of *Bildung* is concerned with nurturing or fostering the self to become somebody, which goes beyond the simple acquisition of knowledge and skills (Biesta, 2002).[4]

Bildungsroman, thus, is a story of one's *Bildung* that focuses on cultivating and forming one's disposition of mind involving intellectual and moral endeavor. It is a story of developing oneself as part of the journey of becoming. Furthermore, *Bildungsroman* refers to a reflexive story about the self, "one in which the problem of *Bildung,* of personal growth, is enacted in the narrator's discursive self-understanding" (Swales, 1978, p. 4). Roberts (2008) also states that the part of the role of a *Bildungsroman* is "to remind us that we all have a story to tell, and that while we can question and wrestle with what life throws at us, we cannot halt the flow of experience" (p. 252).

Wilhelm Dilthey (1833–1911) has been most influential in understanding *Bildungsroman* (Swales, 1978). Dilthey portrayed the *Bildungsroman* in the following manner:

> A regulated development within the life of the individual is observed, each of its stages has its own intrinsic value and is at the same time the basis for a higher stage. The dissonances and conflicts of life appear as the necessary growth points through which the individual must pass on his way to maturity and harmony. (cited in Swales, 1978, p. 3)

Thus, *Bildungsroman* addresses not only the inner development but also the complexity and conflicts of human experience, which eventually leads to personal growth and maturation, while valuing the process more than the end. The *Bildungsroman*, therefore, is written "for the sake of the journey, and not for the sake of the happy ending toward which that journey points" (Swales, 1978, p. 34).

Again, Rousseau's *Emile or On Education* (1762/1979) is known to be one of the first *Bildungsroman*, followed by Goethe's *Wilhelm Meister* (1795/1824). A more contemporary example written in English would be James Joyces's *A Portrait of the Artist as a Young Man* (1956). However, the German Nobel Laureate Herman Hesse, who is one of my favorite writers, is seen as one of the key figures in the evolution of the German *Bildungsroman* (Roberts, 2008; Swales, 1978). Hesse investigated processes of human growth and development through his literary work, for example, *The Glass Bead Game* (1943), *The Journey to the East* (1932), and *Narcissus and Goldmund* (1930). Roberts (2008) argues that *The Glass Bead Game* and *The Journey to the East* provide evidence of Hesse's distinctive contribution to the German tradition of the *Bildungsroman*.

Bildungsroman was not just a German genre. Dunlop (2002) shows us that *Bildungsroman* was also a popular literary form in Britain's Victorian era as a source of the moral and social development of protagonists. For male protagonists, in particular, the moral of the story was usually about how to reconcile the conflict between the man's desire for social aspiration and moral feeling. For female protagonists, however, the main concern was the search for autonomy and self in opposition to social constraints placed upon women as is shown, for example, in Charlotte Brontë's *Jane Eyre* (1847), or Emily Brontë's *Wuthering Heights* (1847). Canadian literary critic and theorist Northrop Frye (1990) also notes that the *Bildungsroman* has traditionally been a main genre for Canadian fiction for the last two centuries. He particularly explores *Bildungsroman* that portray narratives of women to trace how female protagonists develop themselves (see Table 4.2 for some features of *Bildungsroman*).

I believe that *Bildungsroman*, informed by philosophy and literature, has a lot to offer to narrative researchers, and deserves a unique status as a genre of narrative research. For example, narrative researchers in education can write a story of students who work toward personal growth, overcoming adverse life experiences. Or, they can write a story about teachers who work toward personal and professional growth by documenting their challenging teaching experiences.

Below, I'd like to present an excerpt of Matto's story as an example of a male student's *Bildungsroman*. Here is my disclaimer: I didn't know I was writing a *Bildungsroman* when I wrote

Table 4.2 Features of *Bildungsroman*

- The idea of an inner or spiritual journey of personal growth;
- The tension between the ideal and the reality;
- The importance of the context in which the protagonist's personal journey takes place;
- The role of enhancing the *Bildung* of the researcher and the reader;
- The importance of questioning, dialogue, and doubt in the personal journey; and
- The elements of striving, uncertainty, complexity, and transformation.

(Adapted from Roberts, 2008)

this. I only wish I had known about *Bildungsroman* at the time! Matto, one of my participants, went through tumultuous life experiences: he participated in a rite of passage as part of his Sioux tradition at the age of eleven; he was a gang member when he was twelve to fourteen years old; and he was suspended from high school numerous times, until he found himself aspiring to be a football player and worked toward graduation.

Matto's *Bildungsroman:* An Excerpt

Matto was only 11 when he faced the fear of death for the first time. As a part of the Sioux culture into which he was born, he was expected to go through a rite of passage into manhood. Right after his eleventh birthday his grandpa told Matto that it was time. He was to be taken to the forest to stay for a week and survive on his own. He has never forgotten that day when his grandpa hiked with him to the thick forest at the top of a mountain outside Albuquerque, New Mexico.

"Do you know how to use a knife?" Grandpa asked.

"Yeah."

"You're gonna need this," Grandpa handed him a knife.

"Do you know how to use matches?" Grandpa asked again.

"Yeah."

"You're gonna need these too. Use the matches carefully. You will need them for a week." Grandpa handed him a box of matches and a blanket.

Grandpa shook Matto's hand, kissed him on his forehead, and said, "You're a big boy now. You are ready. Good luck, Matto." Then, he promptly turned around and walked slowly back down to the village without ever looking back. Matto watched him until his grandpa became just a speck and finally disappeared from the view.

Left all alone in the wilderness, Matto felt like crying. His mind was suddenly filled with a primordial fear. Looking around, all he could see were the tall trunks of trees reaching skyward and huge rocks scattered here and there with shapes like frightening animals. The forest had an eerie silence, too, except for occasional cries from startled birds. The late afternoon sun began to cover the forest with darkening shadows from the surrounding trees, giving Matto unusual chills for a hot summer.

Matto wished he had somebody to talk to. He was well taught to be a survivor by his elders and buddies, but the fear of being alone in the unknown wilderness where wild, cunning beasts might be hunting for their fresh dinner was quite intimidating and overwhelming. He felt like a small rabbit that would soon to be hunted by a fox. He had thought that the rite of passage would be like going to a haunted house for fun. He used to scorn his peers who were scared to death about having to go through the rite of passage. But now he was being a coward.

Matto slowly began to find his courage and gather himself together. He had to, first, find a safe place to spend the night before it got dark. With a little bit of effort, he discovered a huge, flat rock which jutted out, whose top could be used for sleeping and underneath which could be a shelter that would give him some protection from the possible rainy weather and wild animals. He also picked up some pieces of wood nearby to build a small fire to keep him warm. These activities kept his mind busy and his fear was slowly leaving him. Sitting on the rock's ledge looking out over the fire into the darkness, he felt a sense of safety and even a sense of comfort. "I can do this," he thought to himself. "Yes, I can overcome this fear and loneliness." He was regaining his usual audacity.

His thoughts turned to his grandpa who named him "Matto." "Matto" meant "bear" in the Sioux language, and his grandpa wanted him to be a man who would never be daunted by anything. Matto grinned as he remembered his grandpa one day calling him a grizzly bear. Grandpa was proud of Matto's knowledge about nature, his physical strength which was unusual for such a young age, and his abilities to run fast like the deer of the forest.

Matto sat in front of the fire with his blanket around him and watched the flames from the fire flickering into the night for a long time. He finally lay down on the rock. Totally absorbed in the silence of the night, he started watching the sky. There were so many stars in the sky, it seemed as if they were about to pour down at him. Matto's eyes were searching for the familiar big dipper, the lion and others that he had learned from his grandpa. Stars were good company to Matto. They seemed to be singing a lullaby for him. While he was thinking about food for the next day, sleep took him over without any warning.

Matto was awakened by the early morning sun shining on his face. He could hear the birds singing and felt the excitement of a new day. He was happy that the fear of death was gone and that he had survived his first night alone. His courage had returned. Suddenly he started feeling very hungry. It was time to hunt for food. He picked up the knife his grandpa gave him and searched for a good stick to make a spear. He learned this from his grandpa a long time ago. He found a little stream not far from where he was. Catching fish with the spear he made was not difficult. The fun part was barbequing them on fire. Matto had not had such a delicious meal in ages. (Source: Kim, 2012, pp. 635–636)

———————————————— ๑๑๑๑๑ ————————————————

Life Story/Life History[5]

Life story/life history narrative research, also known as life narratives, the narrative study of lives, and personal history, is a "method of looking at life as a whole and of carrying out an in-depth study of individual lives" (Atkinson, 2012, p. 116). It is a main genre of narrative research used for understanding single lives in detail, and how the individual plays various roles in society. Robert Atkinson, a strong advocate of life story, founded the Center for the Study of Lives (now known as the Life Story Commons) at the University of Southern Maine in 1988 (see http://usm.maine.edu/olli/national/lifestorycenter). Atkinson defines a life story as:

> the story a person chooses to tell about the life he or she has lived, told as completely and honestly as possible, what is remembered of it, and what the teller wants others to know of it, usually as a result of a guided interview by another. (Atkinson, 1998, p. 8)

Grounded in the work of Wilhelm Dilthey, Atkinson believes that everyone has an important story to tell about his or her life that needs to be acknowledged. Dilthey, whose view we discussed briefly regarding *Bildungsroman,* viewed the individual's experience of life as a fundamental human act of narrative understanding, which should not be discarded at the expense of pursuing scientific knowledge. Dilthey believed that each individual lived experience is unique and particular as it is like no one else's; but at the same time, it is universal because it could be like everyone else's. In this sense, a life story is a way to put one's life as a whole, one's entire lived experience, into story form, presenting an understanding of a life lived from an insider's perspective (Atkinson, 2007; van Manen, 1990).

Now, let's take a look at the historical evolution of life story. Sociologists Bertaux and Kohli (1984) provide an extensive overview of the popularity of life story that was spread all over the world in the 1980s, including European countries such as Germany, Italy, France, and Britain, but also in Brazil, Argentina, Mexico, and the United States. Particularly in Western Europe, interest in the life story approach has grown quickly, marking a "biographical movement" (Bertaux & Kohli, 1984, p. 221). Such disciplines as linguistics, history, psychology, and anthropology adopted the life story approach to people's lives based on their narratives as a method of data collection (Bertaux & Kohli, 1984). For example, sociolinguists analyze the narrative structure that undergirds life stories. Historians are interested in life stories, mainly in the form that is called oral history (on which I will elaborate later). Psychologists are interested in life stories in hopes that they will reveal theories about human development across the whole life span.

The life story approach is believed to provide rich ground for the formulation of substantive theories for different disciplines, drawing upon a variety of theoretical orientations, including symbolic interactionism, phenomenology, hermeneutics, structuralism, and Marxism. In particular, the life story approach is appealing to sociology, as a life story can reveal the constraining effects of structural relationships, derived from the structuralist standpoint. Any life story is not just a personal story that is isolated or independent from societal influence. Again, following Mills (1959), life story narratives develop simultaneously at several levels: the historical, the societal, and the personal. So, we need to pay attention to the various levels that one's life story reveals, while being sensitive to the historical and social layers that the story bears.

Franco Ferrarotti, an important figure in life story research from Italy (Bertaux & Kohli, 1984), used life stories as a means of getting to know what was happening to a small, traditional town where large industrial projects were being developed shortly after World War II. He made important points about life stories that we should keep in mind: (a) society is historical; (b) each person is both unique and universal, that is, he or she is a "singular universal"; and (c) there are layers of mediations between macro-social processes and personal lives, such as local institutions, families, and peer groups (Ferrarotti, 1981). It is interesting to note that Ferrarotti was able to make these important points only after realizing his tendency to ignore his participants' frequent complaints about the negativities of industrialization. Ferrarotti, who was a strong believer in industrialization, did not realize how his perspective prevented him from paying attention to those complaints until he became self-conscious of his own bias. After self-critical reflexivity, he became sensitive to whatever personal truths were revealed in his research, understanding that they might reflect sociological truths. This kind of sensitivity is one of the many traits that all narrative researchers should nourish.

However, let's not make the mistake of assuming that all personal stories (personal truths) will become social stories (sociological truths). Another important figure in life story, educational researcher William Tierney (1998), posits two approaches to life story or life history. Following Linde (1993), Tierney distinguishes a *portal approach* and a *process approach*. The portal approach to life story uses an individual's story to mirror some reality in which the larger, societal story is embedded. That is, we can use a personal story as a *portal* to understanding the larger society. From this perspective, our goal is to study someone's life in order to gain insight into not simply the participant's personal life but also as an objective account of the way people live (without involving the researcher's subjective interpretation). In the portal approach, our retelling consists of an objective description of our findings with the goal of informing the reader about the social conditions of people gleaned from the life story.

The process approach, on the other hand, emphasizes the personal story itself. Unlike the portal approach, it stays away from the assumption that if we understand one person's life, we will gain access to the values and norms of the larger society. The process approach focuses on narrative whose meaning needs to be interpreted. Thus our act of retelling is constantly involved in interpretation followed by "thick description" (Geertz, 1983), hoping to provide the reader with some glimpse of narrative experience different from the reader's own. Thus the text itself becomes a central component of the research endeavor, allowing the reader to interpret the text in his or her own way.

Here's a caveat, though, when we use the process approach. If we use the portal approach, we have an easy way out, since we are just recording what was said without much interpretation of the text. But if we use the process approach, we need to think carefully about whose interpretations (or whose voices) are at work in writing a text. Tierney (1998) brings up K. M. Brown's 1991 work *Mama Lola* as an example, to explain how Brown struggled in the writing of the life story of Mama Lola with a text that contained multiple voices: the voice of Mama Lola, Brown's scholarly voice, Brown's personal voice, fictional voices of others, and the voice of Gede, a voodoo spirit (Tierney, 1998). Hence, in the process approach, as we change our role from that of a researcher to that of a writer of someone else's story, we have to be cautious about which perspective we use to interpret the data because different perspectives will lead to different interpretations.

A feminist curriculum scholar and narrative researcher that I admire so much is Petra Munro (now, Petra Munro Hendry). Her work on women teachers' life history narratives, titled *Subject to Fiction* (1998), impacted my own narrative work. Using narrative, she interrogates the nature of the dominant curricular stories we tell, focusing on how teacher (and student) stories can shape and reshape our understanding of the lived experience of schools and teaching. She explains that she was drawn to narrative inquiry and the narrative genre, life history, in particular. According to her, it has potential to "highlight gendered constructions of power, resistance and agency" (p. 7) and its primary goal is to provide an opportunity to "explore not only the effects of social structures on people but to portray the ways in which people themselves create culture" (p. 9). Through the personal voices of three women teachers and their descriptions of their daily lives, she takes the lives of women teachers seriously in order to acknowledge their stories as the way they know themselves, and uses these women's narratives as "a generative space for understanding not only the complexity of women's lives but how women construct a gendered self through narrative" (p. 5). Munro lists the advantages of the life history approach for her study:

- the holistic nature of life history allows for a complete biographical picture
- a life history provides a historical, contextual dimension
- in studying a life history, the dialectical relationship between the self and society can be explored. (p. 9)

Furthermore, Munro states that one of the greatest strengths of life history lies "in its penetration of the subjective reality of the individual; it allows the subject to speak for himself or herself" (p. 9). Munro's work will be further discussed in Chapter 6 as an example of life history. Table 4.3 shows some guidelines for writing a life history.

Table 4.3 Guidelines for Writing a Life History

The researcher needs to:

1. include descriptions of the cultural context in which the storied case study takes place, while attending to the contextual features that give specific meanings to events.

2. attend to the bodily dimension of the protagonist, including the protagonists' personalities and propensities that affect personal goals and life concerns.

3. attend to the importance of relationships between the main character and other people in affecting the actions and goals of the protagonist.

4. concentrate on the choices and actions of the protagonist, which indicate the inner struggles, emotional states, plans, motivations, purposes, and interests.

5. consider the historical continuity of the characters. In considering the protagonist as a biographical being, attention needs to be given to social events that the protagonist and his or her historical cohorts have experienced.

6. mark the beginning point of the story and the point of denouement in the context of time and space.

7. make the story plot plausible and understandable because the story is a reconstruction of a series of events and actions that produced a particular outcome.

8. answer the question, "How is it that this outcome came about; what events and actions contributed to this solution?"

(Adapted from Dollard, cited in Polkinghorne, 1995, pp. 16–18)

Oral History

You might be wondering, then, what would be the difference between life story/life history and oral history. Atkinson (2007) helps us with that by citing Titon, who provided an important distinction between a life story and an oral history:

> In oral history the balance of power between the informants and historian is in the historian's favor, for he asks the questions, sorts through the accounts for the relevant information, and edits his way toward a coherent whole. . . . But in the life story the balance tips the other way, to the storyteller, while the listener is sympathetic and his responses are encouraging and nondirective. If the conversation is printed, it should ideally be printed verbatim. (p. 233)

This distinction is indeed important to us as it determines our roles as researcher and interviewer. In life stories, the subjective meaning of the storyteller's lived experience is paramount.

Hence, our focus in a life story project resides in addressing the question of "What is the story my storyteller wants to tell me and what meaning does my storyteller give to it?" In oral history, on the other hand, it is the researcher who determines how a story told by an interviewee illuminates particular historical moments of interest to the researcher.

Oral history has been a major means of communication in human history. Collective memories and histories are shared in the oral tradition of passing down stories through the generations. For example, think about the histories of Native American tribes, which have been largely transmitted through the oral tradition. "Oral history is a history built around people" (p. 31), so observes Paul Thompson (2006), a British scholar who played a leading role in the creation of the British Oral History Society and the international oral history movement. Thompson further notes that oral history:

> [a]llows heroes not just from the leaders, but also from the unknown majority of the people. . . . It brings history into, and out of, the community. It helps the less privileged, and especially the old, towards dignity and self-confidence. . . . Equally, oral history offers a challenge to the accepted myths of history, to the authoritarian judgment inherent in its tradition. It provides a means for radical transformation of the social meaning of history. (p. 31)

Oral history is a powerful tool for exploring the historical memory of people, including the unknown majority of the people as Thompson notes above. It can show how people make sense of their past, how their past individual or collective lived experiences are connected to the social context, how their past is connected to the present and future, and how they use their past experience to interpret their lives and the world around them. According to anthropologist Elizabeth Tonkin (1992), in oral history, memory becomes an object of investigation as well as the important source of oral history that mediates between the individual and society. In this sense, oral history narratives become social actions that are in a dialogical process between structure and human agency, situated in particular times and places.

Thomson (2007) provides a substantive discussion about the history of oral history, which describes the evolution of the oral history research tradition since World War II, when oral history became popular internationally. The growing significance of personal testimony in political and legal practices, the increasing use of interviewing and memory in interdisciplinary research, and an increasing interest in relationship between history and memory all influenced changes in oral history. In the 1960s, early oral history projects focused on the formerly undocumented or poorly recorded lived experiences of working-class people, women, or people of color, fostered by politically committed social historians in Britain and around the world. In the late 1970s, oral history researchers had to work on establishing the legitimacy of personal memory and its subjectivity in response to criticisms that personal histories include bias and are not objective. During the 1980s, a transformation in the role of the oral historian as interviewer took place, as interviewers became increasingly reflexive about the relationships formed with their interviewees. They became more conscious of how they were affected by their interviews and how the interviewee, in turn, affected the interview relationship, thus affecting the data generated, the interpretative process, and the product. Another significant feature of oral history in the 1980s was its interdisciplinarity (Yow, 1997). Theoretical and methodological developments on narratives in other disciplines such as anthropology, sociology, psychology, literary studies, folklore studies, linguistics, communication, and cultural studies enriched the practice of oral history, and oral historians themselves have made substantial contributions to those developments in qualitative narrative research (Yow, 1997).

We are currently in the middle of the digital revolution in oral history (and in other areas of narrative inquiry), which began in the late 1990s and early 2000s. New technologies such as e-mail, the Internet, webcams, digital recording, and qualitative software are transforming the ways in which we record, preserve, interpret, share, store, and present oral histories. For example, Frisch (2006) argues that digitization of sound and image is challenging the current reliance on text-bound transcription and how the notion of documentary as product is "displaced by a notion of documentary as process, that is, as an ongoing, contextually contingent, fluid construction of meaning" (p. 113).

Through all of these changes in its development, oral history continues to offer an alternative way of knowing and accessing historical truths.

Arts-Based Narrative Inquiry[6]

Some of you might feel strange or even uncomfortable about writing creative nonfiction, fiction, or poetry as part of your research product. "Can this really be research?" you wonder. You also wonder if your advisor would approve of such arts-based work for your dissertation. Moreover, you have committee members who have shiny careers in "scientific" research. You have a hunch that they will not approve your proposal simply because they believe that the arts, or arts-based research, do not belong in the scientific community. If this is the case, bear with me. You might actually be surprised to know how arts-based narrative inquiry is changing the landscape of the qualitative research arena and narrative research in particular.

The Origin of Genre Blurring

Heated debates about the place of nonacademic forms of writing, namely, art as research, or arts-based research, seem to be old stories now. For example, there were debates at the American Educational Research Association (AERA) almost two decades ago (see Eisner, 1995; Phillips, 1995; Saks, 1996) where opponents argued that narrative inquiry cannot be a legitimate methodology because it has a tendency to be art rather than research, and because it is based on talent, intuition, or clinical experience (Lieblich, Tuval-Mashiach, & Zilber, 1998). However, the integration of two genres, art and research or art into research, can be traced back to the anthropologist-storyteller Clifford Geertz, who helped to legitimate the phenomenon of "genre blurring" (Geertz, 1980, p. 165) in the 1970s. Remember Denzin and Lincoln's eight historical moments in qualitative research that we discussed in Chapter 1? The third moment was "blurred genres" (1970–1986) in which social scientists began to realize that they did not need to imitate physicists or other empirical scientists to create social theory. Instead, they started drawing more from the humanities, "looking less for the sort of thing that connects planets and pendulums and more for the sort that connects chrysanthemums and swords" (p. 165). Geertz calls this culture shift of genre blurring "the refiguration of social thought" (p. 165), whose aim is not the manipulation of human behavior, but an understanding of human and social phenomena with recourse to literary analogies and symbols. This genre blurring has led to an effort to dissolve the art-science dichotomy in the social research development known as *the moment of blurred genres* in qualitative research (Denzin & Lincoln, 2000). Spurred by this moment, qualitative social scientists increasingly became interested in exploring the possibilities of combining scientific research with artistic design elements that are more evocative, enabling readers to vicariously experience the lives of people through their stories. Such writings might include forms of writing more commonly associated with the literary arts, fiction or poetry, interweaving facts (events that are believed to have occurred), facticities (descriptions of how those facts were lived and experienced), and fiction (a link between the facts and facticities) (Denzin, 1989).

Here is an example of such a shift. Pat Shipman, a paleoanthropologist who deciphers the fossil evidence of the evolution and origin of humankind, writes that she quit field and laboratory research in paleoanthropology in order to undertake a new role as a "scientific translator" (Shipman, 2001, p. 82). To her, uncommunicated scientific discoveries are a waste with the potential danger of leaving the public uninformed and misinformed. As she believes that there is an urgent need for scientific translators who are fluent in both the language and the practice of science, she takes on a new role to communicate her field's discoveries to the nonscientist public. Her new role as a "scientific translator," she continues, has increasingly sharpened her sensitivity to the complex connections and interactions that contribute to scientific discovery, rather than minimizing her love of science. As a result, she has come to realize even more forcefully that a straightforward recounting of the "facts" is inadequate. Shipman writes:

> Quite simply, science cannot be conveyed as a chronological list of dates and discoveries, theories and experiments; nor do such events incrementally build a cold, objective edifice of knowledge. Scientists are emotional, proud, stubborn, intuitive—Everything, in fact, except dispassionate and objective. Scholars bleed for their discoveries: they fight, risk, and sacrifice. It is the heat of the scientists' passionate conviction that forges shimmering truths out of the dross of dull evidence. (p. 82)

This passage portrays a counter-image of scientists, who are typically considered dry, cold, and distanced from their feelings in order to maintain objectivity. Shipman's seemingly personal sentiment has been verified by Eisner and Powell's study. Eisner and Powell (2002) interviewed 20 social scientists about their research process as well as their research products to explore the artistic and aesthetic qualities of the work of researchers. Contrary to the popular belief that scientists have little to do with emotions and aesthetics, they found out that social scientists frequently engage in artistic modes of thought and aesthetic forms of experience, involving emotional qualities in the research process. They summarize, "the work of science provides an arena for aesthetic forms of experience. Aesthetic experience can be secured in the use of the tools of the trade, in shaping one's thoughts, and exploring one's ideas" (p. 150).

Increasingly, social scientists accept and employ poetic and literary modes of expression in their research, and Ivan Brady (1991) has termed this growing number of social scientists as "artful scientists." Hence, such disciplines as anthropology, journalism, sociology, and education have opened up spaces for arts-based research (see Bochner & Ellis, 2003).

Eisner and Barone's Arts-Based Research

The late Elliot Eisner and Tom Barone, who studied with Eisner, are the main figures in the process of legitimizing arts-based research in academia over the past two decades, particularly in the field of education. They not only vehemently advocate the use of the arts in social science research, but also promote narrative inquiry as a form of arts-based research, seeking more evocative and aesthetic qualities in narrative. They began to refer to research that exhibited a number of aesthetic design elements (see below) in the research and process as *arts-based research*. Barone and Eisner (2012) define arts-based research as a "process that uses the expressive qualities of form to convey meaning" (p. xii).

When narrative inquiry uses the arts, mainly literary and visual art, such as short story, fiction, novel, poem, photography, and video, it becomes what I call *arts-based narrative inquiry*. In **arts-based narrative inquiry**, the arts accompany narratives to convey the meaning of the stories told and retold. Hence, the ways of creating art are incorporated into the whole process of conducting narrative inquiry, including ways of thinking, collecting, analyzing, interpreting, and producing a project. To use art as a mode of narrative inquiry is to move toward a research paradigm in which ideas are as important as forms, the viewer's perceptions as important as the artist-researcher's intentions, and the language and emotions of art as important as its aesthetic qualities (Bochner & Ellis, 2003). Empathy is a necessary condition for understanding meaning in human life, and the arts elicit empathic understanding because of their evocative and compelling nature. In arts-based narrative inquiry, researchers write stories that are presented in a literary art form as a research product, for example, a work of ethnographic fictional writing (Leavy, 2013; Richardson, 1994), creative nonfiction (Barone, 2001), short stories (Ceglowski, 1997), poetry (Ellis & Bochner, 1996; Faulkner, 2009; Sullivan, 2000), visual ethnography (Bach, 2007), novels (Dunlop, 1999), and ethnodramas (Mattingly, 2007; Saldaña, 2005).

Barone and Eisner (1997) discuss seven features of arts-based research, namely literary-based narrative inquiry, which include: (1) *the creation of a virtual reality;* (2) *the presence of ambiguity;* (3) *the use of expressive language;* (4) *the use of contextualized and vernacular language;* (5) *the promotion of empathy;* (6) *personal signature of the researcher/writer;* and (7) *the presence of aesthetic form* (for further discussion, see Barone & Eisner, 1997, 2012; also see Chapter 3 of this book). It is not necessary to exhibit every one of these features in your narrative work because your research is not going to be characterized as full-fledged art. But, the more art-like features your narrative work exhibits, the more rich and engaging its character can be. Created in this way, your narrative work can be "emotionally and politically evocative, captivating, aesthetically powerful, and moving" (Leavy, 2009, p. 12), appealing to a wider audience. Eisner (2008) says that if the arts are about anything, they are about emotion, and emotion has to do with the ways in which we feel, and most importantly with compassion. Our capacity to feel compassion is a "way of discovering our humanity" (p. 10).

With this understanding of what arts-based narrative inquiry can do, we can justify our use of arts-based narrative inquiry to our committee and to our colleagues in the social and human sciences. Some of you are attracted to arts-based narrative inquiry, but you have some reservations, wondering, "Am I qualified to conduct arts-based narrative inquiry?" Your concern is legitimate, as Mello (2007) asks, "Is it necessary to be an artist to produce art in narrative inquiry?" (p. 220). Similarly, Barone and Eisner (2012) ask:

> Can anyone who so desires do arts-based research? Is arts based research solely a domain of those who are already formally trained in an area of the arts? Should anyone, whether formally trained or not, be encouraged to do arts-based research? (p. 56)

The answers to all these questions are a simple YES with three conditions: "dedication, practice, and guidance" (Barone & Eisner, 2012, p. 57). And, I might add, persistence.

Below, I will discuss two main types of *arts-based narrative inquiry:* literary-based narrative inquiry (creative nonfiction, short story, fiction, and novel) and visual-based narrative inquiry that uses visuals (namely, photographs and/or drawings) as a way of storytelling. For those of you who are interested in incorporating any other particular form of the arts into your narrative inquiry, such as poetry, drama, performance, dance, or music, I provide suggested readings on arts-based research (e.g., Cole & Knowles, 2008) for your reference.

Literary-Based Narrative Inquiry

The adoption of literary writing in qualitative research is not new. In Chapter 3, we discussed that it was two decades ago when Laurel Richardson (1994) called for writing as a method of inquiry as well as a method of knowing. She advocated for experimental genres that deploy literary devices, calling them "alternative forms of representation" or "evocative representations" (p. 521). She encouraged qualitative researchers to "experiment" with their research materials, using imagination to meet the literary criteria of coherence and verisimilitude.

Creative Nonfiction and Short Story

For **literary-based narrative inquiry**, I think we can begin with creative nonfiction because it is a rather gradual introduction of an imaginative approach to the reporting of narrative data. We might use creative and imaginative techniques to represent the collected facts and information more interesting and more accessible. For example, in a typical journal report in traditional journalism, you would report factual information in an objective manner where your personal feelings should not enter into the writing of the report. However, in creative nonfiction, you would present factual information using the tools of the fiction writer, while maintaining fidelity to fact and, at the same time, openly communicating the writer's subjectivity or personal feelings about the topic (Caulley, 2008). Creative nonfiction uses an imaginative approach to reporting that requires the skills of a storyteller and the research ability of a fact-finding reporter in order to write about facts in ways that bring the reader to an empathic understanding (Cheney, 2001; Gutkind, 2008). Feminist sociologist and fiction writer Patricia Leavy (2013) notes that creative nonfiction has changed the landscape of academic writing and brought the tools of literary fiction into the researcher's purview.

Creative nonfiction grew out of the so-called New Journalism that was popular in the 1960s and 1970s. New Journalism had a preference for reporters who used evocative and metaphorical description, aiming for an impressionistic reconstruction of actual events, thus defying the entrenched notion of the reporter as a detached and objective recorder of events (Barone, 2008). More specifically, according to Talese (1992), New Journalism is not fiction, although it reads like fiction. Talese writes:

> It is, or should be, as reliable as the most reliable reportage, although it seeks a larger truth than is possible through the mere accumulation of verifiable facts, the use of direct quotations, and adherence to the rigid organizational style of the older form. The new journalism allows, demands in fact, a more imaginative approach to reporting, and it permits the writer to inject himself into the narrative, if he wishes, as many writers do, or to assume the role of a detached observer, as other writers do, including myself. (as cited in Cheney, 2001, p. 3)

Using this creative nonfiction genre as a model for reporting qualitative research, and narrative inquiry in particular, has proliferated in academia and been welcomed by the public since the early 1990s (Caulley, 2008; Schneider, 1997). Qualitative researchers have come to believe that fictional accounts can sometimes portray a research phenomenon more clearly than do the standard representations of qualitative data (Tierney, 1998). The fictionalization of research data provides researchers with the opportunity to work with raw data in order to speak to the heart of the reader's social consciousness, while providing the protection of anonymity to the research participants (Clough, 2002). Barone and Eisner (2012) also justify the use of fictive writing in social science research by problematizing the dichotomous relationship between fantasy and fact that has been prevalent in the Western world. According to them, all activities of human cognition and behavior contain a fictive element, and a synthesis of fact and fiction is indeed apparent in any creation of a work of art. Their belief is that social science can be fictional with the power to disrupt the commonplace and to suggest new ways of thinking, or new possibilities. It is indeed a fascinating idea to straddle the two elements of fact and fiction in a creation of our narrative research work!

Coupled with the features of arts-based narrative inquiry espoused by Barone and Eisner (1997), I think it would be helpful to have some guidelines for writing creative nonfiction; they are in Table 4.4.

Table 4.4 Guidelines for Writing Creative Nonfiction

1. Open with text that is vivid and vital.

2. Capture a subject to hook the reader.

3. Use scenes (vignettes, episodes, and so forth) as a way of creating a verisimilitude.

4. Use realistic details (written in the field notes or in a personal research journal) to conjure emotions and images in the reader.

5. Show, don't tell.

6. Avoid the killer be's (am, is, was, to be, had been) and use the active voice.

7. Capture conversation to enhance action and characterization.

8. Choose an appropriate writing style with word choices, syntax, and tone.

9. Use metaphors and similes to make text rich.

10. Use a list of single words (litany) or short phrases (prose rhythm) to create and leave the impression of a person, place, or thing.

(Adapted from Caulley, 2008)

Fiction and Novel

Ethnographers embraced this literary fictional writing trend in the name of *fictional ethnography* as Rinehart (1998) termed it. Ethnographic narrative researchers came to believe that fiction and fictional devices might in fact be more effective in conveying certain aspects of lived experience, both to academics and the public, than the so-called scientific language (Rinehart, 1998). They began to realize how limiting it was to place one's stories of the lived experience within an existing traditional paradigm that, more often than not, obscured possible alternative interpretations or alternative theoretical engagements. Thus, they turned to fiction as a means of working through or restructuring their ideas, finding the explicit use of fiction more adequate, effective, and evocative (Frank, 2000; Diversi, 1998; Leavy, 2013; Rinehart, 1998).

Fictional ethnography, according to Rinehart (1998), combines the goals of academic ethnography and fiction, using a variety of fictional methods, ranging from point of view to internal monologue to flash-forward and back. Using raw data that we have collected, we can create a work of fiction as a final research product, relying on our intuition, imagination, and creativity, and guided by logical thinking to write an effective story that appeals to the reader. In so doing, we try to get at both the cognitive and affective truth of the lived experience. An affective feel of the lived experience—verisimilitude—is what we are after here, since the complexity of lived experience might not always be possible to convey in a theoretical explanation (Diversi, 1998). Thus, in fictional ethnography, exact recordings of words said are less important than what the teller meant to say. What is paramount is believability. Believability leads to issues of representation, making us think about how well we can represent the lived experience of self and others in a believable way.

How, then, do we make our work of fictional narrative inquiry scholarly and academic? One good example of a fictional narrative that we can emulate is Katherine Frank's "The Management of Hunger" (2000) in the field of anthropology (see Chapter 9 for an excerpt). In her article, Frank first presents her "ethnographically grounded fiction" (p. 481), and then provides a traditional analysis of the story, including a review of the literature and a discussion. Her fiction is about an encounter in a strip club. Frank explains that the characters in her short fiction are composites and constructions consisting of bits and pieces of herself, of the people she has known in her research settings (strip clubs in a large southern U.S. city), and of her fantasies of them. Frank continues that the story is indeed based on her experiences working in strip clubs and is written as part of an attempt to think through complicated relationships that form between dancers and their customers. Furthermore, Frank believes that descriptions of the experience will provide readers who are unfamiliar with this kind of venue or relationship with vicarious experience, which will, in turn, help them discern some of the multiple meanings of the story. Frank claims that her fictional account, which originated from her ethnographic research, presents ongoing emotional relationships between dancers and their regular customers that are commonplace. However, it is not that Frank intends to advocate that her field of anthropology should change its conceptual and methodological approach to a literary enterprise by using fiction. Rather, she uses fictional techniques to evoke a mood, conversation, or setting, derived from fact. Her belief is that it is ethical for the researcher to explicitly state which part is fiction in an academic text. Clough (2002) also echoes this sentiment by saying that he does not "argue that all research should be reported through fictionalized narrative" (p. 9).

In the field of education as well, to write fiction or a novel for a thesis or a dissertation has already been justified and legitimated (Kilbourn, 1999). I first read a dissertation that was written in the novel genre in a graduate coursework, Narrative Inquiry, in 2002, taught by my professor, Tom Barone. What Barone had us read was Rishma Dunlop's *Boundary Bay* (1999), which is known to be the first novel to be accepted as a doctoral dissertation by a Faculty of Education in Canada. It was such an eye-opening experience for me as well as for the rest of my classmates. Writing a novel as dissertation? It was a kind of culture shock for all of us, almost like a Copernican revolution! Dunlop explained that her novel/dissertation began with a narrative inquiry with the purpose of exploring the lived experiences in the first years of teaching and the transition from teacher education training into the classroom. She collected data with traditional qualitative data collection methods of semi-structured interviews (with a group of five volunteer participants among newly graduated teachers from a teacher education program). After realizing that the stories collected over a period of two and a half years revealed some compelling stories about the personal, emotional, and intellectual impact of teachers' lives at multiple levels, Dunlop wanted to tell these stories in the form of fiction, a novel that could represent teachers' stories in powerful, evocative ways, opening up new epistemological and methodological possibilities. For her, fiction writing became a form of inquiry that enabled her to enact and perform theoretical evocations through narrative form. Of course, it was not easy to get it approved by her dissertation committee. Dunlop portrayed the struggle through the story of Evelyn, a character that she created:

> Evelyn remembers struggling with her doctoral dissertation, wanting to intertwine texts of poetry and journals into the text, wanting the power and eloquence of creative work. Arguments with her supervisor about the requirements of a dissertation and what constitutes research. "You cannot excel at both scholarly writing and creative writing. You must choose." Evelyn refuses to choose. She knows this refusal to demarcate, the blurring of genres, marks her in the academy. She does not care. She wants her writing to be plump with blood and bread. (Dunlop, 1999, p. 40)

Dunlop (2001, 2002) further argues that the novel can be a vehicle for an investigation of human life in dissertation research because it provides a deep understanding of human experiences, enabling research participants, researchers, and readers to move into emotional and psychological realms and helping them see things anew. The novel, she argues, provides a more widely accessible form that can extend research findings to a large interdisciplinary discourse community, providing opportunities for multiple perspectives and multiple readings.

Visual-Based Narrative Inquiry

To collect photographs is to collect the world.

—Susan Sontag (1977, p. 3)

The use of visual materials in the study of stories characterizes a growing field in narrative scholarship (Bell, 2013) that I categorize as **visual-based narrative inquiry**. Visual-based narrative inquiry is storytelling research that uses visual methods such as images, photographs, drawings, paintings, collages, cartoons, films, video, signs, symbols, and other visual technology. The marriage between the visual and the narrative is not new, either; the visual method has long been adopted as a way to collect social science data in anthropology and sociology by some of the early pioneers like Bateson and Mead (Riessman, 2008). Photographs have been an integral part of these disciplines since their beginnings, but they were not taken seriously in the social science until the 1960s. New social researchers began to work with professional photographers or filmmakers engaging in social science research, calling for a "visual literacy" especially sensitive to issues of class, race, and gender (Becker, 2004). In fact, visual anthropology and visual sociology are leading sub-disciplines in the development of visual research (Pink, 2004; Weber, 2008). Thus, the use of visual data in narrative inquiry is promising, as it will broaden the field of narrative inquiry to encompass visual images to share the lived experiences of our participants.

Photographic Narrative

I turn to Conceptualism, or Conceptual Art, to explain the marriage between the visual and the narrative in social and human science research. In Conceptual Art, and Conceptual Photography in particular, narratives are an explicit part of the artwork's content, tightly connected to the image. Hence, there is a natural affinity between the two. The idea behind photographic narrative is quite interesting; it deserves some discussion here as a way to inform visual-based narrative inquiry, which is interdisciplinary in its nature. I am grateful to Lucy Soutter, a photographer, art historian, and feminist, for an incisive discussion of **photographic narrative** or narrative photography, which was derived from Conceptual Photography.

Soutter (2000) wrote an article from a feminist perspective that criticizes a particular strand of contemporary photography, which she terms "panty photography" (p. 9), that refers to quasi-narrative art photographs of half-dressed young women. She discusses the role of photographic narrative, which was a prevalent trend in the photography of the 1990s, for example, multi-image serial narratives. According to her, narrative photography is the core of Conceptual Photography in which a photographic work is driven by a narrative that conceptualizes the image. In Conceptual Photography, the artist's ideas are considered more important than photography itself, and photography is only used to convey the artist's ideas, just as various materials serve that purpose in Conceptual Art. In other words, conceptual photographers use photography in new and unexpected ways that prioritize ideas over the art form of photography. In Conceptual Photography, therefore, photography is merely a medium that presents the artist's idea or an illustration of a story that the artist wants to tell. Therefore, stories are told alongside the artwork with a descriptive title. These stories include the activities that constitute the idea of the artwork done by the artist, or intentions or experiences that are related to the creation of the artwork (see Soutter, 1999, for the historical development of Conceptual Photography). Borrowing from the literature and Roland Barthes's terminology of narrative in particular, Soutter points out how a still image can evoke a narrative, or a story, leading to photographic narrative or narrative photography, rather than merely recording whatever the camera captures. Soutter contends, however, that without supplementary narrative, stories in photographs might never come to fruition except in the imagination. The role of photographic narrative, thus, is to connect the image and the text; and narrative becomes an explicit part of the photograph's content, a bonus to the visual information that is provided in the picture.

The importance of photographic narrative is further illustrated in *Storytellers: A Photographer's Guide to Developing Themes and Creating Stories With Pictures* (Foster, 2012). Although Foster does not mention Soutter's photographic narrative in the book, his visual storytelling concept seems closely related. A Texas-based professional photographer, Jared Foster, speaks of the value of visual storytelling and how to go about producing powerful stories through photographs. He reminds readers that what separates a serious photographer from the stereotypical tourist photographer is the photographer's ability to collect images in a way that tells a story and offers a greater understanding of what he or she sees in a particular time and space. He emphasizes that photographers are visual storytellers who record life's dynamics, nuances, ambiguities, and emotions, all presented in the images. For his book, Foster interviewed professional photographers who had inspired him to become a visual storyteller. One of his inspirations is Jim Richardson, a photojournalist working for the National Geographic Society, living in a small rural town, Lindsborg, Kansas, not far from where I live. In the interview, Richardson makes an insightful remark on photographic narrative:

that whole narrative, that whole story, is what drives a huge piece of what is happening in our world. Similarly, you always have to assume that when people look at a photograph, they're going to take a story away from it—whether you intend for them to or not. (Foster, 2012, n.p.)

Coincidentally, I had an opportunity to attend a talk by Richardson, given as part of the Agronomy Seminar Series at Kansas State University on December 14, 2013. The talk was about his work undertaken on assignment for the National Geographic Society, photographing soils of the world and including images of soil erosion, restoration, and other human interventions, and plant roots. He wanted to create a photographic narrative or a visual story that would make viewers, who may never have appreciated soil before, pause and think. The pictures he shared with the audience during his talk were profound and metaphorical, as they symbolize environments that are indispensable to human survival and prosperity. The photographic narratives that he showed the audience deepened my appreciation of soils in a way that I had never considered before. I was deeply touched by his visual stories; they made me pause and rethink, indeed. With Richardson's permission, I share his visual storytelling of the soils and roots.

Jim Richardson's Visual Storytelling

1. Soils: The Roots of Life

©Jim Richardson

Image 4.1   Kansas Prairie Soil Profile.

(Continued)

(Continued)

My challenge photographing this story paralleled the greater challenge faced by all humans: to understand that this humble stuff beneath our feet is the very stuff that makes life on earth what it is. The power of soil to formulate the building blocks of life is (there is no other word that is sufficient) miraculous. What a gift!

2. Roots: The Prairie Survivors

While working on the Soils story for National Geographic we developed the technology for photographing the incredible prairie roots that Jerry Glover has been growing at the Land Institute in Salina. The plants you see here are from nine to sixteen feet long from top to bottom. They survive in the dry prairie lands because they dig deep for water and nutrients. They are remarkable beings, beautiful and worthy of our admiration.

Big Bluestem   Kansas Resinweed   Compass Plant

Image 4.2   Roots: The Prairie Survivors.

Richardson's narratives and images shed fresh light on familiar features of the natural environment we may have taken for granted. Richardson shares his tactic as a visual storyteller, which seems to be in line with his research tactic: He first has a focused topic to explore. For example, in his images he explores how soil has been exploited by human development and how soil is fundamental from an ecological perspective. Before he gets to the images of how soil has been ruined, he focuses on the importance of soil and its organic relationship to plants, a relationship that serves as an analogy for the relationship of soil to the life of human beings. As we observe the images that Richardson took, we understand the compelling story that he wants to convey.

I think there are so many things that we narrative inquirers can learn from visual storytellers such as Soutter and Richardson. Can we consider collecting visual images to tell a story? Can we create photographic narratives to convey the meaning of the lived experience of our participants? Can we enhance the meaning of our written texts by providing visual images? The answers are all positive. I see many possibilities inherent in the visual-based narrative inquiry.

Photovoice

More and more contemporary narrative scholars use visual-based narrative inquiry, which is a partnership of words and images depicting the social texture of the everyday life of people and places. Participants' lived experiences are represented and reflected in visual images to provide vicarious experiences for readers. This multimodal storytelling adds another layer of meaning to narrative inquiry, namely a different "angle of vision" (Bach, 2007, p. 282). When both ways (narrative and visual) are used in combination, they can convey an idea that neither could convey alone, keeping the truthfulness of the stories intact (Johnson, 2004). Just like verbal narrative, visual narrative captures the specificity of social phenomena while illuminating the general in the particular, which allows us to explore the relationship between the two (Knowles & Sweetman, 2004).

In visual-based narrative inquiry, we use images as "texts" to be interpreted. Therefore, attention should be paid not only to how and why the images were produced, but also to how they might be read by different audiences. In other words, we have to understand that the term *visual* is not just about an image or object in and of itself but is more concerned with the perception of and the meanings attributed to it, which requires interpretation by the researcher and the viewer (Soutter, 2000). In addition, we have to remember that the images themselves provide no proof for any one of the interpretations over another. It should be noted that although a picture is worth a thousand words and some say that images "speak for themselves," Riessman (2008) insists that narrative researchers must write about the images, as the written texts can provide information that cannot be gleaned from the image alone. I concur. In visual-based narrative inquiry, written narrative should accompany the visual data.

To take another example of visual-based narrative inquiry, education researcher Bach (2007) uses photographs as a way of sharing lived experience and to make meaning of participants' experiences visually. She begins her visual narrative inquiry by photographing her own storied life to portray the particularities of an autobiographical narrative perspective. And she meets with participants individually and speaks about the ethical issues of working with cameras, discussing the possibilities of composing photographs, collecting photographs, and conversing with/through/about photographs before providing participants with cameras and camerawork tasks. She usually selects participants who are active in their subcultures. She asks them to take pictures as a way to compose their lives through photography and a way to convey what matters to them. Participants take photographs of their lives over a short time span of a week or two and tell stories about those photographs over time. This method is called **Photovoice**, "a strategy that relies on informants to produce images" (Bell, 2013, p. 145). These photographs are made *with* participants as well as *of* them. The photographs that participants take represent the "diverse relationships possible among people, cameras, and images" (Bach, 2007, p. 285). She then studies the photographs and constructs a "field text" about possible meanings before she invites the participant to speak about the photographs of his or her choice. This process of working together is repeated several times. Bach advises that it is important that the researcher remains open and flexible to the inquiry during the recursive process, knowing that there will be shifts and changes. She states:

> I am mindful of my intentions, knowing that they will shift, and that they are negotiated within the narrative inquiry space, depending on what my position is on the landscape and who I am in relation to the participant, the program, and the audience. (p. 285)

Archival Photographs

Another way to do visual-based narrative inquiry is to work with archival photographs (Bell, 2002, 2006; Caswell, 2012). A former graduate student, Heather Caswell, on whose committee I served, worked with archival photographs in the Library of Congress. Caswell (2012) examined photographs taken in American classrooms during the first half of the twentieth century, to explore perspectives about the context of school, pedagogy, and teacher-student relationships during those years. Her semiotic analysis provides rich discussions of what we can learn about education through visual images by considering the social and historical contexts of the images.

Sociologist Susan Bell (2002), to take another example, used thought-provoking autobiographical photographs of British feminist Jo Spence (1934–1992), who took photos of herself to document her experiences of breast cancer from the time of her diagnosis in 1982 until the time of her death in 1992. In her study, Bell makes a case for how the study of illness narratives can go beyond oral and textual accounts by the incorporation of visual elements, which in turn can enhance the understandings of people's experience of illness. Below is an example of an autobiographical photograph taken by Spence (Image 4.3), Spence's description of the photograph, and an excerpt of Bell's analysis of Spence's visual and written texts.

> Passing through the hands of the medical orthodoxy can be terrifying when you have breast cancer. I determined to document for myself what was happening to me. Not to be merely the object of their medical discourse but to be the active subject of my own investigation. Here whilst a mammogram is being done I have persuaded the radiographer to take a picture for me. She was rather unhappy about it, but felt it was preferable to my holding the camera out at arm's length and doing a self portrait. (Spence, 1988, p. 153, cited in Bell, 2002, p. 15)

And, here is Bell's own interpretation of the image:

> The words and images in this photograph bear witness to Spence's interruption of a routine medical event. For adult women—especially those over the age of 40 or those whose bodies

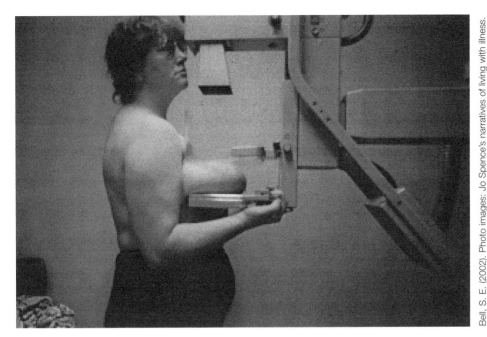

Bell, S. E. (2002). Photo images: Jo Spence's narratives of living with illness. Health: An Interdisciplinary Journal for the Social Study of Health, Illness and Medicine, 6(1), 5–30. p. 15.

Image 4.3   Mammogram

have developed mysterious "lumps"—it also evokes a recognizable story: breast cancer is a common disease. Mammograms detect malignancies. Thus women over the age of 40 should have regular mammograms. In addition, it suggests to me a particular story in progress: Jo Spence is having a mammogram. What will be the outcome? (Bell, 2002, p. 17)

As you can see, the potential of using visual images in narrative inquiry is enormous. Although the use of images in qualitative research is not new, bringing visuals into narrative inquiry has been understudied (Bach, 2007). Johnson (2004) also posits that there has been very little systematic analysis of how the visual text of narrative inquiry can be utilized to produce alternative meanings. To further motivate you, I want to provide a list of values that visual images hold for our research (see Table 4.5 on the next page).

Digital Storytelling

With the advancement of today's digital technology, I would say that the future of narrative inquiry is wide open and more promising than ever. Nowadays, it is much easier and more convenient to collect narrative data using mobile devices, such as smartphones, iPads, or tablets. It is not necessarily "easier" for me, who is not as tech-savvy as you are, but I am sure it is certainly true for

Table 4.5   Why Use Visual Images in Research

1. Images can be used to capture the ineffable, the hard-to-put-into-words.

2. Images can make us pay attention to things in new ways.

3. Images are likely to be memorable.

4. Images can be used to communicate more holistically, incorporating multiple layers, and evoking stories or questions.

5. Images can enhance empathic understanding and generalizability.

6. Through metaphor and symbol, artistic images can carry theory elegantly and eloquently.

7. Images encourage embodied knowledge.

8. Images can be more accessible than most forms of academic discourse.

9. Images can facilitate reflexivity in research design.

10. Images provoke action for social justice.

(Adapted from Weber, 2008, pp. 44–46)

many of you who are digital natives. Indeed, today's technological advancements have influenced what and how we choose to conduct narrative inquiry, therefore, I would be remiss if I didn't bring up digital storytelling, an emerging method for narrative research that you have probably heard of.

The **digital storytelling** method refers to a three- to five-minute visual narrative that synthesizes photo images, artwork, video, audio recordings of voice and music, and text to create compelling accounts of lived experience (A. Gubrium, 2009). It is a newly emerging narrative research genre that uses a variety of digital technologies to document first-person narratives. Digital storytelling is used in community-based participatory research to increase community members' participation in research on local health issues, as their concerns and interests have been typically excluded or placed at the bottom of institutional priorities (A. Gubrium, 2009; Lambert, 2006). It is also used to preserve and promote indigenous oral wisdom as a way to overcome the limits of interview-based narrative research (Willox, Harper, & Edge, 2012). Willox et al. (2012) state:

> We believe that digital storytelling opens up some exciting and innovative new terrain for conducting and sharing narrative research, particularly within indigenous communities. As a method, it not only addresses the conceptual and practical issues and limitations associated with narrative research but it also works to alter, reverse, and/or disrupt the power dynamics often inherent in the research process and in the very roles of the "researcher" and "researched." The stories created, and the voices and lived experiences within, are an important, rich, and powerful source of data that have not been written, prestructured, or altered by the researcher. (p. 141)

The key here is that the stories created are not "altered by the researcher." Hence, one of the merits of digital storytelling resides in that it presents the stories initiated and created by the participants from their perspectives without the researcher's interruption.

This, then, means that digital storytelling involves immersive training and workshops for research participants who are not familiar with the use of technologies, which could be a challenge for some individual researchers who do not have the means to offer such workshops. According to Gubrium (2009), in fact, the digital storytelling process was originally codified by the Center for Digital Storytelling (www.storycenter.org), where experts in digital storytelling train participants to produce their own digital stories, which includes digital story elements, crafting the script of their stories, a tutorial on working with a digital image-editing software program such as Adobe Photoshop Elements, and other technical elements of digital storytelling, such as creating storyboards and recording voice-overs. I do not intend to discourage you from taking an interest in digital storytelling by pointing out this challenge because I have students who present their final papers by making short movies without much training, similar to the digital storytelling method. My point, though, is that although digital storytelling seems to be a cutting-edge method, we should carefully consider what is entailed in carrying out such a method before we employ it.

As you see, today's technology offers many possibilities for expanding the scope of narrative inquiry. However, we should also be aware of some concerns that are particularly pertinent to visual-based narrative inquiry that involve ethics (confidentiality) and legal copyright. Dissemination of visual data can become problematic when reviewed by courts using outdated laws and ethics committees with limited knowledge of visual methods. As mentioned above, visual methods can reveal important information that text or word-based methods cannot. Hence, Prosser (2011) advises that it is critical to know enough about the moral rights of participants and their culture, society, or community through research to "make sound sensitive moral decisions" (p. 493). (See Chapter 3 for more discussion about ethical issues.)

Conclusion: Blurring Genres

In this chapter, we have discussed narrative research genres or forms, including autobiography, autoethnography, biographical research, *Bildungsroman,* life story/life history, oral history, literary-based narrative inquiry, and visual-based narrative inquiry (Chase, 2011).[7] These narrative research genres are possible ways for the narrative inquirer to mediate stories into being. Hence, the role of the narrative inquirer as a metaphorical midwife is strongly suggested here. These narrative research genres, however, should be viewed as a means, not as an end. They are the means with which you mediate stories so that the meanings of the stories will be conveyed in ways that engage the reader.

After reading this chapter, I hope you now sense, even if vaguely, which genre of narrative inquiry appeals to you. But, this attraction to a certain narrative form should not be weighed in isolation. You must consider all factors, from the purpose of your research, research questions, participants, and kind of stories you would like to collect, to data collection methods and implications. You may wish to blur narrative research genres, integrating multiple forms into your narrative inquiry. As you see, writing stories, and by this I mean, writing *compelling* stories that will affect the reader (so that your research makes a difference) requires your imagination, empathy, passion, and compassion. As we deal with stories of our participants, those stories that breathe our participants' past, present, and future, our approach to narrative inquiry should also be as organic, living, fluid, and flexible as possible, because stories will not produce a fixed formula that we can apply uniformly.

Questions for Reflection

- In what ways does each narrative research genre address your research interests?
- Which narrative genre would you choose for your own research and why?
- How would you justify and convince your committee members of the value of your selected narrative research genre?

Activities

1. Listen to these three different classical music pieces: Paganini's *Caprice 24*, Brahms's *Paganini Variations,* and Rachmaninoff's *Rhapsody on a Theme of Paganini.* Try to feel how one main theme can be represented in various forms. And then, try to imagine how your narrative inquiry can be represented in variations.

2. Try to write your own short autobiography.

3. Create two different imaginary groups: one that represents your doctoral committee who are positivists; and the other that advocates multiple forms of narrative inquiry. Create a mock proposal defense for your arts-based narrative inquiry.

Suggested Readings

For Archival Photographs

American Life History Collection (Library of Congress): http://www.loc.gov/collection/federal-writers-project/about-this-collection/#overview

For Drama

Norris, J. (2000). Drama as research: Realizing the potential of drama in education as a research methodology. *Youth Theatre Journal,* 14, 40–51.
Saldaña, J. (Ed.). (2005). *Ethnodrama: An anthology of reality theatre.* Walnut Creek, CA: AltaMira Press.

For Poetry

Faulkner, S. (2009). *Poetry as method: Reporting research through verse.* Walnut Creek, CA. Left Coast Press.

For Creative Nonfiction

Miller, B. & Paola, S. (2004). *Tell it slant: Writing and shaping creative nonfiction.* Boston, MA: McGraw-Hill.

For Fiction

Leavy, P. (2013). *Fiction as research practice: Short stories, novellas, and novels.* Walnut Creek, CA: Left Coast Press.

For Arts-Based Narrative Dissertation

Jacobs, D. (2008). *The authentic dissertation: Alternative ways of knowing, research and representation.* London, UK, and New York, NY: Routledge.

Knowles, G., & Cole, A. (Eds.). (2008). *Handbook of the arts in qualitative research.* Thousand Oaks, CA: Sage.

For Visual Inquiry

Foster, J. (2012). *Storytellers: A photographer's guide to developing themes and creating stories with pictures.* Berkeley, CA: New Riders.

Luttrell, W. (2010). "A camera is a big responsibility": A lens for analyzing children's visual voices. *Visual Studies. 25,* 224–237.

Margolis, E., & Pauwels, L. (Eds.). (2011). *The Sage handbook of visual research methods.* Thousand Oaks, CA: Sage.

NOTES

1. Note that autoethnography has its own offshoots, such as evocative autoethnography (Bochner, 2012; Ellis, 2004; Ronai, 1995), analytic autoethnography (Anderson, 2006), performative autoethnography (Spry, 2001), interpretive autoethnography (Denzin, 2014), and critical autoethnography (Boylorn & Orbe, 2014). See also *Journal of Contemporary Ethnography* (2006), volume 35, issue 4, for more discussion on different types of autoethnography.

2. *Bildungsroman* can be autobiographical if the researcher focuses on the personal growth and development of the researcher's self.

3. Technically, *Bildungsroman* is a literary genre that is part of the novel, a central form of fiction. However, I treat it as a separate narrative research genre because of its strong philosophical orientation, uniquely different from other narrative genres I discuss in this chapter.

4. See Kim (2013) for a more thorough discussion of the concept of *Bildung.*

5. Rosenthal (1993) defines life history as "the lived through life" and life story as "the narrated life as related in a conversation or written in an actual present-time" (p. 59). However, I observe researchers use these two terms interchangeably without any specific distinction, which I follow here.

6. I want to draw a distinction between arts-based narrative inquiry (ABNI) and arts-based research (ABR). ABR is another offshoot of qualitative research that uses the arts as the process and the product of their inquiry. It includes literary writing, poetry, music, performance (drama), dance, visual art, film, and other artistic mediums (Leavy, 2009). In this book, I focus on arts-based narrative inquiry (ABNI) that incorporates the arts into narrative inquiry including literary-based narrative inquiry and visual-based narrative inquiry.

7. For other approaches to narrative genres or forms, see Chase (2011).

CHAPTER TOPICS

- Narrative Thinking
- Interview Logistics
  - o *Informed Consent*
  - o *Confidentiality*
  - o *Sampling and Saturation*
  - o *Trust and Rapport*
- Types of Qualitative Interview
- Narrative Interviewing
  - o *Life Story Interview/Biographical Interview*
  - o *Narrative Interview Phases*
  - o *Narrative Interview Questions*
  - o *Two-Sentence Format Technique*
- Fieldwork
  - o *Gaining Access to the Research Field*
  - o *The Art of Observation—Also Known as Attention*
  - o *Observer's Paradox*
- Artifacts: Cabinets of Curiosities or Cabinets of Wonder
- Visual Data
- (Digital) Archival Data
- Conclusion: Excavating Stories as Data

©Tom Parish, T. Candon—Root Cellar,
Liberty Township, Geary County, KS 2012

CHAPTER 5

Narrative Data Collection Methods

Excavating Stories

QUESTIONS TO CONSIDER

- What are the ways to collect narrative data?
- What are the techniques for narrative interviewing?
- How do we gain access to our research site?

INTRODUCTION

Bryan comes to my office without warning. He seems quite distressed. Puzzled, I ask, "What's wrong?" Bryan ignores my question, but apologizes for showing up without an appointment. I convince him not to worry about it and ask him to shoot. Bryan tells me he had an interview that yielded nothing interesting. The interview was short; the interviewee was neither talkative nor enthusiastic about the interview. Bryan tells me what bothers him the most, though, is his lack of confidence in his interview skills. He didn't know what questions to ask or how to ask them in order to get an interesting story out of his interviewee. There were awkwardly silent moments between him and the interviewee. His questions were not conducive to lengthy answers. The interview ended up much shorter than he anticipated. He tried to ask questions hoping that he would get some stories from the interview but ended up getting short, fragmented answers. When Bryan finally pauses for a long sigh, I reach for my jacket and ask Bryan to go for a walk with me. "Bryan, let's go get some coffee."

I hear many trial-and-error stories like this from student researchers. Fieldwork to collect narrative data does not always go as planned. To minimize those disappointing experiences, we need to hone the skills and techniques required of narrative inquirers doing fieldwork. This chapter is about narrative research methods that will help us collect various types of narrative data based on which we reconstruct or retell stories. The objective of this chapter is, therefore, to prepare you for the research fieldwork you will engage in as a way to excavate stories.

Narrative Thinking

In Chapter 3, we discussed learning to think narratively as a part of the aesthetic play of narrative research design. We as "researcher-storytellers" (Barone, 2007, p. 468) should think narratively, imagining a lifespace, living and telling as starting points for collecting field texts, balancing the commonplaces (temporality, sociality, and place), and investing ourselves in the inquiry (Connelly & Clandinin, 2006). Now, to avoid an interview that yields not much data, like Bryan's case above, we should help our participants (participant-storytellers) think narratively as well by encouraging them to be involved in narrative thinking.

What, then, is narrative thinking? **Narrative thinking** is a method of making a story out of experience, "a heuristic process that requires skill, judgment, and experience" (Robinson & Hawpe, 1986, p. 111). Robinson and Hawpe argue that storytelling involves narrative thinking in which we reflect upon our experiences to construct stories. In other words, narrative thinking is an attempt to create a fit between a situation and a story schema about some experience or event that consists of who, what, how, and why. It describes the flow of events and actions. We employ narrative thinking to understand and analyze how past events and actions led to a past outcome, and to imagine what actions to carry out to achieve future ends (Polkinghorne, 2010). Hence, narrative thinking is a method of creating a story by organizing experiences around our perception, thought, memory, and imagination. It seems paramount, then, for narrative researchers to understand what narrative thinking is before learning narrative methods regarding how to excavate stories.

According to Robinson and Hawpe (1986), three components are involved in the process of narrative thinking: the narrative schema, the storyteller's prior knowledge and experience, and a diverse array of cognitive strategies. The *narrative schema* is an implicit procedural plan that organizes certain types of essential information, linking them by means of causal relations. That is, the storyteller maps out a story situation and structure using the narrative schema that consists of a series of questions to be answered, such as, what happened?, to whom?, why?, and so on (p. 115). These questions require the storyteller to examine the information available about an incident, identifying relevant facts, which then become part of the narrative schema. This narrative schema is, of course, drawn from the second component of narrative thinking, which is the storyteller's *prior knowledge and experience.* And then, the storyteller utilizes the third component, *cognitive strategies,* which include selecting, comparing, inferring, arranging, and revising the past knowledge and experiences. These cognitive strategies play a pivotal role in narrative thinking, as they guide the storyteller's judgment about which details are relevant in the creation of a story.

An act of narrative thinking, elicited through these three components—the storyteller's narrative schema, his or her prior knowledge and experience, and cognitive strategies—yields a story that facilitates an understanding of the actions of others and oneself in relation to others. According to Robinson and Hawpe (1986), narrative thinking is a heuristic device that allows open-endedness, construction, and varying kinds of uncertainty, through which stories are created as "natural mediators between the particular and the general in human experience" (p. 124).

We can further link the components of narrative thinking with two narrative principles proposed by Chase (2003). The first principle is that narration is a major way in which people make sense of experience, construct the self, and create and communicate meaning. And the second principle is that personal narratives are unavoidably social in character, no matter how unique and individual the narratives are.

Our narrative research will be enhanced when narrative thinking and narrative principles are incorporated into our narrative inquiry methods, as these help us excavate stories. Such methods include interviews, fieldwork through observation or participant observation, visual and archival data, and artifacts in a cabinet of curiosities. As we collect narrative data, we should consider narrative thinking grounded in the narrative principles as a foundation for data collection methods for narrative inquiry, which will differentiate narrative methods from general qualitative methods.

Interview Logistics

Interviews provide unique insights into the complex lives of individuals in a society. Individual interviews are the most commonly used data collection method in qualitative research and the foremost method in narrative inquiry in particular, as we understand that our interviewees will tell stories based on their narrative schema that reflects personal knowledge and experiences arranged by their cognitive strategies.

Undergirding the use of the interview is the premise that the individual person is an important source of knowledge (Gubrium, Holstein, Marvasti, & McKinney, 2012). Much of what we claim to know about individuals' beliefs, values, and feelings in particular social contexts will be based on our interviewees' responses to questions we ask them during interviews. Mishler (1986a) writes, "No significant aspect of life has been beyond the pale of inquisitive interviewers" (p. 233). This statement goes to show how critical it is for us to have good interview skills that can evoke responses meaningful enough to generate stories that inform our research purposes and research questions. Hence, a good understanding of the interview method will lead to conducting a successful narrative inquiry.

A basic attitude we should have toward interviews is that we are the knowledge seeker and our interviewee is the knowledge holder. Thus, our approach to narrative interviewing should be:

> I want to understand the world from your point of view. I want to know what you know in the way you know it. I want to understand the meaning of your experience, to walk in your shoes, to feel things as you feel them, to explain things as you explain them. Will you become my teacher and help me understand? (Spradley, 1979, p. 34)

This humble and empathic approach acknowledges that it is an honor to be granted access to your interviewee's life, insights, and viewpoints from which you intend to generate further knowledge to inform your field. The interview method involves some ethical and methodological issues, including informed consent, confidentiality, sample size, and data saturation, which will be discussed below.

Informed Consent

As we discussed in Chapter 3, human research constitutes a number of key ethical principles, most notably respect for human beings, integrity, beneficence, and justice (Heggen & Guillemin, 2012). The very first item you will need to prepare for your interview is a form that acknowledges understanding and grants informed consent, complying with ethical principles stipulated by your school's Institutional Review Board (IRB). Information provided in requesting informed consent furnishes potential research participants with core information about your research study, including the purpose, duration, and methods of the research. It also states possible risks and benefits deriving from participation in the study. Moreover, it should be stated that the participant has the right to withdraw his or her consent at any time without any penalty. Hence, the notion of informed consent is grounded in the principles of confidentiality, individual autonomy, and beneficence (Marzano, 2012).

Confidentiality

Confidentiality is about protecting your research participant's privacy. It refers to the agreement between the researcher and the research participant about what may be done with the interview data. It also ensures that no one other than the researcher knows who participated in a study and no one but the researcher has access to the interview data (Kaiser, 2012). A number of strategies serve to protect participants' confidentiality, including the use of pseudonyms rather than participants' actual names and removing identifying features from research reports, as stated in the informed consent document.

However, the issue of confidentiality is not as straightforward as it seems. We may encounter some difficulties in protecting the identities of our participants, as we provide detailed descriptions of the participants as well as research context. During this process, a breach of confidentiality may occur when the traits and experiences of individuals make them identifiable in research reports despite the use of pseudonyms, a situation that is called deductive disclosure (Kaiser, 2012). For example, Baez (2002) interviewed minority faculty members at a predominantly White university about promotion and tenure experiences (e.g., experiences of isolation, racism, betrayal, and sexism). Baez was concerned about the possibility that these accounts, if published, would cause his study participants to be identified by their colleagues, which could lead to retaliation or other negative career consequences. This kind of concern will arise more frequently when we engage in "backyard research" (Glesne & Peshkin, 1991), which is discussed in more detail in Chapter 8. Hence, we should be aware of the risks of breaching the confidentiality of our participants at every stage of a research project, not just at the start of the interview when we obtain informed consent.

What, then, should we do when we have a participant who shares private, sensitive, and critical information, but asks us not to share with others? This presents an "ethically important moment" (Guillemin & Gillam, 2004), which requires the use of our *phronesis* (ethical judgment) through reflexivity, as discussed in Chapter 3. Kaiser (2012) proposes two procedures that can be added to the end of the interview to deal with confidentiality issues that arise during the interview: First, we can ask our interviewees for permission to contact them in the future to discuss questions about their data. Second, we can use an end-of-interview document to obtain our interviewee's specific wishes for data use and confidentiality. A post-interview confidentiality form is shown in Figure 5.1.

Figure 5.1   Post-Interview Confidentiality Form

Study Title

Study #

Post-Interview Confidentiality Form

It is our goal and responsibility to use the information that you have shared responsibly. Now that you have completed the interview, we would like to give you the opportunity to provide us with additional feedback on how you prefer to have your data handled. Please check one of the following statements:

_____ You may share the information just as I provided it. No details need to be changed and you may use my real name when using my data in publications or presentations.

_____ You may share the information just as I provided it; however, please do not use my real name. I realize that others might identify me based on the data, even though my name will not be used.

(Continued)

(Continued)

_____ You may share the information just as I provided it; however, please do not use my real name and please change details that might make me identifiable to others. In particular, it is my wish that the following specific pieces of my data not be shared without first altering the data so as to make me unidentifiable (describe this data in the space below):

_____

_____

_____

_____ You may contact me if you have any questions about sharing my data with others. The best way to reach me is (provide phone number or email):

_____

_____

_____

Respondent's Signature, Date

_____

Investigator's Signature, Date

(Adapted from Kaiser, 2012, p. 462)

Sampling and Saturation

The issue of sampling or sample size first refers to how researchers decide which informants and how many to include or exclude, which is a core concern for researchers to determine for a successful project (Johnson & Rowlands, 2012). My students frequently asked, "What is a good number of potential interviewees for narrative inquiry?" or "How many interviews should be conducted for each participant?" These are important questions that you will grapple with as you embark your research study. You will realize that it is not easy to determine how many people you need to interview in order to yield sufficiently meaningful data. Unless you clearly justify the number of interviewees (sample size), you will be challenged by one of your dissertation committee members or IRB personnel for an insufficient sample size, which is a typical target of criticism against qualitative research.

However, qualitative theorists have not been able to reach agreement on an optimal sample size[1]; for this reason, continual examination is required (Beitin, 2012). Beitin suggests that an appropriate sample size could range from 6 to 12 participants, provided there is thematic redundancy after 6 interview participants. Kvale (1996) suggests that the number of interviews in current interview studies tends to be around 15 $\pm$ 10, based on a combination of the time and resources available. If your focus is on collecting life stories, the sample of interviewees will usually be smaller and the interviewing may be a lengthy process. If your focus is on exploring themes across interviewees, the sample might be larger and each interview shorter.

However, if your purpose is to understand the world as experienced by one specific person, like writing a *Bildungsroman*, for example, you could rely on a single person. Let's take an example from psychology. A paradox is that if you want to obtain general knowledge, you focus on a few intensive case studies. For instance, Freud claimed to derive a general knowledge of psychoanalysis from Dora's case, a single case study. Piaget's research on children's cognitive development originated from studying his own children. Each case study involved immense amounts of time for observations and interviews of single individuals. Therefore, in determining a sample size for qualitative inquiry, and narrative inquiry in particular, an emphasis should be placed in the quality rather than the quantity of the interviews (Kvale, 1996). Kvale suggests a minimum of three rounds of open or in-depth life story interviews. Furthermore, according to O'Reilly and Parker (2012), the adequacy of the sample is not determined solely by the number of informants, but by the appropriateness of the data. Hence, our aim is to gather a sufficient depth of information from various types of data as a way of fully describing the phenomenon being studied, which is necessary for us to achieve richness and depth of analysis. Therefore, we have to be flexible and realistic in our approach not only to sampling and sample size, but also to the adequacy of sampling in addressing sufficiently our research purpose and the research questions.

How, then, do we know our sampling is adequate and enough? This question is associated with the notion of saturation, which is one of the quality markers of qualitative research. Guest, Bunce, and Johnson (2006) write, "Saturation has, in fact, become the gold standard by which purposive sample sizes are determined in health science research" (p. 60). We reach a point of saturation when new interview data do not yield any new knowledge but merely confirm or are redundant with what has been found in the existing data, or when the interviewee has exhausted all the relevant stories that she or he wanted to share (Suárez-Ortega, 2013). When we say saturation has been reached, it means that depth as well as breadth of information has been achieved. Yet this is not to say that the notion of saturation should be accepted without question. The truth is that qualitative phenomena that deal with human beings are organic and unique; there will always be new things that unfold, depending on your research topic. Hence, data can sometimes never be fully saturated, which is a conundrum for us.

Luckily, O'Reilly and Parker (2012) provide us with a promising explanation for this seeming dilemma. They advise that we need to be transparent about epistemological and methodological positions that have guided our decision-making process. We also need to be transparent about how and why we cannot reach saturation, which can refer to our limitations. O'Reilly and Parker also convince us that our transparency about limitations does not necessarily invalidate the research findings. If saturation is not reached, they state, "it simply means that the phenomenon has not yet fully explored rather than that findings are invalid" (p. 194).

Trust and Rapport

The most important aspect of the interview method is trust and rapport between the interviewer and the interviewee. Kvale (1996) postulates that interview is a way to create knowledge *inter* the points of *view* of the interviewer and the interviewee. It is a way of generating knowledge in which the knowledge evolves through human interaction and where you rely on your interviewee's openness, trust, and generosity to share what he or she knows with you. Hence, your act of collecting stories via interview will depend on the level of trust and rapport in the relationship you have with your interviewee.

How do we build up trust and rapport with our participants? Grinyer and Thomas (2012), for example, discuss the value of multiple or longitudinal interviews, which play a critical role in establishing harmonious, trustworthy relationship (rapport) between the researcher and the research participants. As one example, they provide Cornwell's study, which drew a distinction between "public" and "private" accounts of interview data. Grinyer and Thomas explain that Cornwell, who studied repeat interviews in the field of health and illness in East London, found out that the public accounts tended to be offered in the first interview when rapport between the interviewer and the interviewee was minimal. That is, the interviewee had a tendency of offering an account that he or she thought the interviewer wanted or expected to hear. However, the interview participants tended to offer their private (more interesting and meaningful) accounts in a second or subsequent interview because trust and familiarity with the researcher had been established. Although this does not mean that the first interview will not produce as much meaningful data as the following interviews, the point here is that the importance of rapport and a trustworthy relationship cannot be overemphasized in generating meaningful data. Depending on the quality of relationship we have with our interviewees, we might or might not gain data of high quality.

However, we also need to be warned against over-rapport. Goudy and Potter (1975), for example, argue that we should aim for an optimal level of rapport rather than maximal rapport. That is, when rapport is too high (the researcher and the participant are too close), there may be greater bias in the interview, obscuring the purpose of the interview. Thus, they argue, the purpose of the interview is not simply to establish rapport in and of itself, but to use rapport as a means to generate data of high quality. Darlington and Scott (2002) offer a great insight into this:

> Rapport is often included in research texts as an entity that is established at the beginning of the research, and once this is done the researcher can get on with the business of researching. But rapport is not a finite commodity that can be turned on and off by the researcher. It is relational. . . . Like all relationships, the researcher-participant relationship is subject to continuing negotiation and reworking; this extends to the participant's trust in the researcher's behavior at every stage of the research. (p. 54)

It seems that there should be a happy medium regarding rapport. We cannot take it for granted that there will be a good relationship once we start our "business of researching." Nor should we automatically assume that an extended (longitudinal) interaction with our participants will ensure desirable rapport and trust (Grinyer & Thomas, 2012).

To develop a trustworthy relationship, you the interviewer will need to be willing to open up as well. Your role as an interviewer is not that of a therapist or an interrogator, nor will you be a distanced listener. But, there is also a tension in qualitative research as to how much of themselves researchers should share with participants (Bondy, 2012). Although openness is expected, Bondy posits, researchers sometimes choose not to disclose parts of themselves, such as their sexual orientation, marital status, political views, and the like, to the participants, because they don't want to bias the participants and have them tell the interviewer what they think he or she wants to hear. Hence, it is difficult to determine what an optimal level of rapport and trust is during the course of research. Central to the achievement of trust and rapport, therefore, is the researcher's genuine caring, interest, and respect for the participant's human dignity and integrity, as Shea (2000) states:

> Everyone agrees that among the highest duties of academics is to make sure that the human beings they study—fellow citizens they probe, query, prod, and palpate—are treated with dignity and respect. (p. 28)

Types of Qualitative Interview

Now that we understand the ethics and logistics of interviewing, let's take a look at interview methods. Interviews in qualitative research follow three broad categories in general: structured, semi-structured, and unstructured (open-ended). The main difference between them is the degree to which you as the researcher have control over the process and content of the interview (Corbin & Morse, 2003; Fontana & Frey, 1998). For narrative inquiry, the most typical types of interview are semi-structured and unstructured, open-ended interviews.

First, in structured (close-ended) interviews, you will have a set of pre-determined questions that you will follow exactly, with no flexibility. The general responses for this kind of interview are short answers, like an oral questionnaire. This type of interview can be good if you intend to collect specific answers on a particular theme from various interviewees. However, this method is considered a traditional survey interview and is not highly recommended for narrative researchers. In particular, Elliot Mishler heavily criticized this method, which I will discuss later.

In semi-structured interviews, you prepare general questions that you want to ask, but use them only to guide the interview, helping you maintain its focus rather than dictate its direction. These interviews are also called "guided interviews" or "guided conversations" in which you may prepare six to ten questions providing a general order to guide the course of the interview (Morse, 2012, p. 194). The questions are flexible enough to expand the scope of the interview, as they allow you to ask different but relevant questions depending on the interviewee's responses. You have to think on your feet, so to speak, as you listen to your interviewee, while being sensitive to the content and nature of the interview as it progresses. Your interview skills, how attentive, sensitive, and responsive you are, will be critical in generating interviewee responses that yield meaningful data. Your interviewee may withhold important information simply because relevant questions are not asked, or he or she may answer in a perfunctory manner if your interview skills fall short.

In unstructured, open-ended interviews, which are sometimes referred to as narrative interviews, you the researcher usually have no set agenda other than to listen to whatever your interviewee wants to tell you, barring a tangential story totally unrelated to your research. You often ask just a "grand tour" question (Spradley, 1979) that presents the general topic to focus the participant. The interviewee tells his or her own story in his or her own way with minimal interruption from you. You primarily assume a listening stance because your goal is to obtain the participant's perspective without "leading" (Morse, 2012). It is the interviewee, not you, who controls the content, including where to begin the narrative, what will and will not be disclosed, the scope of the interview, the order in which topics are introduced, the pacing of the interview, and the amount of detail. Your interviewee is the central actor who is telling story. However, this does not mean that you are merely a passive listener. You can play an active role through active listening, and by asking occasionally relevant questions for probing and clarifying during the course of the interview, as long as you are cautious enough not to make any intrusion that might alter it (Corbin & Morse, 2003; Fontana & Frey, 1998). In conducting a semi-structured or an open-ended interview, it is also important to be flexible enough to be prepared for an interview that may end up having less to do with prepared questions than with the exchange of stories. Narayan and George (2012) make a point about this matter:

> How an interview runs its course depends very much on all the participants involved. It is important for the interviewer to be flexible and ready to follow the unexpected paths that emerge in the course of talking together with interviewees. (p. 515)

Therefore, when we encounter some unexpected stories, we should not make quick judgments or interpretations of what we hear, but maintain a critical stance toward the content, as Riessman (2012) notes:

> Personal narratives can emerge at unexpected moments in research interviews, even in response to fixed-response questions. What may appear at the time to be an unrelated response can become important analytically, telling us a great deal about our interviewing practices and participants' preferred topics. (p. 376)

Interviewer flexibility and open-mindedness are important because they will not only let unexpected data emerge but can also contribute to developing good rapport and trust. And delaying our judgments or interpretations of what appears to be irrelevant to the research topic can be beneficial in the long run.

Narrative Interviewing

So far, we have familiarized ourselves with the "hows" and "whats" of qualitative interviews in general, including various interview types (e.g., structured, semi-structured, and open-ended interview); logistics of interviewing (e.g., interview sampling, interview rapport, data saturation); and ethical issues of the interview (e.g., informed consent, protecting the interviewee's confidentiality, and more). But this knowledge is shared with qualitative research in general. In this section, therefore, I'd like to discuss in more depth some aspects of interviewing that are especially pertinent to narrative inquiry.

When we engage in narrative thinking and narrative principles during our interviews, it is unproductive to conduct a survey or questionnaire type of interview in which questions and answers are viewed as "stimuli and responses rather than as forms of speech" (Mishler, 1986b, p. viii). An interview for narrative research that suppresses the interviewee's personal stories embedded in social contexts is counter-productive, for those stories reveal how individuals perceive, organize, and give meaning to their understandings of themselves, their experiences, and the world. Our interviewees may tell interesting stories in response to overarching questions as long as we do not interrupt them. We might have the urge to apply external structure to the interview, but all we need to do in this case is to show engagement with nods or murmurs and be flexible enough to follow the lead of the interviewee while not losing sight of the focus. In the presence of such experienced storytellers, we may at times need to skillfully redirect the stories toward subjects suited to our specific interests.

Mishler (1986a) explains that "stories are a recurrent and prominent feature of respondents' accounts in all types of interviews" (p. 235). Therefore, an interview needs to be designed in a way that it invites our interviewees to speak in their own voices, to express themselves freely, deciding where to start their story as well as the flow of the topics (creating their own narrative schema). Since the interview is an "invitation to narrate" (Narayan & George, 2012, p. 514), we should seize this wonderful opportunity to grasp the complexity of stories that may not be told otherwise. As discussed before, narratives are fluid and unexpected; we should let them emerge in the interviews.

In narrative interviewing, then, it is important to establish such a stance that an interviewer is an attentive listener and our interviewee is a narrator with narrative thinking. This stance is more important than the form and content of a particular question. That is, we are likely to find stories if we allow our interviewees to continue in their own way. The narrative inquirer's job is to listen with attentive care and ask necessary questions that will further inspire the telling of stories. We are unlikely to find stories if we cut our storytellers off with new questions, which could signal that we are not listening to their stories (Mishler, 1986a). This is a conceptual shift away from the idea that "interviewees have answers to researchers' questions" to the idea that "interviewees are narrators with stories to tell and voices of their own" (Chase, 2005, p. 660). Hence, we have to remember that:

> Often, being a good interviewer for stories involves not just asking the right questions but sympathetically listening and holding questions back so that the person being interviewed can

shape stories in his or her own way. Equally, being a good interviewer may involve responding to questions from an interviewee and so entering into a reciprocal exchange. (Narayan & George, 2012, p. 522)

In the traditional, standard practice of interview, like survey interviews or structured interviews, there is a striking asymmetry of power, tilted excessively toward the interviewer. In narrative interviewing, however, it is our interviewee, the narrator, who is the central actor, as discussed above. Before we conduct our interview, some critical questions we want to ask ourselves are: Whose interests are going to be served by the asymmetry of power between my interviewee and me? Who will benefit from my control of the interpretation, dissemination, and use of findings? If our goal is to let stories be told (as it should be), then giving up the power as an interviewer and empowering our storyteller instead is natural. Again, I want to remind you of what Spradley (1979) advised us (the quote cited at the beginning of this chapter).

Although narrative interviewing requires us to give up control and follow the interviewee's leads, it does not mean that we should enter our interview empty-headed. That is, we should not lose sight of our research purposes and theoretical perspectives. It is also important to note that we maintain the standards of research regarding preparation for the interviews, and continue our commitment to ethics in practice (or everyday narrative ethics, discussed in Chapter 3), not to mention the previously mentioned ethical guidelines of approval from an Institutional Review Board (IRB) (Pederson, 2013). But most of all, the key to getting the best interview is our flexibility and ability to adapt to specific circumstances.

Life Story Interview/Biographical Interview

The purpose of the interview in narrative inquiry is to let stories be told, particularly the stories of those who might have been marginalized or alienated from the mainstream, and those whose valuable insights and reflections would not otherwise come to light. Although the way you approach narrative interview will depend on your overall research design, including the purpose of your research and research questions, narrative inquirers can usually begin with what we call a **life story interview** or biographical interview. This is the most common narrative interview we use, and it is based on the concept of one's life story being a social construct comprising both social reality and a personal, experiential world (Rosenthal, 1993). This interview method, which is based on the unstructured, open-ended interview format, has become a central element of narrative inquiry used in a variety of disciplines as a way of carrying out an in-depth study of an individual life as a whole. I would posit that any narrative researcher could/should use the life story interview method as a basic research tool because not only the full life story but also some segments of the life story can be used as data for analysis and interpretation or to illustrate any number of theoretical positions. Within the life story, there may be segments of the life that can tell us more about the individual, and there also may be specific themes or issues that relate to the larger social issues of gender, class, race, and culture. Hence, the life story interview, as Atkinson (2012) posits, turns personal narratives into rigorous research endeavors.

A life story can cover the time from birth to the present as a way of understanding better the past and the present, sometimes shedding light on the future. It includes the important events, experiences, and feelings of a lifetime that the interviewee chooses to tell. The point of the life story interview is to learn the interviewee's life stories as a whole and produce a first-person text in the words of the interviewee. This produced story is examined later for analysis and interpretation through the lens of your theoretical framework to address your research questions. Hence, our initial interest in the life story interview begins with a question like, "What is the story my interviewee wants to tell others and what meaning does it convey?" This allows us to just listen, understand, and accept the story without judgment. Thus the purpose of a life story interview is not to document categories of data (in other words, it is not paradigmatic in Bruner's term, as we discussed in Chapter 1). Rather, it is to look for the wholeness in a person's life. It is a retelling of "one's life as a whole in the voice of the teller, as it is remembered and in a language that is deeply felt" (Atkinson, 2007, p. 237).

Yet it would be naïve to believe that we will get a person's entire life story—that would require ongoing interviewing throughout our interviewee's lifetime. So, the life story interview or biographical interview does not mean a review of every single event that ever took place in a person's life, but, rather, it constitutes selective accounts of an individual's life "to the extent to which it separates the relevant from the irrelevant" (Rosenthal, 1993, p. 61). Thus, the life story represents our interviewee's overall construction of his or her past, present, and future, in which the interviewee makes decisions as to which experiences are relevant, or which experiences should or may be included or excluded (again, think about the three components of narrative thinking).

Life history researchers Goodson and Gill (2011) advise that it is crucial for us to share our research intentions and our methodology with the participants. Sharing the importance of the narrative inquiry methodology and our research purposes helps our participants understand and be aware of the value of their own voice and the importance of sharing their own experiences and stories. Goodson and Gill also ask us to directly confront our selective bias in the choice of our interviewees. For example, it is a common reaction among researchers to select interviewees whose story seems to appeal to the researcher and the researcher most sympathizes with. Hence, "the researchers are effectively telling their own stories" (Goodson & Gill, 2011, p. 37). To avoid this criticism, it is important to be able to justify and be transparent about how we came to select our participants, as O'Reilly and Parker (2012) noted earlier. Benefits of the life story interview are shown in Table 5.1 on the next page.

Narrative Interview Phases

I would recommend that we engage in the interview method for narrative inquiry with two distinct phases, which I call the *narration phase* and the *conversation phase*. The *narration phase* is an extensive narration by the interviewee/narrator, during which the interviewer restricts his or her interventions to the minimum while keeping the narration going, just as in open-ended interviews. We ask our interviewees to give a full narration of events and experiences from their own life, encouraging their narrative thinking processes. This narrative is not interrupted by

Table 5.1   Benefits of the Life Story Interview

1. A clearer perspective on personal experiences and feelings is gained, which brings greater meaning to one's life.

2. Greater self-knowledge, a stronger self-image, and self-esteem are gained.

3. Cherished experiences *and* insights are shared with others.

4. Joy, satisfaction, and inner peace are gained in sharing one's story with others.

5. Sharing one's story is a way of purging, or releasing, certain burdens and validating personal experience.

6. Sharing one's story helps create community and may show that we have more in common with others than we thought.

7. Life stories can help other people see their lives more clearly or differently and perhaps be an inspiration to help them change something in their life.

8. Others will get to know and understand us better, in a way that they hadn't before.

9. A better sense of how we want our story to end, or how we could give it the "good" ending we want, might be gained.

(Adapted from Atkinson, 2012, p. 120)

questions, but can be encouraged by nonverbal expressions of interest and attention. It is best to let the interview take its course naturally to cover all that the interviewee wants to cover of his or her life. Thus, it is almost as if we intend to keep a "vow of silence" (Goodson & Gill, 2011, p. 39), although this does not mean that we will be completely unstructured or unprepared for this kind of an interview.

In the *narration phase,* our main role would be that of a listener and observer. I'd like to reference the renowned psychoanalyst Spence's notion of "active listening" here. Spence (1982) posits that in psychoanalysis "active listening is required" (p. 279) in order to understand the patient's narrative truth from an utterance that might be fragmentary, ambiguous, and disconnected. Although our interview session should not be confused with a counseling session, there is a lesson we can learn here. Just like psychoanalysts (see the section Narrative Inquiry in Psychology in Chapter 1), it is the researcher's responsibility to listen with an ear tuned to sequence, coherence, continuity, meaningfulness, and transformation in our interviewee's story. Narrative inquirers should have what I call a *narrative competence of listening,* borrowing from what Spence calls "the psychoanalytic competence" (p. 280). Active listening or a *narrative competence of listening* also comes with a keen observation of the way the interviewee talks, the use of body language, emotional expressions, feelings, pauses, and more. Through our *narrative competence of listening,* we try to sense, feel, see, hear, and even vicariously experience our narrator's mental, intellectual, cognitive, and emotional engagement with the telling of his or her own life story.

Once the *narration phase* is complete, we can enter the *conversation phase,* although I do not intend to mean that these phases have to be done in a linear fashion, one after the other. The *conversation phase* is a period of semi-structured, in-depth questioning or interchange when the interviewer wants some clarifications on the issues presented in the first narration. In this phase, we also introduce additional topics related to our theoretical interests so that we can get more detail than the narrator's original narrations may have provided (Spence, 1982). We use narrative questions that aim to elicit further narrations, that is, questions that invite more stories about our interviewee's experiences. We ask our interviewee to elaborate in greater detail, if possible, on a previously mentioned experience, event, or period of his or her life. It is in this *conversation phase* where important interaction and collaboration between the interviewer and the interviewee take place. Goodson and Gill (2011) call it a "grounded conversation" (p. 40) where a collaborative meaning-making process between the interviewer and the interviewee occurs. Through our narrative questions, for which we can use other sources of data such as documentaries and historical data to shape what is told and retold in more detail, it is our goal to create a collaborative (re)construction of our interviewee's story. Mishler (1986a) comments, "If we wish to hear respondents' stories, then we must invite them into our work as collaborators, sharing control with them, so that together we try to understand what their stories are about" (p. 249).

The *conversation phase* is an in-depth interview process where questions and responses comprise the interview. That is, the interviewee's responses and the interviewer's relevant questions will continually inform the evolving conversation. The interview is no longer considered a unilaterally guided means of excavating information. The researcher is an active co-constructor rather than a passive collector or recorder of data (Gemignani, 2014). Although the interviewer's aim is to encourage the interviewee to talk, the practice of narrative questioning, or the way the interviewer asks questions and the kinds of questions, will shape the evolving discourse (Paget, 1983). Narrative interview in the conversation phase, therefore, is viewed as discourse (Bertaux & Kohli, 1984; Merrill & West, 2009; Rosenthal, 1993) as well as dialogic interchange (Goodson & Gill, 2011). It involves the creation of meaning as both interviewer and interviewee respond "to features of the ongoing interaction, to nuances of mood, and to the content of the evolving conversation" (Paget, 1983, p. 69). During this conversation phase, solidarity between the interviewer and the interviewee will be established, as both try to understand important aspects of the interviewee's life, which in turn will systematically create knowledge that illuminates human experience.

Narrative Interview Questions

Just because we let our interviewee talk as the central actor of the interview, it does not mean that we don't need any interview techniques. On the contrary. For successful narrative interviews, good preparation is necessary. As narrative researchers, we have to think narratively about how we can generate interview data that will help us accomplish our research purpose and research questions, while leaving room for surprises that might come out of our narrative data. For successful interviews, critical advance preparation includes identifying whom you will interview and why, how, where, and when you are going to collect certain stories from your interviewee(s). Along with these careful advance preparations, knowing how to ask good questions is paramount in generating meaningful narrative data. For example, asking a "grand tour" question such as "Tell me the story of your life" can produce disappointing, brief, and even terse results, like what my student Bryan experienced. Thus, working out some questions beforehand is important (although you may not use them all), even while staying flexible and adaptable.

Then, what types of questions should we ask to elicit stories? As you probably know, the least helpful type of question is the yes-no question, unless you follow it right up with a "what," "why," or "how" question. More useful questions are the open-ended, descriptive, structural, and contrast questions with which you can get to the interviewee's emotional level because they encourage more thoughtful and personally meaningful answers. Oral historian Charles Morrissey (1987) states that good interviewers:

> phrase questions in open- ended language, avoid jargon, pursue in detail, ask for examples, defer sensitive questions until rapport is solid, let the interviewee set the pace of the interview and speak whatever explanations are foremost in the volunteered version of what occurred. (p. 44)

Here are some examples of interview questions (in case of high school experience):

- How would you describe your high school experience? (open-ended)
- What is the most memorable event that happened to you in your high school? How did/do you feel about it? (descriptive)
- How did your high school experience differ from that of your time in middle school? (contrast)

You will ask many other follow-up, probing, clarifying questions, depending on the responses from the interviewee. One interview technique to which I want to bring your attention is a two-sentence format technique.

Two-Sentence Format Technique

Morrissey (1987) argues for the two-sentence format as an effective interviewing technique. The two-sentence format consists of a statement and a question, which works to explain the question before you ask it. For example:

> Knowing as we do what happened and how it happened, we need to consider why the merger happened (*statement*). Would you recount the reasons why you supported the merger (*question*)? (p. 46)

Notice how the first sentence is a statement that predicates the question in the next sentence. The first sentence indicates that both the interviewer and the interviewee know about the merger. And then, notice how the wording in the second sentence closely repeats the wording in the first sentence. Additionally, the second sentence always asks only one question, practicing "the credo that respondents can deal most responsively—and unavoidably—with one question at a time" (p. 46). Here are some examples of the two-sentence format:

- We've talked for a while about discipline in the schools. What do you do to avoid disciplinary punishments of students?
- You've talked about many challenges you face as a new teacher. Can you tell me how you try to overcome those challenges?

See Table 5.2 for the characteristics of the two-sentence format interview technique.

Table 5.2   Characteristics of Two-Sentence Format Interview Technique

- The two-sentence format provides an interviewer with an opportunity to involve the interviewee in the co-creation of the document resulting from their interaction.
- It reaffirms the interviewee's attentiveness and pursuit of detailed recollections.
- It contributes to the relationship between interviewer and interviewee as co-creators of life story or oral history.
- It vitalizes two basic interview qualities, rapport and collaboration.
- It transforms the interviewee's silence into a narrative opportunity by having explained the rationale for the question (first sentence) and then having asked it (second sentence).

(Adapted from Morrissey, 1987)

Fieldwork

Some narrative researchers might think that understanding the interview method should be sufficient for the skilled practice of narrative inquiry. In fact, one of the blind reviewers' comments for my book proposal was that the reviewer did not care about any other data collection methods than interviews. I respect the reviewer's comment, but alas, how strongly do I disagree! In fact, I see more and more doctoral students not wanting to do the fieldwork for observations for their research because going out to a research field for observations is time-consuming. True. Plus, it is not easy to gain access to a research site.

Doing fieldwork for observation or participant observation is another core method of generating data for narrative inquiry, although I would not insist that it is a must. Coming from an educational background, I know my fellow narrative inquirers in education frequently use schools as their research sites; there they explore the stories of teachers and students. This is a way of living the inquiry. For example, as we learned in Chapter 3, Connelly and Clandinin (2006) posit that thinking narratively involves living in the research field, collecting data through observations or participant observations. They also identify three commonplaces of narrative inquiry—*temporality, sociality, and place*—as dimensions of narrative inquiry space. In particular, the third commonplace, place, is "the specific concrete, physical and topological boundaries of place or sequence of places where the inquiry and events take place" (Connelly & Clandinin, 2006, p. 480). Thus, *place* refers to your research site or a place where your participants' experiences and events occurred in the past and/or are taking place in the present. Place or a series of places is your inquiry boundary that delimits the experiences or stories of your participants. In this life space, fieldwork will produce valuable data because "the specificity of location is crucial" (Connelly & Clandinin, 2006, p. 480) in narrative inquiry. We interact with our participants in a natural setting, developing a meaningful relationship with them. The social milieus of the location impact our participants' lived experiences from which we can excavate more stories. As we do the fieldwork, we engage ourselves in keen attention, attuned to the life space of our participants.

Below, I present an excerpt of my dissertation, the part that describes how I gained access to the field. The school, which was my research site (*place*), was the temporary life space of the students (*temporality*) as the study participants and myself as the researcher, where social interactions (*sociality*) continuously evolved and was experienced by all of us. All the happenings that I could observe in the life space were recorded in my field texts as part of my data.

Gaining Access to the Research Field

Contact with Borderlands Alternative High School started in spring 2002 when I took one of the research method classes as a part of my doctoral study. The principal of the school at that time, Mr. Vee, was my classmate. He willingly gave me permission to use his school as a research site for my term paper. I was given an opportunity to do classroom observations in Ms. Dee's class, twice a week for three hours per visit for two months. The assignment for the course was to find out what was going on in the classroom, so I tried to record almost everything I saw and heard as meticulously as possible in writing. I also interviewed Ms. Dee at her house over dinner. She provided me with her personal life story and her valuable insight on her school, Borderlands, and alternative education in general. The assignment became the groundwork for my dissertation.

I revisited the school a year later in May, 2003 to explore the possibility of using the school as my dissertation research site. Mr. Vee had already informed me that he had resigned his position due to some difficulties he encountered with the school district. Keeping the information in mind, I made an appointment with the new principal, Mrs. Steadman. Our appointment was set for 9 o'clock in the morning on the ninth of May, 2003. I arrived 10 minutes early with a little bit of anticipation and trepidation: what if the new principal doesn't want her school to be studied. I could feel some butterflies in my stomach. The administrative assistant asked me to have a seat and told me that Mrs. Steadman was meeting with a parent at the moment. I was glad that I had a time to take a deep breath and relax a little bit before I got to meet the principal. While waiting, I started looking at the banners glued on the wall:

You Are the Author of Your Own Life Story.

An Education Is Your Key to Success.

A Little Respect Goes a Long Way.

Respect. Learn it. Earn it.

Your Teacher's Goal Is Simple: To Help You Reach Yours.

While I was reflecting on the implied meanings of these quotes in the banners, a Hispanic girl came into the office abruptly. She was wearing a mini-skirt, leopard-skin patterned shoes and a hat. Her style was very attractive and fashionable. She handed something to the administrative assistant in an impolite manner and said "School's DUMB!" And then, she left the office. People who were in the room, such as the administrative assistant, secretary to the principal, security guard, and school nurse, looked at each other and shrugged their shoulders.

To me, the comment was very intriguing. Why is school "dumb"? Is it her personal opinion or does everybody here think so? If school is "dumb," how can an education be a key to success? While wondering about the relationship between schooling and the student's perception about schooling, I found myself more motivated and excited about doing research at Borderlands.

Mrs. Steadman became available 30 minutes after the appointment time. After introducing myself, I gave her a brief summary of my dissertation prospectus. She seemed interested. When I told her that one of the aspects I wanted to look at in the school was the hidden curriculum of the school, she said, "Oh, in this school, almost everything is done in the hidden curriculum." "Oh, really?" I didn't dare to ask what she meant by "hidden curriculum." I thought I would probably figure that out later. That was a part of my research.

"You bet," and then, she continued. "Your study sounds very interesting. We'll be happy to have you here." "Oh, thank you very much. Thank you very much." I was happy like a kid at a candy store. I even bowed. Mrs. Steadman smiled at me. "By the way, can I have a copy of your dissertation proposal?" "Sure. Here it is. I brought one for you. Do you think I need to contact the school district too?" "No, you don't need to."

To my surprise, my access to the school was gained without difficulty. Mrs. Steadman was very intelligent, down to earth, and most of all, very kind . . .

I spent most of my observation time in classes that my six interviewees were taking: ninth grade class, tenth grade social studies class, senior English class, and economics class. Interactions between the teacher and students, what they teach and learn in class, how they react to each other, what is happening in classroom, what they say and what they do were documented in my field notes.

Upon the principal's permission and after an IRB approval, I started my fieldwork in August 2003, which lasted for 13 weeks till December 2003, Monday through Thursday, about five to six hours each day. The total observation time I spent at the research site was between 260 and 312 hours. I started my observation in Mrs. Emm's classroom, where senior English and Economics were taught. I chose her class first because she personally told me that I would be welcomed any time to her class. She was easy going and did not seem to be bothered by my presence . . . (Kim, 2005, pp. 48–51)

I was lucky to be able to identify my research site and gain access to it without difficulty. I was allowed to observe and explore the daily lives of my participants, including adults working in that site, without the need for negotiation. However, we should understand that gaining access to a field site can involve challenges and negotiations. Most writings about access center on issues of gatekeepers in addition to practical and ethical challenges of entering fieldwork sites (see Reeves, 2010, for example).

Access to a research site is a process of negotiations, which includes selecting, entering, continuing in the field, and exiting (Bondy, 2012). Although I had relatively "easy" access, once I got to the field, I had to constantly negotiate my position in multiple situations because I was a "stranger" to the population. As I discussed in Chapter 3, I was mistaken as a "spy" by a student. Another time when I was writing my field notes in a classroom, a couple of students came up to me and tried to look at my notes, wondering if I was writing something bad about them. This incident made me realize that writing field notes in front of the participants was a "risky" business that may endanger the relationship and trust I was trying to build up with them. Bondy posits that the role of researcher as stranger means "the researcher must be aware of and negotiate his or her position within the research setting delicately" (p. 582). This was true throughout my research process. Therefore, as Bondy states, we should carefully examine "the connections between how we access research settings and the results of our research. Each part represents a crucial piece of the research puzzle, and one that provides a more complete understanding of a given social setting" (p. 587).

The Art of Observation—Also Known as Attention

When we are in the field, what are we supposed to observe? Do we have observation skills? Do we even have enough patience for an extended observation? Aren't we living in the age of inattention where people are texting, instant messaging, or tweeting while being with their friends, behaviors that are sometimes favorably termed multi-tasking?

Speaking of inattention, I stumbled upon an article with the headline "How to End the Age of Inattention" in *The Wall Street Journal* (Finn, 2012) on a Sunday morning. The article was about an innovative class that Yale's School of Medicine has been offering for the last decade to help future doctors learn the art of observation. This program, called *Enhancing Observational Skills,* was created by collaboration between Yale medical school faculty member Dr. Irwin Braverman and Linda Friedlaender, curator of education at the Yale Center for British Art. The impetus to create the program was their increasing concern about how the art of detailed, careful observation is getting short shrift in an age when physicians rely heavily on high-tech imaging and tests, which results in many misdiagnoses. The so-called museum intervention was created to hone medical students' observational skills. Students are assigned to a painting that they examine for 15 minutes, recording all they see. This is followed by a group discussion about their observations. The purpose is to help students improve their ability to detect important details for a better diagnosis while withholding their initial assumptions and a hasty interpretation of what they see. This program has been so successful that it has expanded to more than 20 other medical schools, including Harvard, Columbia, and Cornell (see also Chapter 1 for narrative medicine).

One of the strategies these programs use to develop observational skills is *Visual Thinking Strategies* (VTS), developed by Harvard-trained cognitive researcher Abigail Housen and veteran art educator Philip Yenawine. VTS employs a discussion facilitation protocol as participants examine and discuss a carefully selected art image. The process helps participants develop observation, language, and thinking skills such as evidence-based reasoning. VTS uses visual art to help learn to express opinions shaped from detailed observations of the art with evidence to back them up. It is being used in higher education (on college campuses and in medical education), as well as in K-12 settings, and is typically taught in collaboration with art museums and different disciplines (Yenawine & Miller, 2014). Students are asked to respond to the very basic meaning-making question, *What's going on in this image?* A second question, *What did you see that makes you say that?* is used when students make interpretive comments or express an opinion. Every response is paraphrased by the facilitator. Over time, students have been shown to develop the following skills that I would say are what we need for good observation and attention:

- Look carefully at complex, intriguing works of art
- Engage in thoughtful, extended examinations of what they find
- Back up their ideas with evidence
- Listen to and consider the views of others, agreeing, disagreeing, or building on what they hear
- Hold a variety of interpretations as possible (Yenawine & Miller, 2014, p. 3)

For more information on Visual Thinking Strategies, you can visit www.vtshome.org. I believe that it is not just medical doctors who need to pay particular attention to their observational skills. We narrative researchers also need to hone observational skills to better understand our participants' stories. We need to be keen observers of our participants' life worlds in order to retell their stories in full, closer to their reality. In addition, observational skills are needed beyond data collection in the field, especially when analyzing data. They are particularly important because visual narrative inquiry is becoming more prevalent, as discussed in Chapter 4.

Observer's Paradox

As we consider the role and importance of observation during our fieldwork, we should also be aware of the effect that the observer's presence may have on the data generated, which is what Labov calls the **observer's paradox**. According to Labov (1972), the aim of research (especially in linguistic research) is "to find out how people talk when they are not being systematically observed; yet we can only obtain this data by systematic observation" (p. 209). Labov's observer's paradox emphasizes the importance of collecting data in a natural setting because the observer's presence, if viewed as an artificial arrangement, might influence how participants behave and act in the research setting, which is referred to as the *Hawthorne Effect*[2] or the *Observer Effect*.

The paradox is that it is important to collect data in a natural setting, but the systematic recording of data, for instance, the observer writing field notes while observing, or taping or video-recording a conversation, may affect how the participant acts or what the participant says.

My student, Jodie, visited me in my office to ask questions about her interview data. She said, "I had a wonderful interview with my participant, today. My participant shared a lot of information about the challenges she's experiencing as a PE teacher. But what's more interesting is that she talked more seriously about her personal insights even after I thought we were done with the interview! I mean, as soon as I turned off my iPhone recorder, she started talking more. She said to me, 'Well, since we are not recording any more, I can talk more freely about what I really think.' Is it common?" I assured Jodie that it is indeed common that interviewees would talk more after a recorder is turned off, and sometimes it can be more interesting than what is recorded. Jodie was perplexed, "Really? Then, would I gather more meaningful data if I don't record the interview at all? Actually, some of my participants didn't like it when I turned on the audio-recorder at the interview. They became a little bit nervous."

Jodie was encountering the observer's paradox. I'm sure you have been in Jodie's situation or you may experience it once you start interviewing or observing. Gordon (2012) posits that the observer's paradox is inescapable because we have to inform our research participants of recording for ethical reasons. Even so, according to Speer (2008), researchers should work to "eliminate extraneous, research-induced 'contaminants'" (p. 511), a term that refers to the presence of an "observer," be it a person, recording device, or both.

There are possible ways to minimize the observer's paradox. First, it is important for us to spend an extended period at a research site or to be in a natural setting where we as observers are treated as a "natural" part of the life space. We can accomplish this by "being there" for an extended period of time, and working as a participant observer, if possible, which will help us establish trustworthy relationships with the participants. Xu and Connelly (2010) call such efforts of becoming a natural part of the setting field-based narrative inquiry. Second, at the beginning of the recording, we should engage in conversational moments with our participant to the point when the recorder is "forgotten" (Speer, 2008). Third, we should embrace the observer's paradox instead of trying to escape it (Gordon, 2012). That is, rather than treating the presence of a researcher and/or a recorder as "contaminants" (Gordon, 2012, p. 300), we should pay greater attention to the interconnections among methods, context, and data, keeping in mind the various ways the data might be influenced by the existence of the researcher/observer/recorder.

Artifacts: Cabinets of Curiosities or Cabinets of Wonder

Recently, the Beach Museum of Art at my institution had a special exhibition titled *Museum of Wonder,* honoring Kansas State University's sesquicentennial celebration (February 12, 2013). For this exhibition, inspired by the traditional cabinets of curiosities or cabinets of wonder (*wunderkammern*), the museum collected over 100 objects from different departments at KSU, consisting of an eclectic mix of objects to represent the university's past, present, and future. The exhibition included objects such as wheat-related products, machines, equipment, books, maps and drawings, prints and paintings, decorative items, furniture, clothing and textiles, and animal fossils and skeletons. Each object had a story of its own representing the diverse fields of research and knowledge pursued at KSU in the last 150 years (http://beach.kstate.edu/explore/exhibitions/museumofwonder.html).

As I enjoyed looking closely at each object displayed at the exhibition, I started imagining what kind of story each one might hold. I wondered about the owner or maker of each object, a person who could tell me an interesting story of the thing and what meaning it might have. My wonderings did not stop there, though. As I looked at the entire exhibition, I began to wonder how this collection of artifacts could be used as a research method. I started seeing much potential in the cabinet of curiosities. How about collecting objects as data from our storytellers, which will go with the life story and lived experiences that our storytellers relay to us? How about creating a cabinet of curiosities full of objects that our storytellers are willing to share?

The traditional **cabinets of curiosities** or cabinets of wonder started in the Baroque period (16th and 17th centuries) with well-to-do European travelers who began collecting extraordinary items from foreign countries they visited, such as natural specimens, items made of precious materials, and instruments of technology. These extraordinary objects or artifacts were stored in special cupboards or actual rooms for viewing enjoyment to inspire the viewer's imagination, curiosity, and wondering about art, other cultures, and the natural world. These groupings and displays became the foundation of the modern museum (MacLure, 2006).

One of the best known cabinets of curiosities is the Museum Wormianum, established by Ole Worm, a seventeenth-century Danish archaeologist, embryologist, natural philosopher, physician, and teacher (Purcell, 2004). Rosamond Purcell,[3] who is a photographer, artist, and scientist, was recently commissioned to re-create Ole Worm's museum at the Harvard University Science Center. Purcell (2004) wrote about how Worm collected artifacts from the daily lives of peoples from the circumpolar region, including baskets, spears, and tools, not to mention natural objects and ethnographic and archaeological artifacts such as coins, corals, fossils, magnifiers, mirrors, stuffed gulls, a polar bear, and so on.

By now, you have probably guessed where I am going with this discussion. I am suggesting that we collect artifacts with the concept of the cabinet of curiosities as a way to excavate further stories from our research participants. The items can be personal journals, diaries, letters, books, photographs, paintings, personal belongings, formal and informal documents, student homework assignments, or any other objects that the storytellers would like to share that are related to the telling of their story. So, we could create our own cabinets of curiosities or cabinets of wonder as part of our research data, with which we tell more stories.

Alas, I am not the original adopter of the cabinet of curiosities as a qualitative research method. MacLure (2006) has explored how a baroque method such as *trompe l'oeil*[4] painting (visual illusion in art) and the cabinets of curiosities that were popular in the Baroque age can be used in postmodern qualitative research. MacLure posits that the baroque method can conjure up possibilities for spaces where difference, wonder, and otherness can emerge. Following

Lambert's (2004) argument for a "return of the baroque" that has recently arrived in fields including art, cultural theory, philosophy and aesthetics, surrealism and literary theory, MacLure posits that a baroque method can be used in qualitative research to "resist clarity, mastery and the single point of view" and to "honor the obligation to get entangled in the details and decorations, rather than rise above them" (p. 731) (see MacLure (2006) for more detailed characteristics of the baroque method).

Here, our interest is in one of the baroque methods, the cabinet of curiosities or *wunderkammer,* for use as an aid to provoke more stories from the storytellers for narrative inquiry. The cabinet of curiosities represents *wonder,* which is a preeminently baroque effect/emotion (Lambert, 2004), or "the contemplation of otherness" (Mauriès, 2002, p. 249). Objects in the cabinet, concealed in nested drawers, shelves, niches, and boxes, would represent our wondering about the storyteller's past, present, and future, evoking our imagination, empathy, and understanding of the other. Indeed, the cabinet of curiosities is the experience of wonder, "designed to spark connections" (MacLure, 2006, p. 738), opening up more stories to whoever experiences it: the researcher, the researched, or the reader.

I posit that collecting artifacts in the spirit of creating a cabinet of curiosities is an important narrative method in which we narrative inquirers should engage. As Miller (2010) states, "Stuff does not merely reflect who we are, but in many respects it actually creates us in the first place" (p. 40). A cabinet of curiosities is full of such "stuff." As you can see, then, there is much to discover, explore, and search through for meaning in the artifacts that our storytellers might share with us. We wonder, mull over, and possibly take another journey with the artifacts collected in the cabinet of curiosities in the hermeneutical excavation of stories through our narrative inquiry.

Visual Data

Today, you see that images and visual artifacts are ubiquitous, and they are produced on a daily basis (e.g., websites, photo images, advertisements, and signs). For most people, such visual images in daily life are taken for granted, and they are not subjects of systematic inquiry for scholarly activities. However, it is our understanding that images convey multiple messages that provide insights into social phenomena (Weber, 2008). We don't always notice the importance of what we see, nor do we attempt to systematically analyze it. It is "the *paying attention,* the looking and the taking note of what we see that makes images especially important to art, scholarship, and research" (Weber, 2008, p. 42, italics in original). Qualitative researchers, therefore, should take advantage of the wide sweep of visual data sources available in society (Margolis & Pauwels, 2011) and pay attention to such visual data sources. If you recall, we discussed in Chapter 4 how visual-based narrative inquiry is becoming increasingly prevalent these days.

Visual data include a wide range of visual forms, including films, video, photographs, drawings, cartoons, graffiti, maps, diagrams, cyber graphics, signs, and symbols (Weber, 2008).

Margolis and Pauwels (2011) suggest that one of the most essential choices we have to make in visual research is whether to use existing visual material ("found" visuals) as primary data for research, or to generate visual data as a researcher.

In fact, if you're interested in visual-based narrative inquiry, it will be helpful to understand that there are three types of visual data to gather: (1) found materials; (2) researcher-generated visual data; and (3) respondent-generated visual data (Margolis & Pauwels, 2011). Found materials are the ones that already exist, or materials that have been produced by other researchers for similar or different research purposes. Researcher-generated visual data means the researcher selects events and phenomena to initiate the production of visual data.

Finally, respondent-generated visual data, which is an increasingly popular data type in the social and human sciences, is generated when participants are asked to produce their own data in a visual form. For example, participants take photographs of their lives over a short time span of a week or two and tell stories about those photographs over time. This method is called Photovoice (see Chapter 4), "a strategy that relies on informants to produce images" (Bell, 2013, p. 145). These photographs are made *with* and by participants as well as *of* them. The researcher still needs to analyze the respondent-generated data, hence "it is important to note that the respondent-generated material, while offering a unique (insider) perspective, is never an end product, but just an intermediate step in the research" (Margolis & Pauwels, 2011, p. 8).

Why, then, do we use visual images? According to Knowles and Sweetman (2004), there are three approaches to the usage of visual images within social and human science research. First, we use images as representations of reality and documentation of already existing phenomena or events from a realist perspective. Photojournalism or taking images while doing fieldwork would be an example of this approach. Second, we use images as evidence to *construct* reality from a poststructuralist perspective. For example, we can use photography to problematize important social issues such as homelessness, immigration, or prisons. An example of this approach would be Richard Ross's work on *Juvenile-in-Justice,* which is shown in Chapter 6. Finally, we use existing images in the archives as texts for a semiotic analysis (or semiology). The existing images can be analyzed to uncover their social and cultural significance that needs to be deconstructed (Pauwels, 2011).

To gain more insights into visual methods, I would highly recommend that you look into the fields of visual sociology and visual anthropology (e.g., http://visualsociology.org and http://www.societyforvisualanthropology.org), as they have done much of the pioneering work on image-based methodologies.

(Digital) Archival Data

Closely related to visual data, another set of technology-driven data that narrative inquirers can use is (digitally) archived data. We can use archival data as a supplementary set of data to support the story we are retelling as we delve into personal stories and histories, making the personal story social. Archival data allow "the individual to write his or her own story of the past—combining his or her own story with the stories represented in the archives" (Morgan-Fleming, Riegle, & Fryer, 2007, p. 82).

In the past, it was challenging to use archival data with primary source materials preserved in the traditional way, not in the digital form. Traditional archival data had limited access and the labor to go through it was costly and time-consuming. However, access to digital archival materials has never been as easy as it is today, transcending limits of time and space with availability on the Internet, and with many digital archives open to the public. These online archives provide us with an opportunity to access a wide range of personal stories, folk tales, audio files, and video files about any genre. We can use primary sources of a particular historical time and an individual's personal experience of that event.

Morgan-Fleming, Riegle, and Fryer (2007) provide wonderful digital archival resources for us in their appendix (p. 98). For example, their institution, Texas Tech University's Southwest Collection, has more than 4,500 tapes of 2,800 interviews, covering a wide range of disciplines such as agriculture, medicine, education, religion, politics, and more. Notably, there is also a movement that demands the principle of open access to all knowledge. The Open Content Alliance (http://www.opencontentalliance.org/), for example, with an effort to build "a digital archive of global content for universal access," has digitized more than 1 million books in OpenLibrary (http://openlibrary.org). Their associated organization, archive.org (http://archive .org), has innumerable video, audio, and text files available to us.

The impact of digitally available resources on the way we conduct our narrative research in an age of open access is huge, leading us to rethink our understanding of what constitutes data and how we collect data.

Conclusion: Excavating Stories as Data

In this chapter, we looked into narrative data collection methods that would elicit narrative thinking to help us in excavating stories. The methods described included interviews, fieldwork, observation (attention), visual data, artifacts (cabinets of curiosities or cabinets of wonder), and (digital) archival data. However, there are other methods available. As Barthes (1975) points out, narrative is present in every age, in every place, and in every society, in an "almost infinite diversity of forms" (p. 251) such as spoken or written language, fixed or moving images, gestures, fables, history, dramas, stained-glass windows, news items, comics, cinema, and more. Therefore, we should use imagination and creativity to find as much meaningful data as possible to accomplish whatever research purpose we have for narrative inquiry. I would say that what is most important to remember during the data collection period is to be an active listener, attentive observer, and empathic person with integrity.

QUESTIONS FOR REFLECTION

- Why is it necessary to give up the authoritative position of a researcher and be a humble listener who honors the voice of your participant?
- What types of interview are you going to conduct? How many informants will you interview to fit your research design? How would you justify your method of sampling and saturation?
- Can you list narrative research methods that you are going to use for your narrative inquiry? What are they?
- Is there any new, creative data collection method you have come up with? If so, how would you justify and theorize it?

ACTIVITIES

1. Let's write an interview guide. Beginning with your "grand tour" question, jot down all of the topics and areas you want to cover in the interview. Then, write a series of questions for each of those topics or areas. After that, organize the questions in order for topical flow. Share them with your classmates and justify how these questions will help you with addressing each of your research questions.

2. Imagine your interview situation and create your interview questions in the two-sentence format based on your research questions.

3. Find a person you can interview for 30 minutes using the interview questions and guide that you have just created. Transcribe the interview.

4. Visit a nearby museum with your classmates. Pick one painting for your observation. Observe the painting for 15 minutes and record the details that you see. What can you tell about the painting?

5. Find more online archival sources and grow the list provided here.

ONLINE ARCHIVAL RESOURCES

http://archive.org

http://www.opencontentalliance.org/

http://openlibrary.org/

http://daln.osu.edu/ (Digital Archive of Literacy Narratives) http://www.saadigitalarchive.org/firstdays (South Asian American Digital Archive, sharing stories from South Asians about their first day in the U.S.)

http://911digitalarchive.org (Collection of stories, images, documents, and videos of September 11, 2011)

http://www.indiana.edu/ ~ libarchm/ (The Archives of Traditional Music; audiovisual archive that documents music and culture from all over the world)

http://www.vietnam.ttu.edu/oralhistory/ (The Oral History Project of the Vietnam Archive)

http://www.digital.swco.ttu.edu/Oral_History/oralhistory.asp (audio, photo, text collection of racial relations in the American Southwest)

http://aton.ttu.edu/ (Archive of Turkish Oral Narrative)

http://loc.gov/ (U.S. Library of Congress)

http://www.nationalarchives.gov.uk/webarchive/archiving-datasets.htm (UK National Digital Archive of Datasets [NDAD])

Digital storytelling (the Center for Digital Storytelling in California): www.storycenter.org

NOTES

1. See Mason (2010) for an in-depth discussion on the issues of sample size and saturation in PhD studies.
2. *Hawthorne Effect* is a term that refers to a phenomenon in which the participants' behavior is affected by the observer's presence. The term came from the Hawthorne experiments done by researchers from the Harvard Business School, whose aim was to find out worker productivity, job satisfaction, and workplace organization at the Hawthorne Works of the Western Electric Company. Gillespie (1991) contends that the findings from the Hawthorne experiments were skewed to benefit the company, hence knowledge was "manufactured" in specific social, institutional, and ideological contexts, in which meaning was imposed rather than discovered (p. 4).
3. Photographer and collage artist Rosamond Purcell was commissioned to re-create Ole Worm's museum for an exhibition opened September 27, 2004, and ran until January 2005 at the Collection of Historical Scientific Instruments, Harvard University Science Center, Cambridge, Massachusetts.
4. MacLure (2006) explains that the *trompe l'oeil* is one of many baroque devices that "invoke the unavoidably compromised and problematic nature of vision" (p. 736) of an observer/viewer/reader, leading to an "inability to tell the difference between representation and reality, original and copy" (p. 734).

CHAPTER TOPICS

CHAPTER 6

Narrative Data Analysis and Interpretation

"Flirting" With Data

QUESTIONS TO CONSIDER

- How do we transform the "messy" data to meaningful stories?
- What are the methods of narrative data analysis and interpretation?
- What does narrative analysis look like in each narrative genre?

INTRODUCTION

Bryan left my office after venting his frustration over his interview skills, and I didn't hear from him for a while. I decided no news was good news, meaning he must have been working hard, collecting data in the field. I knew he would visit me sooner or later, and I was right.

So, on a Monday morning during my office hours, Bryan showed up with a stack of paper along with a thick notebook. His first words came out before even saying hi to me.

Bryan: I am overwhelmed, Dr. Kim. Look at these pages of transcripts and I still have more interviews to transcribe. By the way, how are you?

Me: Fine, thank you for asking. And you?

Bryan: I would feel better if I were done with this stuff.

Me: What stuff?

Bryan: This research stuff. It is so time consuming to get an interview tape transcribed. I have transcribed three so far and I have five more to go. It is so time consuming and overwhelming.

Me: Welcome to my world, Bryan. It's good that you're trying to transcribe your tapes yourself. I commend you. It's tedious, but worth it. Believe me. When I finished my data collection, I was overwhelmed, too. I had a thick notebook filled with observational notes of my fieldwork and had 13, 120-minute-long microtapes to be transcribed. I also had a huge box full of artifacts to look at. Yes, transcribing the interview tapes seemed to take forever. I didn't hire a transcriptionist, not just because of my tight budget but also because of the importance of the initial learning opportunity about my interview data. And then, I had to read, re-read and re-re-read the transcripts and field notes for analyses. This process was really daunting and even depressing. I didn't enjoy it much, I admit. But I felt a tremendous responsibility and accountability, realizing that I was "the" researcher for the first time with a mountain of my own serious data! And, you know something? I didn't know it during the data analysis period, but after finishing it, I felt like I went through a rite of passage to my researcher-hood, and THAT was exciting.

Bryan: Wow, a rite of passage to the researcher-hood!

Me: Yes, Bryan. Think of it as a rite of passage into researcher-hood. You're not the only one. I had other doctoral students literally crying in my office, overwhelmed. But they made it! You'll pass through this, too. So, go have some fun flirting with your data.

You will enjoy doing the fieldwork after finally gaining access to your research site. Like Bryan, however, you will also feel overwhelmed by the amount of data you accumulate over time, not knowing what to do with them. You are about to enter the maze of data analysis and interpretation, which is the focus of this chapter. The purpose of this chapter is to help you with narrative data analysis and interpretation through which you will excavate meaningful stories to (re)tell. We will learn to "flirt" with different methods of narrative data analysis and interpretation to find narrative meanings in the collected data. After going through data analysis and interpretation, you will feel as if you have experienced a rite of passage into researcher-hood. It is an integral process of becoming an independent narrative researcher.

On Flirtation

You have just finished typing the field notes from your final observation of the study and you proceed to file them. There, facing you, is all the material you have diligently collected. An empty feeling comes over you as you ask, "Now what do I do?" (Bogdan & Biklen, 2007, pp. 172–173)

Faced with the data that you have collected through the methods described in Chapter 5, you may have an overwhelming feeling of "Now, what do I do?" It is a common feeling among researchers to feel "terrified and overwhelmed" and "at a loss as to where and how to begin" (Kiesinger, 1998, p. 84). All the textual, visual, and audio data, and the artifacts in the cabinet of curiosities feel like a steep mountain whose trail is strenuous, zigzagged, and unexplored. However, if you don't have such an overwhelming feeling about your collected data, it may be because you don't have much data to analyze, which should be more worrisome. So, I want to assure you that being overwhelmed by the amount of data is a good thing and it is just an initial feeling that will be followed by a sense of accomplishment sooner or later!

Now that we have admitted to being overwhelmed, it is time to find ways to convert our field texts into research texts through the process of data analysis and interpretation, a process that all researchers must go through. Remember I wanted us to think of narrative research design as "aesthetic play" (Chapter 3)? We discussed how aesthetic play encourages us to be open-minded, experimenting with many different, possible ideas out of curiosity. I wanted us to conceive of research design and methods *playfully and seriously* at the same time. In keeping with this spirit, the notion of *flirtation* seems fitting here in the discussion of data analysis and interpretation.

Bear with me for a moment if you think that I am using a "bad" term, as we usually think that the word ***flirtation*** has the negative connotation of being uncommitted, referring to a relationship to people. But in psychoanalysis, flirtation is associated with Freud's notion of free-floating attention, or free association, which is the psychic act of detaching one's devotion to internal censors (Phillips, 1994). That is, the idea of flirtation asks us to undo our commitment to what we already know and question its legitimacy. Thus flirtation is considered an "unconscious form of skepticism" (Phillips, 1994, p. xii). In any transition or in any shift of allegiances, Phillips argues, there may have to be some flirtation. By engaging in flirtation with ideas, we get to know them in different ways since "flirtation keeps things in play" (p. xii). Flirting with ideas allows us to dwell on what is unconvincing, uncertain, and perplexing, rendering surprises and serendipities, and of course, disappointments as well.

To summarize Phillips's ideas on flirtation, flirtation:

- Exploits the idea of surprise and curiosity;
- Creates a space where aims or ends can be worked out;
- Makes time for less familiar possibilities; and
- Is a way of playing with new ideas without letting these new ideas be influence by our wishes.

So, I hope you are on the same page with me on using Phillips's ideas on flirtation as an approach to narrative data analysis and interpretation. Flirting with data is an attempt to analyze and interpret the research data to exploit the idea of surprise and curiosity, as we don't know what is going to evolve and emerge until we deal with the data; it creates a space for us where we can discover ways to reach and negotiate our research aims with data; it encourages us to make time to embrace less familiar possibilities; and it is a way of cultivating ideas for finding yet another story, "one we haven't necessarily bargained for" (p. xxv). Data analysis and interpretation as flirtation is a "transitional performance" (p. xviii), moving from data collection to data analysis and interpretation, allowing room for surprises and curiosities to explore "which ways of knowing, or being known, sustain our interest, our excitement" (p. xviii). This transitional performance as flirtation is important because as you know, we often interpret events "as we wish to see them, not as they are" (Wragg, 2012, p. 51). With that in mind, let's go on to the topic of this chapter, narrative data analysis and interpretation.

Qualitative Data Analysis

Understanding qualitative research data analysis is definitely the first step to conduct narrative data analysis. I always think that we are qualitative researchers before narrative researchers. Hence, understanding qualitative research analysis will greatly inform us, who are about to go into the details of narrative data analysis. I assume that you have taken one or two (or more) qualitative research courses as part of your program of study. As you know, data analysis in qualitative research in general is comprised of: examining raw data; reducing them to themes through coding and recoding processes; and representing the data in figures, tables, and narratives in a final research text. This is the general process that qualitative researchers typically use, with some variations (Creswell, 2007). So, you will first go through multiple coding processes in which you attempt to find a word or short phrase that can be an attribute for a portion of your data (see Saldaña, 2009, for coding manuals). Then, you find relations between similar codes and combine them to make a category. And then, you identify an emerging pattern in each category, which then can be built as a theme (see Figure 6.1).

Qualitative data analysis may look simple because I have just reduced the complex process of analysis to four basic elements: codes, categories, patterns, and themes. But you know that this is just a tip of the iceberg and that each stage involves much deliberation and recursion. Creswell provides a data analysis spiral where these four elements feed into a loop of description, classification, and interpretation (see Creswell, 2007, p. 151). As qualitative researchers go through this data analysis process several times, they will engage in a detailed description of what they discover from the analysis, classify the information for the reader (discussing emergent themes), and provide an interpretation of the findings in light of the literature and their theoretical perspectives.

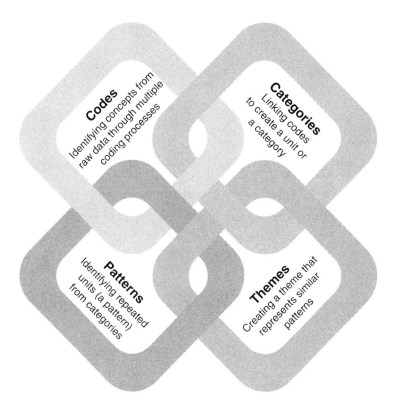

Codes
Identifying concepts from raw data through multiple coding processes

Categories
Linking codes to create a unit or a category

Patterns
Identifying repeated units (a pattern) from categories

Themes
Creating a theme that represents similar patterns

Figure 6.1   Basic Elements of Qualitative Data Analysis

Theorizing Narrative Data Analysis and Interpretation

Narrative researchers point out that much attention has been given to the various issues of narrative research, but relatively less attention to the theoretical concerns that underlie the processes of analysis and interpretation (Josselson, 2004; Polkinghorne, 1995). In an effort to address this concern, I would like to discuss some theoretical issues related to data analysis and interpretation before getting into the methods of analysis.

First of all, I want to point out that data analysis involves interpretation, which in turn affects our choice of representations of stories. Some might think that analysis and interpretation are two different concepts, as analysis implies objectivity and interpretation implies subjectivity. However, although they are not identical concepts, they work in tandem because we analyze narrative data in order to develop an understanding of the meanings our participants give to themselves, to their surroundings, to their lives, and to their lived experiences through storytelling. Narrative researchers try to interpret meanings through an analysis of plotlines, thematic structures, and social and cultural referents. These meanings are to be analyzed and interpreted concurrently in a transitional period to the research text.

Josselson (2006) emphasizes that narrative research is "always interpretive at every stage" (p. 4), from conceptualization of research, to data collection, to writing a research text. That is, we narrative inquirers do not stand outside in a neutral, objective position, merely presenting or analyzing "what was said," says Riessman (2008), who defines narrative analysis as "a family of methods for interpreting texts" (p. 11). Chase (2003)[1] also talks about how she encourages her students to write interpretive comments while analyzing interview data. She suggests: "avoid being too descriptive on the one hand and overinterpreting on the other hand. Do interpret what is being said and try to articulate your reasons—give evidence—for your interpretations" (pp. 92–93).

Narrative Meaning

As we understand that narrative data analysis and interpretation work in tandem, I want to suggest that narrative analysis and interpretation is an act of finding *narrative meaning,* following Polkinghorne (1988). Recall that narrative inquiry is a way of understanding human experience through stories that, in turn, help us better understand the human phenomena and human existence. Polkinghorne equates narrative inquiry with the study of narrative meaning because the aim of narrative inquiry is to understand human experience that is meaningful, and our human actions take place informed by this meaningfulness, projected in stories and narratives. Polkinghorne defines narrative meaning as "a cognitive process that organizes human experiences into temporally meaningful episodes" (p. 1). Narrative meaning concerns diverse aspects of experience that involve human actions or events that affect human beings. Individual stories have their own narrative meanings, and cultures also maintain collections of typical narrative meanings in their myths, folk tales, and histories, accumulated over time. Thus, the aim of the study of narrative meaning, according to Polkinghorne, is to "make explicit the operations that produce its particular kind of meaning, and to draw out the implications this meaning has for understanding human existence" (p. 6). Based on this remark, I would suggest that narrative data analysis and interpretation is a meaning-finding act through which we attempt to elicit implications for a better understanding of human existence.

Polkinghorne posits that research into meaning is "the most basic of all inquiry" (p. 9), and the realm of meaning is "best captured through the qualitative nuances of its expression in ordinary language" (p. 10). However, he also cautions that there are some inherent problems in the study of meaning:

- Meaning is not tangible, nor static, thus it is not easily grasped.
- We do not have direct access to the realm of meaning of others. We are at the mercy of the storyteller's recollection or introspection.

- Information about other people's realms of meaning can be gathered through the narratives and stories. These narratives are context-sensitive, hence, they are not to be treated in isolation.
- The analysis of narrative data makes use of hermeneutic (interpretative) reasoning, thus the analysis methods are not as precise as quantitative tools.
- The realm of meaning appears in various modes of presentation, such as perception, remembrance, and imagination. These complex connections among images and ideas make the realm of meaning difficult to investigate. (pp. 7–8)

I find Polkinghorne's cautions insightful. He reminds us that narrative data analysis and interpretation as an act of finding narrative meaning is not a straightforward enterprise; rather, it may pose challenges and potential dilemmas. However, his intention is not to discourage us from engaging in understanding narrative meaning, but to help us be more attuned to the nuances of narrative meaning that has the following characteristics. According to Polkinghorne, narrative meaning:

1. Functions to give form to the understanding of a purpose to life and to join everyday actions and events into episodic units;

2. Provides a framework for understanding the past events of one's life and for planning future actions; and

3. Is the primary scheme by means of which human existence is rendered meaningful. (p. 11)

With an understanding of narrative meaning, including its challenges and functions, we can better flirt with data through the process of data analysis and interpretation.

Narrative Smoothing

One of the major means of narrative data analysis and interpretation involves narrative smoothing. Last April, I attended a talk by Curator Jorge J. E. Gracia, who organized a very interesting exhibition titled *Painting Borges: Art Interpreting Literature,* at the Beach Museum in my institution. Professor Gracia is also a philosopher teaching at the State University of New York, Buffalo. For this exhibition, Curator Gracia selected 24 paintings done by contemporary Argentinean and Cuban artists, who created their artistic representations based on Jorge Luis Borges's most famous stories about identity and memory, freedom and destiny, and faith and divinity. Gracia calls these artistic representations "painted stories" (Gracia, 2012), which I think is a lovely phrase, and these painted stories showcased the interpretation of literature by the selected visual artists. In his talk, Gracia spoke about the concept of interpretation in lay terms to help the audience (mostly undergraduate students and non-philosophers like me) understand, rather than using complex philosophical terms, like hermeneutics.[2] He said, there are two general types (or goals) of interpretation: one is an *act of understanding* (to develop an effective interpretation to understand); and the other is *instrumental understanding* (to mediate an effective understanding). And, there are usually five strategies involved in interpretation: *focus, omission, addition, appropriation,* and *transposition.*

I think the types of interpretation that professor Gracia addressed can be transferred to an act of interpretation and analysis in narrative research. That is, we can interpret our data (1) to understand the phenomenon under study (as an act of understanding); and (2) to facilitate an understanding of the phenomenon under study for the reader (as an instrumental understanding). For this act of interpretation, we can employ the five strategies: *focus, omission, addition, appropriation,* and *transposition.*

Since narrative data analysis deeply involves interpretation, we are about to engage in arbitrary subjectivity, which puts us in a "tricky" situation. The use of arbitrary interpretation (especially when we "appropriate" data to fit our philosophical orientation, or "transpose" the data from one situation to another) often becomes a mode for saying what we want to say or hear instead of really listening to or seeing what is being said (Munro Hendry, 2007). Further, while undertaking an analysis and interpretation of narrative data, we might find ourselves in a dilemma, realizing that a faithful account (faithful to what the participant said) is not necessarily going to be a "good" story that we'd like to present, or that a "good" story might not be a faithful account. Spence (1986) points out how researchers have a tendency to write "a good story more than a faithful account" (p. 212) through subjective interpretation. Spence calls this involvement of subjective interpretation *narrative smoothing,* which can be used to mask our subjective interpretation as explanation, and to present a "good" story that is not necessarily a "faithful" account (see "fidelity" in Chapter 3).

Narrative smoothing is an interesting concept. It is a necessary method that many narrative researchers including myself use to make our participant's story coherent, engaging, and interesting to the reader. It is like brushing off the rough edges of disconnected raw data. However, it can also be problematic because it involves certain omissions, such as the selective reporting of some data (while ignoring other data), or the lack of context due to the researcher's assumption that what is clear to him or her will also be clear to the reader. Spence (1986) states:

> By failing to provide the background information and context surrounding a particular clinical event, by failing to "unpack" the event in such a way that all its implications become transparent, the author runs the risk of telling a story that is quite different from the original experience. (p. 213)

Spence (1986) gives us an example. Spence argues that Freud presented the story of his patient, Dora, as an "intelligible, consistent, and unbroken" account (p. 212) by filling in the gaps in her account, thus leading to conclusions that were not supported by the evidence.

Spence problematizes this kind of narrative smoothing where we might be able to provide a good, "intelligible, consistent, and unbroken" story, but that it may be a far different story from the original account told by our participant (hence, not a faithful account). This kind of problem—failing to produce a faithful account—creates an ethical issue, which seems to happen to us quite often if we use strictly standardized narrative rules of "deletion-selection-interpretation" (Mishler, 1986a, p. 238), or the five strategies of *focus, omission, addition, appropriation,* and *transposition* that Gracia (2012) mentioned, without paying attention to the nuances that are involved in the interpretation process. Therefore, the ethics of interpretation has to be carefully considered (Squire, 2013). Spence (1986) suggests that we can address the ethics of interpretation (a) by being more nuanced and sensitive, (b) by recognizing the fact that the stories are not fixed and the referents can be ambiguous, (c) by guaranteeing confidentiality at the expense of some of the data's richness, and (d) by taking the participant and the reader into consideration.

In lieu of the ethics of interpretation, we can further consider Josselson's (2006) following question:

> Does the interpreter/researcher privilege the voice of the participant, trying to render the meanings as presented in the interview—or does the researcher try to read beneath—or, in Ricoeur's metaphor—in front of the text—for meanings that are hidden, either unconscious or so embedded in cultural context as to make them seem invisible? (p. 4)

The point Josselson is making here is whether we should look at our data with faith or with suspicion in an effort to find narrative meaning, which I will discuss next.

The Interpretation of Faith and the Interpretation of Suspicion[3]

Josselson (2004) provides an insightful account about interpretation in narrative research drawing upon Ricoeur (1970, 1991, 2007), who distinguishes between two forms of hermeneutics: a *hermeneutics of faith* and a *hermeneutics of suspicion.* Based on Ricoeur's distinction, Josselson proposes a hermeneutics of restoration (faith) and a hermeneutics of demystification (suspicion) that can be applied in the practice of analysis and interpretation in narrative research. This distinction is an issue we will always encounter during the data analysis of our participants' stories, so it needs some elaboration.

First, we can approach our narrative data from the perspective of an **interpretation of faith** in the stories told by our participants. That is, this perspective is operationalized based on the belief that what our participants are telling us is a story that is true and meaningful to their sense of their subjective experience. We take the story at face value. So, the aim of this approach is "to represent, explore and/or understand the subjective world of the participants and/or the social and historical world they feel themselves to be living in" (Josselson, 2004, p. 5). We retell or recount a participant's stories with faith, which is a result of the genuine personal encounter with the participant. Thus, the narrative meaning of the stories represented or retold from this perspective can be found in collaboration between the researcher and the participants through empathic understanding. Most narrative inquirers would initially use this approach, which is probably sufficient to meet most research purposes in narrative inquiry.

Another approach we can take is the **interpretation of suspicion** *in addition to* the interpretation of faith. Please note that I, following Josselson (2004), am trying to outline each approach without subscribing to either-or, binary thinking, in hopes that both approaches will be used in tandem. This approach of suspicion will, along with the interpretation of faith, help us go deeper with our analysis and interpretation as it aims to find hidden narrative meanings that might be lurking in the data. The interpretation of suspicion lets us think again about what we might take for granted in the approach of the interpretation of faith. This is "a less favored mode" (Josselson, 2004, p. 15) because it might give the impression that we have to undermine research relationships with our participants by being "suspicious" or skeptical of what they said. However, let's be clear that this approach is not about suspecting that what our participants told us might not be true, but rather it is about decoding or demystifying the implicit meaning that might go unnoticed in the first approach. For example, we might want to pay extra attention to any play on words, contradictions, or rhetoric. The participants might use their own tactic of "narrative smoothing" in their narration, although Spence did not talk about narrative smoothing from the narrator's perspective, omitting things that they don't want to say for some reason, or assuming that the researcher should know what the participants are talking about, thus not providing sufficient context for the story. Thus with this approach, we are after "surface appearances that mask depth realities; a told story conceals an untold one" (Josselson, 2004, p. 13).

The role of the narrative inquirer as midwife that I discussed in Chapter 3 allows us to pay attention to both approaches to find narrative meaning. We can deliver the stories of our participants at face value, but we should also carefully look for any "red flags," especially if the research topic is about challenging the status quo, or social justice, based on critical theory, critical race theory, or a poststructuralist framework. A good narrative analysis, as Riessman (2008) notes, "prompts the reader to think beyond the surface of a text, and there is a move toward a broader commentary" (p. 13).

Finally, we have to remember that interpretations are fluid and temporal (Gadamer, 1964); that is, our interpretations will change over time as our horizon changes. Thus, we cannot claim that there is a single valid interpretation even within a single researcher. Wolcott (1994) also states, "Qualitative researchers are welcome to their opinions, but focused inquiry is not a soapbox from which researchers may make any pronouncement they wish" (p. 37).

To summarize theoretical issues of narrative analysis and interpretation:

- Narrative analysis and interpretation work in tandem.
- Narrative analysis and interpretation is an act of finding narrative meaning.

- Narrative meaning has inherent problems along with its functions.
- The aims of interpretation are:
  - to understand the phenomenon under study
  - to facilitate an understanding of the phenomenon under study for the reader

- Narrative smoothing is a method of interpretation that involves five tactics: focus, omission, addition, appropriation, and transposition.
- Two approaches to interpreting narrative data are: the interpretation of faith and the interpretation of suspicion.

Methods of Narrative Data Analysis

So, what methods for narrative data analysis are available to us? Methods of analysis do not emerge out of thin air, as Holstein and Gubrium (2012) point out. That is, finding an appropriate method of narrative data analysis for your inquiry should be informed by and contingent upon your narrative research design (Chapter 3) and the narrative inquiry genre you have in mind (Chapter 4), based on the narrative data you have (Chapter 5). Hence, the analysis and interpretation should be done holistically, heuristically, whole-heartedly, and most of all, narratively. I do not intend to present a prescription of one "best" method here, nor do I dare to try to provide you with various "how-to" methods. If I did, I would probably end up pigeonholing each method, causing you to search for where and how you can fit your data analysis into one particular method, like the Procrustean bed that I mentioned in Chapter 2. I encourage you to avoid the Procrustean bed if possible, and find varied narrative meanings through narrative data analysis and interpretation. This is why we should "flirt" with the data during this transitional performance stage from field texts to research texts, exploiting the idea of surprise and curiosity, creating a space where aims can be worked out, allowing room for less-familiar possibilities, and playing with new ideas.

For the methods of narrative data analysis that allow us to engage in flirtation, I will present Polkinghorne's analysis of narratives and narrative analysis, and Mishler's typology of narrative analysis, which encompasses Labov's narrative analysis model. And then I will provide how analysis/interpretation can be done in different narrative genres.

Polkinghorne's Analysis of Narratives and Narrative Analysis

Like many other narrative researchers, I find Polkinghorne's distinction between *analysis of narratives* and *narrative analysis* very useful and I use it quite often as an analytical framework for my work. This distinction is important to us because it points out that narrative research, with its unique and distinctive features, straddles the worlds of both qualitative research and arts-based research.

Based on his understanding of Bruner's two modes of thought, the paradigmatic mode and narrative mode (as discussed in Chapter 1), Polkinghorne (1995) posits that narrative inquiry has two types of analysis: one is an *analysis of narratives* that relies on paradigmatic cognition and the other is *narrative analysis* that depends on narrative cognition.[4]

Analysis of Narratives (Paradigmatic Mode of Analysis)

The **analysis of narratives,** or the **paradigmatic mode of analysis,** relies on paradigmatic cognition, a thinking skill that we humans primarily use to organize experience as ordered and consistent while attending to its general features and common categories and characteristics. A paradigmatic mode of knowing is an effort to classify such general features into different categories. It attempts to fit individual details into a larger pattern. According to Polkinghorne (1995), paradigmatic cognition "produces cognitive networks of concepts that allow people to construct experiences as familiar by emphasizing the common elements that appear over and over" (p. 10). We can use this paradigmatic thinking in narrative data analysis, which Polkinghorne calls an *analysis of narratives* (paradigmatic mode of analysis).

Qualitative research generally employs a paradigmatic type of analysis in which particular pieces of evidence are identified to form general concepts and categories. It seeks to identify common themes or conceptual manifestations discovered in the data. Thus, when we use this method, we examine the narrative data to focus on the discovery of common themes or salient constructs in storied data, and organize them under several categories using stories as data.[5]

Polkinghorne suggests that two types of paradigmatic analysis of narratives are possible: (a) one in which the concepts are derived from previous theory or logical possibilities that can be applied to the data; and (b) one in which concepts are inductively derived from the data (just like Glaser and Strauss's [1967] grounded theory notion). I would also add that another type of paradigmatic analysis of narratives is derived from the predetermined foci of one's study. For example, when we interview several veteran teachers about their teaching experiences, we could predetermine such categories as the first year's teaching experiences, coping strategies, challenges, and the like.

So, in the analysis of narratives (paradigmatic mode of analysis), findings would be arranged around descriptions of themes that are common across collected stories, just like many other qualitative research studies do (Polkinghorne, 1995). Clandinin and Connelly (2000) also note, "An inquirer composing a research text looks for the patterns, narrative threads, tensions, and themes either within or across an individual's experience and in the social setting" (p. 132). By identifying general themes and patterns, the goal of the analysis of narratives will be to minimize ambiguity and emphasize "reference at the expense of sense" (Bruner, 1986, p. 14).

Polkinghorne's analysis of narratives (paradigmatic mode of analysis) can be summarized as follows:

- It describes the categories of particular themes while paying attention to relationships among categories;

- It uncovers the commonalities that exist across the multiple sources of data; and
- It aims to produce general knowledge from a set of evidence or particulars found in a collection of stories, hence underplays the unique aspects of each story.

Narrative Analysis (Narrative Mode of Analysis)

Narrative analysis or narrative mode of analysis is based on narrative cognition that attends to the particular and special characteristics of human action that takes place in a particular setting. Polkinghorne (1995) remarks, "Narrative reasoning operates by noticing the differences and diversity of people's behavior. It attends to the temporal context and complex interaction of the elements that make each situation remarkable" (p. 6). Therefore, *narrative analysis (narrative mode of analysis)* that promotes the narrative mode of thought is about "the configuration of the data into a coherent whole" (Polkinghorne, 1995, p. 15) while sustaining the metaphoric richness of a story. It is a method of emplotting the data, in which we would analyze narrative data that consist of actions, events, and happenings, in order to produce coherent stories as an outcome of the analysis. We create stories (storying and restorying) by integrating events and happenings into a temporally organized whole with a thematic thread, called the plot. In this process, we use the method of narrative smoothing (Spence, 1986), as discussed earlier, to fill in the gaps between events and actions. In such stories we can capture "the richness and the nuances of meaning in human affairs" (Polkinghorne, 1995, p. 11), which cannot be expressed in "definitions, statements of fact, or abstract propositions" (p. 6). The purpose of the narrative mode of analysis is, then, to help the reader understand why and how things happened in the way they did, and why and how our participants acted in the way they did. The final story configured through the narrative mode of analysis has to appeal to readers in a way that helps them empathize with the protagonist's lived experience as understandable human phenomena. Polkinghorne's concept of the narrative mode of analysis has become an impetus of burgeoning "experimentations with a variety of literary genres for emplotting their data" (Barone, 2007, p. 456) (also discussed in Chapter 4). For a more detailed process of narrative mode of analysis, see Coulter and Smith (2009).

Polkinghorne's narrative analysis (narrative mode of analysis) can be summarized as follows:

- It focuses on the events, actions, happenings, and other data elements to put them together in a plot;
- It uses to-and-fro, recursive movement from parts to whole or from whole to parts;
- It fills in the gaps between events and actions using a narrative smoothing process;
- It maintains that narrative analysis is not merely a transcription of the data, but is a means of showing the significance of the lived experience in the final story;
- It makes the range of disconnected data elements coherent in a way that it appeals to the reader;

- It makes the final story congruent with the data while bringing narrative meanings that are not explicit in the data themselves; and
- It emphasizes connotation and sustains the metaphoric richness of a story.

Mishler's Models of Narrative Analysis

Elliot Mishler (1995) proposes a more detailed and comprehensive typology (than Polkinghorne's) of the models of narrative analysis that encompasses most of the narrative approaches available in the field of narrative inquiry. As he states, the models of narrative analysis reviewed in his typology demonstrate "the depth, strength, and diversity of the 'narrative turn' in the many sciences" (p. 117). Mishler's typology attempts to cover the ways in which narrative researchers "story the world," focusing on making meaning of events and experiences through the researcher's tellings and retellings of stories for different purposes in various contexts through various genres. That is, Mishler delineates a comparative perspective on differences of narrative inquiry in terms of theoretical aims and assumptions, types of data, analytic methods and strategies, and genres, based on the triad of language functions proposed by Halliday (1973): "reference, structure, and function" (p. 89). Mishler believes that narrative inquiry is a "problem-centered area of inquiry" (p. 89), hence, the models of narrative analysis we will use depend on our research problems. With his typology in which each model has its central task for narrative analysis, he provides a framework that will allow us to compare the problems, aims, foci, and methods across the different models (see Table 6.1).

I will explain what Mishler's typology entails in a minute, but I find his typology enlightening although Mishler humbly states that his proposed typology is "preliminary, tentative, incomplete" (Mishler, 1995, p. 89) with blurred boundaries. What is more encouraging, though, is that he cautions that narrowly focused approaches can be limiting, hence, it is important "to pursue alternative, more inclusive strategies that would provide a more comprehensive and deeper understanding both of how narratives work and of the work they do" (p. 117). I feel that he gives us permission to flirt with his typology as a departing point to "pursue alternative, more inclusive" methods of narrative analysis.

I have therefore slightly modified[6] his original typology in a way that would help me and other visual learners like some of you make better sense of it (see Figure 6.2). This modified version is also "preliminary, tentative, and incomplete"; therefore, I invite you to flirt with it to fit your analysis frame.

Overview of Mishler's Typology

To briefly provide an overview of Mishler's narrative typology, the methods in the first category, *Reference and temporal order: The "telling" and the "told,"* focus on reference as a problem of representation; specifically, looking for a correspondence between the temporal sequence of

Table 6.1 Mishler's Original Typology

Models of Narrative Analysis: A Typology

Reference and temporal order: The "telling" and the "told"

 Recapitulating the told in the telling

 Reconstructing the told from the telling

 Imposing a told on the telling

 Making a telling from the told

Textual coherence and structure: Narrative strategies

 Textual poetics: Figuration, tropes, and style

 Discourse linguistics: Oral narratives

Narrative functions: Contexts and consequences

 Narrativization of experience: Cognition, memory, self

 Narrative and culture: Myths, rituals, performance

 Storytelling in interactional and institutional contexts

 The politics of narrative: Power, conflict, and resistance

(Mishler, 1995, p. 90)

action events and their order of presentation in the data. The methods in the second category, *Textual coherence and structure: Narrative strategies,* are grounded in the structuralist theory of language, for example, deep structure and surface structure. They correspond with linguistics and narrative strategies, looking for ways in which unity and coherence are maintained in the narrative. These methods are more inclined toward spoken discourse than written texts, thus interested in ways of talking and telling, using the communicative functions of talking in their examination. Finally, the methods in the third category, *Narrative functions: Contexts and consequences,* correspond with "cultural, social and psychological context and functions of stories" (p. 90). The focus of the analysis of these methods is to illuminate the larger society through personal and group stories, using theoretical frameworks.

In this chapter, I focus on Category 1 only because the second category (textual coherence and structure) is extensively addressed in Riessman (2008) and Gee (2011), and it is also beyond the scope of this book. And the methods in the third category (narrative functions) can be explored based on your theoretical framework (see Chapter 2) and the narrative genre you employ (see Chapter 4).

Category 1. Reference and Temporal Order: The "Telling" and the "Told"

In narrative research, we frequently talk about "temporal order." According to Mishler (1995), there are two kinds of temporal order: *the order of the told* and *the order of the telling.* The former

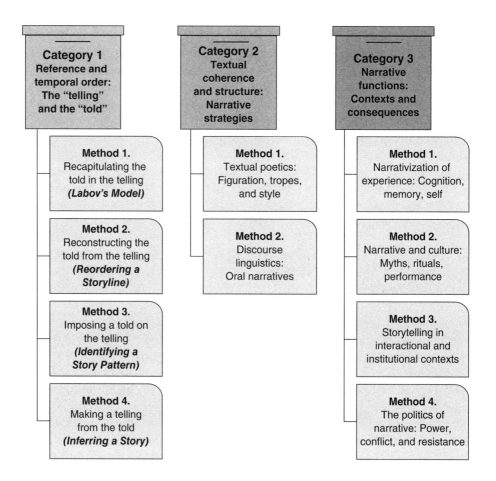

Figure 6.2 Modified Version of Mishler's Typology: Methods of Narrative Analysis

refers to the order of the narratives of events and action that were told by our participants, and the latter refers to the order of the narratives of events and action that we will represent in our research text. Thus, our central task in this category would be to establish a balance between the two kinds of temporal order. The *telling* means the researcher's narrating, and the *told* means the data that are told by the participant. From this perspective, the story (or stories) the researcher (re)tells will be "a series of temporally ordered events" (Mishler, 1995, p. 90) that represents the interpretation of the researcher. This category prioritizes sequences of events and their textual representations for the analysis, which includes four methods: *Recapitulating the told in the telling (Labov's model), Reconstructing the told from the telling, Imposing a told on the telling,* and *Making a telling from the told.*

Labov's Model[7]

Method 1. Recapitulating the Told in the Telling

This analysis method is used to identify what the "told" story is about. For this method, Mishler uses the sociolinguist William Labov's model as a conceptual framework since Labov specialized in an analysis of narratives of personal experience connecting the elements of language, meaning, and action. Mishler (1986a, 1986b, 1995) believes that **Labov's model** is a major resource for a narrative analysis method, and uses it as a point of departure and of reference. Although the limitations and criticisms of the Labovian model have been identified (see, for example, Patterson, 2013; Squire, 2013), his model still remains influential and is being used as a major framework of a method of narrative analysis with some modifications and adjustments (see Mishler, 1986a, 1986b, 1995; McCormack, 2004; Patterson, 2013; Riessman, 2008). It emphasizes recapturing the action and meaning of personal experience. I think that the Labovian model can serve as a narrative mode of thinking (Polkinghorne's narrative analysis) if we use it in a "flirting" manner to overcome possible criticism.

Labov defines narrative as a "recapitulation of experience that maintains the strict temporal ordering of events as they occurred in the real world" (cited in Mishler, 1986a, p. 236). Mishler (1995) adapts Labov and Waletzky's model (1967, cited in Mishler, 1995) in which the structure of a fully developed personal narrative consists of the following six components (see also Mishler, 1986a):

1. *Abstract:* a summary of the story and its points;

2. *Orientation:* providing a context such as place, time, and character to orient the reader;

3. *Complicating Action:* skeleton plot, or an event that causes a problem as in 'And then what happened?';

4. *Evaluation:* evaluative comments on events, justification of its telling, or the meaning that the teller gives to an event;

5. *Result or Resolution:* resolution of the story or the conflict; and

6. *Coda:* bringing the narrator and listener back to the present.

These six elements of a personal narrative give us a framework in which we can analyze the told stories. We could use them to reconstruct stories or to retell stories. Out of these six components, the fourth component, evaluative statements, is the most important element because these statements "reveal the attitude of the narrator towards the narrative by emphasizing the relative importance of some narrative units as compared to others" (Labov & Waletzky, 1967, cited in Mishler, 1995, p. 94). They are critical to our interpretation since they give us clues to understand the meaning that the tellers (our participants) give to their experiences.

The Labovian model has been influential in providing a means to analyze oral storytelling with plot or thematic criteria (the six components) as principles of structural organization in narrative. The main advantage is it helps us answer the question of what the story is about (De Fina & Georgakopoulou, 2012; Mishler, 1986a; Patterson, 2013). Mishler (1986a), for example, points out that determining the point of a story (what the story is about) is an important investigative problem because the main point of the story may not always be stated explicitly by the storyteller. Thus, finding out what the story is about from data requires our inference and interpretation. We can use the Labovian model to extract a core story in the process of narrative analysis by identifying the six elements from the told. We can also identify what our participant intends to communicate as the meaning of his or her narrative account. Another advantage of Labov's model is that it provides a general frame for understanding the narrative structure cross-culturally, bridging the gap between literary and vernacular storytelling (De Fina & Georgakopoulou, 2012). Moreover, it provides guidelines for "comparative analysis of collections of narratives from many respondents" (Mishler, 1986a, p. 236). For example, we could compare the type of evaluation, multiple participants' different evaluations of the same event, or changes of the evaluation within the same interview (Patterson, 2013). Or, we could compare the evaluations of the experience of the same event made by different storytellers based on race, gender, ethnicity, socio-economic status, and more.

However, these advantages come with shortcomings. If you are interested in conversational narratives, interactional discourses, or co-construction of the story between you and the participant, the Labovian model will not fit, hence, you might want to think about using the methods in Category 2. The critique is that Labov's model largely depends on monological narratives told in interviews, such as oral history interviews or life story interviews (De Fina & Georgakopoulou, 2012) rather than conversational interviews.

Now, is it possible to flirt with the Labovian model in an effort to address such criticisms? I think so. How about adding another component? For example, the third component, *Complicating Action,* refers to an event that causes a problem. However, I would say that it's not just an event that will create a problem. Other human issues like anxieties, expectations, desires, wishes, failures, future developments, and the like, which are not considered events by Labov, might have complicated our storyteller's life. Or there might be epiphanies. Turning points. Can we include them as a narrative component? Why not? In fact, Mishler advises us not to follow the Labovian model as fixed and absolute, which is considered one of the problems of the model. He says we can use it as a point of departure. Using the Labovian model as a foundation, we can create our own model, depending on what the focus of our research is. To me, the Labovian model can be expanded, modified, and elaborated. Thus, we can flirt with it. Patterson (2013) seems to agree with me as she states, "There are many ways in which narrative analysts can utilize the valuable aspects of Labov's work by using more inclusive definitional criteria" (p. 43).

Method 2. Reconstructing the Told From the Telling: Reordering a Storyline

This analysis is about putting the told in temporal order, or reordering a storyline. When you analyze the data, you will probably realize that the told (stories told by your participant) is not in order (e.g., chronologically or conceptually) in a way that would make sense to you or the reader, which is a typical problem narrative researchers encounter in data analysis. Participants may not tell their stories in any particular order, hence their stories are somewhat inconsistent, and they often digress from a storyline or make general comments that don't have a clear focus. Our participants may not be linear thinkers; they might zigzag with their stories depending on what they believe is important for the moment. In addition, we have multiple sources of data from which we need to extract sense-making stories. Faced with these issues, we'll have to reassemble or rearrange the told from interviews and other sources of data into chronologically or thematically coherent stories (depending on your research purpose), which is similar to Polkinghorne's narrative mode of analysis (narrative analysis). We have to reorder (reconstruct) a storyline from the telling(s). And this reconstructed story becomes the "narrative for further analysis" (Mishler, 1995, p. 95).

Method 3. Imposing a Told on the Telling: Identifying a Story Pattern

This method is about having predetermined themes for a story, or identifying a story pattern. For example, if you have a large set of data from a large number of participants, you may want to find some commonalities, generalities, and differences across the data (similar to Polkinghorne's analysis of narratives). To be able to compare and contrast different stories, you might want to have a standard format to elicit narrative accounts on the same topics from multiple participants. It is like having structured interviews with many different participants. You will have a list of standardized questions that are constructed around the topics that you want. According to Mishler, this method is effective when we have a large number of participants and want to discover generalities from the large data sets. We will give instructions to our participants to tell a story on certain topics. For example, in Veroff and colleague's study of newlyweds, the selected couples were asked to

> [t]ell a story of their relationship in their own words, following a storyline guide that read: "how you met; how you got interested in one another; becoming a couple; planning to get married; what married life is like right now; and what you think married life will be like in the future." (Veroff, Chadiha, Leber, & Sutherland, cited in Mishler, 1995, p. 99)

Hence, the story patterns identified were the way of a couple's meeting, the way a couple got interested in each other, the way they become a couple, and so on. This method will be good for standard coding procedure because story sequences will be invariant and good for constructing a "prototypical narrative representation" (Mishler, 1995, p. 99) of a certain topic, for example, what it is like to lose the first job.

However, I want to point out that themes are not always predetermined. In fact, often times, themes are later identified as you analyze the data (identifying emergent themes). Hence, I would extend the meaning of "imposing a told on the telling" from predetermined patterns to include emerging ones.

Method 4. Making a Telling From the Told: Inferring a Story

This method is to infer a story from nonverbal data. It will be useful especially when we have multiple types of data, such as visual data or artifacts that are not in a spoken or written form. That is, if you have data that are storied in visual or archival forms, or in artifacts, you will have to *make (infer)* a telling from the told. Making a telling means that you the researcher will write a story inferred from the told in non-textual form. For example, historians will have to use a huge amount of archival data to narrate large-scale social processes and events. If you have visual data, photographs, drawings, or artifacts, you'll have to "make a telling from the told" in a way that complements or counters other types of narratives. In this method, it is you the researcher who is representing a temporal ordering of events and action; as Mishler (1995) states, "It is the researcher who is doing the telling" (p. 102).

Flirting With Polkinghorne, Mishler, and Labov

You see that I embrace Polkinghorne, Mishler, and Labov here. Why? They all help us excavate stories from our data rather than decontextualize them into bits and pieces that we see in qualitative research in general. They ask us to see narrative meanings reflected in recapitulated or reconstructed stories. In particular, what I like about Mishler is that he does not ask us to favor one method over the others. Rather, he encourages us to learn from different methods and value each of them:

> Those of us who study narrative genres and strategies of textualization might strengthen our research, both theoretically and empirically, by attending more explicitly to the contexts of tellings and their personal and social functions. And the parallel point: Analyses of psychological and political functions of narratives might benefit by detailed analyses of their structures and modes of textualization. (Mishler, 1995, p. 117)

Polkinghorne (1995) complements Mishler's open-mindedness by stating:

> Although both types [analysis of narrative and narrative analysis] of narrative inquiry are concerned with stories, they have significant differences. The paradigmatic type collects storied accounts for its data; the narrative type collects description of events, happenings, and actions . . . that produce storied accounts. . . . Both types of narrative inquiry can make important contributions to the body of social science knowledge. (p. 21)

Polkinghorne, Mishler, and Labov allow us to let stories be told in different narrative genres through the methods of narrative analysis, which then become the basis for further discussions and implications.

One good example study that utilizes both Polkinghorne and Mishler's Method 1, *Recapitulating the told in the telling (Labov's model),* is McCormack (2004). She explains how to story stories based on Polkinghorne's distinction between narrative analysis and analysis of narratives, and suggests locating a story in the data that incorporates Labov's model of the six story components. McCormack asks us to compose an interpretive story after each interview as an alternative to the traditional approach. These interpretive stories, then, will be "nested" (p. 13) within a personal experience narrative that is produced as our final product. For McCormack, hence, narrative analysis becomes "the process of storying stories" (p. 13).

Figure 6.3 summarizes my flirtation with Polkinghorne, Mishler, and Labov, echoing their open-mindedness and open-heartedness (like we saw in Dali's sculpture in Chapter 1), which may result in one of the narrative genres.

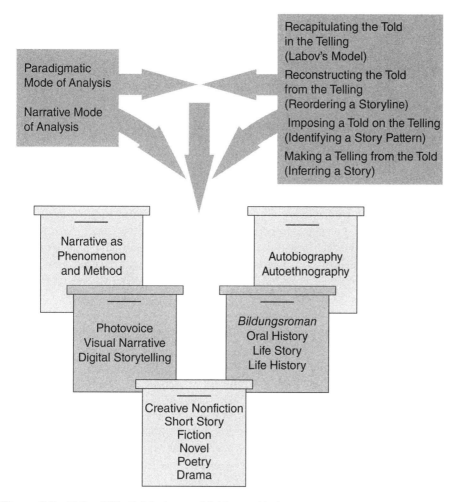

Figure 6.3 Flirting With Polkinghorne, Mishler, and Labov

Narrative Analysis in Narrative Genres

Recall a discussion in Chapter 4 (Narrative Genres) about how our task as "researcher-storytellers" (Barone, 2007, p. 468) is to mediate stories into being as the story is "always mediated" (Abbott, 2002, p. 20). Hence, we are to undertake "this mediation from beginning to end" (Connelly & Clandinin, 1990, p. 8). For the role of mediation of stories, I used a metaphor of a midwife who is positioned as a mediator between the demands of research that addresses the larger landscape and the personal meaning in individual stories. The midwife is to apply her *phronesis* (wise, ethical judgment) as "particular kinds of wakefulness" (Clandinin, Pushor, & Orr, 2007, p. 21) to the stories we mediate, while taking into consideration the three dimensions of narrative inquiry: temporality, the personal and social, and the place. We researcher-storytellers mediate stories, sustaining the spirit of "flirtation" that asks us to challenge our tendency or adherence to what we already know and to question its legitimacy by dwelling on uncertainties and perplexities (interpretation of suspicion).

With this in mind, now, let's look into how these narrative analysis methods are utilized in different narrative genres. Some examples will help.

Analysis in Narrative as Phenomenon and Method:
Broadening, Burrowing, and Restorying

When Connelly and Clandinin (1990) established the importance of narrative inquiry as an educational research methodology, they viewed narrative inquiry as both phenomenon and method. First, narrative inquiry as a phenomenon is the "what" of the study, that is, to study an experience as phenomenon. Hence, we need to think about how to respond to the following questions: What is my narrative inquiry about? What experience am I studying? The "what" of the study as research phenomenon is not like a still life painting. It's always shifting, moving, and complex. Hence, we cannot assume that our research phenomenon will be the same one that was explained clearly in the proposal (Clandinin & Connelly, 2000). It is highly recommended that we identify our inquiry phenomena as they appear in the data during data analysis.

Next, narrative inquiry as method refers to thinking narratively as a way of thinking about phenomena, as we discussed in Chapter 3. Clandinin and Connelly (2000) suggest that thinking narratively during analysis involves "negotiating relationships, negotiating purposes, negotiating ways to be useful, and, negotiating transitions" (p. 129) while keeping in mind theoretical, methodological, and interpretive considerations. To get to a meaningful act of narrative analysis with the approaches of both faith and suspicion without compromising our ethics of interpretation, we will need to *narratively code* our field texts to find narrative meanings (Clandinin & Connelly, 2000). For example, we will pay careful attention to:

names of characters that appear in field texts, places where actions and events occurred, story lines that interweave and interconnect, gaps or silences that become apparent, tensions that emerge, and continuities and discontinuities that appear are all possible codes. . . . However, it is responses to the questions of meaning and social significance that ultimately shape field texts into research texts. (Clandinin & Connelly, 2000, p. 131)

For narrative coding, Connelly and Clandinin (1990) suggest three analytical tools for narrative inquiry: *broadening, burrowing,* and *storying and restorying.* They used these analytical tools to analyze and seam together the narrative material they gathered. With the assistance of these interpretive devices, they transitioned from their interim field texts to research texts (Clandinin & Connelly, 2000).

The first tool, *broadening,* has to do with looking for a (broader) context of the story, including a description of the participant, implied in a told story. It is about making a general description of the participant's character or values, or of the social, historical, or cultural milieus in which your research takes place by looking at your field notes and the literature review. Similarly, Mishler (1986a) calls the concept of broadening *expansion.* He suggests that the narrative researcher introduce more general knowledge of the culture than is contained in the text itself to be able to interpret a broader cultural framework of meaning as part of narrative analysis. Through the analytical tool of broadening or expansion, we are to bring into the analysis "what else we know about the storytellers and their local and general circumstances" (Mishler, 1986a, p. 244).

Another tool is *burrowing.* It is used to focus on more specific details of the data. We make a thorough investigation of our data. For example, we pay attention to the participants' feelings, understandings, or dilemmas, or a certain event's impacts on the participants or the surroundings. We also ask questions about why and how the happenings have influenced the lived experiences of our participants. Burrowing relates to the details that are experienced by our participants from their points of view.

The third analytical tool is *storying and restorying.* After broadening the data and burrowing into them, we find ways to story and restory them so that the significance of the lived experience of the participant comes to the fore. Craig (2012), for example, uses these three analytic tools to excavate teachers' knowledge in context. She transforms the field texts into research texts using the three devices. With broadening, she situates the particular reform endeavor of her research school within the history of school reform in the United States; with burrowing, she concentrates on a certain phenomenon, such as an individual teacher's unfolding image of teaching. As for storying and restorying, Craig captures a story of her participant while revisiting past experiences across time and place.

Some of you might wonder whether to use computer software for narrative analysis, such as Atlas.ti., NVivo, or HyperResearch. More and more qualitative researchers increasingly use them to alleviate the complexity and complication of the analysis process. However, these computer programs should be used with caution and adaptation in narrative research as they are paradigmatic analysis in which codes, patterns, and themes are identified. For example, Clandinin and Connelly (2000) do not find these programs particularly useful for narrative inquiry. You have to determine for yourself how computer software will be helpful in storying and restorying to fit your research agenda.

Analysis in Autoethnography

As I quoted in Chapter 4, Ellis, Adams, and Bochner (2011) state, "Autoethnography is an approach to research and writing that seeks to describe and systematically analyze *(graphy)* personal experience *(auto)* in order to understand cultural experience *(ethno)*" (para. 1, italics added). They posit that autoethnography is not only a process and product but also a method that we use to systematically analyze the researcher's personal experience. Then, how do we systematically analyze our own personal experience, giving rise to the "I," the self? What are the possibilities?

Autoethnography writes about our past experiences in retrospect. We will select particular epiphanies from our past experience. Epiphanies are sudden leaps of understanding of events that have significantly impacted the trajectory of our life. They are "recollections, memories, images, feelings—long after a crucial incident is supposedly finished" (Ellis et al., 2011, para. 6). Epiphanies that reflect a culture, or one's cultural identities, are selected for an analysis. Ellis et al. (2011) maintain:

> Autoethnographers must not only use their methodological tools and research literature to analyze experience, but also must consider ways others may experience similar epiphanies; they must use personal experience to illustrate facets of cultural experience, and, in so doing, make characteristics of a culture familiar for insiders and outsiders. (para. 9)

If you are more inclined to analytic autoethnography in which you would collect data from and about people other than you, the researcher, including other data sources such as official documents and media accounts (see Vryan, 2006), you might want to pay attention to five key features that Anderson (2006) proposes:

- The researcher is a full member in a research group or setting;
- The researcher uses analytic reflexivity;
- The researcher presents narrative visibility of the researcher's self in the written text;
- The researcher engages in dialogue with informants beyond the self; and
- The researcher is committed to developing theoretical understanding of broader social phenomena.

I present Ronai's layered account (1995) as a good example of autoethnographic analysis. It uses methodological tools and research literature to analyze the researcher's personal experience. It is aesthetic, evocative, as well as analytic. It engages the reader, and maintains the characteristics of autoethnography, discussed in Chapter 4.

Example: Autoethnographic Analysis (A Layered Account)

A layered account is a juxtaposition between the author's experience and relevant literature. It is a narrative form designed to present to the reader a continuous dialogue of experience between the author and the author's self, emerging from the multitude of reflexive voices that simultaneously describe, analyze, critique, and interpret a text (Ellis et al., 2011). It presents layers of experience and analysis in which spaces are created for readers to fill with their own interpretation of an autoethnographic story. The layered account illustrates how story and analysis can proceed simultaneously, embodying "a theory of consciousness and a method of reporting in one stroke" (Ronai, 1995, p. 396).

Carol Rambo Ronai (1995), an established autoethnographer in sociology, wrote an autoethnography in a layered account to convey her story of being a survival of child sex abuse. To analyze the participant observational data of her own experience, Ronai used systematic sociological introspection as her method, as she wrote:

> When I write about my social world, I codify myself on paper. I produce an ad-hoc self, . . . reflecting and changing my words in a reflexive manner. I write myself, I edit myself, interacting with the self I wrote by objectifying it, judging it, and rewriting it in response. Each time I write and reflect, I view myself as an object while simultaneously being an active subject. The writing subject interacts with the written object. The written self is adjusted or rewritten in response to changes in the internal dialogue about the self. The dialogue about the written self emerges from being the audience while reading the text, making a judgment while in that pose, and then reflecting on that particular presentation of self. (p. 399)

For her method, the layered accounts are separated by dots between the layers, to compare and contrast her personal experience of child sexual abuse against existing research to make a point that her experience is unique on the one hand, but also how the existing literature shows she is not unique on the other (p. 402). She and her self become the subject and the object of her autoethnography, using her own case as data. Here is an excerpt.

* * *

These memories sicken me. They simultaneously interfere with the righteousness of my victim status and stagger me with the realization of how victimized I was. That I orgasmed makes what he did "not so bad." To my father, that meant I like it and should not complain. The confused little girl I was believed that there was something wrong with her because she did not always like it, that she was "just a big baby."

* * *

Child sex abuse establishes relations between the victim and society. The enforcement of law as against child sex abuse involves serious consequences, such as breaking up the family through arrest of one or both parents (Bagely & King 1990). Social interaction flows more smoothly when child sex abuse is not discussed because it is easier not to take action. (p. 417)

Ronai writes her autoethnography to produce "aesthetic and evocative thick descriptions of personal and interpersonal experience" (Ellis et al., 2011, para. 14). She engages the reader in a way that appeals to "the authority of the readers' own experiences of the text" (Ronai, 1995, p. 399), creating internal dialogues among the readers themselves provoked by her text. Ronai writes an evocative autoethnography to use it as a bridge spanning "the gulf between public and private life" (p. 420) by making intimate details of her life accessible in public discourse. In doing so, she makes the personal social to reach broader and more diverse audiences that traditional research has usually failed to reach.

Analysis in *Bildungsroman*: Story of Personal Growth

In Chapter 4, we discussed that *Bildungsroman* is a story of one's *Bildung* that cultivates and forms one's disposition of mind through intellectual and moral endeavor. It is a story of developing oneself and of one's journey of becoming. It is a story of a quest to find one's true self, whose process consists of life challenges, conflicts between "the protagonist's needs and desires and the views and judgments enforced by social order" (Dunlop, 2002, p. 218). Given the features of *Bildungsroman* that we discussed in Chapter 4, our analysis of *Bildungsroman* will focus on:

- The idea of an inner or spiritual journey of personal growth;
- The tension between the ideal and the reality;
- The importance of context in which the protagonist's personal journey takes place;
- The role of enhancing the *Bildung* of the researcher and the reader;
- The importance of questioning, dialogue, and doubt in personal journey; and
- The elements of striving, uncertainty, complexity, and transformation.

(Adapted from Roberts, 2008)

Example: Female *Bildungsroman*

Boundary Bay (Dunlop, 1999) is Rishma Dunlop's dissertation novel based on her research on the lives of beginning teachers, university professors, and programs of teacher education. It is the story of Evelyn Greene, a newly appointed university professor teaching in a faculty of education. Dunlop (2002) explains the process of how she came to work on a female *Bildungsroman* through her narrative inquiry:

Boundary Bay began with tape-recorded data collection in the form of semi-structured qualitative research interviews with a group of five volunteer participants, newly graduated teachers from the same teacher education program (specializing in secondary art and English). Specific questions were explored, dealing with the nature of the first year of teaching experience and the transition from teacher education training into the classroom. The purpose was to conduct a narrative inquiry into the nature of lived experiences in the first years of teaching, the integration of experiences in teacher education and classroom teaching, and the negotiation of mentorship and educational experiences at the university level. Of particular interest was the implementation of English literature and arts-based curricula.

Over a period of two and a half years, I realized that the narrative inquiry we were collectively engaged in had come to include some difficult stories about the personal, emotional, and intellectual impact of teaching lives at multiple levels of institutional life. I also felt that I could convey these stories in the form of fiction, a novel that could uphold the literary traditions of the *Bildungsroman*, the novel of education or formation, and the *Künstlerroman*, the novel of the artist's growth to maturity. In addition, as a challenge to the conventions of the male hero of the *Bildungsroman*, this novel is a woman's story, told primarily from a female narrator's perspective with a central focus on concerns about women and education. (p. 219)

Dunlop's *Bildungsroman* is a research product that consists of her own interpretation of a broad range of considerations based on her research findings. She states that her work is not a critical analysis; rather, it is a work of art that attempts to interpret the world, and is open to interpretation by readers. She shows us how her dissertation process evolved into a *Bildungsroman,* a move "far beyond her original intention of working with transcribed narratives" (p. 219).

Analysis in Biographical Narrative Inquiry

In Chapter 4, we learned that a biographical movement spread all over the world in the 1980s. We also learned that biographical narrative inquiry informs us of the knowledge that is historical, social, and personal. Biographical narrative inquiry includes oral history, life story, and life history, which focus on people's lives as a way of knowing.

As we attempt to analyze other people's stories, understanding some cautions about biographical narrative approach might be critical. Munro (1998) states that she engages in life history research with some suspicion although she is so attracted to it. First, she understands that life history is a method that would "give voice" to people who have traditionally been marginalized, but the talk of "giving voice" implies an unequal power structure between the researcher and the participants. Second, a focus on the individual story tends to romanticize the participant and thus reify notions of a unitary subject/hero, deviating from the complexities of the individual life that is mired in racism, sexism, and other forms of oppression. Lastly, Munro is concerned about a reiterating potential of colonizing effects of life history research as it might reproduce "positivistic notions of power, knowledge and subjectivity despite claims to the contrary" (p. 12). Munro's point is that narrative does not automatically provide a better way of knowing truth. Therefore, Munro (1998) posits that we need to:

Attend to the silences as well as what is said, that we need to attend to how the story is told as well as what is told or not told, and to attend to the tensions and contradictions rather than to succumb to the temptations to gloss over these in our desire for "the" story. (p. 13)

Example: Life History

Petra Munro's *Subject to Fiction* (1998) is a life history of three women teachers, whom Munro called life historians, including Agnes, Cleo, and Bonnie. Munro states, "The heart of the book is the three narratives that I have constructed" (p. 13). From a poststructural feminist perspective, Munro interrogated ways to think about the agency and resistance that permeate women teachers' stories, challenging the notion of gendered construction of teaching (as "schoolmarms," for example) and ways of treating women teachers as objects of knowledge. The research questions that guided her research were:

- How do women teachers resist the naming of their experiences by others, which distorts and marginalizes their realities?
- How do they construct themselves as subjects despite the fictions constructed about women teachers? (p. 3)

To answer these questions, Munro focused on "the manner of the telling," which she viewed as "the authoring of oneself through story" (p. 5), in which she treated her participants as life historians or authors of their life who gave meanings to their own lives. Munro used interviews as the primary source of data, including in-depth life history interviews. In order to establish a broad context for understanding these life histories, Munro had supplementary interviews with colleagues, administrators, and students. Other sources of data were artifacts, which include teaching materials, photographs, journals, school documents, favorite books, and newspaper articles, and historical data regarding the communities. With this wide range of data sets, here is how Munro worked on her participants' stories:

> My relationships in the field not only provided my primary source of data, but these relationships became the epistemological base from which my interpretations and knowledge claims originated. In constructing the stories of Agnes, Cleo and Bonnie, I incorporate my own story throughout as a means of acknowledging the intersubjective nature of knowledge. I weave my own story of the research process throughout the life histories as a way to create a "tapestry" of our lives, an interweaving of connections, which is not only central to women's survival, but an epistemological act. (p. 11)

The stories of the three women teachers are examples of how Munro reconstructed the told from the telling as in Mishler's method, focusing on the told in the telling. Each story is indeed a "tapestry" of the told (narratives) and Munro's constant reflexive accounts as a way to rethink notions of power, agency, and subjectivity.

Example: Oral History

Leavy and Ross (2006) examined an oral history of Claire, a college student with an eating disorder, to create a link between personal problems and social problems. Their project began because Claire wanted to share a story about her own battle with a life-threatening eating disorder with the hopes of helping others. Claire's story focused on her own question, "How did I get here?" and revealed that "her eating disorder began in college, but her story began in childhood" (p. 66). Using one woman's narrative about a personal eating disorder, Leavy and Ross intended to illuminate a larger social phenomenon, provoking the reader's "sociological imagination" (Mills, 1959) at the intersection of the personal biographical history and the social one. They analyzed Claire's story with a thematic analysis that attended to what is said, or *the told* in Mishler's term, adopting the method of *the analysis of narratives* in Polkinghorne's term. They wrote:

> We analyzed the transcripts from the oral history, which include researcher notes added during transcription, in three phases: 1) line-by-line, 2) thematically, and 3) holistically by hand. First, through line-by-line analysis major code categories began to emerge. Next, we placed excerpts from the transcript under thematic codes that developed inductively out of the analysis process. These codes include perfectionism, control, independence/autonomy, disappointment, and projection of self. When discussing "disappointments" we placed this code under the larger category of "triggers," which is common terminology in regard to eating disorders. (2006, p. 68)

Then Leavy and Ross developed these codes into the themes of: *Striving for Perfection, Yearning for Control, Autonomy as a Central Value,* and *A Web of Pressures: Look at Me, I'm Shrinking,* and each theme was discussed through the analysis of Claire's narratives, interweaving their interpretations in the discussion (see Chapter 9 for more discussion on this article). As they retold Claire's story, they also realized how these themes were interconnected, shedding light on the reasons why some people might be more susceptible to an eating disorder than others. They noted that it was not until data analysis that they were able to understand the presence of particular themes at various moments throughout Claire's life.

Leavy and Ross conclude that during data analysis of the interview transcript both "thematically and holistically" (p. 81), they were able to see how Claire's unique personal story is linked to the general sociological "story" of eating disorders, common among college-age females. They show how oral history narratives can become a vehicle for personalizing social problems or socializing personal problems. They state, "Through the process of interpretation we have been able to use Claire's story to personalize the much more general matrix of eating disorder vulnerability" (p. 81).

The thematic analysis Leavy and Ross adopted for their oral history project is commonly used by narrative inquirers. The emphasis is on "the told," the events or the content of the narratives, paying little attention to how a story unfolds in a conversational exchange between the interviewer and the participant (Riessman, 2008). In thematic narrative analysis, we are not necessarily interested in the form of the narrative, but rather its thematic meanings and points as they emerge in the process of recapitulating the told in the telling (Mishler, 1986a). Thus, the focus is on "the act the narrative reports and the moral of the story" (Riessman, 2008, p. 62).

Example: Life Story

Gubrium and Holstein (1995) analyze their biographical work (life stories) of ethnographic narratives gathered in nursing homes, family therapy, and community mental health agencies. They asked their participants to tell their life stories in relation to the quality of their life and the care they received in nursing homes. With the following focus question, "If residents were asked to be the ethnographers of their own lives in the nursing home, how would the quality of those lives be construed?" (p. 48), they analyzed the interview data using three analytic terms as guides to the participants' interpretive practice through which research participants understand, organize, and represent experience. The three analytic terms are *narrative linkages, local culture,* and *organizational embeddedness.*

First, *narrative linkages* refer to "the experiences that residents linked together to specify the subjective meaning of the qualities of care and nursing home living" (p. 48). The participants' interpretive practice appearing in the narrative linkages becomes the researchers' focus, as the narrative linkages can tell the researchers how the participants came to understand the quality of their nursing home living. Narrative linkages can inform researchers that narratives are carefully constructed communications in a certain time and context, offering a "complex sense of biographical patterning" (p. 48). Through the analysis of narrative linkages, Gubrium and Holstein found that residents' narratives had clear implications for the quality assessment of the nursing home from their own terms, suggesting that a standardized quality assessment system is irrelevant.

Another analytic term is *local culture,* which "refers to the locally shared meanings and interpretive vocabularies" (p. 50) that participants use to construct their experience. Gubrium and Holstein compared how two different family therapy programs have their own local culture that interprets the meaning of functional/dysfunctional families differently from each other. Thus, each local culture provides particular interpretive resources through which participants assign meaning to their life experiences. This local culture, which is diverse and context specific, can illuminate the more abstract, larger culture shared by the general public.

The third, *organizational embeddedness,* shows how the structure of an organization, including its missions, professional visions, and mandates, affects the participants' interpretive practice, projecting "institutionally salient priorities and agendas" (p. 53). Gubrium and Holstein provide the case of Charles, a twelve-year-old client, as an example of how the various departments and programs of a multidisciplinary child guidance clinic interpreted Charles's life and problems differently, eventually referring him to different service programs, from the clinic's delinquency-prevention program, to the psychosocial intervention program, and to medical treatment for hyperactivity. Gubrium and Holstein observed, "As the case moved between these organizational and professional outlooks, its interpretive jurisdiction changed. In the process, Charles's life was alternatively characterized in related biographical vocabularies" (p. 55).

By foregrounding the life stories of participants, Gubrium and Holstein articulated how participants' interpretive understandings are mediated through the three analytic terms, *narrative linkages, local culture,* and *organizational embeddedness,* offering more distinctive and meaningful understandings about social issues and problems.

Analysis in Arts-Based Narrative Inquiry

In Chapter 4, we learned how arts-based narrative inquiry has the benefits of promoting empathy, esthetic experience, and epiphanies that will enlarge the reader's horizon. There are many researchers in the social and human sciences who use the arts as a method and a product of their research. In fact, arts-based research is currently thriving. However, here I limit my discussion of arts-based inquiry to narrative inquiry that uses the arts to enhance its role. I focus on literary-based narrative inquiry (Creative Nonfiction/Short Story/Fiction/Novel) and visual-based narrative inquiry (Photographic Narrative/Photovoice/Archival Photographs).

Example: Literary-Based Narrative Inquiry (Literary Storytelling)

My beloved doctoral advisor, Tom Barone, who has been happily retired to his home state, Louisiana, for a couple of years now, has written numerous influential books and articles on narrative inquiry and curriculum. As I mentioned before, he is the one who helped me develop the love of narrative inquiry through his teaching. His research and teaching have made an enduring influence on me as a teacher and researcher of narrative inquiry. One of his well-known books, *Touching Eternity: The Enduring Outcomes of Teaching* (2001), is an investigation of the meaning of teacher-student encounters within the life narratives of those who lived them. More specifically, it is a quest for the long-term influences a high school teacher in North Carolina, Don Forrister, had on some of his former students. The shape of this book, Barone explains, was influenced by the turn toward "narrative research" and "a literary turn in human studies" (p. 2). The life stories of the teacher and his nine former students, Barone states, "generally exhibit characteristics of imaginative literature, including expressive, evocative language and an aesthetic form. The book may, therefore, be considered a work of *arts-based research*" (p. 2, italics in original). So, what does arts-based narrative research (literary-based) look like?

Based on interviews and other supplementary research materials, Barone presents an exemplary **literary-based narrative inquiry**. To provide life stories of his participants as "literary constructions" (p. 35), he flirts (or "experiments" [p. 35], to use his own word) with the raw data to try out different discursive features such as textual formatting, language style, narrative tone, and emplotment strategies. Barone frequently uses "fashion," "craft," "construct," "compose," and "reconfigure" to signify his engagement with literary-based narrative inquiry. Barone uses Polkinghorne's narrative analysis (or what Barone calls narrative construction) as his main narrative strategy, while incorporating Mishler's models to present biographical and autobiographical stories that are crafted around themes identified by the informants.

Barone emphasizes the use of story titles or subheadings as the theme "related to prominent shifts in life plots" (p 168), which serves as a means to structure the interviews and the emerging story as well as a means for "qualitative control" of each story that helps the researcher determine details to be elicited and included (and those to be ignored and excluded) in the developing story. He uses the *narrative smoothing* strategy based on his interpretation of the data, carefully enough to leave the choice of theme "sacred, untouchable" (p. 169), as he never attempts to influence an informant's judgment about the teacher's significance in his or her life story.

Part II of the book consists of nine students' stories and Part III is the story of Don Forrister. In the beginning of each story, Barone briefly explains his "experiments" with textual formats, some of which I provide below, as they give us valuable insights into how we can flirt with our own literary-based narrative inquiry.

- The Story of the College Teacher[8]

  The life story of former student, now college teacher, Carolyn Wilson (pseudonym) represents a joint effort. The story is crafted primarily out of the information that I gathered in conversations with Carolyn and autobiographical materials previously written by her. In fashioning the life story, I have employed a particular literary conceit in order to avoid a relatively seamless chronological story form. (p. 36)

- The Story of the Waiter

  The following life story is an experimental blend of biography and autobiography. The story is crafted out of the memories of Barry Larson (pseudonym) and the results of his conversations with significant others in his life, as related in several interview sessions. . . . It moves beyond the interview text only in the spirit of Barry's theme. This is primarily a work of nonfiction (in the usual sense of that term). I have, however, taken certain storytelling liberties, while always remaining faithful to Barry's sense of the essential impact of Forrister on his life. (pp. 55–56)

- The Story of the Teacher, Don Forrister[9]

  Composed out of lengthy discussions between Forrister and myself, this section focuses on the person who is Don Forrister, revealing the origins of his artistic nature and the wellsprings of his pedagogy, even the content of his dreams . . .
      Although the story is cast as a biography, written in the third person, it is autobiographical insofar as it recounts an honest version of life experiences from Forrister's perspective. (p. 105)

Barone also notes that Don Forrister's persona is reconstructed and reconfigured through the prisms of the stories of many former students, as well as his own and the researcher's own. In so doing, certain familiar events are revisited, and sometimes rewritten, seen from a different angle, even an opposing slant, thus suggesting the fragility of memories.

Barone's work teaches us how we can transition from field texts to research text using narrative analysis (narrative mode of analysis) to create literary-based narrative inquiry, including creative nonfiction, biography, or life history. While Barone acknowledges that his book does not reach the level of metaphor-laden imaginative literature, he places his work more toward the "narrative/artistic side of the research continuum" (p. 155) than the paradigmatic mode of knowing. For this narrative construction (which is the same as Polkinghorne's concept, narrative analysis), Barone explains that he had to use his imagination to "fill in holes" to compose a vivid story while remaining faithful to the theme of the interview (narrative smoothing method). Thus, Barone becomes "the biographer of teacher and students, even as they tell stories about themselves and others" (p. 167). In so doing, he attempts to "play two games at once" (p. 171). That is, on the one hand, he has a felt need to speak in an analytical voice about motifs confronted within his conversations with the participants. On the other, he wants to honor the life stories of participants before theorizing them.

Example: Visual-Based Narrative Inquiry (Visual Storytelling)[10]

In Chapter 4, I drew upon photographic narratives, originated from Conceptual Art, to discuss how we can use visual data to broaden/deepen/strengthen narrative inquiry. **Visual storytelling** is a powerful means to help us better understand human experiences. The visual turn in narrative studies is an intersection between visual studies in the social sciences and narrative studies. For example, the use of photography (along with other visual images) is valued for its potential to redirect, contest, and unlock the gaze in order to promote social awareness and justice (Luttrell, 2010). Riessman (2013) points out, "Photographers and other visual artists sequence images in ways that invite narrative inquiry" (p. 258). However, according to Riessman, one of the untapped areas in narrative research is using visual materials that tell stories.

Photovoice

A popular method of collecting visual data is **photovoice**, which was briefly discussed in Chapter 4. It is a method that allows participants to produce images, and more specifically, it "puts cameras in the hands of people who have been left out of policy decision-making, or denied access to and participation in matters that concern their daily lives" (Luttrell, 2010, p. 226). Luttrell conducted a longitudinal study in an elementary school that is located in a neighborhood that is racially, ethnically, linguistically, and economically diverse. She used the photovoice method to interrogate the relationships between image, voice, and narrative that were constructed by the child participants from their own perspectives. The participating children, mainly in fifth and sixth grade, were each given a disposable analog camera with 27 exposures and either four days or one to two weeks to take pictures of their school, family, and community lives. They were given little guidance except for basic instructions about using the camera and a discussion about the ethics of picture-taking issues. Following the picture-taking sessions, the participants were interviewed individually and in groups, four times, about their pictures. The aim of the study was "to use the children's photographs, narrations and self representations with teachers and educators-in-training as a means to enhance their awareness of children's funds of knowledge" (p. 226). Luttrell carried out a picture content analysis and an analysis of the children's narratives about their photographs. Below is a list of sample coding systems that Luttrell used for the picture content analysis:

- Setting (e.g., family, school, community, inside, outdoors);
- People (e.g., children/adults, male/female, age and gender mix);
- Things (e.g., technological, household items, personal possessions, toys and games);
- Genre (e.g., snapshot, landscape, portrait);
- Social relationships;

- Activity types (e.g., work, play, socializing);
- Activity level (e.g., low, medium, high);
- Gaze (e.g., looking at the camera, looking away from camera with smile or not), and;
- Things that the children noticed in each other's photographs (e.g., brand name items, hand signs, and babies).

While she provides some cautions about conducting a photovoice project with young people, Luttrell (2010) points out what children's (photo)voices and narratives imply:

> In a context of neo-liberal social policies that have had adverse effects on young people's care worlds—whether immigration policy, welfare reform or a test-driven educational system that pushes out those who cannot measure up—these young people's images and narratives provide a glimpse of the social connections that they see and value, if not fear may be at risk. Perhaps the children's voices and concerns are ahead of social theorists and policy makers who have ignored the centrality and intimacies of care giving and care taking, and we need to take heed. (p. 234)

Archival Photographs: Parallel Stories Between Visual Data[11] and Textual Data

I wish I had incorporated visual images into my narrative inquiry dissertation in the early 2000s. More specifically, I wish I had known Richard Ross at that time. It was serendipity that I had a chance to meet Ross recently. My museum director friend, Linda, encouraged me to attend Ross's talk held at the Beach Museum of Art in February 2014. Ross is a photographer, researcher, and professor at the Department of Art in the University of California, Santa Barbara. His talk was about his recent project, Juvenile-in-Justice, for which he took photographs of youths in 250 prisons in thirty-one states. He interviewed over 1,000 kids in jail. His photographs document "the placement and treatment of American juveniles housed by law in facilities that treat, confine, punish, assist and, occasionally, harm them" (www.richardross.net). In his talk, Ross emphasizes how he uses art as a "weapon to change the future." He further elaborates that as an artist and activist, his goal is to give visual tools to advocates to help reduce mass incarceration and change such ineffective and often harmful practices for our next generations to come. Ross shared a collection of disturbing but powerful images of young teenagers locked down in the jail, along with their narratives. While being struck by parallel stories between his images and my research participants in an alternative school, I was deeply inspired by the power of visual storytelling that Ross presented to the audience on a very cold February evening.

Below, I provide a possibility of combining visual data and textual data by juxtaposing Ross's photos and some part of my research on at-risk students to illustrate similar stories presented in both pictures and written texts. These visual images could have been incorporated into my written texts as a way to make connections between the lives of at-risk students in alternative schools and the larger social structures such as juvenile detention centers. In retrospect, my previous work on alternative schools and the lived experience of students who were at risk of school failure would have benefited from the incorporation of these visual images, since visual data can help the unnoticed aspect of human activity and social organization "become noticed and taken into account in understanding the production of social life" (Bell, 2013, p. 144).

In my previous work (Kim, 2011), I described one of the three images of alternative schools as that of a juvenile detention center, like Image 6.1. I wrote:

> US public schools and alternative schools, in particular, increasingly resemble prisons as they invest in school security apparatus such as metal detectors, police presence, surveillance cameras, chain-link fences, surprise searches, and more (Saltman, 2003). Further, *lockdown* is becoming the pervasive language for "at-risk" youth in public alternative schools in which students are increasingly subjected to physical and psychological surveillance, confinement, and regimentation (Brown, 2003). . . . This concern has resulted in the burgeoning growth of alternative education programs and services directing juvenile delinquents to alternative schools or programs before they end up in prison. (pp. 79–80)

© Richard Ross

Image 6.1   Juvenile Detention Center, Houston, Texas.

Next, take a look at Image 6.2 (S. T., age 15) and Image 6.3 (C. T., age 15). Read their narratives from interviews conducted by Ross.

> S.T's Story: I was with a group of guys when I was 13. We jumped this guy near the lake. We got about $400. They gave me the gun 'cause I was the youngest. I been in Juno cottage for two years. I was coming back from the med unit with a homie and we broke into the canteen through

a window and ate all the candy bars we could find. He got sick and we only had a five-minute pass so they caught us. I got sent to Valis but got played by a staff there so they sent me here to Martin.

C.T's Story: I got kicked out of school for partying and truancy. I use meth. They have had me here for two weeks. I think they keep me here because they think I am a risk of hurting myself. When they want to come in, they come in, they don't knock or anything—this is the observation room. There are five other girls here I think for things like running away and curfew violations . . . lewd and lascivious conduct, selling meth, robbery, weed . . . stuff like that. (http://richardross.net/juvenile-in-justice)

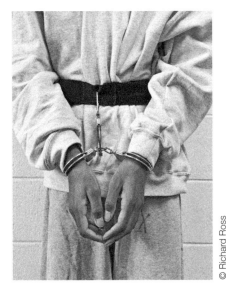

Image 6.2   S.T., age 15, Ethan Allen School, Wales, Wisconsin.

Image 6.3   C.T., age 15, Southwest Idaho Juvenile Detention Center Caldwell, Idaho.

S.T. and C.T. are the kinds of students who would have attended the alternative school that was my research site, as I wrote about the reasons why students were expelled from their regular school and transferred to an alternative school:

In 2001, NCES (National Center for Education Statistics) conducted the first national study of public alternative schools and programs serving at-risk students. . . . Roughly half of all districts with alternative schools and programs identified appropriate reasons for removing at-risk students from a regular school and transferring them to an alternative school. The reasons include: possession, distribution, or use of alcohol or drugs (52 percent); physical attacks or fights (52 percent); chronic truancy (51 percent); possession or use of a weapon other than a firearm (50 percent); continual academic failure (50 percent); disruptive verbal behavior (45 percent); and possession or use of a firearm (44 percent); teen pregnancy/parenthood (28 percent); and mental health (22 percent). (Kim, 2005, p. 11)

Now, take a look at Image 6.4, showing arms that exhibit razor cuts. It reminds me of Kevin in my study, who also had a chronic habit of razor cutting. Kevin narrated:

> We had our own family drama today. Yelling, shouting, cursing. . . . It's part of our home life. I stopped understanding my mom a while ago when she announced her third marriage. Now she's with her fourth husband. I don't trust her any more. I don't feel connected with her any more. Living in this mess—living with my mom's fourth husband and his two children—is just hopeless. Everything looks so meaningless: home, girls, friends, school, and life. . . . Nobody knows me. Nobody cares about me. Nobody understands me. I am so lonely and depressed.
>
> I'm doing it again. I'm cutting myself again. My arms, my belly, and my legs . . . with a razor. . . . I'm bleeding, bleeding a lot. It's painful, but . . . bleeding makes me feel good. I'm numb to pain. If I disappear now, would anybody care? (Kim, 2011, p. 87)

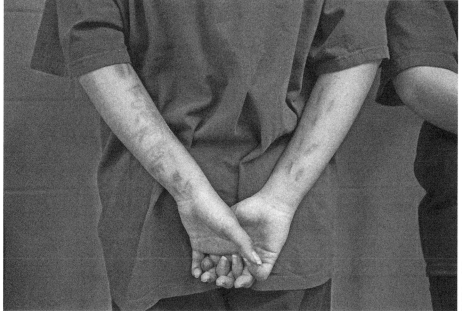

© Richard Ross

Image 6.4 A female juvenile with scars from cutting herself that read "Fuck Me." At Jan Evans Juvenile Justice Center, Reno, Nevada.

Many images and stories from the juvenile detention center that Ross has collected have striking similarities with the kinds of stories that my alternative school research participants shared with me. Ross's photographs preserve fragments of stories that my students shared. Stories in both visual and textual forms present each teenager's unique situation but they all share the common background: teenagers whose life stories simply reflect the lack of surrounding adults' attention, love, and caring for them. The adults are parents, educators, administrators, the public, and society. These intersections between the written texts and the visual texts confirm and affirm research findings.

Working with images, according to Riessman (2008), can deepen and thicken interpretation as images evoke emotions and imaginative understanding, often lacking in social science writing. The use of visual data in narrative inquiry will allow many aspects of human experiences that might otherwise go unnoticed to be recognized and afforded visual voices (Luttrell, 2010).

Conclusion: Variegations of Narrative Analysis and Interpretation

In this chapter, we have discussed issues related to narrative data analysis and interpretation. What is presented here does not cover all the possible ways of narrative analysis methods. Far from it. However, by approaching narrative data analysis and interpretation with a notion of flirtation, using our imagination and creativity, we can adapt, modify, and deepen existing analysis methods to address our individual narrative research design and purpose. I hope that this chapter has provided you with guidance in such a direction.

The variegations of conducting narrative analysis suggest how much can be learned from a narrative perspective on human action and experience. As Mishler (1995) notes, we narrative inquirers have a firm foothold within social and human science research and our job is to continue gaining in depth and significance of the narrative work. Mishler writes:

> The diversity of narrative models invites, and indeed demands, a more reflective stance for researchers. It is clear that we do not *find* stories; we *make* stories. We retell our respondents' accounts through our analytic redescriptions. We too are storytellers and through our concepts and methods—our research strategies, data samples, transcription procedures, specifications of narrative units and structures, and interpretive perspectives—we construct the story and its meaning. In this sense, *the* story is always co-authored, either directly in the process of an interviewer eliciting an account or indirectly. (p. 117, italics in original)

Hence, after flirting with data through the analysis and interpretation process, we'll need to think about writing a text that *desires* the reader, that is, writing a text that invites the reader to play with our narrative writing, framed in one of the narrative genres, presented in Chapter 4. Some of you might be curious how the analytic process can go hand in hand with the creative process. No worries. Richardson and St. Pierre (2005) suggest CAP (creative analytical processes) writing, arguing that "any dinosaurian beliefs that 'creative' and 'analytical' are contradictory and incompatible modes" (p. 962) are doomed for extinction in the wake of postmodernist critiques of traditional qualitative writing practices. So, we have the postmodern thinkers' blessing to write creatively, analytically, narratively, and imaginatively, engaging in one of the narrative research genres.

For further learning about narrative analysis, I would encourage you to check out some of the suggested readings.

SUGGESTED READINGS

FOR NARRATIVE ANALYSIS

De Fina, A., & Georgakopoulou, A. (2012). *Analyzing narrative: Discourse and sociolinguistic perspectives.* Cambridge, UK: Cambridge University Press.

Gee, P. (2011). *An introduction to discourse analysis: Theory and method* (3rd ed.). New York, NY: Routledge.

Holstein, J., & Gubrium, J. (Eds.). (2012). *Varieties of narrative analysis.* Thousand Oaks, CA: Sage.

Riessman, C. K. (2008). *Narrative methods for the human sciences.* Thousand Oaks, CA: Sage.

FOR THE LABOVIAN MODEL

McCormack, C. (2004). Storying stories: A narrative approach to in-depth interview conversations. *International Journal of Social Research Methodology, 7*(3), 219–236.

Patterson, W. (2013). Narratives of events: Labovian narrative analysis and its limitations. In M. Andrews, C. Squire, & M. Tamboukou (Eds.), *Doing narrative research* (pp. 27–46). Thousand Oaks, CA: Sage

FOR VISUAL NARRATIVE ANALYSIS

Bell, S. E. (2002). Photo images: Jo Spence's narratives of living with illness. *Health: An Interdisciplinary Journal for the Social Study of Health, Illness and Medicine, 6*(1), 5–30.

Pink, S. (2004). Visual methods. In C. Seale, G. Gobo, J. Gubrium, & D. Silverman (Eds.), [Special issue] *Qualitative Research Practice* (pp. 361–378). London: Sage.

See also *Visual Studies* (2010), Vol. 25, No. 3.

QUESTIONS FOR REFLECTION

- What type of narrative analysis method will you use?
- How will you flirt between the methods of Polkinghorne and Mishler to address your research purpose?
- What kind of visual data will you have?
- Can you create your own narrative analysis method based on your understanding of data analysis and interpretation?

ACTIVITIES

1. Using the interview transcript you have from one of the activities in Chapter 5, try to analyze it using either the Polkinghorne model or the Mishler model.

2. Using the same interview transcript, write a story or reorder a storyline based on the six components of the Labovian model (Abstract, Orientation, Complicating Action, Evaluation, Result, and Coda).

3. Find a narrative analysis model that fits your research design. Flirt with the model and come up with your own analysis model and justify it.

NOTES

1. See Chase (2003) for wonderful class activities for narrative data analysis and interpretation.
2. If you are interested in a more serious study of interpretation, I would recommend Paul Ricoeur's *The Conflict of Interpretations: Essays in Hermeneutics* (Ricoeur, 2007).
3. Ricoeur's terms are the *hermeneutics of faith* and the *hermeneutics of suspicion,* while Josselson modifies them to the *hermeneutics of restoration* and the *hermeneutics of demystification.* However, for the purpose of this chapter, I have modified the terms to *the interpretations of faith* and *the interpretations of suspicion.*
4. Readers may confuse Polkinghorne's term *narrative analysis* with Mishler's use of narrative analysis. While Polkinghorne uses it to refer to one of the *types* of analyzing narrative data, Mishler uses it to refer to an *act* of analyzing narrative data in general. Most narrative researchers use the term *narrative analysis* to mean the latter, like Mishler does. To minimize the confusion, I use the *paradigmatic mode of analysis* to refer to Polkinghorne's *analysis of narratives,* and the *narrative mode of analysis* for Polkinghorne's *narrative analysis.*
5. Polkinghorne (1995) uses narrative and story interchangeably, as in "storied narrative."
6. Changes are identified in bold and italic font.
7 Although Labov's model is treated as one component of Mishler's typology, I treat Labov's model separately because of Labov's deep influence on narrative.
8. Barone notes that story titles refer to the occupations of protagonists at the time of writing.
9. Barone devotes all of Part III of the book to the life story of Don Forrister, while the nine students' narratives make up Part II.
10. I focus on visual images such as photographs and paintings rather than video clips.
11. All the images here are from Richard Ross's personal website, http://richardross.net/juvenile-in-justice, with his permission.

Chapter Topics

- On Coda
- Research Signature
- Answering the Question "So What?"
- "Desiring" the Audience
- Avoiding an Epic Closure
- Theorizing Findings
- Planting the Seed of Social Justice
- Becoming a Scheherazade
- Conclusion: Ongoing Stories

©Tom Parish, T. Candon—Root Cellar,
Liberty Township, Geary County, KS 2012

CHAPTER 7

Narrative Coda

Theorizing Narrative Meaning

QUESTIONS TO CONSIDER

- How do I write the final stage of my narrative inquiry?
- How do I answer the question of "So what?"
- How do I theorize narrative meaning found in stories?
- How do I (un)finalize my research?

INTRODUCTION

In 2012, the College of Education at my institution began a video series, *A Walk in My Shoes,* featuring compelling stories of a group of people whose lived experience is deemed to deserve public attention. The purpose of this ongoing series, from my understanding, is to raise awareness about the issues of diversity framed in the matter of quality, equality, and equity, in hopes of fostering empathy for the members of a community that is not in the mainstream.

So, a few months ago, we viewed the second series, *Military Life,* which widened my horizon, as I had no idea what it would be like to be a military family until I saw this documentary. Unlike military stories that I used to hear in the media, the personal stories in this video series became particularly real and authentic to me, especially because they were the voices of students and teachers from the local community that I serve. This series truly worked to cultivate *narrative imagination* within me, which we discussed in Chapter 3. To review, narrative imagination, according to Nussbaum (1998), is defined as:

> the ability to think what it might be like to be in the shoes of a person different from oneself, to be an intelligent reader of that person's story, and to understand the emotions and wishes and desires that someone so placed might have. (p. 11)

I think the documentary video series *A Walk in My Shoes* is a great way to promote narrative imagination in the hearts of audiences from the college, the university, and the community.

While being touched by the stories in the movie and admiring the work of my colleague and videographer, Rusty, who put these series together in collaboration with other faculty and staff following our dean's vision, I wondered to myself, "How can I make my storytelling research as compelling as this documentary?" I further wondered, "How is narrative inquiry different from documentary film or any good story?"—in other words, "That's a good story, but is it really research?" (Ceglowski, 1997, p. 198).

Hence, these wonderings become the starting point of this chapter: How can a story become research? More specifically, how do we turn a good story into narrative inquiry? That is, we have a good story, but now what?

The purpose of this chapter is to help you pay attention to the research aspect of storytelling, namely, answering the question of "so what" and to think about how you might approach the final stage (coda) of your research.

On Coda

If you studied music, you would know what coda means. The word *coda* came from Latin, *cauda*, which means *tail*. Not surprisingly, then, a coda in music theory is associated with a finale because it appears toward the end of a musical piece. A coda in a finale is a passage that functions to bring the music piece to an end. It is a musical (or sometimes, magical to me) oomph that gives the audience catharsis with reverberating effects long after the music ends. It is something that the composer might want the listener to take away from his or her music. To me, it is like the composer's signature that he or she signs (musically and metaphorically) to complete the piece. I can feel it when I listen to Mozart's famous last symphony, No. 41 in C, Jupiter Finale, or Tchaikovsky's Swan Lake finale, for example. Perhaps you have other wonderful examples of codas that you cherish.

The meaning of this musical coda has been adopted by literary theorists. For example, if you recall, Labov was the one who included a coda as part of his narrative analysis model that we discussed in Chapter 6. In the Labov model, a coda usually comes at the end of the narrative as a way to bring the storyteller and the listener back to the present time of telling from the retrospective mode of telling and listening. The coda in narrative analysis, thus, is a link between "the past world of the story to the present world of the storytelling" (Patterson, 2013, p. 32).

Then, I am thinking that we can expand this notion of **coda** to a broader context of narrative inquiry. Imagine that you (re)presented compelling stories in one of the narrative genres based on your narrative analysis and interpretation. Then what? What are you going to do next? Are you going to say goodbye to your readers without bringing them together with the why of the stories or the why of your research? In that case, you may risk leaving your readers hanging in the air, shrugging their shoulders, and wondering, "OK, so what?" or "Who cares?" Therefore, we want to have a coda that reverberates in the minds of our readers long after the story is over. So, what is it that you want your readers to take away from your research? What kind of "oomph" do you want to leave your readers with before you sign off?

Bruner (2002) points out that we are good at telling stories but "not very good at grasping how story explicitly transfigures the commonplace" (p. 4). I have seen student dissertations that have a great literature review, well-thought-out research design, and interesting stories and findings, but a dull ending that falls short of transfiguring the story's commonplace in light of a broader context. Bruner further suggests that we need the coda as "a retrospective evaluation of what it all might mean, a feature that also returns the hearer or reader from the there and then of the narrative to the here and now of the telling" (p. 20). It seems to me, then, that a coda is a must-have element that can bring the research a notch up, as the researcher evaluates what the researched stories all might mean, while finding ways to transfigure the story's commonplace to illuminate the larger society, and bringing the readers together with the now of the research phenomenon we have set out to explore. Rather than providing the solution to our research problem, the coda can be presented as an invitation to genuine dialogue among readers for problem finding, because narrative inquiry, as far as I am concerned, is "deeply about plight, about the road rather than about the inn to which it leads" (p. 20).

Hence, the coda as "a final feature of stories" (Bruner, 2002, p. 20), or "what comes *after* the story" (p. 20, italics in original), is a crucial design element that comes in the final stage of our narrative research. By working on how to construct our research coda, we try to find ways to give the reader some sort of catharsis, reverberation, "oomph," or new understandings of the field that should be made available through implications. The coda, as it aims to bring all the parts and pieces of our research together, helps our research make a leap from just a "good" story to fulfilling the inquiry aspect of narrative research. So, understanding what might constitute a coda or how to write your research coda should be given a scholarly importance, which will be discussed next.

Research Signature

Narrative scholars have discussed the concept of coda as the researcher's personal signature (Barone & Eisner, 1997; Clandinin & Connelly, 2000). After analyzing and interpreting the participant's stories, it is now the researcher's turn to provide his or her insights based on existing theories, literature, and personal/professional knowledge about the phenomena under scrutiny. As we discussed in Chapter 4, Barone and Eisner (1997) proposed "personal signature of the researcher/writer" (p. 77) as one of the seven features of arts-based educational research. They argue that the researcher is supposed to "shape the reality" (p. 77) without arriving at a single, "correct" version of reality based on the researcher's thesis because "the characters are, after all, only elements within a virtual world that is the creation of a writer (and re-creation of readers)" (p. 77). According to them, the researcher's particular thesis works as his or her own personal signature, arising out of the negotiations between the researcher himself or herself and the phenomena under examination, and embodying the unique vision of the researcher.

In a similar vein, Clandinin and Connelly (2000) call it the researcher's own "stamp on the work" (p. 148), which is a way of saying it's what he or she wishes to speak and the researcher's way of "being there" in the text. Clandinin and Connelly state, "Being there in the special way that marks each of us as writers constitutes our research signature" (p. 148). Being there in the special way? How are we supposed to "be there in the special way" in the research text, which constitutes our research signature? What does that mean? Clandinin and Connelly explain that it is not as simple as it sounds. There is a dilemma attached to it, as they state:

> The dilemma is the dilemma of how lively our signature should be: too vivid a signature runs the risk of obscuring the field and its participants; too subtle a signature runs the risk of the deception that the research text speaks from the point of view of the participant. (p. 148)

What a great point! What Clandinin and Connelly caution is that while an overly strong researcher signature may be criticized as an abuse of the subjectivity (or misunderstood as the researcher's "propaganda" as in my case, as I will explain in a moment), too weak a signature may also be criticized as a lack of the researcher's intention (research goal). Hence, the text that conveys the research signature requires a balancing act.

Through the balancing act of how to be there in the text where we stamp our signature as narrative inquirers, we attempt to accomplish the research goals that we set out to achieve at the beginning. The balancing act that carries our signature (which is neither too strong nor too weak) is a venture into the unknown possibilities we explore.

Answering the Question "So What?"

In addition to our research signature, we want to make sure that our research coda has substantive discussions about how and why the study is significant, justifying the importance of our study. Clandinin, Pushor, and Orr (2007) suggest this justification as the primary design element for consideration in narrative inquiry. According to them, narrative inquirers need to attend to three kinds of justification: *the personal, the practical,* and *the social.* The personal justification clarifies why the study is important and why it matters personally to you the researcher. You can do this by writing a section called "narrative beginnings" (Clandinin et al., 2007, p. 25) where you situate yourself in the study by discussing how you become interested in the topic of your inquiry. Next, a practical justification is made with a discussion about how the study is going to inform your own and others' practices. And the social justification comes from a discussion about how the study might address the larger social issues. But, I would like to add another justification, *the scholarly.* A scholarly justification will explain the reason why your study is important in your field, discussing how your research findings contribute to your scholarly field. Hence, practical, social, and scholarly justifications that go beyond the personal will allow the researcher to answer the "So what?" and "Who cares?" questions, raised by the reader/audience.

How, then, do we provide these justifications that go beyond the personal importance of the study? We can generally do so by:

- Discussing and theorizing research findings in the context of our respective disciplines,
- Drawing upon theoretical frameworks and the literature to make implications for our respective fields,
- Bridging the gap between the reality in which we live and the virtual reality of the stories where our protagonists (participants) lived,
- Raising more questions to ponder, and
- Making recommendations/suggestions for future research.

"Desiring" the Audience

The issue of justification is deeply related to that of audience, because after reading research findings, a vigilant audience will ask such questions as "Well, it's a good story, but, so what?" "How and why does the study matter to me?" It is the conscious audience that will demand we go beyond the personal boundary of our research and make practical, social, and scholarly contributions. This is where the importance of a coda resides, as it helps us reach the broader audience with our research signature.

When I met with Tom Barone in his office about the draft of the final chapter of my dissertation, his very first question was, *"Who is your audience?" "Audience?"* He caught me off guard. I stumbled over the words. *"Umm, uh, uh . . . I am . . . I am writing for educators. I am writing for at-risk students. Yeah, that's right, I think?"* Barone just smiled at me and said in his typical soft voice, *"Well, it is not clear here."*

I knew my answer was not true. I knew I was writing for the committee, so that they would approve my dissertation and I could graduate! I didn't really think about having an audience in mind other than my committee members. Admittedly, I had a conveniently adopted myopic view of writing a dissertation, and Barone's simple question helped me rethink my final chapter (coda) and urged me to think beyond my immediate audience to reach a broader audience who does not necessarily reside in the academy (Barone & Eisner, 2012). This experience led me to ask the same question of my own students. A lot of times it is not "clear" to me who their audiences are in their dissertations.

Who, then, can be our audiences? Connelly and Clandinin (2006) write:

> There are multiple audiences—participants, imagined reading audience, inquirer. Research texts that emphasize any one to the exclusion of others lose impact. Inquirers who forget their participants and their reading audience, writing only for themselves, become narcissistic; inquirers who write for their imagined audience and neglect their participants run the risks of being unethical and invalid; and inquirers who write only for participants or themselves run the risk of being unable to answer the questions "Who cares?" and "So what?" (p. 485)

Connelly and Clandinin ask us to consider multiple audiences—participants, imagined readers, and inquirers. Writing for the researcher herself or himself only can be, in fact, self-emancipatory, self-transformative, and self-empowering, while taking the risk of self-indulgence, self-absorption, narcissism, and navel-gazing (Barone & Eisner, 2012). Writing for the participants provides an opportunity to let their voice be heard, but it might raise the potential concern that the purpose of narrative research is to "romanticize the individual and thus reify notions of a unitary subject/ hero" (Munro, 1998, p. 12). Writing only for the readers while neglecting the participants would be taking the risks of being unethical because we end up "using" the participants as objects of research. Hence, it is important to consider multiple audiences simultaneously (see Figure 7.1).

The larger the audience we reach, including "an audience of the lay public, or better, the various *publics at large*" (Barone & Eisner, 2012, p. 65, italics in original), the more significant our work will become. It is a way to make a contribution to the larger body of literature and the

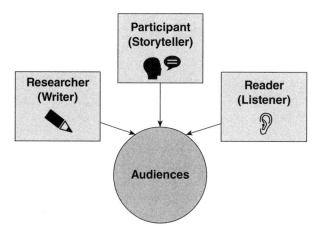

Figure 7.1 Multiple Audiences

society. We can reach multiple audiences by transforming the story's commonplace to its "metaphoric loft" (Bruner, 2002, p. 25).

> The text you write must prove to me that it desires me. (Barthes, 1975, p. 6)

Do you recall this quote? In Chapter 3, we discussed how our writing should "desire" our reader or audience as if we were in a game of aesthetic play with the audience throughout our writing process from the beginning to the end. In this chapter, we want to emphasize that desiring the multiple audiences concomitantly is particularly important in writing a coda. Clandinin and Connelly (2000) speak eloquently of this matter:

> Audience, alive in the researcher's imagination at the outset of inquiry, mostly forgotten during fieldwork, now looms large. It is a necessary condition to be fulfilled by narrative research texts. . . . A sense of an audience peering over the writer's shoulder needs to pervade the writing and the written text. It is excusable to misjudge an audience and write a text that is not read as meaningful by others. But it is inexcusable not to have a sense of audience and a sense of what it is about one's research text that might be valuable for them. (p. 149)

Imagine "a sense of an audience peering over" our shoulder when we write the coda. We don't have any excuse for not having this sense of an audience for our writing! Having an audience alive in our imagination at the outset of inquiry or in our coda is a way of respecting the audience, who is vigilant and has his or her own autonomy and agency (Barone, 1995). By the time we have arrived at the stage of writing a coda, we must have earned the trust and respect from the reader.[1] Hence, it is now time to reciprocate the reader's respect for us. Therefore, in the coda, we are going to create a space in which the reader can participate in a game of narrative imagination with us, fostering empathy for each other. But, it is not a good idea if we supply the whole story that tells the reader what to do because, if we do, there will be nothing left for the reader to do (to imagine), in which case, his or her imagination will never enter the field of our research text (Iser, 1974). Then there will be no (imaginative) dialogue between the reader and the writer, which is counterproductive of our research purpose. It is "only by activating the reader's imagination" (Iser, 1974, p. 282) that we writers can hope to involve the reader in understanding the other through a game of imagination.

In a coda, the goal is to help our reader to have an empathic understanding of the lived experience of our protagonists. To do so, we want the reader to confront his or her own prejudice rather than hiding/ignoring it, because it is the "hidden prejudice that makes us deaf to what speaks to us" (Gadamer, 1975/2006, p. 272). Then, we need to work on helping our readers to reveal their prejudices, so that they will not be deaf to the stories we are (re)telling. If we "desire" the reader in the way Barthes wants us to in our writing of a coda, it is possible that the reader is willing to confront and unveil his or her hidden prejudice. According to Gadamer, there is a false prejudice by which we misunderstand, and true prejudice by which we understand. We can help the reader filter or sort out these different prejudices by providing a "temporal distance" between the prejudice the reader has and the story that he or she just read. This, in turn, will help broaden the reader's horizon to where the reader can transpose himself or herself into the other's situation, fostering narrative imagination.

Avoiding an Epic Closure

Closely related to the topic of "desiring the reader" is avoiding your epic signature. Here's my lesson. More than 10 years ago, I submitted my first AERA proposal. It was flatly rejected. However, it was not the rejection that surprised me. What surprised me was one of the three blind reviewers' comments. My proposal was about something having to do with a social justice theme using critical theory. As a beginning doctoral student, I was full of energy, passion, and almost blind faith in the work of social justice. I do not remember what the exact topic of the proposal was, but I still remember how I ended the proposal. In George Counts's social reconstructionist tone, I wrote "passionately" how the people in power abuse their authority to reproduce the existing social order, hence how we, educational researchers, *must* work to abolish social and educational inequalities and work to "give" voice and "empower" the marginalized group of people in the society. I totally believed in my claim. So, the comment from the reviewer shocked me; it read, *"It seems as if the author tries to use the AERA site to disseminate his/her own propaganda."* Gasp. Isn't propaganda something that extreme conservative politicians disseminate to win the public's consent to their hegemonic ideas? I didn't have any propaganda but wanted to show the world how passionate I was in doing social justice work. I didn't know what I did wrong until I learned about Bakhtin's theory of epic much later in my academic program.

Remember Mikhail Bakhtin from Chapter 2? (I will wait right here if you would like to go back to reread the section on Bakhtin.) When we discussed Bakhtin's theory of novelness, we learned that not all stories are the same. Depending on what kind of purpose a story has, it becomes either an epic or a novel, and Bakhtin is a strong advocate of the latter. Given the historical and social context of high Stalinism in which Bakhtin lived, it is not surprising that Bakhtin was quite reserved about the epic style of writing.

Bakhtin (1981) explains that the epic is a literary genre that is typically used in societies in which diversity and change are either unrecognized or actively suppressed. Thus, the problem with the epic does not reside in its content, such as historical events or factual sources; rather, it resides in its reliance on the authoritative view or approach toward the content and the language of tradition that excludes any possibility of another approach. He remarks:

> The epic world is an utterly finished thing, not only as an authentic event of the distant past but also on its own terms and by its own standards; it is impossible to change, to re-think, to reevaluate anything in it. It is completed, conclusive and immutable, as a fact, an idea and a value. (p. 17)

That means, in the epic world, there is no place for any open-endedness, indecision, and incompleteness, hence no aesthetic play! It is a closed circle in which everything is finished. Thus, in an epic, stories are told with a centripetal force that imposes unity and order on a heterogeneous and diverse world, spoken from one point of view. Truth is presented as "absolute and complete" (p. 16). Further, a singular authoritative point of view is presented as an "official view" to represent one dominant reality. The problem with such an epic world is also pointed out by Dewey, who states, "a world that is finished, ended, would offer no opportunity for resolution. Where everything is already complete, there is no fulfillment" (Dewey, 1934/1980, p. 17).

So, the reason one of the blind reviewers felt that I was disseminating my "propaganda" was because of my epic writing, which was as closed as a circle, and I was presenting my authoritarian, myopic view without any open-endedness. My research signature was presented as absolute truth. So, from Bakhtin's perspective, I was clearly an epic writer. Instead of taking the "stance of epistemological humility," where the researcher "challenges orthodox views without insisting upon a new orthodoxy" (Barone & Eisner, 2012, p. 128), I was imposing my own orthodoxy on the reader with my strong research signature. From the anonymous reviewer, I learned a lesson about how epic writing could shut down the reader and create a gulf between the writer and the reader as a result. Narrative researchers, Barone and Eisner (2012) state, "would refuse to present an alternative master narrative in their own work. They would not purport to have discovered a final truth" (p. 129). Instead, they would offer a variety of alternative perspectives within their research text. It turned out that my proposal was offering my own master narrative as final truth, and lacking the kind of Bakhtinian novelness that allows room for other possibilities to grow and emerge. I was imposing my own Procrustean bed or "propaganda" on the reader.

One of the purposes of narrative research is "to stimulate critical thinking by opening up possibilities for critique and to provoke multiple interpretations, rather than lead the reader to a solitary conclusion" (Rosiek & Atkinson, 2007, p. 508). More specifically, it is to invite readers to a sphere of possible contact with a developing, incomplete and evolving situation, allowing them to re-think and re-evaluate their own views, prejudices, and experiences.

Hence, for the coda of our research, we should avoid an **epic closure**, but possibly incorporate Bakhtinian novelness as our research signature, allowing multiple voices or multiple interpretations to emerge, and yielding no final and complete truth. Such a coda will produce unfinalizable truths that are open to potentiality, freedom, creativity, and surprise, evolving from the dialogic sense of truth (see Chapter 2 for novelness). It goes against domination by a meta-narrative, which is frequently advocated by scientifically based research that attempts to provide a clear-cut solution to human problems. The nature of novelness is well captured in Bakhtin's following remark:

> The novel, after all, has no canon of its own. It is, by its very nature, not canonic. It is plasticity itself. It is a genre that is ever questing, ever examining itself and subjecting its established forms to review. (Bakhtin, 1981, p. 39)

Theorizing Findings

If we embrace the novelness of narrative inquiry as remarked by Bakhtin above, which is "ever questing, ever examining itself and subjecting its established forms to review," we understand that narrative inquiry involves theorizing. We can frame our coda to reflect our ongoing quest for truth and knowledge as a way to examine our established field in order to enhance it. However, this inquiry aspect in narrative inquiry is often forgotten by fresh narrative inquirers (Conle, 2000b), as they tend to enjoy the doing of narrative inquiry while not much "interested in characterizing its inquiry quality abstractly" (p. 190). Conle views this visible lack of the inquiry aspect in narrative research as a possible culprit causing critics to dismiss narrative research as mere storytelling, hence, an "easy" kind of research of "just telling stories" as Clandinin et al. (2007, p. 21) also cautioned.

Narrative inquiry is a quest for knowledge about one's life through narrative, indeed. This quest is not only philosophical and ontological, but also theoretical. It is about a discovery and an exploration of "germs and roots," the "active seeds" (Dewey, 1934/1980, p. 12), lurking in stories and experiences, with which we theoretically understand the why or "causal conditions" (p. 12) of the phenomena under study. Here is Dewey's (1934/1980) analogy:

> It is quite possible to enjoy flowers in their colored form and delicate fragrance without knowing anything about plants theoretically. But if one sets out to *understand* the flowering of plants, he [sic] is committed to finding out something about the interactions of soil, air, water and sunlight that condition the growth of plants. (Dewey, 1934/1980, p. 4, italics in original)

Dewey is asking us to engage in the inquiry aspect (theoretical aspect) to be able to "understand" the phenomena we enjoy on the surface. Certainly, we can enjoy the story as presented. However, if we truly want to *understand* the story, we should be committed to discovering other factors, such as historical, political, environmental, personal, and all things that have influenced the story and anyone involved with the story. To take my college's video series, *A Walk in My Shoes,* as an example, the audience enjoyed or appreciated the film but if we set out to *understand* the lived experiences of the people in the film, we have to be committed to finding all of the causes, influences, factors, and conditions created within the social, political, and historical contexts in which the personal stories reside. This is what differentiates narrative inquiry from mere storytelling because, as Dewey points out, no work can of itself assist the understanding of the nature of the work itself; the work has to be researched, analyzed, interpreted, theorized, and foremost, understood.

Similarly, it has been noted that there is nothing inherently liberatory about stories by themselves (Bowman, 2006; Goodson, 1995). Stories are surely not innocent; stories themselves may be repressive myths that promote a "tyranny of the local" (Harvey, 1989), which fails to address the diverse and complex social life in which different types of oppression such as racism, sexism, and classism continue to exist. Personal stories can be ironically incapacitating when they are placed out of theoretical and social context, disempowering the very people narrative inquirers seek to serve (Goodson, 1995). As Goodson (1995) remarks, "It is not sufficient to say we wanted 'to listen to people,' 'to capture their voices,' 'to let them tell their stories'" (p. 95), if the stories are divorced from understandings of social context and social process. Hence, in our narrative coda, we need to be able to develop the story's linkages to a broader social context in order to *understand* in a Deweyan sense.

To delve further into this issue, I borrow the French term *narratologie* ("narratology"), coined by Tzvetan Todorov, who used the word in parallel with *biology, sociology,* and so forth, to denote "the science of narrative" (Herman, 2005). Narratology is "the theory of narratives, narrative texts, images, spectacles, events; cultural artifacts that 'tell a story'" (Bal, 1997, p. 3). According to narrative theorists, narratology is both an applied science and a theory of narrative texts in its own right (Fludernik, 2005). Fludernik writes that narratology "highlights *how* the text manages to have certain effects and explain *why* these occur, thus providing arguments for existing interpretations of the text" (p. 39).

Thus, narrative inquiry, in a sense, is a narratology, the science of narrative, in which we use stories as a beginning point to understand, analyze, evaluate, and theorize the human and social phenomena. The coda is significant in fulfilling this role, as we provide the implications of research findings, employing social science theory to be connected to the larger society so as to interrogate the historical, social, political world in which stories are embedded (Eisner, 1991). The coda is the emblem of narrative inquiry as the science of narrative or narratology, where we substantiate our knowledge claims through narrative, making scholarly contributions to advancing our respective fields.

Planting the Seed of Social Justice

The role of coda as an emblem of narratology is not just to expand the existing literature. The ultimate goal of our theorizing, I think, is to make a difference in society by planting a seed for social justice. Clandinin, who edited the seminal volume *Handbook of Narrative Inquiry* (2007), posits one of the pressing debates in the field of narrative inquiry, which is whether or not narrative research is "descriptive or interventionist" (p. xv). She asks, "Does narrative inquiry set out to change the world as people engage in the processes of narrative inquiry with their participants, or is it a more descriptive kind of inquiry?" (p. xv). Her intention is not to answer the question for us, but rather to let us think about our position in relation to this debate.

If you ask me, "Is narrative inquiry descriptive or interventionist?" my answer would be, "Yes, please!"

Imagine the answer, "Yes, please!"—the answer Groucho gave to the standard question "Tea or coffee?" in a well-known Marx Brothers' joke (Žižek, 2000). Slavoj Žižek, a Slovenian postmodern philosopher, uses this answer, "Yes, please," as a refusal to choose a false alternative because the answer is "both and more" (p. 90). Although our narrative inquiry may remain either descriptive or interventionist, I would say that it can be both and more. The ultimate goal of doing research, in my humble opinion, no matter what research purposes we have for our individual research, is to make the world a better place or to improve the human condition to the extent that we breathe social justice just as we breathe air in our daily lives.

To be fair, then, we'd better check into what we mean by social justice. I turn to American political philosopher John Rawls, who wrote a groundbreaking book, *A Theory of Justice*

(1999), based on the philosophies of Locke, Rousseau, and Kant. Justice, according to Rawls, is the first virtue of social institutions as truth is the first virtue of systems of thought. Rawls contends:

> Justice denies that the loss of freedom for some is made right by a greater good shared by others. It does not allow that the sacrifices imposed on a few are outweighed by the larger sum of advantages enjoyed by many. Therefore in a just society the liberties of equal citizenship are taken as settled; the rights secured by justice are not subject to political bargaining or to the calculus of social interests. The only thing that permits us to acquiesce in an erroneous theory is the lack of a better one; analogously, an injustice is tolerable only when it is necessary to avoid an even greater injustice. Being first virtues of human activities, truth and justice are *uncompromising*. (pp. 3–4, italics added)

According to Rawls, justice does not approve the democratic majority rule where the rights of a minority are ignored and oppressed for the sake of advancing the interests of the majority. The rights of minorities, under the concept of justice, are not supposed to be used for political bargaining or calculated social interests. Justice as the most fundamental virtue and right of human well-being is uncompromising. This notion of justice is the bottom line for humanity.

Rawls further connects justice to fairness, not in the sense that the concepts of justice and fairness are the same but, rather, on the idea that the principles of justice exist in an initial situation that is fair. Thus, he posits two principles of justice, equality and equity. The first principle, equality, is that "each person is to have an equal right to the most extensive scheme of equal basic liberties compatible with a similar scheme of liberties for others" (p. 53). This requires equality in the assignment of basic rights and duties. And the second principle, equity, is that "social and economic inequalities are to be arranged so that they are both (a) reasonably expected to be to everyone's advantage, and (b) attached to positions and offices open to all" (p. 53). This principle foregrounds the idea that "social and economic inequalities, for example, inequalities of wealth and authority, are just only if they result in compensating benefits for everyone, and in particular for the least advantaged members of society" (p. 13). This equity principle should be applied to other inequalities based on gender, race, sexual orientation, disability, language, and more.

Stories are about human plights, personally experienced. Stories of those who experience human plights every day tend to get buried. The role of narrative inquiry, then, is to excavate those stories and use them as seeds for social justice. Bruner (2002) remarks, "It is the conversion of private Trouble in Burke's sense into public plight that makes well-wrought narrative so powerful, so comforting, so dangerous, so culturally essential" (p. 35). In the coda of our research text, then, we can have personal plights become metaphors writ large to shed light on public plights. This would bring narrative inquiry up a notch to the next level of research that the public calls for. Then, narrative research that reaches out to the heart of the public will plant the seeds of a Rawlsian theory of social justice—to maximize the advantage of the least advantaged, which will become, indeed, a sacred human endeavor.

Becoming a Scheherazade

We know that planting seeds of social justice will not end with a few stories we present in our research. We have to keep the stories going. Perhaps the best storyteller we know of would be Scheherazade, who kept stories going for one thousand and one nights! What are the lessons we narrative inquirers can learn from her?

You may not be familiar with Scheherazade, although you might have read *The Arabian Nights,* or watched Hollywood movies such as *Ali Baba and the Forty Thieves, Aladdin,* and the *Sinbad* series, in your childhood. I remember my daughter and I watched the video *Aladdin* together when she was about 5 years old, but we never talked about Scheherazade. I did not know much about Scheherazade other than the beautiful symphonic suite, *Scheherazade,* Op. 35, by the Russian composer Rimsky-Korsakov. It was through feminist theorist Suzanne Gauch's book *Liberating Shahrazad: Feminism, Postcolonialism, and Islam* (2007) that I learned more about Scheherazade and, further, how her image has been distorted as seductive and sexual by the Western media.

Scheherazade, or Shahrazad as Arabic speakers commonly call her, is the legendary story-teller who tells the tales of *The Thousand and One Nights,* or *The Arabian Nights,* which is a collection of stories, both Persian and Arabic in their origin. It was first translated into French by Antoine Galland, between 1704 and 1712 (Housman, 1981). Gauch (2007) explains that Scheherazade was the brave and intelligent woman who was able to dissolve King Shahrayar's murderous rage that had preoccupied him ever since he had seen his first wife's infidelity with a slave. Before Scheherazade, the king used to marry a virgin every evening and put her to death the following morning. But, offering herself as the king's next victim, Scheherazade had a plan. She told an interesting and intricate story every night to keep the king's attention, leaving it unfinished as dawn broke. The king couldn't kill Scheherazade the next day because he wanted to continue hearing the story. The storytelling went on for one thousand and one nights. The legend has it that the king fell in love with Scheherazade eventually, gave up on the idea of killing his bride, and finally made Scheherazade his queen, living happily ever after.

I am fascinated by the legendary storyteller, Scheherazade. How was she able to divert the stubborn king from his vicious obsession with murder to embracing the stories? How was she able to transform the king through stories? How was this possible? Gauch explains:

> Shahrazad is no political radical; the changes at which her storytelling ultimately aims are not violent. Rather, her stories bit by bit overcome what were once seemingly insurmountable boundaries and limitations to change. They begin by aiming at the transformation of her audience's most intimate experience of themselves. (p. xviii)

Through her storytelling, neither political nor radical nor violent, bit by bit Scheherazade saved not only her own life but also the lives of countless other women. Scheherazade was *liberating,* indeed. Our storyteller, Scheherazade, took a risk to take the killer King Shahrayar to the story world where he was able to catch sight of his own behavior and reflect on the characters of the stories, which were brought to life for him by Scheherazade (Gauch, 2007). Scheherazade was able to do so with stories that "represent a compendium of cross-cultural, transnational influences" (p. 2).

I think Scheherazade gives us valuable lessons about storytelling. To me, Scheherazade's story has the metaphoric loft that Bruner speaks of. First, the eventual transformation of the king was possible thanks to Scheherazade's narrative skill in keeping the stories going (for one thousand and one nights!). Second, the goal of her storytelling, however insurmountable it looked, was achieved bit by bit, on a consistent and constant basis. Third, Scheherazade kept each story's ending open (suspense unresolved), so that the king would be left curious, waiting for the next story. And finally, Scheherazade provided the stories as models of the world so that the king could reflect upon himself, resulting in a transformation.

Scheherazade is our storytelling teacher. According to Gauch (2007), new writers and artists from the Arab and Islamic worlds revisit the symbolic role of Scheherazade as "a speaking agent whose stories have never ended and whose resolve has only increased" (p. xi). These writers resist narrative closure and, like Scheherazade, "they endlessly defer the final word, promising always that the next tale will supersede the previous one in as yet unheard of ways" (p. 12). Isn't this what Bakhtin's unfinalizability is about?

Our research will therefore never provide a final story. Our coda should invite a next story that is better than the previous ones. Through an accumulation of our ongoing stories, we are participating in the process of transforming the world into a better place, little by little, although the change may take place with the speed of water dripping upon a stone, whose definite erosion is not noted until many years later.

Conclusion: Ongoing Stories

How can I conclude?

Our story is not over yet.

Our stories are ongoing.

QUESTIONS FOR REFLECTION

- What do you imagine your research signature is going to be?
- Who will be your targeted audiences?
- How do you understand the concept of social justice?
- How are you going to answer the question "So what?"

- How are you going to avoid an epic closure?
- What else would you add to your research coda?

ACTIVITY

With the story you wrote as part of the activities you did in Chapter 6, try to write a coda, addressing the following questions:

o Is your personal signature as researcher appropriate? How?
o In what ways are you answering the question of "So what?"
o What is the evidence that you "desire" your audiences in your story?
o How do you leave your coda open-ended?
o How do you theorize your story?
o How is your story a seed for social justice?
o How will you keep your story going?

NOTE

1. Here, the reader indicates multiple audiences: the research participant, the reader, the listener, and the researcher.

CHAPTER TOPICS

©Tom Parish, T. Candon—Root Cellar, Liberty Township, Geary County, KS 2012

CHAPTER 8

Critical Issues in Narrative Inquiry

Looking Into a Kaleidoscope

QUESTIONS TO CONSIDER

- What are critical issues that may challenge the status quo of narrative inquiry?
- What are the ways to push the boundary of narrative inquiry?

INTRODUCTION

For this chapter, I will discuss several important topics about which narrative inquirers and perhaps qualitative researchers in general need to think hard. Even in seemingly commonsensical and taken-for-granted knowledge in narrative inquiry, there may be "ifs and buts" lurking behind it, to which we need to give careful consideration. As I write this, I am thinking of my students who visit me with their research problems. They bring "what-should-I-do" questions and expect me to have right answers for them. I answer their questions as best as I could, but quite often, I fail to give them satisfying answers they like to hear. I have one particular student who does not hesitate to tell me, when unsatisfied, quite politely and patiently, "Well, Dr. Kim, that's not what you said last time." Then, I have to bail myself out by saying, "Hmm, well, it's because we are talking about a similar issue in a different context now." But I don't always convince the student fully. It is hard for some of us to think that some research issues are not cut and dry; they are contingent upon varying situations, unbeknownst to us. The same solution might have worked yesterday, but it may not work tomorrow.

In this chapter, I will address some critical issues in narrative inquiry that require us to employ an imaginary kaleidoscope through which we embrace unexpected patterns and changes, depending on how we look at it. As you know, the metaphor of a kaleidoscope is meant to broaden our ways of thinking and understanding, so that we can push the boundaries of narrative inquiry and become as thoughtful and ethical as we can.

Looking Into a Kaleidoscope

Image 8.1   A Mural in Songkwang-sa, Buddhist Temple in South Korea

Last summer, I had a chance to pay a visit to a temple in South Korea with my daughter. It is a small, beautiful temple that is about 1,000 years old, located in Mt. Chogye nearby my hometown. We took many point-and-shoot pictures. Image 8.1 is one of the pictures we took, a mural painted on one of the outside walls right below the roof. I took a particular interest in this mural as it had a legendary story of the famous Korean Buddhist monk Wonhyo (617–686 AD), about whom we learned in Korean history class in middle school. Although I am not a Buddhist, the legendary story of Wonhyo is still vivid in my memory. So, here goes the legend, reconstructed from my memory:

Wonhyo, a Buddhist monk in the Shilla Kingdom that existed between BC 57 and AD 935 in Korean history, was on his way to China to study Buddhism with his colleague. One night as they slept in a cave, Wonhyo woke up in the middle of night, feeling thirsty. He wanted to look for water, but couldn't see anything in the dark. He slowly crawled on all fours in hopes that he would find water nearby. After few movements, he touched an object that seemed to have water in it. He grabbed it and drank the water (see the upper right hand corner of the image). The water tasted so good that he couldn't remember drinking such tasty water before. Satisfied, he went back to sleep. Next morning, when he woke up and looked around, he found himself surrounded by dead human skulls. What was more startling was that each skull had water in it! He suddenly started vomiting to no end at the thought that what he drank was actually something from a dead body!

But an epiphany came to his mind (see the monk with a halo looking at the skull in front of him). His realization was: How is it possible that such a horrible thing could taste so good? What has happened here? He came to a profound realization that anything one acts/thinks/feels can be determined only by his/her mind/perception, hence, his philosophy of "일체유심조" (il-che-you-shim-cho, which literally means everything depends on your mind). With this realization, he immediately turned around to return to Shilla and founded a sect of Korean Buddhism. His 일체유심조 became one of the fundamental principles of Wonhyo's Buddhism.

I am guilty of making the profound Wonhyo's philosophy too simple here. But you've got the idea, I hope. I also wonder if Wonhyo's idea was the beginning of Wittgenstein's rabbit-duck illusion, a notion of multiple ways of seeing, which then seems to become the backbone of Merleau-Ponty's theory of perception. I cannot claim it for sure, but I think this might be one of the junctures where East meets West. But, I'm digressing here.

I bring up this Korean legend because it has implications for what we are going to discuss in this chapter. Some critical issues in narrative inquiry do not present themselves clearly and straightforwardly. The same issue can be approached differently, yielding different results, based on how you look at it or how you turn your kaleidoscope. Many times, it depends on you the researcher (일체유심조), who takes subtle issues (ifs and buts) into careful consideration, be the issue a situation/view of the researcher yourself, that of the participants, that of the reader, or that of the research context. Hence, we have to be flexible and open-minded toward issues that arise during our research as if we are looking into a kaleidoscope. As you rotate the kaleidoscope tube while you're viewing through it, you will see colorful symmetrical patterns emerge and change. As we realize there are many angles that we can choose from, I hope that we are ready to try out an imaginary kaleidoscope when dealing with complex issues arising from our research processes.

Contradicting Stories: The Rashomon Effect

Speaking of a kaleidoscope, let's begin with the **Rashomon effect**, a concept that's known in anthropology, psychology, and the movie industry. It refers to a situation where different people provide different stories of the same event. Hence, we cannot be sure whose story is true. The origin of this term comes from a 1950 Japanese movie, *Rashomon,* set in twelfth-century Japan, directed by Akira

Kurosawa, who is considered one of the most talented directors of the twentieth century. I am grateful for living in the age of the Internet, as I was able to watch the black and white movie online. I found the movie philosophical and symbolic, as it depicts a human's fragility, reflected in the statement made by the priest, one of the main characters: "This time I may finally lose my faith in the human soul." In the movie, four storytellers gave four different accounts of the same event, the death of a husband, at a court trial. Each provides a plausible, believable account of how, by whom, and why the husband had been killed, while refuting the story told by the others. The movie ended with no final answer as to whose story was true about the killing, leaving the audience to wonder.

Based on this movie, anthropologists began to use the term *Rashomon effect* to refer to influences, biases, or personal justifications that might be at work in qualitative research (Heider, 1988). I think it has significant implications, particularly for us narrative researchers, as we mainly work with stories told by our participants. We may hear contradicting stories more often than we realize, particularly if we get stories about the same event from multiple participants in different power positions, for example. What if they provide stories that are self-serving, based on their personal interests, biases, and other factors? Whose account should we believe? How are we going to make a valid claim based on such stories?

The Rashomon effect helps us be careful with our choices for research design and methods as well as the interpretations and knowledge claims we make based on stories. Heider (1988), drawing upon the Rashomon effect, lists the following possible reasons why researchers would have different findings or interpretations of the same phenomena under study:

- We have to understand the possibility that we might be examining only one part of an elephant (as in the old tale of the blind men, each touching a different part of the elephant).
- We have to understand the possibility that our research findings might yield different results if they took place at different times.
- The researcher's personalities, value systems, cultures, traits (e.g., the researcher's gender, age, race, sexual orientation, etc.), theoretical orientations, and worldviews might affect the findings.
- The length of the research time in the field, as Heider points out and different degrees of rapport between the researcher and the participant might affect the findings.

The Rashomon effect helps us realize some of the limitations that our research may entail. Thinking about those limitations from different angles will be a worthwhile effort, especially when we have contradicting stories. Although we understand that it is impossible to address all the possible limitations, we can take some of these issues into consideration during our research processes to make more meaningful and thoughtful knowledge claims.

Temptation of "Backyard Research"

The Rashomon effect may be further influenced by "Backyard Research," where emic views (insider perspectives) are the key sources of information. "Backyard research" refers to conducting research in "your own backyard" (Glesne & Peshkin, 1991, p. 21), which is part of your daily life. Conducting a study within your school, church, department, or neighborhood, involving your colleagues, family, and friends, is considered backyard research, which is convenient and efficient, hence, very tempting. For example, you would have comparatively easy access; there is a certain relationship already established between you and your potential participants (you are not researching complete strangers), you don't need to go too far to do fieldwork, and most of all, research findings might inform your practice if done carefully. More and more researchers conduct backyard research for different reasons. In the current postmodern age, understanding multiple voices, multiple subjectivities, and particularities of the local community where we live, is paramount in generating new knowledge, and so **backyard research** is legitimate and valid.

However, when/if we choose to conduct research in our own backyard, we need to use caution. In fact, Glesne and Peshkin (1991) advise against conducting backyard research for many reasons. First, there might be a conflict between your roles as a researcher and a nonresearcher (such as friend, colleague, or supervisor). You may find these two roles at odds and role-switching back and forth might be confusing to both you and your participant. Second, backyard research can also create ethical and political dilemmas as it might involve "dangerous knowledge" (p. 23) that is politically dicey to hold or to reveal.

I just recently received an email solicitation requesting my participation in a study. The email came from a faculty member and a graduate student in our college. They were recruiting a number of faculty of color to examine the participants' lived experience as faculty. There is only a handful of faculty of color in our college, so the researchers would have a hard time maintaining the anonymity of the participants. One of my colleagues, a faculty of color, who also received the solicitation email, came to me and asked whether or not to participate in the study. We understood their research intent, which was highly valuable, but decided not to participate in this backyard study because we were not sure how honest we could be with our stories without jeopardizing our career in the college unless we only valorized our experience. We had an interesting discussion about this (see Chapter 5 about the confidentiality issue).

Glesne and Peshkin (1991) state that action research is a type of research that is good for backyard research. But I think it also depends. I have a doctoral student, Steve, who is a progressive principal. After getting the principal position in a new school that was part of a district undergoing educational reform, Steve wanted to examine how the faculty and staff viewed the reform effort. He wanted to get a better understanding of the situation at first hand through his action research. It involved interviewing teachers and district-level administrators, including the district curriculum director as well as the superintendent. In the middle of his action research, he called me:

> Dr. Kim, I am in dilemma. I didn't know what mess I got into when I got this position. Administrators are blaming teachers as incompetent, and teachers are blaming the administrators for imposing their agenda without proper communication. Nobody is happy here. This place is a mess. How should I report my research findings? I am more empathic with teachers, but I don't want to upset the administration, either. What should I do?

Steve, the action researcher, had a well-meaning intention to find out how his school was experiencing the reform effort. Because of his position as principal, however, he got mired in "dangerous knowledge" that was politically and ethically high-stakes for him as the principal and researcher. The contradicting interests of the two different roles he played did not bode well for his action research agenda. He had to compromise the scope of his research to avoid jeopardizing his administrative position.

Increasingly, more and more doctoral students are working full time or part time while conducting their dissertation research. Even faculty, for that matter, are crunched for research time. Hence, a lot of us, who are busy individuals, are inclined to conduct backyard research because of its advantages, not to mention that there are times when "backyard research" is necessary to find out what is going on in our own "backyard." Although not all backyard research would involve "dangerous knowledge" (some can produce "helpful" knowledge), we will have to keep in mind how our multiple roles (the researcher's and the insider's role) might compete against each other in the backyard research setting. Unless we take this opportunity to see through a kaleidoscope, which will allow us to observe the same event from different angles, our research might end up being self-serving rather than creating new, meaningful knowledge.

On Reflexivity

I would suggest using a researcher's reflexivity as our imaginative kaleidoscope. There is increased attention to the researcher's reflexivity under the influence of postmodernism and poststructuralism, and qualitative researchers routinely use reflexivity as a methodological tool to better represent and justify their work (Pillow, 2003). In the complex historical field of qualitative research, according to Denzin and Lincoln (2011), more frequent use of reflexivity came with the crisis of representation (1986–1990) that followed the blurred genres phase (1970–1986), as researchers struggled with how to locate themselves and how to represent their participants within research (see Chapter 1). Since then, more and more qualitative researchers place reflexivity at the crux of every stage of all qualitative research, from the research design stage, fieldwork stage, and interpretation stage (Guillemin & Gillam, 2004; Mosselson, 2010; Pillow, 2003). Reflexive research, according to Mason (1996), means that "the researcher should constantly take stock of their actions and their role in the research process and subject these to the same critical scrutiny as the rest of their 'data'" (p. 6). Because we narrative researchers are engaged in making meaning of the stories told by our participants, we are increasingly required to engage in such reflexive research, hence, we need to pay attention to this topic in greater depth, although we briefly touched on the subject in Chapter 3 where we discussed reflexivity as a part of narrative ethics in practice.

Reflexivity is more than reflection in that, whereas reflection is to take one step back from the phenomena under examination, reflexivity is to take one more step back from reflection. That is, reflexivity involves two steps back: a reflection on the reflection (Jenkins, 1992). It is a constant "mirroring of the self" (Foley, 2002, p. 473), through which we researchers make ourselves an object of our own gaze. This gaze, defined as "an attitude of curiosity or observation" (Merleau-Ponty, 1962/2007, p. 263), is directed to our own experience and makes it possible to regard our self as the "other." Hence, reflexivity is founded in "the call to constitute oneself as an object to be known in order to have access to the truth" (Geerinck, Masschelein, & Simons, 2010, p. 380).

The notion of reflexivity as a methodological construct originally evolved from philosophy. British philosopher Lawson (1985) posits that reflexivity was part of philosophy in its inception, beginning with the Greeks. However, since Kant and the Enlightenment, philosophy took part in "the great enterprise of knowledge" (p. 13) of positivism to pursue objective, scientific knowledge, which prevented researchers from engaging in subjectivity and reflexivity. Lawson argues that philosophers such as Nietzsche, Heidegger, and Derrida began to question the foundational role of philosophy in scientific knowledge claims, when they challenged reason, the empirical method, and the distinction between fact and value. These philosophers, according to Lawson, claimed that the enterprise of scientific knowledge must fail and they raised such perpetual questions as what is truth and/or who can claim the final truth, which no one could ever answer in a traditional sense. Hence, Lawson claims that the postmodern predicament is a "crisis of our truths, our values, and our most cherished beliefs . . . [a] crisis that owes to reflexivity its origin, its necessity, and its force" (p. 9).

Therefore, reflexivity is one of the central themes of postmodern philosophy, which, in turn, has influenced qualitative research methodology, including ethnography and narrative inquiry, which intend to discover the meaning of knowledge and truths from different angles. For example, Foley (2002), who points out how reflexive practices have taken place in recent ethnographic writing, argues that (critical) ethnography should move toward a "more engaging, useful, public storytelling genre" (p. 469) through more reflexive narrative practices. Hence, for Foley, reflexivity is a major confluence of the two research methodologies of ethnography and narrative inquiry.

Subjectivist, Confessional Reflexivity

Geertz (1973) argues that all ethnography is part philosophy and a good deal of the rest is confession. Although reflexivity exists in many guises (Foley, 2002),[1] subjectivist reflexivity, or **confessional reflexivity,** is the most common type of reflexivity used by qualitative researchers as an interrogation of subjectivity to challenge supposedly value-free objectivist discourse. The well-known anthropologist George Marcus (1998) calls this confessional type a "subjectivist kind of reflexivity" that focuses on the "self-critique, the personal quest, playing on the subjective, the experiential, and the idea of empathy" (p. 193). This kind of reflexivity was pioneered in feminist writing and autobiography or autoethnography (Marcus, 1998) although the publication of Malinowski's (1967) frank diary could be viewed as the first sign of confessional reflexivity, followed by many other mini-diaries and personal journals (Foley, 2002). As we discussed in Chapter 4, autobiography or autoethnography is one of the narrative inquiry genres in which the author/writer/researcher employs confessional, subjectivist reflexivity to explore "a living, contradictory, vulnerable, evolving multiple self, who speaks in a partial, subjective, culture-bound voice" (Foley, 2002, p. 474).

Ruth Behar's seminal work, *The Vulnerable Observer: Anthropology That Breaks Your Heart* (1996), is a case in point although there are many others. Drawing upon heartfelt autobiographical memories and her feelings of sorrow, shame, fear, and guilt, Behar uses subjectivist reflexivity in a compellingly vulnerable and evocative way. She argues that exploring and retelling the other's stories require emotion and vulnerability so that the researcher can reveal the hidden dialectic between connection and otherness (Foley, 2002). Hence, for Behar, anthropology that does not break one's heart is not worth doing. It is about "getting down in the mud" or "embarking on a voyage through a long tunnel" (Behar, 1996, p. 2), which, she notices, is not the kind of anthropology or any other social science being taught in academia, or the kind that the National Science Foundation or other national agencies want for a grant proposal.

However, this subjectivist, confessional reflexivity is not a realm that belongs to only autoethnographers. As we noted in the beginning of this section, all qualitative researchers should engage in some degree of reflexivity in every stage of research, although reflexivity might not be employed as a main method as in autoethnography. One of the reasons for incorporating reflexivity in research is to keep our subjectivity in check, and make it visible and explicit in the research process. That is, we reveal and question concomitantly our subjective social, political views, research interests, our choice of research design, theoretical framework, research participants, and interpretations, including all the biases, prejudices, and assumptions we possess that might influence the shaping of our research. That is, we keep the Rashomon effect in check, using reflexivity as a kaleidoscope. Reflexivity in research is thus "a process of critical reflection both on the kind of knowledge produced from research and how that knowledge is generated" (Guillemin & Gillam, 2004, p. 274). For example, Marcus (1998) notes how reflexivity is used in ethnography as "common currency to stand for possible but as-yet unrealized alternatives" (p. 190). Marcus states in regard to the crucial turn to reflexivity:

> The sometimes heated debate over the desirability of reflexivity marks the opening up of the ethnographic tradition to new possibilities, to a departure from the ideology of objectivity, distance, and the transparency of reality to concepts, toward a recognition of the need to explore the ethical, political, and epistemological dimensions of ethnographic research as an integral part of producing knowledge about others. (p. 189)

Clearly, reflexivity is necessary when we intend to produce knowledge about others. It has multiple uses as a measure of legitimacy, validity, rigor, and the politics of representation used by feminist scholars, ethnographers, anthropologists, sociologists, poststructuralists, phenomenologists, critical theorists, and critical race theorists (Pillow, 2003). Hence, I would posit that being reflexive is not only a skill but also a disposition that we should demonstrate in our work along with our *phronesis* (ethical, wise judgment). We need to incorporate reflexivity into our narrative research not only to achieve the rigor of research, but also to maintain our own as well as our participants' integrity.

A Paradox of Reflexivity: Whose Story Is It?

However, the concept of reflexivity as the subjective nature in qualitative research is a "slippery" term (Guillemin & Gillam, 2004, p. 274) that needs more speculation. In fact, Marcus (1998) points out that there is an intense polemics about reflexivity going on in academic departments among the dissertation committees of graduate students. According to Marcus, subjectivist reflexivity in anthropology, for example, opened the way for subjective interpretations to become a major method of anthropological theory and research practice, but once its critical function became well absorbed, "it lost its power and fell prey to those who would nervously dismiss reflexivity altogether" (p. 193). Hence, the argument goes: "Is reflexivity a license or a method?" (p. 189), which begs the question, "How do we know whether we are too reflexive or not reflexive enough?"

If you are a graduate student, you might encounter a committee member who urges you to dismiss reflexivity because it is too subjective (i.e., you are not allowed this *license*), or a committee member who encourages you to be more reflexive because you are not sufficiently self-critical (i.e., you are asked to use it as a systemic *method*). But, since we know why we need to embrace reflexivity in our research, we can justify its use to committee members who challenge us. However, we should also keep in mind that too much subjectivity, that is, confessional reflexivity, could be regarded as dead-end self-indulgence or narcissism. Furthermore, it could give the reader "the impression of an excessive self-consciousness" (Lawson, 1985, p. 125) with which the researcher seems to avoid making any assertions at all. Furthermore, when we use too much reflexivity in genres other than autobiography/autoethnography, we might be questioned by the reader, "Whose story is this, the researcher's or the participant's?" We might get carried away with our own reflexivity, busy talking about ourselves for the sake of being transparent, rather than talking about our participants.

An irony is that doing social science more subjectively is believed to lead to more objectivity (Devereux, 1967). That is, we engage in self-reflexivity in order to overcome the subjective nature of all social science knowledge, hence, the real goal of reflexivity in qualitative research is to achieve a significant level of objectivity (by being transparent about the research process, including the researcher's beliefs and attitudes). However, the more reflexive we are about our subjective influences on the research process, the more personal (the more subjective) we will be, as reflected in Behar's (1996) question, "Should we be worried that a smoke alarm will blare in our ears when the ethnography grows perilously hot and 'too personal'?" (p. 7). We are torn here, then, as reflexivity seems to be the "burden that we can neither carry nor throw off" (Lawson, 1985, p. 8). We have, alas, encountered "the paradoxes of reflexivity" (Lawson, 1985, p. 125).

Reflexivity as *Askēsis:* Self as an Object of Care

How, then, do we overcome the paradoxes, letting them cease to be paradoxical? How do we reach a balance between the two diverse functions of reflexivity, that is, on the one hand, "a means of critique, a weapon to be used against the great enterprise of knowledge, and on the other, a positive movement in the proposed alternative" (Lawson, 1985, p. 15)? How can we seek ways to render reflexivity into a positive force, saving it from being paradoxical reflexivity in our narrative research? I will not dare to pretend that I have answers for these questions. But, kindly allow me, if you will, to dwell on the notion of reflexivity a little longer as an attempt to address these lingering questions.

So far, the discussion of reflexivity has focused on the self as an object of knowledge. However, Foucault's notion of reflexivity, reflexivity as *askēsis* (ascesis or exercise in Greek) offers a different understanding of reflexivity, which I think can be used as a positive alternative en route to the balance between the dialectical/paradoxical functions of reflexivity. I am grateful for McGushin's work (2007) that introduced me to Foucault's *askēsis* in which the self is not seen as "object of knowledge" but as "object of care." Let me elaborate.

According to McGushin (2007), Foucault understood *askēsis* simply to mean exercise as in its original Greek context, as in training, practice, or development. Furthermore, for Foucault, in the Greek context, *askēsis* always had a "positive and productive meaning—exercising meant perfecting oneself, developing one's capacities, becoming who one is" (McGushin, 2007, p. xiii). Thus, *askēsis* refers to a philosophical exercise to develop oneself for the better.

Foucault, in one of his lecture series that he offered at the College de France, which later was published as the book *The Hermeneutics of the Subject* (2005), defines the notion of reflexivity as "an exercise of thought, of looking at oneself" (p. 460). He states, "In the West, we have known and practiced three major forms of the exercise of thought, of thought's reflection on itself; three major forms of reflexivity" (Foucault, 2005, p. 460). What, then, are the three major forms of reflexivity that Foucault speaks of? To briefly explain, they are the three M's: *memory, meditation,* and *method.* The first form of reflexivity, *memory,* is what gives access to the truth, to truth known in the form of recognition. In this form, we constantly seek truth through our recollections where we return to our "homeland" (p. 460) and our own being. The second form is *meditation* in which we carry out the test of what we think, "the test of oneself as the subject who actually thinks what he [*sic*] thinks and acts as he thinks, with the objective of the subject's transformation and constitution as, let's say, an ethical subject of the truth" (p. 460). Finally, the third form, *method,* is a form of reflexivity that makes it possible to fix what we believe as truth, providing an alternative that will advance the field of knowledge and truth. According to Foucault, these three forms of reflexivity (what I call the three M's) have dominated the practice and exercise of philosophy, hence, *askēsis.*

However, what Foucault wants to show us through this understanding of the three M's is the permanent relation between knowledge of the self and care of the self in ancient (Greek) thought. According to him, the three forms of reflexivity that we have used to analyze the problems of the subject since Descartes have always privileged the *knowledge of the self* as the guiding principle, unlike the Greeks who emphasized *the care of the self,* instead. For example, in Plato, the care of self was the center of the Platonic dialogue. Elsewhere, Foucault (1988) argues how our philosophical tradition has overemphasized the principle "Know yourself" and forgotten "Take care of yourself." He explains that in the modern world since Descartes, knowledge of the self (the thinking subject, as in Descartes's famous quote, *I think; therefore I am*) has taken on an "ever-increasing importance as the first step in the theory of knowledge" (p. 22). But for Foucault, this Western focus on the knowledge of the self, rather than the care of the self, is what prevented a theory of the subject from being further developed. He postulates that for the Ancients, *askēsis* involved constituting oneself, or more precisely, "arriving at the formation of a full, perfect, complete, and self-sufficient relationship with oneself, capable of producing the self-transfiguration that is the happiness one takes in oneself. Such was the objective of *askēsis*" (pp. 319–320). Thus, he argues that we need to reorient ourselves to focus on the care of the self for happiness that permeated ancient thought, because if one must know oneself, one must take care of the self. Foucault (2005) emphasizes, "Care of the self, precisely, is not just a knowledge, . . . It is a complex practice, which gives rise to completely different forms of reflexivity" (p. 462). His thesis, therefore, is that the care of the self must precede the modern imperative "know yourself," and knowledge of oneself should appear as the consequence of taking care of oneself. Hence, in the act of *askēsis* that takes place through the three M's of memory, meditation, and method, the self is an object of care before being an object of knowledge (Geerinck et al., 2010).

So, when we exercise our reflexivity through the three forms of reflexivity as a practice of care of the self in the notion of *askēsis,* we undertake a journey of transformation of self, as Foucault states, "Sure of having traveled far, one finds that one is looking down on oneself from above. The journey rejuvenates things, and ages the relationship with oneself" (cited in McGushin, 2007, p. xiii). For Foucault, constant exercise of reflexivity as *askēsis* or **reflexive askēsis,** is what helps us grow enough to "look down on ourselves from above"; therefore, it is what constitutes an "ethic of the self" and it is an "urgent, fundamental, and politically indispensable task" (cited in McGushin, 2007, p. xv).

Now, you ask, "What does this understanding of Foucault have to do with paradoxical reflexivity?" Yes, you are asking me to revisit the question we posed at the beginning of this section: How do we seek ways to render reflexivity into a positive force, saving it from being paradoxical reflexivity in our narrative research?

I think that Foucauldian *askēsis* offers a strong alternative to paradoxical reflexivity that might otherwise put us into a "rabbit hole" where there is no easy escape. When we exercise reflexivity as *askēsis,* a care of the self, it becomes our fundamental task of being an ethic of the self as well as that of others. This way, reflexivity will become a positive force that will allow us to overcome the dilemma or paradox of reflexivity. When we take care of ourselves through Foucauldian reflexivity, we also pay attention to others, which is an indispensable, ethical task.

An Example of Reflexive *Askēsis* Through *Currere*

Perhaps an example would be helpful here. As previously mentioned, *askēsis,* for Foucault, meant physical training in athletics as well as spiritual, philosophical training (McGushin, 2007). I wondered if reflexivity could be taught, as Pillow (2003) did:

I must admit that I do remain puzzled by how to teach students how to be reflexive. Is reflexivity a skill, a set of methods that can be taught? If so, what are the methods of reflexivity—is it keeping a research journal or the inclusion of a questioning researcher voice in the text? What should we be reflexive about? The other? Ourselves? The place? (p. 177)

For me as well, how to teach reflexivity was a puzzle, especially as a way to take care of the self and others. I mulled over the ways to incorporate the three forms of reflexivity, the three M's: *memory, meditation,* and *method.* Since Foucauldian reflexivity is a care of self, I thought that my students could start with an autobiographical essay in the form of *currere,* which refers to the running of the course. **Currere**, according to Pinar (2011), is the verb form of curriculum, emphasizes each individual's action, process, and experience. Indeed, *currere* emphasizes:

the everyday experience of the individual and his or her capacity to learn from that experience; to reconstruct experience through thought and dialogue to enable understanding. Such understanding, achieved by working through history and lived experience can help us reconstruct our own subjective and social lives. (Pinar, 2011, p. 2)

So, I wanted to "experiment" with this idea of having students "exercise" their reflexivity, or their reflexive *askēsis,* as a way to take care of self and others. Students in my doctoral seminar, Curriculum Theory, became my innocent "guinea pigs" for this experiment. One of the assignments I gave them was to work on their *currere* in writing, their personal journey of becoming, through reflexivity as *askēsis.* To my surprise, the students' presentation of that assignment became an outpouring of emotions. Imagine, these adult students, three female and five male students, their ages ranging (I'm guessing) between approximately the late twenties and early sixties, choking up during their presentations (although not all of them cried). I also had a huge lump in my throat, listening to their presentations of their autobiographical reflexive essays. I was touched by their candor and the vulnerability that they embodied during their presentations. It was not a "pity-me" session by any means. Rather, it was a critical examination of their growth and learning in light of reflexivity. They showed how their understanding of their own self was deeply involved with an act of "care" grounded in a variety of the curriculum theory literature that we read during the semester. They became (quite naturally) emotional talking about themselves, making themselves vulnerable, while bending back upon their self, encountering their true self, through the exercise of being reflexive, as in "an exercise of thought, of thought's reflection on itself, of looking at oneself" (Foucault, 2005, p. 460). It was a moment of evidence of releasing a self from the self that they have known or they have not known.

One of these surprising outcomes came from Kevin, who kindly gave me permission to use an excerpt of his work, which I present below:

"Go Ahead! Kill yourself!"

   Those were my wife's words resonating through the door after I had barricaded myself in the bathroom during the Summer of 2005. It was at that darkest moment in my life that I began the long journey of searching for myself at the age of 32. Arthur Bochner (1997) clarifies my position by quoting David Carr (1986):

This is the work of self-narration: to make a life that seems to be falling apart come together again, by retelling and "restorying" the events of one's life. At certain junctures in life, this narrative challenge can be a terrible struggle, and we do not always succeed. The unity of life, its apparent wholeness across time, is simply there—sometimes figure, sometimes ground (p. 418).

Bochner's (1997) personal narrative entitled, It's About Time: Narrative and the Divided Self, is a call to action. It is a voice from the field that encourages us to slow down and take the time to recount our lives in such a way that transforms ourselves as well as others. The intersubjective nature of this communal proposition, whereby we encourage others to take part in the subjective analysis of oneself and share it with others, is where personal narratives can be prescribed. That is what Bochner did with his personal narrative about how his father's death changed his life. These narratives are reflexive in nature. Being reflexive is a process that not only asks us to reflect upon past events but pushes us to criticize and subjectify our own thinking of those events in order to grow. Aristotle said, "if you would understand anything, observe its beginning and its development." By deconstructing the way we internalize past events, we sometimes painfully open wounds in an attempt to cleanse and purify so that strength and endurance can emerge.

Autobiographical text in curricular discourse emerged in the 1970s through, what Pinar (1974) expressed as Currere. Currere is an account of one's life, or in Pinar and Grumet's (1976) words, "to run the course" of one's life (p. vii). For Pinar and Grumet, the course of one's life should encompass a shift from biographical text to autobiographical text. This means that we must avoid the simple act of reflecting on one's life through biographical text and explore the deeper meaning of one's life through a reflexive approach in autobiographical processes. This can be accomplished through currere, which is a "systematic search of our inner experience" (Pinar, 1974, p. 3; quoted in Pinar, Reynolds, Slattery, & Taubman, 2008, p. 519). Through this analysis of inner experience one must account for past memories as an integral component of the present. In so doing, the self becomes reflexive. "The analysis of currere is like phenomenological bracketing; one distances oneself from past and future so to be more free of the present" (Pinar, et. al., 2008, p. 520). This is the focus of autobiographical narratives. They should create a new future through the transformative opening of wounds. That deconstructive process is where we move ourselves inward, outward, forward, backward, diagonally, and circularly in an attempt to find our being. Grumet (1981) continues by expressing that, "currere represents a wrestling of individual experience" (quoted in Pinar, et. al., 2008, p. 521). . . .

The life that was falling apart for me in the Summer of 2005 came to a critical juncture that day in the bathroom. My life in 2005, a terrible struggle, was indeed falling apart, as Carr (1986) pointed out. It would not come together again for many years. "How to encompass in our minds the complexity of some lived moments of life? You don't do that with theories. You don't do that with a system of ideas. You do it with a story" (Coles, 1989, p. 128; quoted in Bochner, 1997, p. 418). What follows is my archeological story of self.

(An Excerpt of Kevin's *Currere*)

What followed this excerpt was Kevin's deeply personal story of a life that was "falling apart," which then eventually evolved into a story of himself as a caring teacher who became more attentive to students' voices. As we can see from his writing, it is obvious that Kevin was "exer-cising" his reflexivity as *askēsis,* considering the self as the object of care, as he stated, "This means that we must avoid the simple act of reflecting on one's life through biographical text and explore the deeper meaning of one's life through a reflexive approach in autobiographical pro-cesses." By going deeper, beyond the simple act of reflecting, he struck a chord for his self and others, including me, in class, evoking emotions that connected all of us with unspoken cama-raderie about an understanding of what it means to be human. Once again, it was a great reminder of what Ruth Behar (1996) said: "Call it sentimental, call it Victorian and nineteenth century, but I say that anthropology that doesn't break your heart just isn't worth doing any-more" (p. 177). Although we were not doing anthropology, the reflexive exercise *(askēsis)* we experimented through *currere* had a surprising effect on all of us, perhaps more enlightening than any other course readings. I will continue this reflexive exercise so as to help students to work on their reflexivity as *askēsis,* an act of taking care of oneself and others, which I believe is an indispensable, ethical task.

I have spent much space here discussing the role of reflexivity. Although the question of how much or how little reflexivity to use remains unanswered, my point is that we should use reflex-ivity in narrative inquiry in order to avoid the "danger of drowning in a tsunami of solipsistic studies" (Josselson, 2006, p. 5). There are several types of reflexivity that we narrative inquirers need to employ. I suggest Foucauldian reflexive *askēsis* can be used to overcome the paradox of reflexivity, as it urges us to take care of self and others as a way of pursuing subjective knowledge.

On Bricolage and Bricoleur

The next issue I would like to discuss is the notion of **bricolage** and **bricoleur**. A few weeks ago I had a chance to observe my new colleague's qualitative research class for peer evaluation. I enjoyed the observation very much, as there was rich dialogue going on in the class. Students were asked to share what they learned from the book they had chosen to read for their book review assignment. One student raised her hand and said:

> I read Ruth Lindin's "Making Stories, Making Selves." I enjoyed it a lot, and learned a lot. But I have a question. The author talks about her qualitative study being phenomenological, but then she also talks about her study being symbolic interaction and grounded theory. How is it possi-ble? How do these different methodologies go together? How can a researcher choose more than one methodology in her study? It was confusing to me. I didn't get it. I was like, is she a terrible methodologist or what?

Students burst into laughter at her last statement. It was clear that this student had learned much about different types of qualitative research and that some of the methodologies were not supposed to be used together in a single study unless the researcher was a "terrible methodolo-gist." Other students nodded at her question as if they had meant to ask the same question.

They all looked at their professor who was also wearing a smile on her face. She cheerfully said, "Good question! Some qualitative researchers would mix different methodologies and epistemologies within their research. What you have to do is to *justify* your choices." She emphasized the word *justify.* I agreed with her wholeheartedly, as we are living in the world of a "technology of justification" (Kincheloe & Berry, 2004, p. 3).

For me, the student's question also presented a teachable moment to talk about the notion of bricolage that Denzin and Lincoln (1994) brought up in their first *Handbook of Qualitative Research.* They state:

> The multiple methodologies of qualitative research may be viewed as a bricolage, and the researcher as bricoleur . . . the combination of multiple methods . . . within a single study is best understood, then, as a strategy that adds rigor, breadth, and depth to any investigation. (p. 2)

So, the notion of bricolage in qualitative research has been around for a while. More specifically, Denzin and Lincoln (2011) point out that qualitative researchers became bricoleurs in the blurred genre phase (1970–1986), "learning how to borrow from many different disciplines" (p. 3). They posit that qualitative research can be viewed as a bricolage as qualitative researchers may use multiple methods, multiple epistemological and philosophical frameworks, and/or multiple forms of representations in their study. A qualitative researcher as a bricoleur, then, would "produce a bricolage, a pieced-together set of representations that are fitted to the specifics of a complex situation" (p. 4).

If you recall, we discussed how narrative inquiry is interdisciplinary in Chapter 1 and how there is a diversity of theories, methods, genres, and interpretations and analyses in other chapters. Should a narrative inquirer insist on one grand theory, one methodology/method, or one type of analysis in a single study without crossing the boundary of his or her own discipline? If so, then, how would it be possible for us to address the issues of intersectionality between class, race, and gender, genre blurring of representations, and multiple truths and different voices? Perhaps there is a need for a narrative inquirer to use multiple epistemologies or multiple forms of representations, and become a bricoleur. Kincheloe and Berry (2004) write:

> Bricoleurs in their appreciation of the complexity of the research process view research method as involving far more than procedure. In this mode of analysis bricoleurs come to understand research method as also a *technology of justification,* meaning a way of defending what we assert we know and the process by which we know it. (p. 3, italics added)

Again, the key here is a "technology of justification" as a way of justifying logically, empathically, and metaphorically our complex choices of methods, combinations, or genre blurrings. This is "far more than procedure." OK, I think I am getting ahead of myself. I should first explain exactly what bricolage is and where it originally came from.

Lévi-Strauss's Use of Bricolage and Bricoleur

The French terms *bricolage* and *bricoleur* were first used as an analogy in the academic field by the father of anthropology and a structuralist, Claude Lévi-Strauss, in his book *The Savage Mind* (1966). Lévi-Strauss used these concepts to explain how myths or mythical thoughts are produced in a form of "intellectual bricolage" (p. 17). Lévi-Strauss explains that in his time in France, the bricoleur means "someone who works with his [sic] hands and uses devious means compared to those of a craftsman" (p. 17),[2] and a bricolage is the creation of a bricoleur, in which a new arrangement of elements that come in handy is put together. In this case, the bricoleur does not need all the equipment and knowledge of all trades and professions, but understands that these elements he or she collects have multiple functions. Lévi-Strauss uses these terms as an analogy to understand and analyze mythological structure in anthropology: Myth is created by a bricoleur, and bricolage is the mythological world created by the bricoleur. That is, a bricoleur collects the elements and things to build up a mythical thought as a bricolage. Further, according to Lévi-Strauss, the bricoleur is "adept at performing a large number of diverse tasks" (p. 17):

> Indeed principally, derives his [sic] poetry from the fact that he does not confine himself to accomplishment and execution: he "speaks" not only *with* things . . . but also through the medium of things: giving an account of his personality and life by the choices he makes between the limited possibilities. The "bricoleur" may not ever complete his purpose but he always puts something of himself into it. Mythical thought appears to be an intellectual form of "bricolage" in this sense also. (p. 21, italics in original)

Employing the notion of bricolage, Lévi-Strauss theorizes how mythical thought, as valid as scientific thought, is an intellectual act formed by a bricoleur who builds up structures by fitting together events, using whatever is left over (second-hand sources) from events.

Here is a good example of a latter-day, American version of bricoleur in Lévi-Strauss's sense. Recently, I read an article about Tyler Hays in the *Wall Street Journal Magazine* (Haskell, 2014). Hays is an American furniture maker, ceramicist, painter, woodworker, and founder of a high-end design firm, BDDW. Before he became a successful entrepreneur, he was a manual laborer, construction worker, handyman, electrician, woodchopper, and did other odd jobs. He is currently in the middle of a plan to design a dining table that converts into a table tennis table. Hays is described as having "a child's curiosity with adult taste" (p. 104), being compared to Charles and Ray Eames, who are among the most important American designers of the twentieth century. What has made Hays a distinctive artisan is his hankering for experimentation: Trying things out with his imagination and creativity in his own way. In fact, Hays says his artistic process is organic (read, messy) rather than building anything start to finish. Like what Lévi-Strauss states, Hays, an American "bricoleur," may "not ever complete his purpose" but it seems that he "always puts something of himself into it."

Then, imagine yourself, narrative inquirer, as a bricoleur who longs to experiment, to try things out with imagination and creativity. You would be "adept" at performing different tasks, and you would put something of yourself into it although you may not ever complete your purpose (just like Bakhtin's unfinalizability). Before we get into the notion of narrative inquirer as a bricoleur, let's discuss in more detail how the notion has been advanced in qualitative research.

Bricolage in Interdisciplinary Qualitative Research

The analogy of bricolage was taken seriously by Kincheloe as a concept to be applied to qualitative research, following Denzin and Lincoln, discussed earlier. At his Egon Guba Lecture delivered in 2001, Kincheloe remarked of bricolage: "No concept better captures the possibility of the future of qualitative research" (Kincheloe, 2001, p. 679). In his lecture, he specified the notion of bricolage and bricoleur to push qualitative research to the next conceptual level beyond what Denzin and Lincoln used. He emphasizes how a qualitative researcher as a bricoleur recognizes the limitations of a single method, and delves into multiple methods of inquiry as well as diverse theoretical and philosophical notions of the various research design elements. Thus, he situates bricolage in the "cosmos of disciplinarity and interdisciplinarity" (p, 680).

However, we need to be aware of a constant tension between disciplinarians and interdisciplinarians. Kincheloe (2001) states:

> Disciplinarians maintain that interdisciplinary approaches to analysis and research result in superficiality, interdisciplinary proponents argue that disciplinarity produces naïve overspecialization. The vision of the bricolage promoted here recognizes the dialectical nature of this disciplinary and interdisciplinary relationship and calls for a synergistic interaction between the two concepts. (p. 683)

What Kincheloe (2001; Kincheloe & Berry, 2004) emphasizes is that we cannot engage in the work of bricolage successfully unless we have a rigorous understanding of the particular discipline of our own, for example, acknowledging positive contributions as well as avoiding disciplinary dogmatism. Hence, the interdisciplinary nature of bricolage is not and cannot be superficial. In fact, true interdisciplinary qualitative research is where "disciplinary boundaries are crossed and the analytical frames of more than one discipline are employed by the researcher" (2001, p. 685). Kellner (1995) in cultural studies also maintains the importance of multiperspectival, interdisciplinary features, because any single research perspective is laden with narrowly defined assumptions and blindnesses. To avoid the deficits of a single perspective, according to Kellner, researchers must learn a variety of ways of seeing and interpreting in the pursuit of knowledge, leading to interdisciplinary research and blurred genres.

Qualitative researchers who embrace the complex view of bricolage seek to broaden the restrictive disciplines using an interdisciplinary approach, thus becoming bricoleurs. Bricoleurs would utilize knowledge from philosophy, history, literary theory, the arts, and so on, to inform their own disciplinary field, as already shown in interdisciplinary fields such as women's and gender studies, African American studies, queer theory, and studies in popular culture, among others. Hence, Kincheloe (2001) argues for "bricolage as deep interdisciplinarity: the synergy of multiple perspectives" (p. 686).

Narrative Inquirer as Bricoleur

It may sound like a tall order if I urge you, especially if you are a beginner in narrative inquiry, to be a bricoleur who is conversant with multiple perspectives, methods, and methodologies, along with recent developments in your discipline. But don't let it overwhelm you. In fact, I think that it is at the beginning stage of becoming a narrative inquirer that we should start learning to be bricoleurs, because I don't see that becoming a bricoleur is a linear developmental process, moving from one step to the next. I have observed some students developing a narrow, myopic view of research early on, unwilling to step outside their own disciplines, which is concerning. As we have learned in this book, there are multiple genres in narrative inquiry, multiple theoretical frameworks, multiple narrative analyses and methods, informed by literary theory, anthropology, sociology, history, philosophy, education, and more. Perhaps this multiplicity is one of the unique features of narrative inquiry that enriches the field of qualitative research, distinct from other types of qualitative methodology. This inherently interdisciplinary nature of narrative inquiry is not surprising, though, as narrative is embedded in every aspect of our life. Hence, becoming a narrative bricoleur is perhaps a natural destination as "a lifetime endeavor" (Kincheloe & Berry, 2004, p. 4), an effort we all should exert in order to make a difference in the lives of people that we serve.

Narrative bricoleurs learn from differences, as they are not chained to the same assumptions. They are willing to look through a kaleidoscope. Therefore, they understand that "all methods are subject to questioning and analysis, especially in light of so many other strategies designed for similar purposes" (Kincheloe, 2001, p. 686). They will transcend certain forms and rules that confine the researcher's ability to think beyond boundaries. Hence, a narrative bricoleur does not "simply *tolerate* difference but *cultivates* it as a spark to researcher creativity" (Kincheloe, 2001, p. 687, emphasis added). Such a bricoleur is sensitive to ontological, philosophical, epistemological, historical, hermeneutical, methodological, and analytical differences. Synergized by the interaction with other possibilities (unknown territories), the resulting bricolage of narrative inquiry would provide a new angle of research, pushing the boundaries of narrative research.

On "Small" Stories

As narrative bricoleurs, we want to make ourselves familiar with a contemporary trend in narrative inquiry. In recent years, there has been a growing interest in "small" stories in narrative inquiry (Freeman, 2006), especially in the field of socio-linguistics and psychology, around the topics of identity development. This trend is now overflowing into the field of education (see, for example, Olson & Craig, 2009). The terms "small" and "big" stories have emerged as a "new narrative turn" (Bamberg, 2006, p. 128), offering a different approach to narrative inquiry and analysis (Bamberg, 2006; De Fina & Georgakopoulou, 2012; Georgakopoulou, 2006). The focus on small stories comes with the criticism that life story or biographical and autobiographical research tends to ignore small stories that reside in everyday conversations that do not necessarily make up a part of the big story. For instance, Bamberg (2006) posits that life story or biographical research (representing big stories) seems to be "resting on assumptions that are not moving narrative inquiry forward but rather holding it back" although it is "alive and well—possibly a little too well" (p. 139).

Well, the criticism of life story or (auto)biographical research as something that is "holding narrative inquiry back" does not sit well with me, or with Freeman (2006).[3] However, small story advocates have a good point, as they poignantly ask, "What do you do with stories in your data that do not quite fit the theme or a plotline?" (Georgakopoulou, 2006). As a "big" story advocate, I admit that I have wondered about that, too.

According to Georgakopoulou (2006), while big stories are mainly used in life history or (auto) biographical narrative research,[4] derived from in-depth interviews about the past, small stories are atypical, non-canonical, underrepresented narrative data that include "tellings of ongoing events, future or hypothetical events, shared (known) events, but also allusions to (previous) tellings, deferrals of tellings, and refusals to tell" (De Fina & Georgakopoulou, 2012, p. 116). These tellings, according to small story advocates, tend to be easily skipped by narrative researchers because they are typically "small," fragmented, unpredictable, and multifaceted, compared to a "big," long, coherent narrative of life history, for example.

Small stories, derived from everyday social exchange, are mostly about very recent ("this morning," "last night") events, such as breaking news, which, in today's technological era, is frequently reported in email, texting, mobile phone calls, and tweeting with peers (Georgakopoulou, 2006). Georgakopoulou proposes that such breaking news leads to small stories of projections that involve near-future encounters and happenings (as in an "I will say" or "She [He] will say" type of narrative). When they are shared through conversations, they turn into shared stories, family of stories, or intertextual stories linking story to story. Hence, this interest in small stories has moved narrative inquiry from "the study of narrative as text (first wave) to the study of narrative-in-context" (Georgakopoulou, 2006, p. 123). More specifically, it is a new narrative turn, one that does not prioritize a unified, coherent, reflected-upon self within a retroactive view of narrative.

This narrative shift to studying small stories or the study of narrative-in-context reminds me of a conversation I had with a fellow narrative researcher who came to my session at the annual meeting of the American Educational Research Association a few years ago. I was talking about how important it was to make a story coherent in temporal ordering from data that were inconsistent and fragmented. I was big on writing a "big story"! This fellow researcher asked, "Then, what do you do when you have children's stories that are not necessarily coherent but fragmented due to their story nature? Wouldn't it be too artificial if we try to make such data coherent? Can't we use the data as they are (being fragmented)?" We had an interesting conversation about how to use "small" stories although we didn't use the term at that time.

Small story proponents challenge the narrative tradition of privileging (auto)biographic narratives as the means par excellence to sort out one's past, self, identity, and life. They argue that orienting toward narrative (small stories) that focuses on what is done in interaction and context, and how it is done, would provide a new direction for narrative research, as it can provide a needed meeting point for narrative analysis and narrative inquiry (Bamberg, 2006; Georgakopoulou, 2006). In particular, Georgakopoulou (2006) proposes that small stories be considered mainstream narrative research that establishes connections between their interactional features and their sites of engagement (context). According to her, the significance of small stories resides in the representation of narrators' social practice presented in the talk-in-interaction or in everyday dialogue and conversation among friends, family, and others.

I find the discussion of small stories as a new narrative turn quite important. In fact, I am grateful for it because it complements narrative genres discussed in Chapter 4, which focus on the retrospective narrative of the past and lived experience, what Georgakopoulou (2006) and Bamberg (2006) call mainstream narrative research. This new narrative turn seems fitting and timely, given the current emphasis in conversational or dialogic interviews between the researcher and the researched. It certainly contributes to extending the trajectories of narrative inquiry, as it allows us to pay attention to inconsistent, fragmented, immediate yet important short everyday conversational narratives that may otherwise go unnoticed. Furthermore, this narrative turn has become the impetus for conversational analysis, interactive analysis, dialogic analysis, or performance analysis to be included in narrative inquiry.[5]

"Living Narratives": The Origin of "Small" Stories

Georgakopoulou (2006) credits Ochs and Capps (2001) with blazing a trail to the beginning of small stories, as they emphasize creating the life of narrative in everyday storytelling, which they call **living narratives**. According to Ochs and Capps, *living narratives* are everyday conversational narratives of personal experience that can be regarded as "unrehearsed renderings of events close to the time of the telling" that contain "hesitations, unfinished thoughts, interruptions, and often contradictions" (p. 56). They point out that existing narrative research has centered around narratives with coherent temporal orderings of events and a plot line with a beginning, a middle, and an end, conveying a particular perspective. They argue that narrative research should go beyond these central topics and instead explore *living narratives* as "a hallmark of the human condition" (p. 57), that is less polished, less coherent, but pervasive in ordinary social encounters. Hence, the boundaries of *living narratives* reach beyond the past to include present issues that may be carried out to the future. The plotline of *living narratives* is built collaboratively in a conversation between the two storytellers, and it may or may not encompass a beginning, middle, and end, given that life events are neither necessarily coherent nor immediately resolvable. Therefore, *living narratives* are considered "rough works in progress" (p. 57) that indicate the research participant's ongoing, unresolved life experiences.

Ochs and Capps (2001) further theorize the notion of *living narratives* drawing upon linguistics, anthropology, and psychology, while incorporating literary and philosophical reflections of self, text, and social life. They postulate that the practice of narrative inquiry that renders personal experience entails de-personalization with the potential to broaden the personal experience to social experience. They write:

Though the experiences may be unique, they become socially forged. Idiosyncratic experiences become co-narrated according to local narrative formats, recognizable types of situations and people, and prevailing moral frameworks, which inevitably constrain representation and interpretation. It is in this sense that narratives of personal experience are at the same time narratives of impersonal experience. (p. 55)

Hence, conversational narratives of personal experience projected in the living narratives become paradoxically depersonalized because personal narratives share unique features that are recognizable by other people (the social). Their premise is that when a storyteller relates an experience, the experience becomes the object of public discourse. The experience is then given shape and meaning by those participating in ordinary social exchanges or interactions between the teller and the researcher, rendering the dialogic character of everyday narrative, which calls attention to dialogic and performative narrative.

Storytelling as Performance

Viewing small stories as *living narratives* in a conversation or in interaction among friends, family members, neighbors, or community groups extends our understanding of narratives to performative storytelling. Narrative inquiry is currently extended to the realm of performative inquiry, as scholars have called upon performance as a way of knowing how to understand human phenomena (Pelias, 2008). In fact, we are living in the age of performance where "the buzz over performance is nearly everywhere in the academy" (Madison & Hamera, 2006, p. xiii). Performative storytelling becomes a critical part of narrative inquiry beginning with Goffman's notion of the presentation of self to others (Goffman, 1972), where Goffman defines performance as "all the activity of a given participant on a given occasion which serves to influence in any way any of the other participants (audience, observers, or co-participants)" (p. 244).

For example, autobiographical performance is characterized as "the direct communication of the personal between the writer or performer and the reader/spectator" (Miller & Taylor, 2006, p. 169). Miller and Taylor further explicate two forms that autobiographical performance encompasses: personal narrative performance and auto/biographical performance. While both narrative forms address an audience directly, they differ in some marked ways: In personal narrative, performers stage crafted narratives of themselves, hence the writer is also the performer, whereas in auto/biography, performers present "the intersection of a contemporary life with an historical one" (p. 170), where the central focus is the historical figure and the writer/performer's story becomes secondary. In both forms of performative storytelling, the performer "risks exposure and vulnerability in the effort to breach rigid prohibitions that perpetuate silence" (Park-Fuller, 2000, p. 24).

Langellier and Peterson (2004) also theorize a practice of narrative that moved from story text to storytelling performance, drawing upon semiotic phenomenology. According to them, storytelling practices are rooted in people's daily lives, families, and communities, as we see in the statement, "Let me tell you a story." Thus, the emphasis on storytelling performance conceptualizes narrative "as act, event, and discourse—a site for understanding and intervening in the ways culture produces, maintains, and transforms relations of identity and difference" (p. 3). This narrative turn to performance comes with the understanding that narrative is performed everywhere, as people make sense of their experiences and construct identities while interacting with each other and participating in cultural conversations through acts of storytelling. Drawing heavily upon Benjamin's (1969) notion of storytelling as performance, Peterson and Langellier (2006), further explicate how "Benjamin combines a description of narrative as a making (of experience for listeners) with a description of narrative as a doing (talking, telling, and listening)" (p. 174). Therefore, according to them, there are two ways of understanding narrative as performance: narrative as a *making* and narrative as a *doing*. First, the understanding of narrative as *a making* is evident in investigations into the elements, aspects, and structures that make up narrative, including making arguments, making small talk, and making decisions. The second way of understanding narrative is narrative as *a doing* as evidenced in "explorations of the behaviors, habits, practices, and institutions which enact, execute, or do narrative" (p, 174). Therefore, they observe that "performance turns up in narrative studies at the confluence of two ways of understanding narrative: that is, narrative is both a making and a doing" (p. 173).

Exactly what is it that we narrative inquirers should look for in storytelling as performance? Since the performance turn situates narrative as both a making and a doing, we should attend to "the bodies of participants as well as to bodies of knowledge, to the materiality and the situationality of narrative practice" (Peterson & Langellier, 2006, p. 174). More specifically, as Riessman (2008) explains, performative narrative, including the audience as an active presence, interrogates "how talk among speakers is interactively (dialogically) produced and performed as narrative" (p. 105). Hence, we pay attention to contexts in which a dialogue/conversation takes place including place, time, and social and cultural circumstances, in addition to nonverbal aspects of communication such as gesture, facial expression, pause, and silence. Performative stories would be investigated in contexts that are interactional, historical, institutional, and discursive, to name a few, focusing on to whom, when, why, and for what purposes a conversation is carried out and addressed.

The first and most interesting performative storytelling I encountered was when I took Barone's narrative inquiry class. We were asked to watch the "guru" of ethnodrama, Johnny Saldaña's play as a part of the class assignment, which was in performance at that time at the ASU theatre. Saldaña's ethnodrama was a story about the well-known ethnographer Harry Wolcott's intimate relationship with his life history participant, Brad, the young man known as the "sneaky kid." When I watched the performance, I didn't have any background information about the play. In my ignorance, I didn't know who Wolcott was, not to mention Saldaña. It was in the class we had following the performance that I learned about Wolcott, Saldaña, and ethnodrama. I still vividly remember my shock when I saw how the researcher (Wolcott) had an intimate relationship with his participant, Brad, and how Brad came back to the researcher's house later and set it on fire. The ethnodrama taught me, in the audience, that conducting qualitative research and doing fieldwork is a serious business, posing many potential problems to researchers, especially ethical issues pertinent to the relationship between the researcher and the researched (see Wolcott, 2002, for the complete script of Saldana's ethnodrama, which is available as an appendix). To me, it is the most compelling performative storytelling I have ever experienced.

As we see performative storytelling gaining increasing attention among narrative inquirers, I would like to leave you with some critical questions that the performance study pioneer Conquergood (2006) raised in his seminal work on performance, *Rethinking Ethnography*, originally published in 1991:

- What happens to our thinking about performance when we move it outside of aesthetics and situate it at the center of lived experience?
- What are the methodological implications of thinking about fieldwork as the collaborative performance of an enabling fiction between observer and observed, knower and known?
- How does thinking about fieldwork as performance differ from thinking about fieldwork as the collection of data?
- What kinds of knowledge are privileged or displaced when performed experience becomes a way of knowing, a method of critical inquiry, a mode of understanding?
- What are the rhetorical problematics of performance as a complementary or alternative form of "publishing" research?
- What is the relationship between performance and power?
- How does performance simultaneously reproduce and resist hegemony?

(Adapted from Conquergood, 2006, p. 361)

Conclusion: Pushing the Boundary of Narrative Inquiry

Reading this chapter, you might feel as if you were in an endless maze of issues of narrative inquiry although only a few of them are addressed here. Some issues seem as elusive as a mirage, escaping our full grasp, as they branch out in so many different directions depending on the angle from which you look at them. But this is not to discourage our exploration; rather, it is to acknowledge the kind of joyful, awe-filled moments we might experience by looking through a kaleidoscope. There are multiple ways of seeing, understanding, theorizing, and philosophizing the very human phenomena we like to story. I hope that the issues we discuss here will give you some food for thought, some ways to think about how to push the boundaries of narrative inquiry, which will take us to a brighter future for narrative inquiry. I certainly don't want us to be stagnant, just enjoying the status quo of the renaissance of narrative inquiry. There are much more complex and uncharted narrative areas and issues that need to be tapped into by emerging narrative inquirers like you. The future of narrative inquiry truly depends on you.

QUESTIONS FOR REFLECTION

- How will you negotiate using your "backyard" for your research site?
- What will you do if you get contradicting stories from your participants?
- What is your understanding of reflexivity and what kind of reflexivity are you going to use?
- How will you suppose yourself to be a bricoleur?
- What are your thoughts on "small" stories?

ACTIVITIES

1. Write your own *currere*, exercising your reflexivity as *askēsis*.

2. Attend a talk, an exhibit, or a concert that is outside your discipline. Find ways to become a narrative bricoleur.

3. Experience performative storytelling by performing the story you have written.

4. Bring up any other critical issues in narrative inquiry that are missing here, discuss them with your classmates, and try to theorize them for a journal article.

SUGGESTED READINGS

ON REFLEXIVITY

Mosselson, J. (2010). Subjectivity and reflexivity: Locating the self in research on dislocation. *International Journal of Qualitative Studies in Education, 23*(4), 479–494.
Pillow, W. (2003). Rethinking the uses of reflexivity as methodological power in qualitative research. *International Journal of Qualitative Studies in Education, 16*(2), 175–196.

ON BRICOLAGE AND BRICOLEUR

Kincheloe, J. L. (2001). Describing the bricolage: Conceptualizing a new rigor in qualitative research. *Qualitative Inquiry, 7*(6), 679–696.

ON SMALL STORIES

Bamberg, M. (2006). Stories: Big or small. *Narrative Inquiry, 16*(1), 139–147.
Georgakopoulou, A. (2006). Thinking big with small stories in narrative and identity analysis. *Narrative Inquiry, 16*(1), 122–130.

On Performative Storytelling

Madison, D. S., & Hamera, J. (2006). *The SAGE handbook of performance studies.* Thousand Oaks, CA: Sage.

Park-Fuller, L. (2000). Performing absence: The staged personal narrative as testimony. *Text and Performance Quarterly, 20,* 20–42.

Peterson, E., & Langellier, K. (2006). The performance turn in narrative studies. *Narrative Inquiry, 16*(1), 173–180.

NOTES

1. Foley (2002) delineates four types of reflexivity: confessional, theoretical, textual, and deconstructive, grounded in Marcus's (1998) discussion about three styles of reflexivity: sociological, anthropological, and feminist. Also, see Pillow (2003) for a more comprehensive discussion on reflexivity.
2. The translator notes that the "bricoleur" has no precise equivalent in English. In French, it refers to a person who is a "Jack of all trades or a kind of professional do-it-yourself person" (p. 17). Lévi-Strauss uses the term, as an analogy to represent a creator of myth or mythical thought.
3. Please see Freeman (2006) for the logical defense of "big stories" or (auto)biographical research against Bamberg's criticism.
4. Georgakopoulou (2006) refers "big stories" to narrative canon (canonical narrative), or grand narratives (Lyotard, 1984), but from my understanding, grand narratives or master narratives in postmodern sense refer to hegemonic ideas that are disseminated by people in power. Hence, in this chapter, I narrow the scope of big stories to mean biographical or autobiographical narrative research in general.
5. Please see Riessman (2008) for the discussion of dialogic and performative narrative analysis.

CHAPTER TOPICS

©Tom Parish, T. Candon—Root Cellar,
Liberty Township, Geary County, KS 2012

CHAPTER 9

Examples of Narrative Inquiry

Theory Into Practice

QUESTIONS TO CONSIDER

- What particular issues of narrative inquiry from previous chapters have you found most interesting?
- In what ways are those issues reflected (or not reflected) in the examples provided in this chapter?
- How would you critique the examples provided in this chapter based on the knowledge you have gained?

INTRODUCTION

Some of you might be wondering what happened to Bryan, whose research experience I was sharing with you. Well, I regret to tell you that he decided not to use narrative inquiry and went ahead with a qualitative case study, the method his advisor was most familiar with, after finishing collecting data through interviews. Bryan came to my office to tell me that.

Bryan: Dr. Kim, I'm sorry but my dissertation advisor doesn't want me to pursue narrative inquiry any more.

Me: (My eyes got big) Huh? What do you mean? What happened?

Bryan: (Scratching his head) Well, you know, I played, I mean, I flirted with my data to craft a story, you know, using Polkinghorne's narrative analysis. I was trying to sort of "fictionalize" my participants' experiences of our local community counseling center based on the interview transcripts. Well, I showed some of the draft story to my advisor and he was not happy with it. He was almost suspicious of me.

Me: (My eyes got bigger) Suspicious of you?

Bryan: He didn't think fictionalization was a good idea. He had serious misgivings about "validity" and "trustworthiness" of my analysis and interpretation. He wanted to see the evidence. He didn't think that the story I was fictionalizing was warranted. He thought it was all coming out of my bias and imagination. He kept asking, while pointing his index finger at my paper, "How do I know this actually happened? How do I know which is true and which is not? Is this what you narrative people do?"

Gulp. My heart sank. I didn't take it personally, though. (Oh, really?) To make a long story short, Bryan's advisor ended up requesting that Bryan do "traditional" qualitative research, namely case study, focusing on finding emergent themes and providing concrete examples from data. To Bryan's advisor, perhaps, fictionalization was equal to unfounded and biased research practice. Out of respect for his decision, I read Bryan's draft carefully, and I actually understood why Bryan's advisor became "suspicious." The story Bryan (re)constructed was premature, which was very understandable given that it was Bryan's first try. The story plot (see, for example, the Labovian model in Chapter 6) was loose, and Spence's narrative smoothing (see also Chapter 6) was not incorporated in a way that made the story plausible, engaging, and evocative (see Chapter 3 and 4 for story criteria). There were many loopholes, eyebrow-raising incidences, and descriptions that did not hang together. Although I gave a lot of credit to Bryan for his effort, the draft was not good enough to convince his advisor, who was not a narrative inquirer. I learned much from this experience: we have to design our narrative inquiry carefully (including a selection of narrative genres, analysis and interpretation), and most important, we need a lot of practice in narrative writing.

Some examples would be helpful for our practice. So, this chapter presents some narrative inquiry examples that are published in peer reviewed academic journals. Please note that these examples do not necessarily represent the best narrative articles. Rather, they are possibilities that you can learn from as you consider whether they are good models, or not-so-good models, for you. We can use this opportunity as a way to practice, question, adapt, and create the narrative inquiry format that may best suit your research agenda.

Due to the space limit, I provide an excerpt of each example, following general information about the article. These excerpts typically skip the introduction and the literature review section. After each excerpt, a few questions follow to help guide a discussion.

Example of Narrative Inquiry as Phenomenon and Method

Clandinin, D. J., & Huber, J. (2002). Narrative Inquiry: Toward Understanding Life's Artistry. *Curriculum Inquiry, 32*(2), 161–169. Reproduced with permission of Blackwell Publishing Ltd.

- **About the article:** It is about how Darlene, a mother in an inner-city school context, was engaged in an artistic and aesthetic composition of her life experience along with the authors. It illustrates a metaphorical three-dimensional narrative inquiry space as a way to attend more closely to the artistic and aesthetic dimensions of stories to live by.
- **Why narrative inquiry as phenomenon and method?:** The authors note how they have come to understand experience as narratively constructed and narratively lived (phenomenon), which led them to study experience narratively (method). Hence, narrative inquiry becomes both phenomenon and method.
- **Research questions:** There is no explicit research question, but the authors note that their research intentions are to learn about the experiences of diverse children, families, and teacher-researchers.
- **Theoretical framework:** A metaphorical three-dimensional narrative inquiry space, drawing upon Dewey's concept of experience: interaction (personal and social dimension); continuity (past, present, and future); and situation (place).
- **Methods:** Tape-recorded research conversation with Darlene, whose child attends an inner-city school, City Heights, where the authors worked for their year-long research. Darlene, also an artist, was frequently involved in school activities and worked on the parent advisory council.
- **Data representation:** Darlene's life story as artistic and aesthetic compositions is presented in the three-dimensional narrative inquiry space.
- **Conclusion:** The authors conclude that in living, telling, and retelling her stories to live by, Darlene guided them toward deeper thinking about school landscapes as places intimately textured with a multiplicity of life-story possibilities.

Excerpt of the Article (Clandinin & Huber, 2002)

—————————————————— ❧❧❧❧❧ ——————————————————

Attending to Darlene's Story to Live By

* * * * *

> I mean I was a foster child and it wasn't easy learning the different cultures and learning a different life. Since I was two until I was eight I learned from living in a French family and I learned French. I spoke English and then I spoke French at home. Speaking English was outside the home. [Then I went to a Ukrainian home]. But in the Ukrainian family it was, "you work hard and you do your school work." Your values aren't as lenient. . . . I didn't really have a culture living with a French family, then a Ukrainian family.

In her telling, Darlene described a sense of having other cultural narratives written on her body, of being given other culture's stories to live by. She had no sense of her own place but tried to situate herself in the cultures of her many foster families. She lived this way until she found a picture in a school textbook of someone who, she realized, looked like her and began to ask questions about who she was. As Darlene composed her life in these early years, we see her struggling for a coherent plotline as she moved from one family, from one culture, to another family, to another culture. In this narrative fragment of her life she only hinted at how deep the emotional reaction was to this dislocation of who she was.

> I think the only way I learned my culture was in school. I realized at 16 or 18 that I was Eskimo. I realized I looked Eskimo. So I was left with the choice just knowing that I was different. I spoke English, I read English. I felt English wasn't forced on me. [At 16 or 18] I had the choice. . . . I didn't want to let go, because that was my home. . . . When I found out I was Eskimo I really wanted children. . . . You can still hold onto your culture.

As Darlene learned that she did have a physical and cultural place, she struggled with what she had to give up of the other cultural narratives she had tried to claim as her own. By now she was an English speaker and familiar with urban landscapes. Any memory she might have carried forward from her earliest years was written over, blanked out. She had no story to guide her into the future if she were to choose to return to the place of her birth. However, she eventually returned to her homeland in the North and described her homecoming in the following way:

> [I returned to my Inuit culture when I was 16 or 18]. I didn't know until I was 16 that I was from Inuvik. When someone said that I was from Inuvik, I said, "What's that place?" They said, "You don't know your place?" And I said, "No, I've been in another place." And then I looked it up on a map to find out where I was from. So to me I think the most important thing wasn't the language or the food. The most important thing to me is culture. [When I returned to an Inuit community] my most fear, I think, was drowning, you know. So I didn't want to drown so I had better learn quick the values of my culture. My parents or aunts and uncles said, "You need to think things twice or a few

times over before you go into the bush. Bring your supplies out here and then we will check your supplies." You know, you've got to know you've got your supplies. So for me to learn that, I was just used to living in a house, always had water, electricity. All I had to do was turn a light on. . . .

We metaphorically traveled with Darlene as she shared stories of this time in her life—a time significantly attached with learning where she had come from, who she was, and who she might become. As she shared memories of these experiences, we sense she stood on uncertain ground, already knowing herself as multicultured. Now, she was awakened to another possible story of herself, a story of herself as "Eskimo." She realized that when someone named her birth place she did not know that place but said, "I've been in another place." While she did not share her inner reaction at this moment, we can only imagine her emotional response to finding out she could be someone other than the person who was in a story she had told herself for 16 or 18 years.

The artistry of Darlene's narrative life composition is strongly visible in this section of the research conversation. Thoughtfully attending to Janice's story of learning how to be a teacher, Darlene laid Janice's expression of the tenuous, uncertain nature of life in classrooms and schools alongside her memories of learning her birth culture. As she described this experience of reimagining and retelling herself, Darlene brought to this new story—a story of living among her birth people—all the other stories she had learned to live. She took who she was as an English-speaking urban dweller and opened herself to learning from other people, from the land, and from attending closely to the knowing she carried in her body.

When she left the North as an adult, she became a mother and thought hard about the stories she wanted to live by. Having lived so long without a place for her story to live by, she seemed awake to the possibility of creating places for others to figure out their own stories to live by. For example, she talked in the following transcript fragment about the need for a multicultural narrative in which all people can find a place:

Ever since [my son] has gone to school here, since grade 2, I see all these mothers who are Vietnamese, Chinese, Native. Because I'm Eskimo, Inuit, I'm labeled as Vietnamese, Chinese, Cambodian. They come to me. They speak their language but I'm not able to respond so their reaction is, "Why didn't she say anything? Why isn't she doing anything?" They come to me because they think I'm one of them. [Even though Darlene can't understand them] I don't want to shy away from that cause I'm used to it but for other cultures we are told not to speak to a certain person or not to associate with other people and there again it's something that's been going on for thousands of years. "Don't you speak with people of that culture. You don't do this." Nowadays it's different . . . for Canada to be a gateway for everyone.

When she told of how she now lives in a multicultural community, Darlene brought forward her intimate bodily knowledge, learned as a child and young adult, of the possibility of embodying different cultural narratives. When people of visible minorities approached her she knew the importance of not "shy[ing] away." Even when language was a barrier, as it was in her childhood, she stayed open to encouraging connection across diversity. In one place in our research conversation, Darlene described that one of the ways she tried to become connected with mothers on the playground with whom she could not yet speak was through drawing messages "out on the sand." Reaching out for connections across cultures was something Darlene wanted people in the school to do. When Janice described her ethical concerns about whether she could teach the Inuit culture to children in the Year 3–4 classroom or whether another person of Inuit culture, such as Darlene, needed to teach her culture, Darlene said:

> Yes, you can't take my place and I can't take your place. It's good to be open and find out facts about different cultures. That's the only way each one of us can learn no matter where you go in the world or what you are doing or what you hear. . . . It would be really neat for you and I or any other teacher, no matter who they are, to learn different cultures in school because children are from different cultures. That way we could teach other children the values. And you respect that, you learn from experience so that they can't say they haven't learned this.

* * * * *

An Inukshuk As a Metaphor for Darlene's Story to Live By

Attending to Darlene's life through the three-dimensional narrative inquiry space allowed us to see the unfolding (temporal), situatedness (place) of stories to live by. As we attended to Darlene's life composition narratively, we noticed a fluid movement between what was happening in her body, the personal, and what was happening in the social situations around her, the social. Because our research is about studying lives, the metaphor of a three-dimensional space provides a way to attend to the inner emotions, to the aesthetic reactions woven across time, place, and events. It is a metaphor that allows us, as researchers, to understand Darlene's and others' life compositions as filled with artistic and aesthetic dimensions.

———————————————— ᐊᐊᐊᐊᐊ ————————————————

Questions for Discussion

1. What are the characteristics of narrative inquiry as phenomenon and method and how do the authors transpire them in this article?

2. How do the authors present Darlene's story in a metaphorical three-dimensional space?

3. What kinds of narrative analysis and interpretation are used?

4. What are the merits/limitations of this article?

5. In what ways does this article appeal to you or not?

6. How do the authors present their narrative coda?

Example of Narrative Inquiry as Oral History

Leavy, P. & Ross, L. (2006). The Matrix of Eating Disorder Vulnerability: Oral History and the Link between Personal and Social Problems. *The Oral History Review* 33(1): 65–81. Reproduced with permission of Blackwell Publishing Ltd.

- ***About the article:*** It is an oral history of Claire, a Caucasian, suburban upper-middle-class, college student, suffering from a life-threatening eating disorder, anorexia nervosa.
- ***Why oral history?:*** The authors note that it is the appropriate research method for this project because of their interest in understanding Claire's body image story within the context of her relationships and experiences, from childhood through college.
- ***Research questions:*** How is this woman's body image story enmeshed within her life? What are the various relationships of importance to her? How is her story a part of a larger matrix of social relations, roles, and pressures? In what ways are the themes in her story representative of women's stories?
- ***Theoretical framework:*** Feminist theory to interrogate a gendered social order through the personal meaning as well as the larger questions of social justice.
- ***Methods:*** Oral history interviews during two tape-recorded sessions in the participant's home and in informal discussions over a two-month period.
- ***Data analysis process by hand (three phases):***

  1. Line-by-Line Analysis: Major code categories emerged.

  2. Thematic Analysis: Placing excerpts from the transcript under thematic codes that developed inductively out of the analysis process. These codes include perfectionism, control, independence/autonomy, disappointment, and projection of self.

  3. Holistic Analysis: Identifying broader themes constituting her narrative as formulating a web or "matrix" that culminated in her eating disorder: Striving for Perfection, Yearning for Control, Autonomy as a Central Value, and A Web of Pressures: Look at Me, I'm Shrinking.

- ***Conclusion:*** The authors conclude that oral history can be beneficial as a method of personalizing social problems.

Excerpt of the Article (Leavy & Ross, 2006)

————————————— ༒༒༒༒༒ —————————————

Claire's Narrative: A Thematic Analysis

Striving for Perfection

Claire explained that she always wanted to excel, and in fact, perform flawlessly. As such, perfectionism was a dominant theme in her narrative. Through this theme we can see internal and external pressures operating together, including familial pressures and a desire to succeed. In one discussion in which Claire described her academic life in middle school, she stated:

> I always pushed myself harder than anyone else pushed me, like I remember when I was in fifth grade my school had this special like gifted program even above and beyond the ones that they already had like for the classroom setting and it was an after-school program.

In this instance, Claire is noting the perfectionism in her academic life, and the pressure she put on herself to achieve. Other statements Claire made concerning her attempt for perfectionism center on the high expectations she believed her parents had for her:

> I can remember calling my dad when I was in eighth grade and I got a B+ in calculus or something, I mean I don't even remember what it was. I remember being so bummed out and I was so scared to tell him and everything and he was like, well, you know, you'll just work harder next you know gives you something to shoot for, or whatever, but to me it was like, such, that was, I couldn't believe it you know, what I had missed. It wasn't that I got a B+ like that was good it was like I could have gotten an A I should have worked harder I could have done more you know? Um, so I was always kind of like that.

During one of the toughest times in her life, when she was battling an eating disorder that almost killed her, the same mentality manifested itself:

> I knew I needed help, but, the people who I kept seeing just didn't get it, they were, they just didn't get it, and I, they wanted to put me on all sorts of medications, and I'm so anti-drug, just because I still have this, like, superwoman syndrome thing, that like I can do it, I don't need help, you know?

Scholarly research suggests that many women who develop eating disorders in their lifetimes often have feelings of needing to be a "superwoman;" that is, that women, based on our cultural standards, are covertly forced into believing that they should be able to complete multiple tasks simultaneously, without asking for assistance. In other words, women are expected to be able to carry on a professional career as well as be able to raise a family and complete housework, without their partner contributing an equal amount of time to maintaining familial ties. While Claire was not starting a family, she was faced with multiple situations in which she felt she had to be totally committed; she was devoted to her academics as well as to maintaining positive relationships within her family. Thus Claire feeds into a cultural notion that women should be able to multitask without asking for help. The oral history storytelling process was a critical space for her to name this problem—"superwoman syndrome"—as opposed to having others categorize it for her. In this way, the oral history process was helpful to our participant.

Yearning for Control

Another pervasive theme emerging from Claire's oral history is "control." Based on the vivid descriptions of her childhood that oral history evokes, we are able to start to see the process by which she developed a need for control in her life—so often, she had absolutely no control over the events that transgressed, and she grasped any moment in which she could hope to control her own life. There were many life events she was unable to control, which became "triggers" (which commonly bring on the onset of an eating disorder), such as the painful divorce of her parents, a major mistake her high school made which effectively delayed her process of attending college, and the passing away of loved ones in a short period of time. However, what she could control was her own body—and it was controlled to such a degree that it brought her close to death. Speaking to this issue, Claire said:

> And I was just like, ok, well at least I can, I can control my health. You know? Like, even though I don't really have much I can do about this decision, and now looking back I can see that I, that I did have a voice.

By "voice" Claire is referring to personal autonomy and control. It is in this point in the narration process that a paradox emerges:

> And as soon as he said that, like as soon as people wanted me to do something, I didn't want to do it anymore. I was like, I don't want to do this you know and so . . .

The more familial pressure she seemed to live up to the less autonomy she felt. The only way she could conceive to regain authority over her own life was to ritualistically and severely transform her body. Triggers in the form of "disappointments" were a persistent theme in her story as well, which we believe is intimately connected to her feelings of self-worth, and especially to perfectionism and autonomy, which were her two major markers of self-worth. Although she did not discuss it directly, her self-worth also developed in a cultural context, which in this case is media-driven. Due to the significant life markers we have noted, she often felt an overwhelming amount of disappointment. She focused heavily on familial disappointment, noting difficulties in her relationship with her father.

* * * * *

Autonomy as a Central Value

Claire frequently discussed "independence," and the related concepts of intelligence and maturity, which she believed were important traits to have. Accordingly she pushed herself to appear older and wiser than other children her age. To Claire, being seen as wiser or more mature was a part of a value-system by which she constantly judged herself; she believed that maturity was the sign of productivity, and thus value. Claire excelled as a student, which made her confident during difficult times. Although she knew her parents were unhappy, she desperately wanted their approval, and as a result she often acted as the mediator between them after the dissolution of the marriage. Because she was put in such an emotionally taxing position, and had perfectionist tendencies, she exerted herself physically and mentally to succeed in both academics and athletics. Here we can see how the body, even if peripherally, began to become some of the focus of her perfectionism. To Claire, being mature was an important aspect of her personality. Often she stated how much she enjoyed being around older people:

> I mean, I guess I always grew up wanting to do things older because I never wanted to be thought of as young. I was always worried (voice softens and becomes higher pitched) like would they think this is silly (voice returns to as before) or whatever.

Not only did she want to be mature in her own right, but she also wanted others to know that she was a mature person.

* * * * *

A Web of Pressures: Look at Me, I'm Shrinking

Looking at the internal and external pressures on this young woman, combined with a value-system that emphasizes perfectionism, control, and autonomy (often conflicting values), we can begin to understand the web of pressures and attitudes Claire responded to via her body. But the selection of a coping strategy that would quickly distort her physical body is also important because Claire was deeply concerned with how she projected herself to others. "Projection of self" is similar to the metaphor of the mask. It involves the individual appearing to be a certain way outwardly, while concealing many inner problems or insecurities. An individual may choose to don certain masks in particular situations to mold themselves into the appropriate personality that could handle such circumstances. Similarly, Charles Horton Cooley's looking-glass self theory posits that individuals imagine how others see them and their perception impacts their self concept and behaviors in order to be seen in a way they deem desirable. In Claire's case, it was important to her to appear to others as mature, wise, and in control of herself. She frequently based her decisions on the intricate balance of pleasing herself and conforming to a notion of what others expect. She noted:

> I mean I loved the fact that they thought I was so cool you know for helping my mom, but like I always wanted (brief pause) people to respect me, for what I could do and what I could say and what I thought, more than like, just being a tangent to some-one else's life. Do you know what I mean?

Claire often spoke about how it was important for her to remain silent or invisible, so as not to cause trouble by being who she was. For someone desperate for autonomy this became a high-wire act. She wanted to be heard and to be silent, to be seen and to be invisible. A disorder which would grotesquely shrink her body is almost the logical response to such contradictory attitudes. In fact, some scholars explain that anorexia is the logical, albeit it grotesque, response to a cultural context that pressures women to be hyper-thin. In effect, anorexia made her smaller and more noticeable all at once. She began to occupy less and more space in the social world and her within her family.

But when I weighed the pros and the cons, especially because I was always someone to keep the peace in my house, to disrupt a balance, or to make unnecessary trouble, wasn't something I was willing to do.

Claire is exhibiting a characteristic trait among many American women—the desire to silence themselves and to act as the peace-makers within the familial structure. In the media women are commonly depicted with their mouths covered or having a muted expression, as if more desirable in silence. Thus, the woman, though still in competition with other women for male affection, is forced to remain silent and complacent with the larger society. As the body becomes thinner, as it actually takes up less space, the woman gives the impression of being less of a presence and thus, less of her own entity.

_____ ❧❧❧❧❧ _____

Questions for Discussion

1. What are the characteristics of oral history and how does this article interweave such characteristics?

2. How does Claire's personal story become a social story?

3. What are the merits/limitations of this article?

4. In what ways does this article appeal to you or not?

5. How do the authors present their narrative coda?

6. Which topics would fit the oral history genre?

Example of Narrative Inquiry as Life Story

Lieblich, A. (2013). Healing Plots: Writing and Reading in Life-Stories Groups. *Qualitative Inquiry, 19*(1) 46–52.

- ***About the article:*** It is about how life stories written by a group of mature people work as the healing and curative potential although the group is not about therapy but about remembering, writing, and sharing their stories.
- ***Why life stories?:*** The author notes that remembered episodes or events in one's life can be enlarged and elaborated with the aid of the imagination. When shared with a group, life story can nourish empathy, solace, and support for each other.

(Continued)

(Continued)

- **Research question:** There is no explicitly stated research question in the article. However, the author aims to demonstrate how life-writing often travels to the lands of the writer's pain.
- **Theoretical framework:** There is no explicitly stated theoretical framework in the article.
- **Methods:** Participants are a writing group of eight adults that meets for three hours every fortnight. They reflect upon and read aloud their writing samples, which are accumulated passages in their private notebooks.
- **Data representation:** Life stories written on the topic of "What people throw out to the street."
- **Conclusion:** The author concludes that life stories demonstrate the deep need to dwell upon our human weaknesses, our moments of loss, humiliation, or helplessness. In doing so, the value of catharsis has been manifested and amplified for the benefit of the participants in constructing autobiographical narratives.

Excerpt of the Article (Lieblich, 2013)

_____ ᷽᷽᷽᷽᷽ _____

Esther, 68

Esther volunteers to read first. She starts with the introduction:

I am so glad to have received this assignment, because it gave me the opportunity to tell you something that I didn't share with you so far: I am a collector of glass art, and this is a very important part of my life.

This is what she reads: "I don't quite remember how it all started. Maybe after the war, when we were refugees in Germany, and I, a child of 8, loved to play outside of our camp in a field completely covered by shreds of broken glass. Hills and piles of it, in all colors—probably bombing debris, but we children didn't care. I loved to catch sight of the sun as reflected in these glass shreds and the rainbows that appeared and disappeared with the light. Anyway, years later, as the wife of an Israeli Air Force pilot, when I finally was able to afford it, I started to collect glass objects of all kinds—colored flower vases, drinking glasses, and paper weights. This collection provided a purpose to all our trips, for wherever we went I set out on a hunt after glass objects, and then carried them home, where I displayed many of them all over the place. They filled my life with interest and joy. As I became more of an expert, I specialized in collecting American Depression Glass, which has unique characteristics. But I love all kinds of glass, its transparency, the way it changes and reflects light. I cherish my collection.

One day I saw an ad for an auction of art objects, and I went to have a look. My budget was naturally quite modest, but I enjoyed watching others making their biddings. When I entered the gallery, right away I saw a glass sculpture of incredible beauty. It was a sculpture of a man and a woman embracing, about 40-cm tall. The artist managed to capture in white glass the position of lovers, who to remain together forever. It looked like a museum piece.

I knew that buying it was out of the question. Just the same I approached the attendant and asked meekly for the price. The lady said—it goes for 800 Shekels, which was, at the time, about US$200—a sum that I could easily spend. When she realized how surprised I was, she lifted the sculpture and showed me that it had been broken and glued in the very bottom of the piece. 'It is defected. The former owners threw it out of their home. They didn't want to keep it, since it was damaged.'

I was trembling with excitement and asked if I could purchase the sculpture then and there, and the lady, realizing my passion for it, sold it to me before the auction even started. For me, it was a miracle. People threw such a treasure away, imagine! But in my house it has a place of honor; it is the diamond of my collection. I love it even more because of this small defect, which is my secret."

Esther is quiet for a moment, holding on to her notebook. "I should have brought you a photograph of my sculpture, but it only occurred to me this very moment. And another thing that I realized just now, as I was reading, is that I think I am attracted to glass works also because they are so fragile. They survive only if we provide total security for them—something I never had as a child. They epitomize impermanence as well as survival for me. How come I have never realized this before. . . ."

Hanna, 70

Hanna is a kibbutz member and makes a 2-hour trip every time to meet our group. She starts to read without any introduction and announces her title "Thrown."

"When my partner and I reached the age of 60, ten years ago, we took leave of our family and the kibbutz, and like youngsters went off for a 6-month backpack trip to South America. We didn't have enough money, so Sammy prearranged with a friend in New York to replace him as a taxi driver in the city. And that was it: a month in New York, saving money, 4 months of tracking, and a final month in New York, to cover our debts, before our return home.

I am bringing back three episodes from that trip.

In New York, some remote relatives allowed us to sleep in a small studio apartment that they didn't use, and we found there only a sofa bed, which was terribly uncomfortable. After two very bad nights, we were about to spend some of our precious dollars for buying a mattress. It was a big expense for our budget, but we felt we had no choice.

In the morning, Sammy went for his shift as a driver. I was planning to spend my day at the Metropolitan, as I did every day. To my surprise, Sammy returned home right away. He was all flushed and exclaimed: Put on some clothes, and come down with me right away.

"What happened? Why? I asked, but he refused to answer and just urged me to hurry up."

I followed him down the four floors, and in the entrance to the building saw immediately what had made him so excited. Near the garbage ally, there lay a brand new mattress, discarded, thrown away, a gift for us from an unknown source. We laughed and said: Look what the rich throw away in the big apple! With big effort and many laughs we hauled the mattress all the way to our tiny room and felt the happiest people ever. During that month in NY, we always found in the streets exactly the items that we needed in our flat.

Then in Brazil, I will never forget my first day in Rio . . . Everywhere we walked or drove, there were bands of children in the street, living on the sidewalks, in the bus stations, babies and toddlers with hungry eyes, little boys and girls, almost naked, wild like animals. All were so very dirty! Some looked rather well fed, while others were starving, but they were hanging together in the corners, in the shade of big buildings, or along the main roads. I have never seen such a sight. Who threw them away? How come their mothers did not care for them? There are these photographs of the survivors of the concentration camps, you know? So this was it, the same sight, and no hope of being rescued. I could not bear the sight and soon escaped to the mountains. This could never happen at home; my husband and I comforted each other.

We had a great hike, I managed to forget the Brazilian kids—(in fact I forgot them till last week, she added while looking at us) and then—back to New York. As I was walking to the museum one morning while Sammy was doing his driver's rounds, I saw a little crowd, some cops and an ambulance around a young woman, lying in the street. Passers-by told me that she had fallen; perhaps she was sick, drunk, or addicted to some poison, who knows. I walked on to my new day of the arts. But like in Brazil, it didn't feel right. I felt guilty. It is very nice to find a pot or a mattress, but what do I do when I find a baby, or a young woman? I take what I like, what I need, what pleases me, and discard of all the rest . . . Isn't life cruel?"

Nobody comments on Hanna's story, and the room remains silent.

Finally Esther says: "Don't torture yourself, you are only human!"

* * * * *

Final Comments

These examples of autobiographical stories demonstrate the deep need we have to dwell upon our human weaknesses, our moments of loss, humiliation, or helplessness. Even in cases where pride or courage is involved, as in the narratives of Andy and Dalia, the stories provided also a so-called negative side of having to give up previous expectations.

This phenomenon can be attributed to the underlying mechanism whereby writing and sharing such stories provides relief to the narrators (see Lieblich, Josselson, & McAdams, 2004). Moreover, as Esther's story exemplifies, the storied form of their life events help narrators construct their identity and give meaning to some of their choices or habits. In conveying the message that we were all only humans, the group afforded empathy, solace, and support to the participants.

My experience is usually with older persons, most of the women, who have attended my writing groups. They can afford the time and money for such activity, and it comes natural to them. The above account is by no means unusual in terms of the depth and emotional level revealed in the writing-reading tasks. The prompts we use are of great variety, and some of the examples are: "A door or gate in my life," "Write up a conversation with a significant other: How would you change your part if you had a chance to do it?," "Describe your dinner table and an event that occurred around it," "Childhood sins," "My siblings and me," "I lost it/I found it," and many more. Since ancient times, we believe in the value of catharsis, in other words—that the mere expression of pain has healing potential. In constructing autobiographical narratives, writing them, sharing them, and getting responded to them, this effect is amplified many times for the benefit of all involved.

_____ ৵৵৵৵৵ _____

Questions for Discussion

1. What are the characteristics of life story and how do they transpire in the article?

2. What is the role of writing and how does it enhance narrative inquiry?

3. What are the merits/limitations of this article?

4. In what ways does this article help you understand narrative inquiry as life stories?

5. What implications might this article have for life story and life history?

6. How is the coda presented?

Example of Narrative Inquiry as Autoethnography

Sparkes, A. (1996). The Fatal Flaw: A Narrative of the Fragile Body-Self. *Qualitative Inquiry, 2*(4), 463–494.

- *About the article:* It explores how autoethnography can be utilized to explore the reflexive relationships between the body and the self over time in ways that fuse the personal and the social.
- *Why autoethnography?:* The author notes that he wants to engage the reader by presenting moments from his narrative of self (subjectivity) in a provocative, disruptive, fragmented, and emotionally charged manner. The goal is to take the reader into the intimacies of his world in a way that stimulates the reader to reflect upon the reader's own life in relation to the author's.
- *Research question:* There is no explicitly stated research question in the article.
- *Theoretical framework:* Theories of embodiment and the body.
- *Methods:* Medical reports, diaries, artifacts, and the existing literature on body.
- *Conclusion:* The author does not have a conclusion; however, he presents discussions with such subheadings as "No Conclusion," "The Problem of the Epilogue," and "Left Wondering: What Has He Learned?"

Excerpt of the Article (Sparkes, 1996)

—————————————————— ๙๙๙๙๙ ——————————————————

Thoughts From an Untidy Office

It is May 1994. I have walked down this hospital corridor many times before. The navy blue carpet is familiar as are the polished handrails on either side. Determined not to use these handrails for support, I hobble down an imaginary center line. My body is unable to stand up straight, the hips are pulled to one side, and each time I take a step a searing burst of pain unleashes itself in the lumbar region of my back and travels down my right leg. It's hot in the hospital and I'm sweating. I'm also crying and afraid. In 1988 I had surgery on my lumbar spine here for a prolapsed disc and now I have the feeling that the hospital is soon going to swallow me up again. I want it to; I want this pain to be taken away.

Stopping for a rest I turn toward Kitty, my wife, who is 6 months pregnant. "Deja vu," I say to her, "It's happening again." The tears well up in her eyes, and we hold each other close in the corridor. I kiss the tears on her cheeks. I kiss her eyes; I want to drown and be saved in the blueness of those eyes. As the roundness of her stomach presses against me, a wave of guilt washes over me. Kitty is pregnant, so tired, caring for Jessica our daughter (3 years old at the time), and now having to worry and cope with the stress of me and my body failure. My uselessness makes me angry with my body. At that moment I hate it intensely.

That night, as in previous nights since this latest episode with my back started, I lie there focused on pain. It is impossible to lie on my back. The only position I can get "comfortable" in is on my side with several pillows tucked between my knees and my thighs. Despite the painkillers, the electric shocks bombard my lumbar area, shoot down both legs, and sometimes intrude into my groin. After an hour, sleep has still not arrived, so I roll myself out of bed as quietly as I can so as not to wake Kitty. Going next door into my "office" (the only undecorated room in the house with all my books and my computer), I make myself as comfortable as I can in the orthopedic chair that the Social Services supplied me with in 1988 following my first back operation. I sit there, holding some vague notion that if I can do some "work," that is, academic writing or reading, then I'd be making "good use" of my time. It would be a defiant gesture to my back that it hadn't taken over my life completely; it might also take my mind off the pain. I reflect how, in moments like these, I see the lumbar region of my back and the pain it generates as both part of me and not part of me, as both intimate and alien, as self and other, but one powerful symbol among many of the multiple dualisms and contradictions that I inhabit in relation to my body (p. 468)

* * * * *

No Conclusion

In surgical terms my operations in 1988 and 1994 were successful. The prolapsed discs removed from my L3/L4 and L4/L5 lumbar spine now reside in two bottles of preservative on a bathroom shelf. On good days I walk or cycle the 7-mile round trip from my house to work. However, the chronic back problem remains. Intense physical training is out as are the kinds of sporting activity normally undertaken by many men in their early 40s. Yet deep inside I still want to push myself in the domain of intense physical activity and experience the elation it can sometimes produce. If I do push myself too hard physically the fatal flaw visits me again, my lower back goes into spasm, and I experience acute pain. Sometimes, it just seems to visit for fun, like the episode that was set off recently in July 1995 when I lifted my son, Alexander (aged 11 months) out of his pram. In short, there is no rhyme or reason, no pattern, to how the fatal flaw works itself in and through my life. Even as I write these words in October of 1995, the dull pain in my lower back I get from sitting for long periods deflects my concentration. I wait for my manipulation with the osteopath in a few days time, and the possibility of more sclerosing injections into my lumbar region from the specialist at the end of the month. I'm also thinking about trying the Alexander technique. As a consequence, I am not sure how to end this story. Like Ellis (1995a), I have to request that you the reader, "exist for a time within uncertainty, where plot lines circle round and round, where endings are multiple and often unfinished, and where selves are fractured and often contradictory" (p. 162).

Having set out with the intention to write about moments from my narrative of self in a disruptive, fragmented, and emotionally charged way, I am, like Bloom and Munro (1995), concerned to construct a final text in such a way as to resist an authoritative final interpretation. To accomplish this I have, following Plummer (1995), to drench my story in ambiguity and shun the all too tempting desire to place the fragments of my story into a coherent and totalizing narrative structure. Consequently, the sections that follow, "The Problem of the Epilogue" and "Left Wondering: What Has He Learned?" have intentionally been written in a stop-start, fragmentary, and apparently unfocused manner, which may appear disjointed and unsettling to readers more accustomed to coherent endings and closures in academic papers. As part of this process, I have begun to recognize the implications of Richardson's (1994) thoughts on writing as a method of inquiry and her recent call to extend our reflexivity to the study of our writing practices. Here, we are invited to reflect on and share with other researchers our "writing stories," or stories about how we came to construct the particular texts that we did. For Richardson (1995), this means that, "Rather than hiding the struggle, concealing the very human labor that creates the text, writing-stories would reveal emotional, social, physical, and political bases of the labor" (p. 191).

Reflecting upon my writing-story enables me to avoid an ending and accentuate myself as a multiple reader of my own narrative of self. In Iser's (1978) terms, my task as interpreter/reader then becomes that of elucidating the process of meaning production rather than identifying a single referential or authorized meaning. Adopting this stance, I become increasingly aware of the performative element of my telling and the opportunities this has provided me with for reliving, reshaping, and realigning past events and experiences in order to give them new meaning in relation to the present. As part of the "identity work" that goes with the reflexive project of the self, I acknowledge my engagement in a fictive process of self-invention as part of an attempt to rewrite the self and serve the present needs of consciousness (Eakin, 1985; Freeman, 1993; James, 1994; Temple, 1994). These needs include, according to Linde (1993) and McAdams (1985), the creation of coherence in the lives of people and groups via the telling of stories. This process has been identified as being of vital importance in the lives of those who have experienced (chronic) illness (see Charmaz, 1991; Frank, 1995; Kleinman, 1988; Riessman, 1990; Robinson, 1990). However, as Good and Good (1994) illustrate in their consideration of the subjunctive qualities of illness narratives regarding epilepsy in Turkey, this search for coherence does not mean closure. Rather, the subjunctivizing elements of the stories they heard meant that the narratives maintained multiple perspectives and the potential for multiple readings and endings. That is, they trafficked in human possibilities rather than in settled certainties. I have only just begun to recognize these features in my own narrative, while at the same time becoming aware of how the structure of previous drafts of my story have attempted to deny such features.

——————————————— ✍✍✍✍✍ ———————————————

Questions for Discussion

1. What are the characteristics of autoethnography and how does the author incorporate them into the article?
2. How does the author maintain his reflexivity and what is the role of his reflexivity?
3. What are the merits/limitations of this article?
4. How does the author theorize his personal story?
5. In what ways does this article help you understand narrative inquiry as autoethnography?
6. What are your thoughts on "No Conclusion"?

Example of Narrative Inquiry as Creative Nonfiction

Kim, J. H. (2006). For whom the school bell tolls: Conflicting voices inside an alternative high school. *International Journal of Education & the Arts*, 7 (6). Retrieved from http://ijea.org/v7n6/

- **About the article:** It is about conflicting voices existing inside an alternative high school among different stakeholders, including the principal, school security guard, two students, and a teacher.
- **Why creative nonfiction?:** The author notes that creative nonfiction text would create a virtual reality where stories seem real to the reader. This genre allows the five protagonists share their views, emotions, and reflections about their alternative school experiences in the first person using expressive, contextualized, and vernacular language.
- **Research question:** There is no explicitly stated research question in the article. However, the author notes that the purpose of the article is to provide readers with vicarious access to tensions in the school and to promote dialogic conversation about "best practice" for disenfranchised students who frequently experience educational inequalities.

- **Theoretical framework:** Bakhtinian novelness of polyphony (multiple voices), chronotope (time and space), and carnival (equally valued different voices).
- **Methods:** Ethnographic method for five months. Field observation and participant observation, conversation as research, and semi-structured interviews with participants.
- **Data Analysis:** Polkinghorne's narrative mode of analysis
- **Conclusion:** The author's conclusion is represented in the Voice of the Researcher. She leaves the carnival of the multiple voices open-ended so that it can serve as a starting point for genuine dialogue among educators.

Excerpt of the Article (Kim, 2006)

———————————————— ෨෨෨෨෨ ————————————————

The Voice of Mr. Hard, the Security Guard

I am the security guard at this alternative high school. I got retired from a police department where I worked for 20 years before I came here. My wife is a director at a hospital here in Phoenix. Her job brought us here from Pittsburgh two years ago. I have two sons and a daughter. Two of them are happily married, and my youngest son is in college. My hobby is fixing and building stuff around the house on weekends, and Home Depot is my favorite shopping place.

This is my second year in this school, and I've been enjoying my job so far. My main responsibility is to make sure that our school is a safe place. As you know, kids these days can be dangerous. Especially kids in this school have a lot of problems that regular schools don't want to deal with. That's why they are here. A lot of kids have a criminal history. Some kids have already been to jail. My previous career working as a cop has helped me a lot dealing with these kids who have a potential to commit a crime. That's why I got hired so quickly. Our principal whom I'm closely working with gave me the authority to be in charge of the student discipline. My position here is to be a hard-liner. I'm the final set of rules that students have to abide by. That's my background. I spent a lot of money on my education at the police academy and I'm bringing that knowledge to discipline these kids. That's what I like about my job. I try to help them succeed by using my resources. If a student fails to go by [the] rules, then he or she has to deal with me. You know, they're here because they can't control their attitudes. They can't control what they're saying. They are violent, throw temper tantrums, and talk back. There are different ways to deal with them and they are not in the textbook.

Teachers can be flexible. When they don't want to deal with disruptive students, they can send them to me. My job here is to inculcate rules to kids. Some of you go to football games Sunday afternoon. When there are no referees, what kind of game is it? It's going to be a mess, right? With referees and rules, we have an organized game. Likewise, I'm the referee here. I'm the rules. Students have to face me if they don't follow the rules. I'm the one who keeps the game organized, and keeps the game from getting out of hand. My responsibility is to maintain the rules.

We're trying to help these kids become successful young adults in the society. In that sense, we've been very productive. I've seen a lot of difference among students since I started working here.

Kids try to avoid me at school. Out of sight, out of fight. I know they don't like me. That's fine with me. I don't want to be liked. I just want to be respected. Don't get me wrong. I'm not saying that I don't have sympathy for them. I do feel sorry for these kids because they have a lot of baggage. They come from broken, poor, and abusive families. They don't fit the mainstream. They have lost the idea of where the main road is. So, our job is to put them back on the right track. It can be done only by strict discipline. They need to learn how to behave so that they can function in a society as a cashier or something. If they don't follow the rules, we kick them out of school. In fact, we suspended a lot of students this year. It's our way of showing them they are wrong.

As you can imagine, we have a zero-tolerance policy for students who violate school rules. Holly has been my target these days. She is just impossible. I don't know what she's gonna turn into in the future. She's violent and gets into trouble every other day. She smokes, violates dress codes, and talks back to teachers, just to name a few. We have given her several warnings. She's quite smart, but being smart doesn't count here. What matters is whether or not one obeys the rules. On the first week of October, I caught her smoking in the restroom again. When I asked her to come with me, she wouldn't. So I tried to call the police, but Holly picked up a handful of rocks and started throwing them at me. She was ferocious! We gave her a five-day suspension.

And then, our school threw a Halloween party for students three weeks later. Teachers and staff donated money to buy hamburger patties, sausages, and other stuff for students. I brought my own barbeque grill and tools from home and took charge of barbequing. I was happy to be the chef of the day. I was happy to see students relaxing, having fun, and enjoying food that I cooked. It was so nice to see students and teachers mingling together, playing basketball and other games. It was a nice change. The party was going well for the most part. But, right before the party was over, Holly got into an argument with this Black girl, Shawnee. Holly got mad at her and mooned Shawnee who was with other ninth graders. This incident was reported to the principal, who called Holly's mom to ask her to appear at the school the next day. Holly got expelled after the "happy" Halloween party. Hope this expulsion will teach her something!

The Voice of Holly, the Goofy Snoopy

My name is Holly. I just turned fifteen in July. I was born in Mesa, Arizona, and have never moved out of Arizona. I'm a White girl with a little bit of Native American descent from my mom's side. I heard my mom's great-grandma was some sort of a Native American. I don't know what tribe, though. I'm tall, about five feet seven inches, and have long blonde hair with red highlights. I like to wear tight, low-rise jeans and a black "dead-rose" shirt that has a picture of a human skull surrounded by roses. I used to wear the Gothic style of clothes in my junior high, all in black from head to toe, wearing heavy, clumpy army boots. But I got tired of it, so, now I'm into Punk. I have a tattoo on my lower back and have a silver ring on the center of my tongue. I got my tongue pierced on my 15th birthday. I like it a lot. My mom hates it, though. But I don't care. She hates whatever I do, anyway. She's a bitch. She works at a car body shop, buffing and painting old cars with her boyfriend who is living with us. I can't wait to leave home. As soon as I turn 18, I'll say bye to them and leave home. I'm tired of them ordering me to do this and that.

Anyways . . . My nickname is snoopy. I got it in eighth grade for jumping and dancing like Snoopy at the Fiesta Shopping Mall. I just felt like doing it. People gathered around me and shouted, "Snoopy, Snoopy!" I did that for an hour. I didn't feel embarrassed at all. Since then, my friends started calling me Snoopy. They think I'm goofy. Yes, I am goofy. I don't care what others think about me. If I feel like doing something, I just do it. No second thought. But at school, I get into trouble because of that. Teachers don't like my personality. They think I'm just acting out. In fact, I was very upset when Ms. Bose told me the other day to change my personality. Do you know what she told me? She said, "I don't like your personality. You need to stop acting out. You need to change your personality. Then, your school life will be a lot easier." I said to myself, "Bullshit!" Change my personality? It took me fifteen years to develop it, for Christ's sake! I don't care if she likes it or not. I'm unique. I'm different. I have my own opinions unlike other kids. But teachers think I'm acting out, disruptive, unruly, and rude. Because I like to speak up, I have a history of being kicked out of classrooms and sent to ALC (Alternative Learning Center) where other "disruptive" kids are isolated, supposedly working on their individual assignments.

My friends like to talk to me about their personal issues because I give them a solution. Having said that, I think I have a leadership personality. I want to be a lawyer. I like to argue with people: my mom, her boyfriend, teachers, and my classmates. I win them all. Teachers are actually my worst enemies, but I'm not scared of them. A lot of times, they don't make sense. Last week, for example, I whistled in Ms. Bose's math class because I was happy to finish my work sheet earlier than other kids. Well, we're supposed to be ninth graders, but we were learning things that I had already learned in seventh grade. So this worksheet was super easy for me. So, I whistled to let everybody know that I finished my assignment. But here goes Ms. Bose. "Holly! Stop whistling. You're getting a zero point for today for being disruptive." "What? I'm getting a zero point even though I finished my assignment? That doesn't make sense!" "Yes, you're getting a zero point no matter what, because you are being disruptive." "Fine! If I'm getting a zero point for the day, I might as well keep whistling. What the hell!" I just kept whistling. Ms. Bose started yelling at me, "Holly, stop whistling right now! Otherwise, I'm gonna call the office." "Whatever!" It was one heck of a yelling match. Finally, Ms. Bose called the office. Five minutes later, Mr. Hard came to our classroom to get me. He took me to the ALC. So, the day became another "do-nothing-at-school" day.

This school sucks, if you ask me. They put a bunch of "bad" kids here all together like a warehouse. There is nothing attractive here. Look at these ugly portable buildings without any windows. They are called "classrooms." We don't have a cafeteria, so we have to eat our lunch at outdoor picnic tables near the restrooms. We get to enjoy this picnic every single day even under the hot temperature of one hundred five degree heat of the desert. Go figure. We use old, "hand-me-down" textbooks that came from a neighboring high school. It's like we are the disposables of education. We don't mean much. Our classes have six or seven students. I like this small class. But we don't really cover all the stuff in the textbook. We learn easy stuff, and I get bored with that. I had to do the multiplication table again because our Mexican boy, Guillermo, didn't know how to do multiplications! When I run into difficult stuff, I just copy answers from the textbook to fill out the worksheets without understanding. And I get a good point for that as long as I behave. I want to be a lawyer. But I don't know if I will ever be able to achieve my dream. I know I'm not stupid. But there is no counselor I can talk to about it.

There are more rules and regulations here than regular schools. Look at Mr. Hard, the old, fat, security guard who retired from the police department. I hate that guy. He is obsessed with rules. He goes, "Follow the rules, follow the rules. That's the rule number one here, otherwise you deal with me." We try to avoid running into him because he will make sure to find something wrong with us. He randomly calls one or two kids into his office and starts searching their backpacks. We hate it. It's such an insult. Recently, Mr. Hard has been watching me like a hawk. I don't know when I became his target. Somehow, he decided to pick on me. On a gloomy day in October, I felt like smoking. The weather was weird, and I had a fight with my mom again that morning. I was having a bad day, you know. I needed to smoke to release my stress. When I was smoking in the restroom, Mr. Hard caught me on the spot. He asked me to come with him to his office. I said no. He asked me again. I said no again. Then, he started calling the police. I quickly grabbed some rocks on the ground and threw them at the son of bitch. He ran away like a chicken with his head chopped off. I beat him finally! That night, I had a dream of him. I had a screw driver and shoved it into his neck, saying, "Leave me alone!" He was scared of me!

Questions for Discussion

1. What are the characteristics of creative nonfiction and how does the author incorporate them into the article?

2. How is virtual reality created?

3. In what ways does the author invite the reader to engage in a dialogue?

4. How has the author's theoretical framework, Bakhtinian novelness, been achieved?

5. Why is the theoretical framework appropriate or not appropriate in this article?

6. What are the merits/limitations of this article?

7. What other data analysis methods could have been used in this article?

Example of Narrative Inquiry as Fiction

Frank, K. (2000). "The Management of Hunger": Using Fiction in Writing Anthropology, *Qualitative Inquiry,* 6 (4), pp. 474–488.

> • ***About the article:*** It is a short-story fiction created based on the author's fieldwork in U.S. strip clubs, reflecting the multiple manifestations of hunger and desire—for food, for money, for intimacy, for recognition, for the desire of the Other, and for power.

- **Why fiction?:** The author notes that when factual representation obscures possible alternative interpretations, the explicit use of fiction might be appropriate and evocative. Fiction allows the author to portray a complexity of lived experience that might not always come across in a theoretical explication.
- **Research question:** There is no explicitly stated research question in the article. However, the author aims to interrogate the relationship between intimacy, sexuality, and power by using metaphors, elucidating the complexity of power relations and human interactions.
- **Theoretical framework:** There is no explicitly stated theoretical framework in the article. However, the author notes that she turns to fiction to work out problems for which she is unable to find the appropriate theoretical language or framework since there are times when academic language is incomplete or deficient in some way to translate a certain experience.
- **Methods:** Ethnography, participant observation, 30 multiple, in-depth interviews with the regular male customers of the clubs as well as conducting shorter interviews with nonregular customers, dancers, managers, advertisers, and other club employees.
- **Data Representation:** Fiction. The author notes that none of the characters have an objective existence. They are composites and constructions.
- **Conclusion:** The author concludes that in order to respond to the crisis of representation in anthropology, fiction could be practiced as ethnographic representation.

Excerpt of the Article (Frank, 2000)

————————————— 🐦🐦🐦🐦🐦 —————————————

The Management of Hunger

I am pulling a gold knit dress carefully over the rollers in my hair when my friend Maya enters the dressing room of the strip club where we work. She is still in her street clothes and looks like a young boy—a baseball cap, baggy jeans, and a T-shirt. She has a duffel bag slung over her shoulder and is carrying her hair attachment in one hand, a long, shiny black ponytail.

She throws something at me and it hits me lightly on the arm. "Hey, Kenzie," she says, "one for me, one for you." I bend down and pick a small stuffed animal off the floor. It is a kangaroo beanie baby, with a baby kangaroo tucked into its pouch.

"How cute," I say. "From the Doctor?"

"Of course," she says. "One of the door girls was on her way back to give them to us, and I saved her the trouble. I think he's early." She sets her bag heavily down on a chair and lays the ponytail carefully on top of it.

I check the clock, and it is 6:15. "Thanks," I say. "I'm almost ready anyway."

Every Friday night, the Doctor and I have a dinner date at 6:30, and though my shift doesn't actually start until 7, I am always dressed and ready to go when he arrives. He has to be home by 8:30 or his wife gets suspicious.

The club that I work in has a main room with four stages, a VIP room with couches, and a dining room where the customers can take dancers to dinner or for drinks. Most dancers charge a hundred dollars an hour to go to dinner with a customer, and I am no exception. Seeing the Doctor early on Fridays means that I still have a chance to try to get someone else to take me to dinner after he leaves, before the restaurant section closes at 11.

* * * * *

"Do you want to come to dinner with us tonight?" I ask her. Although the Doctor has been taking me to dinner weekly for more than 6 months, he thinks that Maya and I are roommates and often asks her to join us. As with most of the customers, I could never tell him that I really live with my boyfriend, Seth. Maya and I are very convincing at being roommates, though, sometimes even staging fights about dirty dishes or borrowed clothes to seem more realistic. Several times the Doctor has given us grocery money after we've described the sorry state of our refrigerator to him—imaginary baby carrot sticks, sour milk, ketchup, and Slim Fast. We always split that money evenly.

"Not tonight," she says. "I think I'll make more than a hundred an hour working the floor." Then she pauses. "I shouldn't say that—I might jinx myself and end up with the Plague." I laugh, having experienced "the Plague" myself as often as any other dancer. Some nights everyone in the club thinks that you are ravishing. Other nights, the exact same look and moves can't turn a single head. A bout with the Plague has sent many a dancer home empty handed at the end of a long shift after paying out the mandatory taxes, tips, and house fees. But empty pockets are an occasional job hazard—just like swollen knees, razor bumps, and periodic cynicism. When I started dancing, I learned quickly never to spend my money before it was earned, to put bags of frozen peas on my knees after particularly busy nights (works better than ice to calm the swelling), and to rub Secret deodorant on my bikini line to make unsightly razor rash recede. I have not yet, however, found a remedy for the cynicism. Perhaps that is best.

"Well, at least come do some dances with me," I say, and she nods. Sitting down on the floor, I fasten the ankle straps on my high heels. Then I take one of my small sequined evening bags out of my locker and slip a lipstick in it. Besides the lipstick, the purse is completely empty to leave room for my money. This was one of the things I found most amusing about dancing when I first started—walking into a nightclub at the beginning of the evening with an empty purse and leaving at the end with a roll of smoky cash.

The club is still nearly empty, and I immediately spot the Doctor at the bar.

He is drinking a gin and tonic and talking to the bartender, whom he's known for years. He turns to look at me as I approach. "You look great, Kenzie," he says, using my real name instead of my stage name. I've been letting him call me Kenzie for several months now at Maya's suggestion.

I give him a quick hug. "Thanks for the kangaroo."

"Sure. Can I get you a drink?" he asks. "Or would you like to go to dinner?"

"Dinner," I say. "Can we have wine at the table?" He nods and picks up his glass. We make our way through the club to the dining room, and I wave at a few of the dancers showing up for the night shift.

This early in the evening there are only a few couples in the dining area. This section is lush and intimate—mostly tables for two or semicircular booths, decorated with candles and fresh-cut flowers. The tables are wide enough to do table dances on, which is also just wide enough to make the geometry of the room seem odd. Although the dancers wear long gowns, their "dates" are sometimes wearing shorts, also making the scene peculiar to the eye. A brunette dancer I don't recognize sways high above the breadbasket and centerpiece on one of the tables, naked except for her high heels. Because we serve food, high heels, strangely enough, are required at all times by the health department. The two customers staring up at her barely notice us enter the room.

The hostess recognizes the Doctor and leads us to our usual table in the corner. As we slide into the booth, I make sure that he is sitting on my right side, my better side. We sit close together, and I ask him about his week. He tells me stories about work, absently drumming a finger on the table. Unlike some of the customers, he makes no attempt to hide his wedding band. The waitress takes our order—grilled mahi-mahi for me, rare steak for the Doctor. The irony of a doctor ordering red meat is not lost on him, and he has told me that this is the only place where he doesn't have to worry about reproach. He picks out a bottle of Merlot from the wine list and orders another gin and tonic. The Doctor always spends more than a hundred dollars on our food and drinks, and some nights I wish that he would just give me the money or let me dance for it instead. But that isn't how our relationship works, and with the stiff competition for good customers here, I don't complain out loud to anyone, much less to him.

* * * * *

I sense that the Doctor is in a melancholy mood tonight and try to cheer him up by talking nonstop about things we might do together if he ever takes a vacation. I suggest swing dancing, horseback riding, and the beach. I tell him that if he takes me to the beach, I'll make him get up every morning at 5 a.m. and go jogging with me. He laughs and looks down at his softening abdomen. I tell him that in the afternoon I'll bring him piña coladas by the pool and walk around in a thong, making all of the other men at the pool jealous and the women mad. I show him that I am wearing a gold t-back that matches my shoes, trying to get him to relax by being silly and childlike.

But nothing is working tonight, and I worry that he has lost interest in me. I've heard that the Doctor gets sick of dancers after a while—one day he'll just show up and choose someone new to spend his money on. That's how it happened when we first began sitting together, and the dancer who used to sit with him got so angry that I had stolen her regular that she left the club for 3 weeks until the managers talked her into coming back. Now she refuses to speak to me if we end up on the same shift.

"Let me dance for you," I say finally, and he helps me to the table.

I take off my dress and dance two songs for him to the smell of our dinners cooking in the kitchen. This early in the evening, the room is cold and goose bumps rise on my legs and arms, making me feel exposed. I never feel naked unless my body doesn't cooperate with my plans for it. During my second dance, Maya weaves her way over to our table and kisses the Doctor on the cheek. She is completely transformed, wearing a floor-length blue dress and black velvet gloves. Her hair is slicked back into the luxurious ponytail attachment, which swings behind her as she walks. "Thank you for the kangaroo, Tom," she says sweetly. "It's adorable." Then she wipes the lipstick off his cheek with a gloved finger. "Don't want to get anyone in trouble," she says dramatically. The Doctor stiffens, and from my precarious stance on the table, I give her a dirty look. Maya always forgets that the Doctor hates to be reminded that our dates are clandestine.

He motions for her to get on the table, and we dance for him together—black and blonde, a contrast he likes—placing our feet carefully around the bread plates and wine glasses with each move. We are so close together on the small table that when she turns her back to me, her fake hair whisks across my stomach. Then we turn in the other direction, and she steadies me by putting her hands on my hips. The table rocks slightly as we move back and forth.

"Why don't you ever wear your hair down?" the Doctor asks her.

"It's too thick," she lies with a smile. "It looks more glamorous up."

When she leaves with several 20s folded into her garter, I dance one more song. Then he helps me back down onto the bench and hands me his snakeskin wallet like he always does. I take the money out for my dances, $20 each, and for the time we will spend at dinner in advance. He knows I won't cheat him. "We need to trust each other," he told me the first night that we were together in the club. "That's the only way these relationships work."

He still seems too serious.

"What can I do to cheer you up?" I ask, sliding the wallet back to him.

"I would love to cook dinner for you sometime," the Doctor says, ignoring my question and continuing to slowly drum the tabletop with his fingers. "Maybe at my summer home in the mountains."

"Anytime," I say brightly, knowing that all of our plans are safely impossible.

Although I am glad to get him daydreaming, I am surprised that he mentions one of his houses. Usually we just talk about being together in public places, faraway or exotic travel spots.

The Doctor, after all, is married with two daughters nearly my age, Lisha and Kaila. Although they are both attending the same college and are far from being children, I know that he buys them beanie babies like he does for Maya and me. Once when I was taking money out of his wallet, I came across a picture of Lisha in her dorm room that was clearly taken just for him. Blonde and tan, just like me, she was sitting on the side of her bed and wearing a red sundress with small white flowers on it. She was smiling and pointing to a pile of stuffed animals on her bed, many of them the same beanie babies that I have in my locker—the Siamese cat, the snake, the floppy orange giraffe. I remember the photo and picture him at the cash register of a kiosk in the mall, four identical little animals in his hands—two that will be shipped off to Auburn University in a small brown box, two that will be hand delivered to the Sin City Cabaret.

The Doctor always talks very protectively of his daughters. I know so much about Lisha and Kaila: I've heard about their majors, their grades, their sorority, their propensity to date boys that the Doctor thinks have no promise. Sometimes I feel like a Peeping Tom, someone that looks periodically into their lives while always remaining hidden in the shadows.

He talks less about his wife, but I know that they've been together for 27 years, longer than I've been alive. I wonder whether she knows or suspects how he spends his Friday nights. There are only so many "meetings" one can attend, only so many nights of working late that seem believable. Perhaps she no longer cares how he spends his evenings, or perhaps it no longer crosses her mind that he might be interested in the theatrics of romance, in candlelit dinners, in pursuing and being pursued. Or maybe he won't let her give him any of those things, ignoring her when she puts on a silky negligee or scrap of a thong, unable to see her as anything but a mother, a friend, a roommate.

That experience is not unfamiliar to me, I realize. There are nights that I arrive home from work with my head still full of whispers of praise and passionate promises from my customers, my body still electrified with the beat of the dance music and the thrill of the money. "You smell like smoke," Seth says flatly from our bed, even before he can see me or smell me. He is annoyed that I have awoken him from his dreams. "You need to shower or you'll get that god-damn glitter all over the sheets."

"I don't cook much anymore," the Doctor says, breaking my reverie. "I can't remember why I stopped. No time, I guess."

While we wait for our dinner to arrive, the Doctor begins to tell me stories of food that he will cook for me if I join him in the mountains, describing dishes that he used to make during his bachelor days. He had actually considered culinary school instead of medical school at one point in his life but knew that there was no money in it. Now, in this place where he feels beyond reproach for his decisions, he freely dreams up plates of linguini with pesto and chicken, fresh boiled lobsters with melted butter, elaborate salads with melon and walnuts.

"I can't watch you boil a lobster," I say.

"Oh, they don't feel pain," he says. He makes a motion with his hand, dunking an invisible kicking lobster into a kettle. "That kicking is a reflex."

In his fantasy kitchen, the Doctor prepares regions, ethnicities, whole countries—Northern and Southern, French and Greek, Italian and Indian, Thai and Japanese. He bakes for me—cooking up visions of banana bread, zucchini bread, focaccia with olives and onions. He puts me to work in the kitchen chopping, grating, and washing and pictures me fresh faced and ponytailed, wearing flat sandals instead of stilettos. He talks of fresh crushed spices, of garlic and cumin, cayenne and ginger—each with its own objective and attitude. He pours Chiantis and Cabernets, sweet wine from Sauternes and miniature glasses of port. And desserts, of course—he'll serve cheesecake with raspberries, a light tiramisu, carrot cake with thick sweet frosting, homemade baklava layered and brushed with pounds of butter.

"You'll make me fat," I say, smiling and patting my stomach.

"Of course," he says. "Did you know that in Tibet, some mothers rub their babies with butter twice a day? Pure hedonism, no?" I shake my head. I didn't know, but I remember hearing a dancer talk backstage about how to naturally enlarge your breasts by rubbing them each with a full stick of butter every night until it was gone. The fat molecules, she told us, are absorbed by your skin and become part of your body. Maya and I had vowed to try it but gave up after one attempt because it took so long to make a stick of butter dissolve.

* * * * *

He isn't tired of me, yet. He asks me to do four more table dances as we eat our meal, point-ing to the places where the food has settled in my stomach. There. And there. And there. "Really?" I say, running my hands over my abdomen. We taunt each other. A modern-day Persephone, I know what he is looking for. Only so much, I think. Only so much.

But it's just dinner, after all, and this isn't his mountain home or his home in the city. We are still on safe ground, exactly where we both want to be. And when he returns home and his wife asks, What did you have for dinner, dear? it will only be the bloody tangibility of the steak that will weigh on his conscience.

At 8:15, I walk the Doctor to the front door of the club and give him a quick hug good-bye. "I'll see you on Friday if I'm hungry," he says, and I smile at him, sliding my purse underneath one arm. I know that he'll be here.

I move back out onto the main floor, hoping to stir up another dinner date or a couple of table dances before I have to go onstage. As I prepare to transform myself into whatever the next customer is looking for, I remind myself that my value here lies in what I am not as much as in what I am. Not a lover, not a wife. Not a daughter. Never a daughter.

A feast without food, a paradox of sustenance.

Questions for Discussion

1. What are the characteristics of narrative inquiry as fiction and what is the value of the genre?

2. Is this article art or research or both?

3. In what ways does this genre appeal to you or not?

4. What are the merits/limitations of this article?

5. What is the inquiry aspect of this article?

Conclusion: Learning to Be a Storyteller

In this chapter, we have looked at several narrative research examples. I hope that these examples prompted you to go back to previous chapters to see how some of the narrative theories and concepts we have discussed in the book are "applied" or realized in narrative research practice. As you can see, depending on the authors' research paradigms, research topics, and purposes, their choices of narrative research design and process are different from study to study. You could choose a narrative study that can work as a model, but you will quickly find it limiting because your research idea is not exactly the same as the model study that you have in mind. Hence, it is important for all of us to have strong foundational knowledge on narrative inquiry and build up our own narrative research skills, knowledge, and *phronesis* (wise judgment). We will have to be as eclectic as a bricoleur, learning to be as great a storyteller as Scheherazade, so as to appeal to postmodern readers who demand the right to know and wish to expand their knowledge through our research stories. However, no matter how diverse and creative our narrative research process is, our common aim is to understand and explore what it means to be human. Narrative research is deeply rooted in who we are as human because narrative is the most fundamental means by which we human beings understand who we are. That common aim is what brings us together to the field of narrative inquiry. I hope that we are open-minded and open-hearted enough to embrace the unity in the diversity as well as the diversity in the unity of narrative inquiry. To borrow Tolstoy again, narrative inquiry begins where scarcely begins, where a true life begins.

ACTIVITIES

1. Identify some other narrative inquiry examples and share them with your classmates or colleagues.

2. I provide a matrix (Table 9.1) for your review of the articles that I list below. Read the following three articles, and try to fill in the matrix with your analysis:

Patterson, W. (2013). Narratives of events: Labovian narrative analysis and its limitations. In M. Andrews, C. Squire, & M. Tamboukou (Eds.), *Doing narrative research* (pp. 27–46). Thousand Oaks, CA: Sage.

Sermijn, J., Devlieger, P., & Loots, G. (2008). The narrative construction of the self: Selfhood as a rhizomatic story. *Qualitative Inquiry, 14*(4), 632–650.

Yates, L. (2010). The story they want to tell, and the visual story as evidence: Young people, research authority and research purposes in the education and health domains. *Visual Studies, 25*(3), 280–291.

Table 9.1 Article Review Activity

	Patterson (2013)	Sermijn et. al (2008)	Yates (2010)
About the Article			
Narrative Genre			
Research Question			
Theoretical Framework			
Data Collection Methods			
Data Analysis & Interpretation			
Conclusion			
Your Questions About the Article			

©Tom Parish, T. Candon—Root Cellar,
Liberty Township, Geary County, KS 2012

CHAPTER 10

Epilogue

Dear Readers,

We have been together on this journey of becoming narrative inquirers for quite some time now! I hope you have found it illuminating. On this journey, we covered familiar and fundamental issues that piqued our intellectual curiosities. However, I know the journey was sometimes rocky and tiring, as we explored untrodden areas, territories, and boundaries. We attempted to survey the vast field of narrative inquiry as broadly and deeply as we possibly could within limited time and space. I hope that this journey has provided you with epiphanies, joys, inspirations, and motivations to become narrative inquirers.

It would be presumptuous of me to say that you are now well equipped to become narrative inquirers. Until the meaning of the journey truly sinks in, which will take some time, some of you may feel still insecure. We could go on in this journey longer, but I think it is time to stop and pause to look back where we have traveled and what meanings we can gather from our time together. This processing time is an indispensable part of becoming a well-grounded narrative inquirer.

Thinking about the meaning of this journey, I hope its ups and downs have prepared you for the rite of passage to "researcher-hood" that you will go through sooner or later. One of my former research participants, Matto, to whom you were introduced in Chapter 4, told me during his interview how he went through his rite of passage as a Sioux Indian boy when he was eleven years old. His rite of passage to adulthood required him to survive a week alone in wilderness with a small box of matches, a knife, and a blanket. Matto told me how his grandpa taught him survival skills. However, Matto could not have survived if he had not possessed more than such basic skills. Even more important were the wisdom, courage, and strength Grandpa nourished in Matto, which allowed him to complete the process of becoming an adult.

I hope this journey is similar. As you are about to go through a symbolic rite of passage to your own "researcher-hood," I hope you feel that you have been given the skills and tools, but more important, that you are nourished and supported in developing the wisdom you will need to overcome unforeseen challenges that you may encounter in the practice of narrative inquiry. I know you will eventually thrive and flourish as narrative inquirers, who will pass on compelling stories to future generations. In the meantime, you and I have built up some strong camaraderie as narrative inquirers through this journey together.

Ernest Hemingway, in his acceptance letter of the Nobel Prize, wrote that for a true writer, each book is a new beginning where the writer tries again for something that is beyond attainment.[1] To me, then, for a true narrative inquirer, each inquiry is a new beginning where we try again for something that is beyond attainment. In that sense, we are all perpetual beginners. As perpetual beginners, we dare to engage in narrative inquiry to develop bridges that will connect us with other human beings. More than anything, narrative inquiry is about what it means to be human. It is a journey of becoming.

Before I say farewell to you, here is an assignment I want to give you. Write a short story about your deepest secret, one that you have never shared with anyone. Write it in the third person as if you are writing about someone else's secret that you happen to know. Make it as mysterious, compelling, and interesting as you possibly can. Once done, don't show it to anybody. Just give it another read, tear it up into tiny pieces, and discard them into a recycling bin. In this secret assignment, I want you to feel liberated and to experience becoming. This will be the reward for your courage to confront yourself and to be willing to become a perpetual beginner of narrative inquiry, who learns:

To see a world in a grain of sand,

And a heaven in a wild flower,

Hold infinity in the palm of your hand

And eternity in an hour.

     — William Blake (1757–1827)

Now, please do me a favor. Go online and google Andrea Bocelli, *Con te Partiro,* and listen to his song. I will see you around. Be good and be well, in the meantime.

With camaraderie,

J. H. Kim, a perpetual beginner

NOTE

1. See http://www.nobelprize.org/nobel_prizes/literature/laureates/1954/hemingway-speech.html.

Glossary

Aesthetic play: A play of ideas with an artistic meaning-making spirit that is playful and serious at the same time. It is an approach to narrative research design in which the narrative inquirer embodies curiosity and open-mindedness to the research process, allowing room for deliberation, intuition, and anticipation.

Analysis of narratives (Paradigmatic mode of analysis): Polkinghorne's term that refers to a method of analysis in which narrative data are categorized based on the common themes that are derived from previous theory, collected data, or predetermined foci of one's study.

Arts-based narrative inquiry: Narrative inquiry that uses the arts to enhance and deepen research, which includes literary-based (literary storytelling) and visual-based (visual storytelling) narrative inquiry.

Autobiography: A genre of narrative inquiry in which the narrative inquirer's personal life story is told, while giving rise to the "I," the self. It is the inquirer's narrative construction of self-identity.

Autoethnography: A genre of narrative inquiry in which the narrative inquirer systematically analyzes personal experience to illuminate broader cultural, social, and political issues.

Backyard research: Conducting qualitative research in the site that is part of the researcher's daily life where the researcher has personal relationships with research participants.

Bakhtinian novelness: A feature of a story that emphasizes the importance of openness. It includes essential concepts such as *polyphony* (multiple voices), *chronotope* (time and space), and *carnival* (celebration of openness and invisible hierarchy).

Bildung: A philosophical concept that is concerned with nurturing or developing the self to become somebody.

Bildungsroman: A story of one's *Bildung,* or personal growth, that values the process of one's self-development through intellectual and moral endeavor involving the complexity and conflicts of human experience.

Bricolage: A creation or a product done by a bricoleur.

Bricoleur: A person who is a jack-of-all-trades and is adept at performing diverse tasks while integrating multiple sources in the creation. In qualitative research and narrative inquiry in particular, bricoleur refers to a researcher who is adept at multiple methods and multiple epistemological and philosophical frameworks with interdisciplinarity.

Cabinet of curiosities: A baroque method of collecting objects or artifacts that represent the storyteller's past, present, and future, which are used to provoke more stories.

Coda: A final feature of narrative research that aims to bring all the parts of research together in order to fulfill the inquiry aspect of narrative inquiry, providing new understandings of the field.

Confessional reflexivity: The most common type of reflexivity that is used to explore and analyze the vulnerable, evolving self as a way to self-critique and as a personal quest typically used in autobiography or autoethnography.

Critical race theory: An interpretive paradigm that places race at the center of analysis to explain how racial minority groups experience racial oppression and inequalities within White supremacy.

Critical theory: An interpretive paradigm that examines class relationships of domination and subordination that create inequality in society and raises critical consciousness in people for individual empowerment and social transformation.

Currere: A verb form of *curriculum* that means to run the course of one's life. In curriculum theory, it is used as an autobiographical account of one's life that emphasizes the everyday experience of the individual and explores how the experience shapes one's life.

Deconstruction: A branch of poststructuralism, espoused by Derrida, that seeks to understand the deeper meaning of a text to reestablish ethical issues toward the self and the other.

Digital storytelling: A narrative inquiry genre that uses a variety of digital technologies to document personal narratives.

Epic closure: A story that has an ending that presents an "official view," or an absolute solution, without allowing any room to change, rethink, and reevaluate.

Ethics in practice: Ethical issues that arise locally while conducting research. It is also called micro-ethics.

Experience, theory of: According to Dewey, experience is a combination of doings (we do something to the thing) and undergoings (it does something to us in return). Experience has the principles of continuity and interaction in situations, and these two principles are inseparable.

Feminist theory: An interpretive paradigm that places gender at the center of analysis to explain how gender inequality and sexism are pervasive in society.

Flirtation: An approach to data analysis and interpretation that requires researchers to undo their commitment to what they already know and question its legitimacy, while opening up to what appears to be unconvincing and perplexing, and exploiting the idea of surprise and curiosity.

Interdisciplinarity: An approach whereby the researcher explores knowledge in other disciplines outside his or her home discipline, brings back new knowledge, and integrates it into the researcher's discipline.

Interpretation of faith: An approach to data interpretation in which the researcher takes the participant's story at face value, with the belief that the participant is telling a story that is true and meaningful in his or her experience.

Interpretation of suspicion: An approach to data interpretation in which the researcher seeks to find hidden narrative meanings that may not have been told by the participant.

Intersectionality: An understanding of how issues of gender, race, class, and other categories of difference intersect, and how they create a nuanced and complex research phenomenon as a result.

Labov's model: A narrative analysis model that consists of six components: abstract (a summary of the story), orientation (story context), complicating action (an event that causes a problem), evaluation (justification or meaning of the event), result (resolution of the conflict), and coda (a final section that brings the narrator and the listener back to the present).

Life story/Life history: A narrative inquiry genre that is an in-depth study of one's individual life as a whole. It has been popular since the 1980s as a part of biographical movement.

Life story interview: An interview method of narrative inquiry that is based on an unstructured, open-ended format in which the interviewee shares his or her individual life experience.

Literary-based narrative inquiry (literary storytelling): Narrative inquiry that uses literary genres such as creative nonfiction, fiction, short story, novel, drama, or poetry.

Living narratives: Everyday conversational narratives of personal experience or events happening close to the time of the telling. They focus on present happenings that are ongoing or on unresolved life experiences that may not have a beginning, middle, and end. Living narratives are considered the origin of small stories.

Macro-level theory (interpretive paradigm): Big "T" (grand) theory in social and human genres or overarching theoretical and philosophical perspective that the researcher employs for the interpretation of his or her study.

Meso-level theory (methodological paradigm): Theory that is involved with methodological choices that the researcher employs for his or her study.

Micro-level theory (disciplinary paradigm): Theory that is concerned with the researcher's discipline or content/topic area.

Narrative: Etymologically, narrative has two meanings: "to tell" (*narrare*) and "to know" (*gnārus*). It is a way of telling and knowing about human life experiences.

Narrative analysis (or Narrative mode of analysis): An analysis method posited by Polkinghorne, in which the data are configured or emplotted to a whole story that consists of actions and events, in order to sustain the metaphoric richness of a story.

Narrative imagination: An ability to think what it might be like to be in someone else's shoes, taking the perspective of others compassionately and being capable of love and imagination.

Narrative inquiry: A storytelling methodology that inquires into narratives and stories of people's life experiences.

Narrative inquiry genres: Forms that narrative inquiry takes, which include autobiography, autoethnography, *Bildungsroman,* life story/life history, oral history, literary-based narrative inquiry (creative nonfiction, fiction, poetry, drama, etc.), and visual-based narrative inquiry (photographic narrative, photovoice, archival photographs, digital storytelling, etc.)

Narrative smoothing: A method of data analysis and interpretation that is used to make disconnected raw data a coherent story by filling in gaps with imagination.

Narrative thinking: A storytelling tactic with three components: the storyteller's narrative schema (organizing essential information), prior knowledge and past experience, and cognitive strategies (skills that are used for selecting, comparing, and revising the prior knowledge and past experience).

Observer's paradox: A methodological paradox that researchers may encounter while collecting data. Although it is important to collect data in a natural setting, it is paradoxical that the data should be collected systematically by the observer despite his or her potential influence on the data itself.

Oral history: A narrative inquiry genre in which the historical memories of people are explored through oral tradition. The researcher can ask the interviewee to share particular historical moments of the researcher's interest.

Phenomenology: An interpretive paradigm that focuses on the essence of one's lived experience, through the meaning given by one's own subjectivity.

Photographic narrative: A narrative inquiry genre (visual-based) in which photographs are used to illustrate a story that the researcher wants to tell.

Photovoice: A narrative inquiry genre (visual-based) in which participants are given cameras to produce images that reflect the participants' stories.

Phronesis: Ethical judgment or practical wisdom that helps the researcher to do the right thing in a particular time and space during research process.

Poststructuralism: An interpretive paradigm that is opposed to seeking universal truth and unity based on reason. It emphasizes particularities, multiple truths, and differences, while analyzing how knowledge is produced through different power relations embedded in language and discourse.

Rashomon effect: A concept in qualitative research that refers to a situation where different people provide different stories about the same event based on their biases or personal justifications.

Reflexive *askēsis:* A Foucauldian concept of reflexivity that views self as an object of care rather than an object of knowledge. It is a philosophical exercise that utilizes three forms of reflexivity: memory (giving access to truth), meditation (testing of what one believes as truth), and method (fixing what one believes as truth and providing an alternative).

Reflexivity: The researcher's subjectivity that involves critical reflection upon the factors that may influence the research planning and findings, including the role of the researcher.

Reproduction theory: A sub-category of critical theory that explains how social systems function to maintain or reproduce the existing social order.

Resistance theory: A sub-category of critical theory that explains why there are oppositions among people that challenge the oppressive nature of social systems.

Rhizomatic thinking: A branch of poststructuralism espoused by Deleuze and Guattari, with principles of connection, heterogeneity, multiplicity, and multiple entries. It has neither beginning nor end, but always a middle between things (interbeing). The rhizome does not reproduce, but operates by variation, expansion, rupture, and offshoots.

Small stories: Narratives that are performed in everyday conversations, which are not necessarily a part of the big story that is used in life story or life history. Small stories are atypical, non-canonical, unpredictable, and fragmented. Focusing on small stories is considered a new narrative turn.

Story: A detailed organization of events, arranged in a plot with a beginning, middle, and end. It has the connotation of a "full" description of lived experience, unlike narrative. Story is a higher category than narrative, as narratives make up a story.

Visual-based narrative inquiry: Narrative inquiry that uses visual genres, such as photographic narrative, photovoice, or digital storytelling. It is an intersection between visual studies and narrative research in which visual data are used to strengthen narrative inquiry.

References

Abbott, H. P. (2002). *The Cambridge introduction to narrative.* Cambridge, UK: Cambridge University Press.

Acker, S. (1987). Feminist theory and the study of gender and education. *International Review of Education, 33*(4), 419–435.

Adams, T. (2008). A review of narrative ethics. *Qualitative Inquiry, 14*(2), 175–194.

AERA. (2009). Standards for reporting on humanities-oriented research in AERA publications: American Educational Research Association. *Educational Researcher, 38*(6), 481–486.

Agee, J. (2009). Developing qualitative research questions: A reflective process. *International Journal of Qualitative Studies in Education, 22*(4), 431–447.

Allen, J., & Kitch, S. (1998). Disciplined by disciplines? The need for an interdisciplinary research mission in women's studies. *Feminist Studies, 24*(2), 275–299.

Alpert, B. (1991). Students' resistance in the classroom. *Anthropology and Education Quarterly, 22*(4), 350–366.

Altman, R. (2008). *A theory of narrative.* New York, NY: Columbia University Press.

American Sociological Association. (2003). *The importance of collecting data and doing social scientific research on race.* Washington, DC: Author.

Anderson, L. (2006). Analytic autoethnography. *Journal of Contemporary Ethnography, 35*(4), 373–395.

Andrews, M., Squire, C., & Tamboukou, M. (2011). Interfaces in teaching narratives. In S. Trahar (Ed.), *Learning and teaching narrative inquiry: Travelling in the Borderlands.* Amsterdam, The Netherlands: John Benjamins.

Angelou, M. (1969). *I know why the caged bird sings.* New York, NY: Random House.

Anyon, J. (1980). Social class and the hidden curriculum of Work. *Journal of Education, 162,* 67–92.

Anyon, J. (1994). The retreat of Marxism and socialist feminism: Postmodern and poststructural theories in education. *Curriculum Inquiry, 24*(2), 115–133.

Anzaldúa, G. (1990). Haciendo caras, una entrada. In G. Anzaldúa (Ed.), *Making face, making soul: Creative and critical perspectives by feminists of color* (pp. xv–xxviii). San Francisco, CA: Aunt Lute Books.

Aristotle. (1985). *Nicomachean ethics* (T. Irwin, Trans.). Indianapolis, IN: Hackett.

Atkinson, R. (1998). *The life story interview.* Thousand Oaks, CA: Sage.

Atkinson, R. (2007). The life story interview as a bridge in narrative inquiry. In D. J. Clandinin (Ed.), *Handbook of narrative inquiry: Mapping a methodology* (pp. 224–246). Thousand Oaks, CA: Sage.

Atkinson, R. (2012). The life story interview as a mutually equitable relationship. In J. Gubrium, J. Holstein, A. Marvasti, & K. McKinney (Eds.), *The SAGE handbook of interview research: The complexity of the craft* (2nd ed., pp. 115–128). Thousand Oaks: Sage.

Bach, H. (2007). Composing a visual narrative inquiry. In D. J. Clandinin (Ed.), *Handbook of narrative inquiry* (pp. 280–307). Thousand Oaks, CA: Sage.

Baez, B. (2002). Confidentiality in qualitative research: Reflections on secrets, power and agency. *Qualitative Research, 2,* 35–38.

Bakhtin, M. M. (1981). *The dialogic imagination: Four essays by M. M. Bakhtin.* Austin, TX: University of Texas Press.

Bakhtin, M. M. (1984). *Problems of Dostoevsky's poetics* (C. Emerson, Trans. & Ed.). Minneapolis: University of Minnesota Press.

Bal, M. (1997). *Narratology: Introduction to the theory of narrative* (2nd ed.). Toronto, Ontario, Canada: University of Toronto Press.

Bamberg, M. (2006). Stories: Big or small. *Narrative Inquiry, 16*(1), 139–147.

Barone, T. (1995). Persuasive writings, vigilant readings, and reconstructed characters: The paradox of trust in educational storysharing. In J. A. Hatch & R. Wisniewski (Eds.), *Life history and narrative* (pp. 63–74). London, UK: Falmer Press.

Barone, T. (2000). *Aesthetics, politics, and educational inquiry: Essays and examples.* New York, NY: Peter Lang.

Barone, T. (2001). *Touching eternity: The enduring outcomes of teaching.* New York, NY: Teachers College Press.

Barone, T. (2007). A return to the gold standard? Questioning the future of narrative construction as educational research. *Qualitative Inquiry, 13*(4), 454–470.

Barone, T. (2008). Creative nonfiction and social research. In G. Knowles & A. Cole (Eds.), *Handbook of the arts in qualitative research* (pp. 105–116). Thousand Oaks, CA: Sage.

Barone, T. (2010). Commonalities and variegations: Notes on the maturation of the field of narrative research. *Journal of Educational Research, 103*(2), 149–153.

Barone, T., & Eisner, E. (1997). Arts-based educational research. In R. M. Jaeger (Ed.), *Complementary methods for research in education* (2nd ed., pp. 75–116). Washington, DC: American Educational Research Association.

Barone, T., & Eisner, E. (2012). *Arts based research.* Thousand Oaks, CA: Sage.

Barthes, R. (1975). *The pleasure of the text* (R. Miller, Trans.). New York, NY: Hill and Wang.

Barthes, R. (1982). Introduction to the structural analysis of narratives. In S. Sontag (Ed.), *A Barthes reader* (pp. 251–295). New York, NY: Hill and Wang.

Baxter, L. A. (1992). Interpersonal communication as dialogue: A response to the "Social Approaches" forum. *Communication Theory, 2,* 230–337.

Becker, H. (1986). *Writing for social scientists: How to start and finish your thesis, book, or article.* Chicago, IL: University of Chicago Press.

Becker, H. (2004). Afterword: Photography as evidence, photographs as exposition. In C. Knowles & P. Sweetman (Eds.), *Picturing the social landscape: Visual methods and the sociological imagination* (pp. 193–197). London, UK, & New York, NY: Routledge.

Behar, R. (1996). *The vulnerable observer: Anthropology that breaks your heart.* Boston, MA: Beacon.

Behar, R. (1999). Ethnography: Cherishing our second-fiddle genre. *Journal of Contemporary Ethnography, 28*(5), 472–484.

Behar-Horenstein, L. S., & Morgan, R. R. (1995). Narrative research, teaching, and teacher thinking: Perspectives and possibilities. *Peabody Journal of Education, 70*(2), 139–161.

Beitin, B. (2012). Interview and sampling. In J. Gubrium, J. Holstein, A. Marvasti, & K. McKinney (Eds.), *The SAGE handbook of interview research: The complexity of the craft* (pp. 243–253). Thousand Oaks, CA: Sage.

Bell, D. (1987). *And we are not saved: The elusive quest for racial justice.* New York, NY: Basic Books.

Bell, S. E. (2002). Photo images: Jo Spence's narratives of living with illness. *Health: An Interdisciplinary Journal for the Social Study of Health, Illness and Medicine, 6*(1), 5–30.

Bell, S. E. (2006). Living with breast cancer in text and image: Making art to make sense. *Qualitative Research in Psychology, 3,* 31–44.

Bell, S. E. (2013). Seeing narratives. In M. Andrews, C. Squire, & M. Tamboukou (Eds.), *Doing narrative research* (pp. 142–158). Thousand Oaks, CA: Sage.

Benjamin, W. (1969). The storyteller (H. Zohn, Trans.). In H. Arendt (Ed.), *Illuminations* (pp. 83–109). New York, NY: Schocken.

Bertaux, D., & Kohli, M. (1984). The life story approach: A continental view. *Annual Review of Sociology, 10,* 215–237.

Biesta, G. (2002). *Bildung* and modernity: The future of *Bildung* in a world of difference. *Philosophy and Education, 21,* 343–351.

Biesta, G. (2009). Deconstruction, justice, and the vocation of education. In M. Peters & G. Biesta (Eds.), *Derrida, deconstruction, and the politics of pedagogy* (pp. 15–38). New York, NY: Peter Lang.

Blumenfeld-Jones, D. (1995). Fidelity as a criterion for practicing and evaluating narrative inquiry. In J. A. Hatch & R. Wisniewski (Eds.), *Life history and narrative* (pp. 25–36). Washington, DC: Falmer Press.

Bochner, A. P. (2012). On first-person narrative scholarship: Autoethnography as acts of meaning. *Narrative Inquiry, 22*(1), 155–164.

Bochner, A. P., & Ellis, C. (1992). Personal narrative as a social approach to interpersonal communication. *Communication Theory, 2*(2), 165–172.

Bochner, A. P., & Ellis, C. (2003). An introduction to the arts and narrative research. *Qualitative Inquiry, 9*(4), 506–514.

Bogdan, R., & Biklen, S. (1998). *Qualitative research for education* (3rd ed.). Boston, MA: Allyn & Bacon.

Bogdan, R. , & Biklen, S. K. (2007). *Qualitative research for education: An introduction to theories and methods* (5th ed.). Boston, MA: Pearson Education.

Boje, D. (1991). The story-telling organization: A study of story performance in an office supply firm. *Administrative Science Quarterly, 36,* 106–126.

Bondy, C. (2012). How did I get here? The social process of accessing field sites. *Qualitative Research, 13*(5), 578–590.

Boote, D., & Beile, P. (2005). Scholars before researchers: On the centrality of the dissertation literature review in research preparation. *Educational Researcher, 34*(6), 3–15.

Bowles, S., & Gintis, H. (1976). *Schooling in capitalist America: Educational reform and the contradictions of economic life.* New York, NY: Basic Books.

Bowman, W. D. (2006). Why narrative? Why now? *Research Studies in Music Education, 27,* 5–20.

Boyd, B. (2009). *On the origin of stories: Evolution, cognition, and fiction.* Cambridge, MA: The Belknap Press of Harvard University Press.

Boylorn, R., & Orbe, M. (Eds.). (2014). *Critical autoethnography: Intersecting cultural identities in everyday life.* Walnut Creek, CA: Left Coast Press.

Brady, I. (Ed.). (1991). *Anthropological poetics.* Savage, MD: Rowman & Littlefield.

Brinthaupt, T., & Lipka, R. (Eds.). (1992). *The self: Definitional and methodological issues.* Albany: State University of New York Press.

Brooks, P. (2005). Narrative in and of the law. In A. Phelan & P. Rabinowitz (Eds.), *A companion to narrative theory* (pp. 415–426). Malden, MA: Blackwell.

Brown, K. M. (1991). *Mama Lola: A Vodou priestess in Brooklyn.* Berkeley: University of California Press.

Brown, L. M., & Gilligan, C. (1992). *Meeting at the crossroads: Women's psychology and girls' development.* Cambridge, MA: Harvard University Press.

Bruner, J. (1986). *Actual minds, possible worlds.* Cambridge, MA: Harvard University Press.

Bruner, J. (1994). Life as narrative. In A. H. Dyson & C. Genishi (Eds.), *The need for story: Cultural diversity in classroom and community* (pp. 28–37). Urbana, IL: National Council of Teachers of English.

Bruner, J. (2002). *Making stories: Law, literature, life.* New York, NY: Farrar, Straus and Giroux.

Bury, M. (2001). Illness narratives: Fact or fiction? *Sociology of Health & Illness, 23*(3), 263–285.

Butler, J. (1990). *Gender trouble: Feminism and the subversion of identity.* London, UK: Routledge.

Butler, J. (1992). Contingent foundations: Feminism and the question of "postmodernism." In J. Butler & J. Scott (Eds.), *Feminists theorize the political* (pp. 3–21). New York, NY: Routledge.

Carman, T. (2008). Foreword. In M. Heidegger, *Being and time* (J. Macquarrie & E. Robinson, Trans.) (pp. xiii–xxi). New York, NY: Harper & Row.

Carr, W. (2004). Philosophy and education. *Journal of Philosophy of Education, 38*(1), 55–73.

Casey, K. (1993). *I answer with my life: Life histories of women teachers working for social change.* New York, NY: Routledge.

Casey, K. (1995). The new narrative research in education. *Review of Research in Education, 21,* 211–253.

Caswell, H. C. (2012). *Captured images: A semiotic analysis of early 20th century American schools* (Unpublished doctoral dissertation). Kansas State University, Manhattan, KS.

Caulley, C. (2008). Making qualitative research reports less boring: The techniques of writing creative non-fiction. *Qualitative Inquiry, 14*(3), 424–449.

Ceglowski, D. (1997). That's a good story, but is it really research? *Qualitative Inquiry, 3*(2), 188–205.

Chakrabarty, N., Roberts, L., & Preston, J. (2012). Critical race theory in England [Editorial]. *Race Ethnicity and Education, 15*(1), 1–3.

Chamberlayne, P., Bornat, J., & Wengraf, T. (Eds.). (2000). *The turn to biographical methods in social science.* London. UK: Routledge.

Charon, R. (2006). *Narrative medicine: Honoring the stories of illness.* New York, NY: Oxford University Press.

Charon, R., & DasGupta, S. (2011). Editors' preface: Narrative medicine, or a sense of story. *Literature and Medicine, 29*(2), vii–xiii.

Chase, S. (2003). Learning to listen: Narrative principles in a qualitative research methods course. In R. Josselson, A. Lieblich, & D. McAdams (Eds.), *Up close and personal: The teaching and learning of narrative research* (pp. 79–100). Washington, DC: American Psychological Association.

Chase, S. (2005). Narrative inquiry: Multiple lenses, approaches, voices. In N. K. Denzin & Y. S. Lincoln (Eds.), *The SAGE handbook of qualitative research* (3rd ed., pp. 651–680). Thousand Oaks, CA: Sage.

Chase, S. (2011). Narrative inquiry: Still a field in the making. In N. K. Denzin & Y. S. Lincoln (Eds.), *The SAGE handbook of qualitative research* (4th ed., pp. 421–434). Thousand Oaks, CA: Sage.

Cheney, T. (2001). *Writing creative nonfiction: Fiction techniques for crafting great nonfiction.* Berkeley, CA: Ten Speed Press.

Clandinin, D. J. (Ed.). (2007). *Handbook of narrative inquiry.* Thousand Oaks, CA: Sage.

Clandinin, D. J., & Connelly, M. (2000). *Narrative inquiry: Experience and story in qualitative research.* San Francisco, CA: Jossey-Bass.

Clandinin, D. J., & Huber, J. (2002). Narrative inquiry: Toward understanding life's artistry. *Curriculum Inquiry, 32*(2), 161–169.

Clandinin, D. J., & Murphy, M. S. (2007). Looking ahead: Conversations with Elliot Mishler, Don Polkinghorne, and Amia Lieblich. In D. J. Clandinin (Ed.), *Handbook of narrative inquiry* (pp. 632–650). Thousand Oaks, CA: Sage.

Clandinin, D. J., & Murphy, M. S. (2009). Relational ontological commitments in narrative research. *Educational Researcher, 38*(8), 598–602.

Clandinin, D. J., Pushor, D., & Orr, A. M. (2007). Navigating sites for narrative inquiry. *Journal of Teacher Education, 58*(1), 21–35.

Clark, C., & Medina, C. (2000). How reading and writing literacy narratives affect preservice teachers' understandings of literacy, pedagogy, and multiculturalism. *Journal of Teacher Education, 51*(1), 63–76.

Clinton, H. (2014, June 30). Briefing. *Time, 183*(25), 9.

Clough, P. (2002). *Narratives and fictions in educational research.* London, UK: Open University Press.

Cohan, S., & Shires, L. (1988). *Telling stories: A theoretical analysis of narrative fiction.* New York, NY: Routledge.

Cole, A., & Knowles, G. (2008). Arts-informed research. In G. Knowles & A. Cole (Eds.), *Handbook of the arts in qualitative research* (pp. 55–70). Thousand Oaks, CA: Sage.

Cole, B. (2009). Gender, narrative and intersectionality: Can personal experience approaches to research contribute to "undoing gender"? *International Review of Education, 55,* 561–578.

Cole, M., & Maisuria, A. (2007). "Shut the f***up," "you have no rights here": Critical race theory and racialisation in post-7/7 racist Britain. *Journal for Critical Education Policy Studies, 5*(1). Available at http://www.jceps.com/?pageID = article&articleID = 85

Coles, R. (1989). *The call of stories: Teaching and the moral imagination.* Boston, MA: Houghton Mifflin.

Collins, P. H. (1986). Learning from the outsider within: The sociological significance of Black feminist thought. *Social Problems, 33*(6), S14–S32.

Conle, C. (2000a). Narrative inquiry: Research tool and medium for professional development. *European Journal of Teacher Education, 23*(1), 49–63.

Conle, C. (2000b). Thesis as narrative or "What is the inquiry in narrative inquiry?" *Curriculum Inquiry, 30*(2), 190–214.

Conle, C. (2003). An anatomy of narrative curricula. *Educational Researcher, 32*(3), 3–15.

Connelly, F. M., & Clandinin, D. J. (1990). Stories of experience and narrative inquiry. *Educational Researcher, 19*(4), 2–14.

Connelly, F. M., & Clandinin, D. J. (2006). Narrative inquiry. In J. L. Green, G. Camilli, & P. Elmore (Eds.), *Handbook of complementary methods in education research* (3rd ed., pp. 477–487). Mahwah, NJ: Lawrence Erlbaum.

Conquergood, D. (2006). Rethinking ethnography: Towards a critical cultural politics. In D. S. Madison & J. Hamera (Eds.), *The SAGE handbook of performance studies* (pp. 351–365). Thousand Oaks, CA: Sage.

Corbin, J., & Morse, J. (2003). The unstructured interactive interview: Issues of reciprocity and risks when dealing with sensitive topics. *Qualitative Inquiry, 9*(3), 335–354.

Coulter, C., Michael, C., & Poynor, L. (2007). Storytelling as pedagogy: An unexpected outcome of narrative inquiry. *Curriculum Inquiry, 37*(2), 103–122.

Coulter, C., & Smith, M. L. (2009). The construction zone: Literary elements in narrative research. *Educational Researcher, 38*(8), 577–590.

Coulter, D. (1999). The epic and the novel: Dialogism and teacher research. *Educational Researcher, 28*(3), 4–13.

Coulter, C., & Smith, M. L. (2009). The construction zone: Literary elements in narrative research. *Educational Researcher, 38*(8), 577–590.

Cover, R. (1983). The Supreme Court 1982 term: Nomos and narrative. *Harvard Law Review, 97*(1), 4–68.

Craig, C. (2012). "Butterfly under a pin": An emergent teacher image amid mandated curriculum reform. *Journal of Educational Research, 105*(2), 90–101.

Crenshaw, K. (1988). Race, reform, and retrenchment: Transformation and legitimation in antidiscrimination law. *Harvard Law Review, 101*(7), 1331–1387.

Crenshaw, K. (1989). Demarginalizing the intersection of race and sex: A Black feminist critique of antidiscrimination doctrine, feminist theory and antiracist politics. *University of Chicago Legal Forum, 14,* 538–554.

Creswell, J. (2007). *Qualitative inquiry and research design: Choosing among five approaches.* Thousand Oaks, CA: Sage.

Cusick, P. (1973). *Inside high school: The student's world.* New York, NY: Holt, Rinehart and Winston.

Czarniawska, B. (1997). *Narrating the organization: Dramas of institutional identity.* Chicago, IL: University of Chicago Press.

Czarniawska, B. (2007). Narrative inquiry in and about organizations. In D. J. Clandinin (Ed.), *Handbook of narrative inquiry* (pp. 383–404). Thousand Oaks, CA: Sage.

Daiute, C., & Fine, M. (2003). Researchers as protagonists in teaching and learning qualitative research. In R. Josselson, A. Lieblich, & D. McAdams (Eds.), *Up close and personal: The teaching and learning of narrative research* (pp. 61–77). Washington, DC: American Psychological Association.

Dall'Alba, G. (2009). Phenomenology and education: An introduction. *Educational Philosophy and Theory, 41*(1), 7–9.

Darlington, Y., & Scott, D. (2002). *Qualitative research in practice: Stories from the field.* Buckingham, UK: Open University Press.

Davey, N. (2006). *Unquiet understanding: Gadamer's philosophical hermeneutics.* Albany: State University of New York Press.

Davis, K. (2008). Intersectionality as buzzword: A sociology of science perspective on what makes a feminist theory successful. *Feminist Theory, 9*(1), 67–85.

De Fina, A., & Georgakopoulou, A. (2012). *Analyzing narrative: Discourse and sociolinguistic perspectives.* Cambridge, UK: Cambridge University Press.

Deleuze, G., & Guattari, F. (1987). *A thousand plateaus: Capitalism and schizophrenia* (B. Massumi, Trans.). Minneapolis: University of Minnesota Press.

Delgado, R. (1989). Storytelling for oppositionists and others: A plea for narrative. *Michigan Law Review, 87*(8), 2411–2441.

Delgado, R. (Ed.). (1995). *Critical race theory: The cutting edge.* Philadelphia, PA: Temple University Press.

Delgado, R. (2003). Crossroads and blind alleys: A critical examination of recent writing about race. *Texas Law Review, 82*(1), 121–152.

Dennings, S. (2005). *The leader's guide to story telling: Mastering the art of business narrative.* New York, NY: John Wiley.

Denzin, N. K. (1989). *Interpretive biography.* Newbury Park, CA: Sage.

Denzin, N. K. (2005). Emancipatory discourses and the ethics and politics of interpretation. In N. K. Denzin & Y. S. Lincoln (Eds.), *The Sage handbook of qualitative research* (3 ed., pp. 933–958). Thousand Oaks, CA: Sage.

Denzin, N. K. (2014). *Interpretive autoethnography* (2nd ed.). Thousand Oaks, CA: Sage.

Denzin, N. K., & Lincoln, Y. S. (1994). Introduction: Entering the field of qualitative research. In N. Denzin & Y. Lincoln (Eds.), *Handbook of qualitative research* (pp. 1–17). Thousand Oaks, CA: Sage.

Denzin, N. K., & Lincoln, Y. S. (2000). *Handbook of qualitative research.* Thousand Oaks, CA: Sage.

Denzin, N. K., & Lincoln, Y. S. (2011). Introduction: The discipline and practice of qualitative research. In N. K. Denzin & Y. S. Lincoln (Eds.), *The SAGE handbook of qualitative research* (4th ed., pp. 1–20). Thousand Oaks, CA: Sage.

Derrida, J. (1972). Discussion: Structure, sign, and play in the discourse of the human sciences. In R. Macksey & E. Donato (Eds.), *The structuralist controversy* (pp. 247–272). Baltimore, MD: Johns Hopkins University Press.

Devereux, G. (1967). *From anxiety to method in the behavioral sciences.* The Hague, The Netherlands: Mouton.

Dewey, J. (1980). *Art as experience.* New York, NY: Perigee Books. (Original work published 1934)

Dewey, J. (1997). *Experience and education.* New York, NY: Touchstone. (Original work published 1938)

Dewey, J. (2011). *Democracy and education*. LaVergne, TN: Simon & Brown. (Original work published 1916)

Diversi, M. (1998). Glimpses of street life: Representing lived experience through short stories. *Qualitative Inquiry, 4*(2), 131–147.

Dixson, A., & Rousseau, C. (2005). And we are still not saved: Critical race theory in education ten years later. *Race Ethnicity and Education, 8*(1), 7–27.

Drummond, K. (2012). "I feel like his dealer": Narratives underlying a case discussion in a palliative medicine rotation. *Literature and Medicine, 30*(1), 124–143.

DuBois, J., Iltis, A., & Anderson, E. (2011). Introducing *Narrative Inquiry in Bioethics: A Journal of Qualitative Research. Narrative Inquiry in Bioethics: A Journal of Qualitative Research, 1*(1), v–viii.

DuBois, W. E. B. (1990). *The souls of Black folks*. New York, NY: Vintage Books. (Original work published 1906)

Dunlop, R. (1999). *Boundary Bay: A novel as educational research* (Doctoral dissertation). The University of British Columbia, Vancouver, British Columbia, Canada.

Dunlop, R. (2001). *Boundary Bay: A* novel as educational research. In A. Cole, G. Knowles, & L. Neilsen (Eds.), *The art of writing inquiry*. Halifax, Nova Scotia, Canada: Backalong Books.

Dunlop, R. (2002). A story of her own: Female Bildungsroman as arts-based educational research. *The Alberta Journal of Educational Research, 48*(3), 215–228.

Dunne, J. (2003). Arguing for teaching as a practice: A reply to Alasdair MacIntyre. *Journal of Philosophy of Education, 37*(2), 353–369.

Dunne, J. (2005). An intricate fabric: Understanding the rationality of practice. *Pedagogy, Culture and Society, 13*(3), 367–389.

Eagleton, T. (1983). *Literary theory: An introduction*. Oxford, UK: Basil Blackwell.

Eagleton, T. (2008). *Literary theory: An introduction*. Minneapolis: University of Minnesota Press.

Eisner, E. (1991). *The enlightened eye: Qualitative inquiry and the enhancement of educational practice*. New York, NY: Macmillan.

Eisner, E. (1995). What artistically crafted research can help us to understand about schools. *Educational Theory, 45*(1), 1–7.

Eisner, E. (2008). Art and knowledge. In G. Knowles & A. Cole (Eds.), *Handbook of the arts in qualitative research* (pp. 3–12). Thousand Oaks, CA: Sage.

Eisner, E., & Powell, K. (2002). Art in science? *Curriculum Inquiry, 32*(2), 131–159.

Elbaz-Luwisch, F. (2007). Studying teachers' lives and experience: Narrative inquiry into K-12 teaching. In D. J. Clandinin (Ed.), *Handbook of narrative inquiry: Mapping a methodology* (pp. 357–382). Thousand Oaks, CA: Sage.

Ellis, C. (2004). *The ethnographic-I: A methodological novel about autoethnography*. Walnut Creek, CA: AltaMira Press.

Ellis, C. (2007). Telling secrets, revealing lives: Relational ethics in research with intimate others. *Qualitative Inquiry, 13*(1), 3–29.

Ellis, C., Adams, T., & Bochner, A. P. (2011). *Autoethnography: An overview*. Retrieved from http://www.qualitative-research.net/index.php/fqs/rt/printerFriendly/1589/3095-gcit

Ellis, C., & Bochner, A. P. (Eds.). (1996). *Composing ethnography: Alternative forms of qualitative writing*. Walnut Creek, CA: AltaMira Press.

Ellis, C., & Bochner, A. P. (2000). Autoethnography, personal narrative, reflexivity. In N. Denzin & Y. Lincoln (Eds.), *Handbook of qualitative research* (2nd ed., pp. 733–768). Thousand Oaks, CA: Sage.

Ellsworth, E. (1989). Why doesn't this feel empowering? Working through the repressive myths of critical pedagogy. *Harvard Educational Review, 59*(3), 297–324.

Faulkner, S. (2009). *Poetry as method: Reporting research through verse.* Walnut Creek, CA: Left Coast Press.

Ferrarotti, F. (1981). On the autonomy of the biographical method. In D. Bertaux (Ed.), *Biography and society: The life-history approach in the social sciences* (pp. 19–27). Beverly Hills, CA: Sage

Finn, H. (2012, June 1). How to end the age of inattention. *The Wall Street Journal.* http://online.wsj.com/news/articles/SB10001424052702303640104577436323276530002?mg=reno64-wsj

Fludernik, M. (2005). Histories of narrative theory (II): From structuralism to the present. In J. Phelan & P. Rabinowitz (Eds.), *A companion to narrative theory* (pp. 36–59). Malden, MA: Blackwell.

Foley, D. (2002). Critical ethnography: The reflexive turn. *International Journal of Qualitative Studies in Education, 15*(4), 469–490.

Fontana, A., & Frey, J. (1998). Interviewing: The art of science. In N. K. Denzin & Y. S. Lincoln (Eds.), *Collecting and interpreting qualitative materials* (pp. 47–78). Thousand Oaks, CA: Sage.

Foster, J. (2012). *Storytellers: A photographer's guide to developing themes and creating stories with pictures.* Berkeley, CA: New Riders.

Foucault, M. (1970). *The order of things: An archaelogy of the human sciences.* New York, NY: Pantheon Books. (Original work published 1966)

Foucault, M. (1979). *Discipline and punish: The birth of the prison* (A. Sheridan, Trans.). New York, NY: Vintage Books.

Foucault, M. (1983). Structuralism and poststructuralism: An interview with Michel Foucault by G. Raulet, Trans. J. Harding. *Telos, 55,* 195–211.

Foucault, M. (1984). Polemics, politics and problematization. In P. Rabinow (Ed.), *The Foucault reader* (pp. 381–393). New York, NY: Pantheon.

Foucault, M. (1988). *Technologies of the self: A seminar with Michel Foucault* (L. Martin, H. Gutman, & P. Hutton, Eds.). Amherst: University of Massachusetts Press.

Foucault, M. (2005). *The hermeneutics of the subject: Lectures at the College de France, 1981–1984* (G. Burchell, Trans.). New York, NY: Palgrave Macmillan.

Foucault, M., & Deleuze, G. (1977). Intellectuals and power. In D. Bouchard (Ed.), *Language, counter-memory, practice: Selected essays and interviews* (pp. 205–217). Ithaca, NY: Cornell University Press.

Frank, K. (2000). The management of hunger: Using fiction in writing anthropology. *Qualitative Inquiry, 6*(4), 474–488.

Freeman, M. (2006). Life "on holiday"? In defense of big stories. *Narrative Inquiry, 16*(1), 131–138.

Freire, P. (1997). *Pedagogy of the oppressed.* New York, NY: Continuum. (Original work published 1970)

Friedman, S. (1998). (Inter)disciplinarity and the question of the women's studies PhD. *Feminist Studies, 24*(2), 301–325.

Frisch, M. (2006). Oral history and the digital revolution: Toward a post-documentary sensibility. In R. Perks & A. Thomson (Eds.), *The oral history reader* (pp. 102–114). New York, NY: Routledge.

Frye, N. (1990). Culture and society in Ontario 1784–1984. In *On education* (pp. 168–182). Markham, Ontario, Canada: Fitzhenry & Whiteside.

Gadamer, H.-G. (2008). *Philosophical hermeneutics* (D. E. Linge, Trans.). Berkeley: University of California Press.

Gadamer, H.-G. (1975/2006). *Truth and method* (J. Weinsheimer & D. Marshall, Trans., 2nd ed.). New York, NY: Continuum.

Gauch, S. (2007). *Liberating Shahrazad: Feminism, postcolonialism, and Islam.* Minneapolis: University of Minnesota Press.

Gee, P. (2011). *An introduction to discourse analysis: Theory and method* (3rd ed.). New York, NY: Routledge.

Geerinck, I., Masschelein, J., & Simons, M. (2010). Teaching and knowledge: A necessary combination? An elaboration of forms of teachers' reflexivity. *Studies in Philosophy and Education, 29,* 379–393.

Geertz, C. (1973). *The interpretation of cultures.* New York, NY: Basic Books.

Geertz, C. (1980). Blurred genres: The refiguration of social thought. *The American Scholar, 49*(2), 165–179.

Geertz, C. (1983). *Local knowledge: Further essays in interpretive ethnography.* New York, NY: Basic Books.

Geertz, C. (1988). *Works and lives: The anthropologist as author.* Stanford, CA: Stanford University Press.

Gemignani, M. (2014). Memory, remembering, and oblivion in active narrative interviewing. *Qualitative Inquiry, 20*(2), 127–135.

Georgakopoulou, A. (2006). Thinking big with small stories in narrative and identity analysis. *Narrative Inquiry, 16*(1), 122–130.

Gergen, K. J., & Gergen, M. M. (1986). Narrative form and the construction of psychological science. In T. R. Sarbin (Ed.), *Narrative psychology: The storied nature of human conduct* (pp. 22–44). New York, NY: Praeger.

Gillborn, D. (2011). Once upon a time in the UK: Race, class, hope and Whiteness in the academy: Personal reflections on the birth of "Britcrit." In K. Hylton, A. Pilkington, P. Warmington, & S. Housee (Eds.), *Atlantic crossings: International dialogues on critical race theory* (pp. 21–38). Birmingham, UK: CSAP.

Gillespie, R. (1991). *Manufacturing knowledge: A history of the Hawthorne experiments.* Cambridge. UK: Cambridge University Press.

Giroux, H. (1983a). Theories of reproduction and resistance in the new sociology of education: A critical analysis. *Harvard Educational Review, 53*(3), 257–293.

Giroux, H. (1983b). *Theory and resistance in education: A pedagogy for the opposition.* New York, NY: Bergin & Garvey.

Giroux, H. (2001). *Theory and resistance in education: Towards a pedagogy for the opposition.* Westport, CT: Bergin & Garvey.

Glaser, B. G., & Strauss, A. (1967). *The discovery of grounded theory: Strategies for qualitative research.* Chicago, IL: Aldine.

Glesne, C., & Peshkin, A. (1991). *Becoming qualitative researchers.* White Plains, NY: Longman.

Goethe, J. W. (1824). *Wilhelm Meister's apprenticeship and travels* (T. Carlyle, Trans.). London: Chapman & Hall. (Original work published 1795)

Goffman, E. (1972). The presentation of self to others. In J. Manis & B. Meltzer (Eds.), *Symbolic interaction: A reader in social psychology* (2nd ed., pp. 234–244). Boston, MA: Allyn and Bacon.

Goodson, I. (Ed.). (1992). *Studying teachers' lives.* New York, NY: Teachers College Press.

Goodson, I. (1995). The story so far: Personal knowledge and the political. In J. A. Hatch & R. Wisniewski (Eds.), *Life history and narrative* (pp. 86–97). London, UK: Falmer Press.

Goodson, I. (2000). Professional knowledge and the teacher's life and work. In C. Day, A. Fernandez, T. Hauge, & J. Møller (Eds.), *The life and work of teachers: International perspectives in changing times* (pp. 13–25). London, UK: Falmer Press.

Goodson, I., & Gill, S. (2011). *Narrative pedagogy: Life history and learning.* New York, NY: Peter Lang.

Gordon, C. (2012). Beyond the observer's paradox: The audio-recorder as a resource for the display of identity. *Qualitative Research, 13*(3), 299–317.

Gotham, K., & Staples, W. (1996). Narrative analysis and the new historical sociology. *The Sociological Quarterly, 37*(3), 481–501.

Goudy, W. J., & Potter, H. R. (1975). Interview rapport: Demise of a concept. *Public Opinion Quarterly, 39,* 529–543.

Gracia, J. (2012). *Painting Borges: Philosophy interpreting art interpreting literature.* Albany: State University of New York Press.

Grinberg, J. G. A. (2002). "I had never been exposed to teaching like that": Progressive teacher education at Bank Street during the 1930's. *Teachers College Record, 104*(7), 1422–1460.

Grinyer, A., & Thomas, C. (2012). The value of interviewing on multiple occasions or longitudinally. In J. Gubrium, J. Holstein, A. Marvasti, & K. McKinney (Eds.), *The SAGE handbook of interview research: The complexity of the craft* (pp. 219–230). Thousand Oaks, CA: Sage.

Gubrium, A. (2009). Digital storytelling: An emergent method for health promotion research and practice. *Health Promotion Practice, 10*(2), 186–191.

Gubrium, J., & Holstein, J. (1995). Biographical work and new ethnography. In R. Josselson & A. Lieblich (Eds.), *Interpreting experience* (pp. 45–58). Thousand Oaks, CA: Sage.

Gubrium, J., Holstein, J., Marvasti, A., & McKinney, K. (Eds.). (2012). *The SAGE handbook of interview research: The complexity of the craft* (2 ed.). Thousand Oaks, CA: Sage.

Guest, G., Bunce, A., & Johnson, L. (2006). How many interviews are enough? An experiment with data saturation. *Field Methods, 18,* 58–82.

Guillemin, M., & Gillam, L. (2004). Ethics, reflexivity, and "ethically important moments" in research. *Qualitative Inquiry, 10*(2), 261–280.

Gur-Ze'ev, I. (2005). Critical theory, critical pedagogy and diaspora today: Toward a new critical language in education [Introduction]. In I. Gur-Ze'ev (Ed.), *Critical theory and critical pedagogy today: Toward a new critical language in education* (pp. 7–34). Haifa, Israel: University of Haifa.

Gutkind, L. (2008). Private and public: The range and scope of creative nonfiction. In L. Gutkind (Ed.), *Keep it real: Everything you need to know about researching and writing creative nonfiction* (pp. 11–25). New York, NY: W. W. Norton.

Gutman, H. (1988). Rousseau's *Confessions:* A technology of the self. In L. Martin, H. Gutman, & P. Hutton (Eds.), *Technologies of the self: A seminar with Michel Foucault* (pp. 99–120). Amherst: University of Massachusetts Press.

Halliday, M. (1973). *Explorations in the functions of language.* London, UK: Edward Arnold.

Hardin, J. (Ed.). (1991). *Reflection and action: Essays on the bildungsroman.* Columbia: University of South Carolina Pres.

Hart, C. (1999). *Doing a literature review: Releasing the social science research imagination.* London, UK: Sage.

Harvey, D. (1989). *The condition of postmodernity.* Oxford, UK: Basil Blackwell.

Haskell, R. (2014, May). The tinkerer. *Wall Street Journal Magazine,* pp. 100–105.

Hatch, J. A., & Wisniewski, R. (1995). Life history and narrative: questions, issues, and exemplary works. In A. Hatch & R. Wisniewski (Eds.), *Life history and narrative* (pp. 113–136). Washington, DC: Falmer Press.

Heggen, K., & Guillemin, M. (2012). Protecting participants' confidentiality using a situated research ethics approach. In J. Gubrium, J. Holstein, A. Marvasti, & K. McKinney (Eds.), *The SAGE handbook of interview research: The complexity of the craft* (pp. 465–476). Thousand Oaks, CA: Sage.

Heidegger, M. (2008). *Being and time* (J. Macquarrie & E. Robinson, Trans.). New York, NY: Harper & Row. (Original work published 1962)

Heider, K. (1988). The Rashomon effect: When ethnographers disagree. *American Anthropologist, 90*(1), 73–81.

Hendry, P. M. (2010). Narrative as inquiry. *The Journal of Educational Research, 103*(2), 72–80.

Herman, D. (2005). Histories of narrative theory (I): A genealogy of early developments. In J. Phelan & P. Rabinowitz (Eds.), *A companion to narrative theory* (pp. 19–35). Malden, MA: Blackwell.

Herrnstein Smith, B. (1981). Narrative versions, narrative theories. In W. J. T. Mitchell (Ed.), *On narrative* (pp. 209–232). Chicago, IL: University of Chicago Press.

Hertz, R. (1997). Introduction: Reflexivity and voice. In R. Hertz (Ed.), *Reflexivity and voice* (pp. vi–xviii). Thousand Oaks, CA: Sage.

Hollingsworth, S., & Dybdahl, M. (2007). Talking to learn: The critical role of conversation in narrative inquiry. In D. J. Clandinin (Ed.), *Handbook of narrative inquiry* (pp. 146–176). Thousand Oaks, CA: Sage.

Holman Jones, S. (2005). Autoethnography: Making the personal political. In N. K. Denzin & Y. S. Lincoln (Eds.), *Handbook of qualitative research.* Thousand Oaks, CA: Sage.

Holquist, M. (1994). *Dialogism: Bakhtin and his world.* New York, NY: Routledge.

Holquist, M. (2011). Narrative reflections—After *"After Virtue." Narrative Inquiry, 21*(2), 358–366.

Holstein, J., & Gubrium, J. (2012). Introduction. In J. Holstein & J. Gubrium (Eds.), *Varieties of narrative analysis* (pp. 1–11). Thousand Oaks, CA: Sage.

hooks, b. (1994). *Teaching to transgress: Education as the practice of freedom.* New York, NY: Routledge.

hooks, b. (2000). *Feminism is for everybody: Passionate politics.* Cambridge, MA: South End Press.

Housman, L. (1981). *Arabian Nights: Stories told by Scheherazade.* New York, NY: Abaris Books.

Hughes, S., Pennington, J., & Markris, S. (2012). Translating autoethnography across the AERA standards: Toward understanding autoethnographic scholarship as empirical research. *Educational Researcher, 41*(6), 209–219.

Hunter, K. M. (1986). "There was this one guy . . . ": The uses of anecdotes in medicine. *Perspectives in Biology & Medicine, 29,* 619–630.

Hunter, K. M. (1989). A science of individuals: Medicine and casuistry. *Journal of Medicine & Philosophy, 14,* 193–212.

Hylton, K. (2012). Talk the talk, walk the walk: Defining critical race theory in research. *Race Ethnicity and Education, 15*(1), 23–41.

Ingram, D., & Simon-Ingram, J. (Eds.). (1992). *Critical theory: The essential readings.* St. Paul, MN: Paragon House.

Iser, W. (1974). *The implied reader.* Baltimore, MD: Johns Hopkins University Press.

Iser, W. (2006). *How to do theory.* Malden, MA: Blackwell.

Jackson, B. (2007). *The story is true: The art and meaning of telling stories.* Philadelphia, PA: Temple University Press.

Jacobs, D. (2008). *The authentic dissertation: Alternative ways of knowing, research and representation.* London, UK, and New York, NY: Routledge.

Jardine, D. (1992). *Speaking with a boneless tongue.* Bragg Creek, Alberta, Canada: Makyo Press.

Jenkins, R. (1992). *Pierre Bourdieu.* London, UK: Routledge & Kegan Paul.

Johnson, G. (2004). Reconceptualising the visual in narrative inquiry into teaching. *Teaching and Teacher Education, 20*(5), 423–234.

Johnson, J., & Rowlands, T. (2012). The interpersonal dynamics of in-depth interviewing. In J. Gubrium, J. Holstein, A. Marvasti, & K. McKinney (Eds.), *The SAGE handbook of interview research: The complexity of the craft* (pp. 99–113). Thousand Oaks, CA: Sage.

Josselson, R. (2004). The hermeneutics of faith and the hermeneutics of suspicion. *Narrative Inquiry, 14*(1), 1–28.

Josselson, R. (2006). Narrative research and the challenge of accumulating knowledge. *Narrative Inquiry, 16*(1), 3–10.

Josselson, R. (2007). The ethical attitude in narrative research: Principles and practicalities. In D. J. Clandinin (Ed.), *Handbook of narrative inquiry: Mapping a methodology* (pp. 537–566). Thousand Oaks, CA: Sage.

Josselson, R., & Lieblich, A. (2003). A framework for narrative research proposals in psychology. In R. Josselson, A. Lieblich, & D. McAdams (Eds.), *Up close and personal: The teaching and learning of narrative research* (pp. 259–274). Washington, DC: American Psychological Association.

Joyce, J. (1956). *A portrait of the artist as a young man.* New York, NY: Viking.

Juzwik, M. (2010). Over-stating claims for story and for narrative inquiry: A cautionary note. *Narrative Inquiry, 20*(2), 375–380.

Kaiser, K. (2012). Protecting confidentiality. In J. Gubrium, J. Holstein, A. Marvasti, & K. McKinney (Eds.), *The SAGE handbook of interview research: The complexity of the craft* (pp. 457–476). Thousand Oaks, CA: Sage.

Kearney, R. (1993). Derrida's ethical re-turn. In G. Madison (Ed.), *Working through Derrida* (pp. 28–50). Evanston, IL: Northwestern University Press.

Kearney, R. (2002). *On stories.* London, UK, and New York, NY: Routledge.

Kellner, D. (1995). *Media culture: Cultural studies, identity and politics between the modern and postmodern.* New York, NY: Routledge.

Kemmis, S., & Smith, T. (2008). Praxis and praxis development. In S. Kemmis & T. Smith (Eds.), *Enabling praxis: Challenges for education* (pp. 3–14). Rotterdam, The Netherlands: Sense Publishers.

Kermode, F. (1981). Secrets and narrative sequence. In W. J. T. Mitchell (Ed.), *On narrative* (pp. 79–97). Chicago, IL: University of Chicago Press.

Kessels, J. P. A. M., & Korthagen, F. A. J. (1996). The relationship between theory and practice: Back to the classics. *Educational Researcher, 25*(3), 17–22.

Kiesinger, C. (1998). From interview to story: Writing Abbie's life. *Qualitative Inquiry, 4*(1), 71–95.

Kilbourn, B. (1999). Fictional theses. *Educational Researcher, 28*(9), 27–32.

Kim, J. H. (2005). *A narrative inquiry into the lives of at-risk students at an alternative high school: The experienced curriculum and the hidden curriculum* (Unpublished doctoral dissertation). Arizona State University, Tempe.

Kim, J. H. (2006). For whom the school bell tolls: Conflicting voices inside an alternative high school. *International Journal of Education & the Arts, 7*(6), 1–18.

Kim, J. H. (2008). A romance with narrative inquiry: Toward an act of narrative theorizing. *Curriculum and Teaching Dialogue, 10*(1 & 2), 251–267.

Kim, J. H. (2010a). Understanding student resistance as a communicative act. *Ethnography and Education, 5*(3), 261–276.

Kim, J. H. (2010b). Walking in the "swampy lowlands": What it means to be a middle level narrative inquirer. In K. Malu (Ed.), *Voices from the middle: Narrative inquiry by, for, and about the middle level community* (pp. 1–17). Charlotte, NC: Information Age.

Kim, J. H. (2011). Teacher inquiry as a phenomenological *Bildungsroman.* In I. M. Saleh & M. S. Khine (Eds.), *Practitioner research in teacher education: Theory and best practices* (pp. 221–238). Frankfurt, Germany: Peter Lang.

Kim, J. H. (2012). Understanding the lived experience of a Sioux Indian adolescent boy: Toward a pedagogy of hermeneutical phenomenology in education. *Educational Philosophy and Theory, 44*(6), 630–648.

Kim, J. H. (2013). Teacher action research as *Bildung:* An application of Gadamer's philosophical hermeneutics to teacher professional development. *Journal of Curriculum Studies, 45*(3), 379–393.

Kim, J. H., & Macintyre Latta, M. (2010). Narrative inquiry: Seeking relations as modes of interactions. *Journal of Educational Research, 103,* 69–71.

Kincaid, J. (1996). *The autobiography of my mother.* New York, NY: Farrar, Straus and Giroux.

Kincheloe, J. L. (2001). Describing the bricolage: Conceptualizing a new rigor in qualitative research. *Qualitative Inquiry, 7*(6), 679–696.

Kincheloe, J. L., & Berry, K. (2004). *Rigour and complexity in educational research: Conceptualizing the bricolage.* New York, NY: Open University Press.

Kincheloe, J. L., & McLaren, P. (2011). Rethinking critical theory and qualitative research. In K. Hayes, S. R. Steinberg, & K. Tobin (Eds.), *Key works in critical pedagogy* (pp. 285–326). Rotterdam, The Netherlands: Sense Publishers.

Klein, J. (1990). *Interdisciplinarity: Histories, theories, and methods.* Detroit, MI: Wayne State University Press.

Kleinman, A. (1988). *The illness narratives: Suffering, healing, and the human condition.* New York, NY: Basic Books.

Knight Abowitz, K. (2000). A pragmatist revisioning of resistance theory. *American Educational Research Journal, 37*(4), 877–907.

Knowles, C., & Sweetman, P. (Eds.). (2004). *Picturing the social landscape: Visual methods and the sociological imagination* London, UK, & New York, NY: Routledge.

Kohl, H. (1967). *36 children.* New York, NY: Signet.

Komesaroff, P. (1995). From bioethics to microethics: Ethical debate and clinical medicine. In P. Komesaroff (Ed.), *Troubled bodies: Critical perspectives on postmodernism, medical ethics and the body* (pp. 62–86). Melbourne, Australia: Melbourne University Press.

Kontje, T. (1993). *The German Bildungsroman: History of a national genre.* Columbia, SC: Camden House.

Korthagen, F. A. J., & Kessels, J. P. A. M. (1999). Linking theory and practice: Changing the pedagogy of teacher education. *Educational Researcher, 28*(4), 4–17.

Kozol, J. (1991). *Savage inequalities: Children in America's schools.* New York, NY: HarperPerennial.

Kristjansson, K. (2005). Smoothing it: Some Aristotelian misgivings about the *phronesis-praxis* perspective on education. *Educational Philosophy and Theory, 37*(4), 455–473.

Kuhn, T. S. (1962). *The structure of scientific revolutions* (2 ed.). Chicago, IL: University of Chicago Press.

Kuhn, T. S. (1970). *The structure of scientific revolutions* (2nd enlarged ed.). Chicago, IL, & London, UK: University of Chicago Press.

Kvale, S. (1996). *InterViews.* Thousand Oaks, CA: Sage.

Labov, W. (1972). *Sociolinguistic patterns.* Philadelphia: University of Pennsylvania Press.

Lakoff, G., & Johnson, M. (1980). *Metaphors we live by.* Chicago, IL: University of Chicago Press.

Ladson-Billings, G. (1998). Just what is critical race theory and what's it doing in a nice field like education? *International Journal of Qualitative Studies in Education, 11*(1), 7–24.

Ladson-Billings, G. (2012). Through a glass darkly: The persistence of race in education research & scholarship. *Educational Researcher, 41*(4), 115–120.

Ladson-Billings, G., & Tate, W. F., IV. (1995). Toward a critical race theory of education. *Teachers College Record, 97,* 47–68.

Lambert, G. (2004). *The return of the baroque in modern culture.* London, UK: Continuum.

Lambert, J. (2006). *Digital storytelling: Capturing lives, creating community.* Berkeley, CA: Digital Diner Press.

Langellier, K., & Peterson, E. (2004). *Storytelling in daily life: Performing narrative.* Philadelphia, PA: Temple University Press.

Lareau, A. (1989). *Home advantage: Social class and parental intervention in elementary education.* London, UK: Falmer Press.

Lather, P. (1997). Creating a multilayered text: Women, AIDS, and angels. In W. Tierney & Y. Lincoln (Eds.), *Representation and the text: Re-framing the narrative voice* (pp. 233–258). Albany: State University of New York Press

Lather, P. (1999). To be of use: The work of reviewing. *Review of Educational Research, 69*(1), 2–7.

Lather, P. (2008). New wave utilization research: (Re)Imagining the research/policy nexus. *Educational Researcher, 37*(6), 361–364.

Lawson, H. (1985). *Reflexivity: The post-modern predicament.* London, UK: Hutchinson.

Leach, M., & Boler, M. (1998). Gilles Deleuze: Practicing education through flight and gossip. In M. Peters (Ed.), *Naming the multiple: Poststructuralism and education* (pp. 149–172). Westport, CT: Bergin & Garvey.

Leavy, P. (2009). *Method meets art: Arts-based research practice.* New York, NY: Guilford.

Leavy, P. (2013). *Fiction as research practice: Short stories, novellas, and novels.* Walnut Creek, CA: Left Coast Press.

Leavy, P., & Ross, L. (2006). The matrix of eating disorder vulnerability: Oral history and the link between personal and social problems. *The Oral History Review, 33*(1), 65–81.

LeCompte, M. D., Klingner, J. K., Campbell, S. A., & Menk, D. W. (2003). Editor's introduction. *Review of Educational Research, 73*(2), 123–124.

Levering, B. (2006). Epistemological issues in phenomenological research: How authoritative are people's accounts of their own perceptions? *Journal of Philosophy of Education, 40*(4), 451–462.

Lévi-Strauss, C. (1966). *The savage mind.* Chicago, IL: University of Chicago Press.

Lieblich, A. (2013). Healing plots: Writing and reading in life-stories groups. *Qualitative Inquiry, 19*(1), 46–52.

Lieblich, A., Tuval-Mashiach, R., & Zilber, T. (1998). *Narrative research: Reading, analysis and interpretation.* Thousand Oaks, CA: Sage.

Linde, C. (1993). *Life stories: The creation of coherence.* New York, NY: Oxford University Press.

Lindquist, B. (1994). Beyond student resistance: A pedagogy of possibility. *Teaching Education, 6*(2), 1–8.

Loots, G., Coppens, K., & Sermijn, J. (2013). Practicing a rhizomatic perspective in narrative research. In M. Andrews, C. Squire, & M. Tamboukou (Eds.), *Doing narrative research* (2nd ed., pp. 108–125). Thousand Oaks, CA: Sage.

Luttrell, W. (2010). "A camera is a big responsibility": A lens for analyzing children's visual voices. *Visual Studies, 25*(3), 224–237.

Lyon, A. (1992). Interdisciplinarity: Giving up territory. *College English, 54,* 681–694.

Lyons, N., & LaBoskey, V. K. (2002). Why narrative inquiry or exemplars for a scholarship of teaching? In N. Lyons & V. K. LaBoskey (Eds.), *Narrative inquiry in practice: Advancing the knowledge of teaching* (pp. 11–30). New York, NY: Teachers College Press.

Lyotard, J.-F. (1979/1984). *The postmodern condition: A report on knowledge* (G. M. Bennington & B. Massumi Trans.). Minneapolis: University of Minnesota Press.

MacIntyre, A. (2007). *After virtue* (3rd ed.). Notre Dame, IN: University of Notre Dame Press.

MacIntyre, A., & Dunne, J. (2002). Alasdair MacIntyre on education: In dialogue with Joseph Dunne. *Journal of Philosophy of Education, 36*(1), 1–19.

Macintyre Latta, M. (2013). *Curricular conversations: Play is the (missing) thing.* New York, NY: Routledge.

MacLure, M. (2006). The bone in the throat: Some uncertain thoughts on Baroque method. *International Journal of Qualitative Studies in Education, 19*(6), 729–745.

Madison, D. S., & Hamera, J. (2006). *The SAGE handbook of performance studies.* Thousand Oaks, CA: Sage.

Mahon, M. (1992). *Foucault's Nietzschean genealogy: Truth, power, and the subject.* New York: State University of New York Press.

Mahoney, D. (2007). Constructing reflexive fieldwork relationships: Narrating my collaborative storytelling methodology. *Qualitative Inquiry, 13*(4), 573–594.

Malinowski, B. (1967). *A diary in the strict sense of the term.* London, UK: Routledge & Kegan Paul.

Marable, M. (1992). *Black America.* Westfield, NJ: Open Media.

Marcus, G. E. (1998). On ideologies of reflexivity in contemporary efforts to remake the human sciences. In G. E. Marcus (Ed.), *Ethnography through thick and thin* (pp. 181–202). Princeton, NJ: Princeton University Press.

Margolis, E., & Pauwels, L. (Eds.). (2011). *The SAGE handbook of visual research methods.* Thousand Oaks, CA: Sage.

Marshall, J. (1998). Michel Foucault: Philosophy, education, and freedom as an exercise upon the self. In M. Peters (Ed.), *Naming the multiple: Poststructuralism and education* (pp. 65–83). Westport, CT: Bergin & Garvey.

Marshall, J. (2005). Michel Foucault: From critical "theory" to critical pedagogy. In I. Gur-Ze'ev (Ed.), *Critical theory and critical pedagogy today: Toward a new critical language in education* (pp. 289–299). Haifa, Israel: University of Haifa.

Martin, W. (1986). *Recent theories of narrative.* Ithaca, NY: Cornell University Press.

Marzano, M. (2012). Informed consent. In J. Gubrium, J. Holstein, A. Marvasti, & K. McKinney (Eds.), *The SAGE handbook of interview research: The complexity of the craft* (pp. 443–456). Thousand Oaks, CA: Sage.

Mason, J. (1996). *Qualitative researching.* London, UK: Sage.

Mason, M. (2010). Sample size and saturation in PhD studies using qualitative interviews. *Forum: Qualitative Social Research. 11*(3). Available from http://www.qualitative-research.net/index.php/fqs/article/view/1428/3027

Matsuda, M., Lawrence, C., Delgado, R., & Crenshaw, K. (Eds.). (1993). *Words that wound: Critical race theory, assaultive speech and the First Amendment.* Boulder, CO: Westview Press.

Mattingly, C. (1998a). *Healing dramas and clinical plots: The narrative construction of experience.* Cambridge, UK: Cambridge University Press.

Mattingly, C. (1998b). In search of the good: Narrative reasoning in clinical practice. *Medical Anthropology Quarterly, 12*(3), 273–297.

Mattingly, C. (2007). Acted narratives: From storytelling to emergent dramas. In D. J. Clandinin (Ed.), *Handbook of narrative inquiry: Mapping a methodology* (pp. 405–425). Thousand Oaks, CA: Sage.

Mauriès, P. (2002). *Cabinets of curiosities.* London, UK: Thames & Hudson.

Maxwell, J. (2004). Causal explanation, qualitative research, and scientific inquiry in education. *Educational Researcher, 33*(2), 3–11.

Maxwell, J. (2005). *Qualitative research: An interactive design* (2nd ed.). Thousand Oaks, CA: Sage.

Maxwell, J. (2006). Literature reviews of, and for, educational research: A commentary on Boote and Beile's "Scholars before researchers." *Educational Researcher, 35*(9), 28–31.

Maynes, M. J., Pierce, J. L., & Laslett, B. (2008). *Telling stories: The use of personal narratives in the social sciences and history.* Ithaca, NY: Cornell University Press.

McCall, L. (2005). The complexity of intersectionality. *Signs, 30*(3), 1771–1800.

McCarthy, T. (2001). Critical theory today: An interview with Thomas McCarthy by Shane O'Neill & Nicholas Smith. In W. Rehg & J. Bohman (Eds.), *Pluralism and the pragmatic turn: The transformation of critical theory: Essays in honor of Thomas McCarthy* (pp. 413–429). Cambridge, MA: MIT Press.

McCormack, C. (2004). Storying stories: A narrative approach to in-depth interview conversations. *International Journal of Social Research Methodology, 7*(3), 219–236.

McGraw, L., Zvonkovic, A., & Walker, A. (2000). Studying postmodern families: A feminist analysis of ethical tensions in work and family research. *Journal of Marriage and Family, 62*(1), 68–77.

McGushin, E. (2007). *Foucault's askēsis: An introduction to the philosophical life.* Evanston, IL: Northwestern University Press.

McHale, B. (2005). Ghosts and monsters: On the (im)possibility of narrating the history of narrative theory. In A. Phelan & P. Rabinowitz (Eds.), *A companion to narrative theory* (pp. 60–71). Malden, MA: Blackwell.

McQuillan, M. (Ed.). (2000). *The narrative reader.* London, UK, & New York, NY: Routledge.

Mello, D. M. (2007). The language of arts in a narrative inquiry landscape. In D. J. Clandinin (Ed.), *Handbook of narrative inquiry: Mapping a methodology* (pp. 203–223). Thousand Oaks, CA: Sage.

Merleau-Ponty, M. (1962/2007). *Phenomenology of perception* (C. Smith, Trans.). New York, NY: Routledge.

Merrill, B., & West, L. (2009). *Using biographical methods in social research.* Thousand Oaks, CA: Sage.

Miller, D. (2010). *Stuff.* Cambridge, UK: Polity Press.

Miller, L., & Taylor, J. (2006). The constructed self: Strategic and aesthetic choices in autobiographical performance. In D. S. Madison & J. Hamera (Eds.), *The SAGE handbook of performance studies* (pp. 169–187). Thousand Oaks, CA: Sage.

Mills, C. W. (1959). *The sociological imagination.* New York, NY: Oxford University Press.

Miron, L. F., & Lauria, M. (1995). Identity politics and student resistance to inner-city public schooling. *Youth and Society, 27*(1), 29–53.

Mishler, E. G. (1986a). The analysis of interview-narratives. In T. R. Sarbin (Ed.), *Narrative psychology: The storied nature of human conduct* (pp. 233–255). New York, NY: Praeger.

Mishler, E. G. (1986b). *Research interviewing: Context and narrative.* Cambridge, MA: Harvard University Press.

Mishler, E. G. (1995). Models of narrative analysis: A typology. *Journal of Narrative and Life History, 5,* 87–123.

Mitchell, J. (1971). *Woman's estate.* New York, NY: Pantheon Books.

Mitchell, W. J. T. (Ed.). (1981). *On narrative.* Chicago, IL: University of Chicago Press.

Moran, D. (2000). *Introduction to phenomenology.* London, UK: Routledge.

Morgan-Fleming, B., Riegle, S., & Fryer, W. (2007). Narrative inquiry in archival work. In D. J. Clandinin (Ed.), *Handbook of narrative inquiry: Mapping a methodology* (pp. 81–98). Thousand Oaks, CA: Sage.

Morrissey, C. (1987). The two-sentence format as an interviewing technique in oral history fieldwork. *Oral History Review, 15*(1), 43–53.

Morse, J. (2012). The implications of interview type and structure in mixed-method designs. In J. Gubrium, J. Holstein, A. Marvasti, & K. McKinney (Eds.), *The SAGE handbook of interview research: The complexity of the craft* (pp. 193–204). Thousand Oaks, CA: Sage.

Morson, G. S., & Emerson, C. (1990). *Mikhail Bakhtin: Creation of a prosaics.* Stanford, CA: Stanford University Press.

Mortensen, K. P. (2002). The double call: On *Bildung* in a literary and reflective perspective. *Journal of Philosophy of Education, 36*(3), 437–456.

Mosselson, J. (2010). Subjectivity and reflexivity: Locating the self in research on dislocation. *International Journal of Qualitative Studies in Education, 23*(4), 479–494.

Moustakas, C. (1994). *Phenomenological research methods.* Thousand Oaks, CA: Sage.

Munro Hendry, P. (2007). The future of narrative. *Qualitative Inquiry, 13*(4), 487–498.

Munro, P. (1998). *Subject to fiction: Women teachers' life history narratives and the cultural politics of resistance.* Philadelphia, PA: Open University Press.

Narayan, K., & George, K. (2012). Stories about getting stories. In J. Gubrium, J. Holstein, A. Marvasti, & K. McKinney (Eds.), *The SAGE handbook of interview research: The complexity of the craft* (pp. 511–524). Thousand Oaks, CA: Sage.

National Research Council. (2002). *Scientific research in education.* Washington, DC: National Academy Press.

Nussbaum, M. C. (1998). *Cultivating humanity: A classical defense of reform in liberal education.* Cambridge, MA: Harvard University Press.

O'Reilly, M., & Parker, N. (2012). "Unsatisfactory saturation": A critical exploration of the notion of saturated sample sizes in qualitative research. *Qualitative Research, 13*(2), 190–197.

Ochs, E., & Capps, L. (2001). *Living narrative.* Cambridge, MA: Harvard University Press.

Olson, M., & Craig, C. (2009). "Small" stories and meganarratives: Accountability in balance. *Teachers College Record, 111*(2), 547–572.

Paget, M. (1983). Experience and knowledge. *Human Studies, 6*(2), 67–90.

Paley, V. G. (1986). On listening to what the children say. *Harvard Educational Review, 56*(2), 122–131.

Park-Fuller, L. (2000). Performing absence: The staged personal narrative as testimony. *Text and Performance Quarterly, 20,* 20–42.

Parsons, T. (1959). The school class as a social system: Some of its functions in American society. *Harvard Educational Review, 29,* 297–313.

Patterson, W. (2013). Narratives of events: Labovian narrative analysis and its limitations. In M. Andrews, C. Squire, & M. Tamboukou (Eds.), *Doing narrative research* (pp. 27–46). Thousand Oaks, CA: Sage.

Pauwels, L. (2011). An integrated conceptual framework for visual social research. In E. Margolis & L. Pauwels (Eds.), *The SAGE handbook of visual research methods* (pp. 3–23). Thousand Oaks, CA: Sage.

Pederson, S. (2013). To be welcome: A call for narrative interviewing methods in illness contexts. *Qualitative Inquiry, 19*(6), 411–418.

Pelias, R. (2008). Performative inquiry: Embodiment and its challenges. In C. Knowles & A. Cole (Eds.), *Handbook of the arts in qualitative research* (pp. 185–194). Thousand Oaks, CA: Sage.

Personal Narratives Group. (Ed.). (1989). *Interpreting women's lives: Feminist theory and personal narratives.* Bloomington and Indianapolis: Indiana University Press.

Peterkin, A. (2011). Primum non nocere: On accountability in narrative-based medicine. *Literature and Medicine, 29*(2), 396–411.

Peters, M. A. (1998). Introduction—Naming the multiple: Poststructuralism and education. In M. A. Peters (Ed.), *Naming the multiple: Poststructuralism and education* (pp. 1–24). Westport, CT: Bergin & Garvey.

Peters, M. A. (2005). Critical pedagogy and the futures of critical theory. In I. Gur-Ze'ev (Ed.), *Critical theory and critical pedagogy today: Toward a new critical language in education* (pp. 35–48). Haifa, Israel: University of Haifa.

Peters, M. A. (2009a). Derrida, Nietzsche, and the return to the subject. In M. A. Peters & G. Biesta (Eds.), *Derrida, deconstruction, and the politics of pedagogy* (pp. 59–79). New York, NY: Peter Lang.

Peters, M. A. (2009b). Heidegger, phenomenology, education [Editorial]. *Educational Philosophy and Theory, 41*(1), 1–6.

Peterson, E., & Langellier, K. (2006). The performance turn in narrative studies. *Narrative Inquiry, 16*(1), 173–180.

Phillion, J., He, M. F., & Connelly, F. M. (Eds.). (2005). *Narrative & experience in multicultural education.* Thousand Oaks, CA: Sage.

Phillips, A. (1994). *On flirtation.* Cambridge, MA: Harvard University Press.

Phillips, D. C. (1995). Art as research, research as art. *Educational Theory, 45*(1), 1–7.

Pillow, W. (2003). Rethinking the uses of reflexivity as methodological power in qualitative research. *International Journal of Qualitative Studies in Education, 16*(2), 175–196.

Pinar, W. F. (1997). Regimes of reason and the male narrative voice. In W. Tierney & Y. Lincoln (Eds.), *Representation and the text: Re-framing the narrative voice* (pp. 81–114). Albany: State University of New York Press

Pinar, W. F., Reynolds, W. M., Slattery, P., & Taubman, P. (2008). *Understanding curriculum: An introduction to the study of historical and contemporary curriculum discourses.* New York, NY: Peter Lang.

Pinar, W. F. (2011). *The character of curriculum studies: Bildung, currere, and the recurring question of the subject.* New York, NY: Palgrave Macmillan.

Pinar, W. F., & Reynolds, W. M. (Eds.). (1991). *Understanding curriculum as phenomenological and deconstructed text.* New York, NY: Teachers College Press.

Pink, S. (2004). Visual methods. In C. Seale, G. Gobo, J. Gubrium, & D. Silverman (Eds.), *Qualitative research practice* (pp. 361–378). London, UK: Sage.

Pinnegar, S., & Daynes, J. G. (2007). Locating narrative inquiry historically. In D. J. Clandinin (Ed.), *Handbook of narrative inquiry: Mapping a methodology* (pp. 3–34). Thousand Oaks, CA: Sage.

Polkinghorne, D. E. (1988). *Narrative knowing and the human sciences.* Albany: State University of New York Press.

Polkinghorne, D. E. (1995). Narrative configuration as qualitative analysis. In J. A. Hatch & R. Wisniewski (Eds.), *Life history and narrative* (pp. 5–25). London, UK: Falmer Press.

Polkinghorne, D. E. (2010). The practice of narrative. *Narrative Inquiry, 20*(2), 392–396. Poster, M. (1989). *Critical theory and poststructuralism: In search of a context.* Ithaca, NY: Cornell University Press.

Poster, M. (1989). *Critical theory and postructuralism: In search of a context.* Ithaca, NY: Cornell University Press.

Prosser, J. (2011). Visual methodology: Toward a more seeing research. In N. K. Denzin & Y. S. Lincoln (Eds.), *The SAGE handbook of qualitative research* (pp. 479–496). Thousand Oaks, CA: Sage.

Purcell, R. (2004). A room revisited. *Natural History, 113*(7), 46–48.

Rabaté, J.-M. (2003). Introduction 2003: Are you history? In J. Sturrock (Ed.), *Structuralism* (pp. 1–16). Oxford, UK: Blackwell.

Rabinow, P. (1984). Introduction. In P. Rabinow (Ed.), *The Foucault reader* (pp. 3–29). New York, NY: Pantheon.

Rajagopalan, K. (1998). On the theoretical trappings of the thesis of anti-theory; or, why the idea of theory may not, after all, be all that bad: A response to Gary Thomas. *Harvard Educational Review, 68*(3), 335–352.

Rajchman, J. (1985). *Michel Foucault: The freedom of philosophy.* New York, NY: Columbia University Press.

Rallis, S., & Rossman, G. (2010). Caring reflexivity. *International Journal of Qualitative Studies in Education, 23*(4), 495–499.

Rawls, J. (1999). *A theory of justice* (Rev. ed.). Cambridge, MA: The Belknap Press of Harvard University Press.

Reed-Danahay, D. (1997). *Auto/ethnography: Rewriting the self and the social.* Oxford, UK: Berg.

Reeves, C. (2010). A difficult negotiation: Fieldwork relations with gatekeepers. *Qualitative Research, 10*(3), 315–331.

Reilly, J. M., Ring, J., & Duke, L. (2005). Visual thinking strategies: A new role for art in medical education. *Literature and the Arts in Medical Education, 37*(4), 250–252.

Richardson, L. (1990). *Writing strategies: Reaching diverse audiences.* Newbury Park, CA: Sage.

Richardson, L. (1994). Writing: A method of inquiry. In N. K. Denzin & Y. S. Lincoln (Eds.), *Handbook of qualitative research* (pp. 516–529). Thousand Oaks, CA: Sage.

Richardson, L., & St. Pierre, E. (2005). Writing: A method of inquiry. In N. K. Denzin & Y. S. Lincoln (Eds.), *Handbook of qualitative research* (3rd ed., pp. 959–978). Thousand Oaks, CA: Sage

Ricoeur, P. (1970). *Freud and philosophy: An essay on interpretation* (D. Savage, Trans.). New Haven, CT: Yale University Press.

Ricoeur, P. (1991). *From text to action: Essays on hermeneutics.* Evanston, IL: Northwestern University Press.

Ricoeur, P. (2007). *The conflict of interpretations: Essays in hermeneutics.* Evanston, IL: Northwestern University Press.

Riessman, C. K. (2008). *Narrative methods for the human sciences.* Thousand Oaks, CA: Sage.

Riessman, C. K. (2012). Analysis of personal narratives. In J. Gubrium, J. Holstein, A. Marvasti, & K. McKinney (Eds.), *The SAGE handbook of interview research: The complexity of the craft* (pp. 367–380). Thousand Oaks, CA: Sage.

Riessman, C. K. (2013). Concluding comments. In M. Andrews, C. Squire, & M. Tamboukou (Eds.), *Doing narrative research* (pp. 255–260). Thousand Oaks, CA: Sage.

Rinehart, R. E. (1998). Fictional methods in ethnography: Believability, specks of glass, and Chekhov. *Qualitative Inquiry, 4*(2), 200–224.

Roberts, P. (2008). From west to east and back again: Faith, doubt and education in Hermann Hesse's later work. *Journal of Philosophy of Education, 42*(2), 249–268.

Robinson, J. A., & Hawpe, L. (1986). Narrative thinking as a heuristic process. In T. R. Sarbin (Ed.), *Narrative psychology: The storied nature of human conduct* (pp. 111–125). New York, NY: Praeger.

Robinson, T. L., & Kennington, P. D. (2002). Holding up half the sky: Women and psychological resistance. *Journal of Humanistic Counseling, Education and Development, 41*(2), 164–177.

Robinson, T. L., & Ward, J. V. (1991). "A belief in self far greater than anyone's disbelief": Cultivating resistance among African American female adolescents. *Women & Therapy, 11,* 87–103.

Rodrik, D. (Ed.). (2011). *In search of prosperity: Analytic narratives on economic growth.* Princeton, NJ: Princeton University Press.

Rogers, A. (2003). Qualitative research in psychology: Teaching an interpretive process. In R. Josselson, A. Lieblich, & D. McAdams (Eds.), *Up close and personal: The teaching and learning of narrative research* (pp. 49–60). Washington, DC: American Psychological Association.

Romer, C., & Romer, D. (2010). The macroeconomic effects of tax changes: Estimates based on a new measure of fiscal shocks. *American Economic Review, 100,* 763–801.

Ronai, C. R. (1995). Multiple reflections of child sex abuse: An argument for a layered account. *Journal of Contemporary Ethnography, 23,* 395–426.

Rorty, R. (1991). *Essays on Heidegger and others: Philosophical papers* (Vol. 2). Cambridge, UK, & New York, NY: Cambridge University Press.

Rosenthal, G. (1993). Reconstruction of life stories. *The Narrative Study of Lives, 1*(1), 59–91.

Rosiek, J., & Atkinson, B. (2007). The inevitability and importance of genres in narrative research on teaching practice. *Qualitative Inquiry, 13*(4), 499–521.

Rossman, G., & Rallis, S. (2010). Everyday ethics: Reflections on practice. *International Journal of Qualitative Studies in Education, 23*(4), 379–391.

Rousseau, J. (1762/1979). *Emile or on education* (A. Bloom, Trans.). New York, NY: Basic Books.

Rudestam, K. E., & Newton, R. R. (2001). *Surviving your dissertation* (2nd ed.). Thousand Oaks, CA: Sage.

Saks, A. L. (1996). Viewpoints: Should novels count as dissertations in education? *Research in the Teaching of English, 30*(4), 403–427.

Saldaña, J. (2009). *The coding manual for qualitative researchers.* Thousand Oaks, CA: Sage.

Saldaña, J. (Ed.). (2005). *Ethnodrama: An anthology of reality theatre.* Walnut Creek, CA: AltaMira Press.

Santostefano, S. (1985). Metaphor: Integrating action, fantasy, and language in development. *Imagination, Cognition and Personality, 4,* 127–146.

Sarbin, T. R. (1986). The narrative as a root metaphor for psychology. In T. R. Sarbin (Ed.), *Narrative psychology: The storied nature of human conduct* (pp. 3–21). New York, NY: Praeger.

Schafer, R. (1981). Narration in the psychoanalytic dialogue. In W. J. T. Mitchell (Ed.), *On narrative* (pp. 25–49). Chicago, IL: University of Chicago Press.

Schafer, R. (1992). *Retelling a life.* New York, NY: Basic Books.

Scheppele, K. (1989). Foreword: Telling stories. *Michigan Law Review, 87*(8), 2073–2098.

Schneider, A. (November, 1997). As "creative nonfiction" programs proliferate, their critics warn of trendy solipsism. *The Chronicle of Higher Education,* pp. A12–A14.

Schneider, K. (2010). The subject-object transformations and "Bildung." *Educational Philosophy and Theory.* doi: 10.1111/j.1469-5812.2010.00696.x

Schön, D. A. (1983). *The reflective practitioner: How professionals think in action:* New York, NY: Basic Books.

Schrift, A. (1995). *Nietzsche's French legacy: A genealogy of poststructuralism.* New York, NY: Routledge.

Sermijn, J., Devlieger, P., & Loots, G. (2008). The narrative construction of the self: Selfhood as a rhizomatic story. *Qualitative Inquiry, 14*(4), 632–650.

Shea, C. (2000). Don't talk to humans: The crackdown on social science research. *Lingua Franca, 10*(6), 27–34.

Shipman, P. (2001). Missing links: A scientist reconstructs biography. *The American Scholar, 70*(1), 81–86.

Shuman, A. (2005). *Other people's stories: Entitlement claims and the critique of empathy.* Urbana and Chicago: University of Illinois Press.

Smith, D. (2007, January 23). A career in letters, 50 years and counting. *The New York Times.* Retrieved from http://www.nytimes.com/2007/01/23/books/23loom.html?_r = 0

Smith, D., & Thomasson, A. (2005). Introduction. In D. Smith & A. Thomasson (Eds.), *Phenomenology and philosophy of mind* (pp. 1–15). New York, NY: Oxford University Press.

Smith, S., & Watson, J. (2005). The trouble with autobiography: Cautionary notes for narrative theorists. In A. Phelan & P. Rabinowitz (Eds.), *A companion to narrative theory* (pp. 356–371). Malden, MA: Blackwell.

Smith, T. (2008). Fostering a praxis stance in pre-service teacher education. In S. Kemmis & T. Smith (Eds.), *Enabling praxis: Challenges for education* (pp. 65–84). Rotterdam, The Netherlands: Sense Publishers.

Solórzano, D. (1997). Images and words that wound: Critical race theory, racial stereotyping and teacher education. *Teacher Education Quarterly, 24,* 5–19.

Solórzano, D., & Yosso, T. (2009). Counter-storytelling as an analytical framework for educational research. In E. Taylor, D. Gillborn, & G. Ladson-Billings (Eds.), *Foundations of critical race theory in education* (pp. 131–147). New York, NY: Routledge.

Solórzano, D., & Yosso, T. J. (2001). Critical race and LatCrit theory and method: Counter-storytelling. *International Journal of Qualitative Studies in Education, 14*(4), 471–495.

Sontag, S. (1977). *On photography.* New York, NY: Delta.

Soutter, L. (1999). The photographic idea: Reconsidering conceptual photography. *Afterimage, 26*(5), 8–10.

Soutter, L. (2000). Dial "P" for panties: Narrative photography in the 1990s. *Afterimage, 27*(4), 9–12.

Sparkes, A. C. (1994). Self, silence and invisibility as a beginning teacher: A life history of lesbian experience. *British Journal of Sociology of Education, 15*(1), 93–118.

Sparkes, A. C. (1996). The fatal flaw: A narrative of the fragile body-self. *Qualitative Inquiry, 2*(4), 463–494.

Speer, S. (2008). Natural and contrived data. In A. Bickman & J. Brannen (Eds.), *The SAGE handbook of social research methods* (pp. 290–312). London, UK: Sage

Spence, D. P. (1982). *Narrative truth and historical truth.* New York, NY: W. W. Norton.

Spence, D. P. (1986). Narrative smoothing and clinical wisdom. In T. R. Sarbin (Ed.), *Narrative psychology: The storied nature of human conduct* (pp. 211–232). New York, NY: Praeger.

Spradley, J. P. (1979). *The ethnographic interview.* New York, NY: Holt, Rinehart & Winston.

Spring, J. (1989). *The sorting machine revisited: National educational policy since 1945.* New York, NY, & London, UK: Longman.

Spry, T. (2001). Performing autoethnography: An embodied methodological praxis. *Qualitative Inquiry, 7,* 706–732.

Squire, C. (2013). From experience-centred to socioculturally-oriented approaches to narrative. In M. Andrews, C. Squire, & M. Tamboukou (Eds.), *Doing narrative research* (pp. 47–71). Thousand Oaks, CA: Sage.

Steele, R. S. (1986). Deconstructing histories: Toward a systematic criticism of psychological narratives. In T. R. Sarbin (Ed.), *Narrative psychology: The storied nature of human conduct* (pp. 256–275). New York, NY: Praeger.

Sturrock, J. (1986). *Structuralism.* London, UK: Paladin.

Sturrock, J. (2003). *Structuralism* (2nd ed.). Oxford, UK: Blackwell.

Suárez-Ortega, M. (2013). Performance, reflexivity, and learning through biographical-narrative research. *Qualitative Inquiry, 19*(3), 189–200.

Sullivan, A. M. (2000). Notes from a marine biologist's daughter: On the art and science of attention. *Harvard Educational Review, 70*(2), 221–227.

Swales, M. (1978). *The German bildungsroman from Wieland to Hesse.* Princeton, NJ: Princeton University Press.

Sword, H. (2012). *Stylish academic writing.* Cambridge, MA: Harvard University Press.

Talese, G. (1992). *Honor thy father.* New York, NY: Ivy Books.

Tamboukou, M. (2003). *Women, education and the self: A Foucauldian perspective.* Basingstoke, UK: Palgrave Macmillan.

Tamboukou, M. (2013). A Foucauldian approach to narratives. In M. Andrews, C. Squire, & M. Tamboukou (Eds.), *Doing narrative research* (pp. 88–107). Thousand Oaks, CA: Sage.

Tanaka, G. (1997). Pico College. In W. Tierney & Y. Lincoln (Eds.), *Representation and the text* (pp. 259–299). Albany: State University of New York Press

Tate, W. (1997). Critical race theory and education: History, theory, and implications. *Review of Research in Education, 22,* 195–247.

Taylor, E. (2009). The foundations of critical race theory in education: An introduction. In E. Taylor, D. Gillborn, & G. Ladson-Billings (Eds.), *Foundations of critical race theory in education* (pp. 1–16). New York, NY: Routledge.

Tedlock, B. (1991). From participant observation to the observation of participation: The emergence of narrative ethnography. *Journal of Anthropological Research, 47*(1), 69–74.

Thomas, G. (1997). What's the use of theory? *Harvard Educational Review, 67*(1), 75–104.

Thomasson, A. (2005). First-person knowledge in phenomenology. In D. Smith & A. Thomasson (Eds.), *Phenomenology and philosophy of mind* (pp. 115–139). Oxford, UK: Oxford University Press.

Thompson, A. (1998). Not *The Color Purple:* Black feminist lessons for educational caring. *Harvard Educational Review, 68*(4), 522–554.

Thompson, P. (2006). The voice of the past: Oral history. In R. Perks & A. Thomson (Eds.), *The oral history reader* (pp. 25–31). New York, NY: Routledge.

Thomson, A. (2007). Four paradigm transformations in oral history. *The Oral History Review, 34*(1), 49–70.

Tierney, W. (1998). Life history's history: Subjects foretold. *Qualitative Inquiry, 4*(1), 49.

Tolstoy, L. (1998). Why do people stupefy themselves? *New England Review, 19*(1), 142–154.

Tonkin, E. (1992). *Narrating our pasts: The social construction of oral history.* Cambridge, UK: Cambridge University Press.

Tubbs, N. (2005). The philosophy of critical pedagogy. In I. Gur-Ze'ev (Ed.), *Critical theory and critical pedagogy today: Toward a new critical language in education* (pp. 226–240). Haifa, Israel: University of Haifa.

Tyack, D., & Hansot, E. (1990). *Learning together: A history of coeducation in American schools.* New Haven, CT: Yale University Press.

Valencia, R. (1997). *The evolution of deficit thinking: Educational thought and practice.* Washington, DC: Falmer Press.

van Manen, M. (1990). *Researching lived experience: Human science for an action sensitive pedagogy.* Albany: State University of New York Press.

Verhesschen, P. (2003). "The poem's invitation": Ricoeur's concept of mimesis and its consequences for narrative educational research. *Journal of Philosophy of Education, 37*(3), 449–465.

Villenas, S., & Deyhle, D. (1999). Critical race theory and ethnographies challenging the stereotypes: Latino families, schooling, resilience and resistance. *Curriculum Inquiry, 29*(4), 413–445.

von Wright, M. (2002). Narrative imagination and taking the perspective of others. *Studies in Philosophy and Education, 21,* 407–416.

Vryan, K. (2006). Expanding analytic autoethnography and enhancing its potential. *Journal of Contemporary Ethnography, 35*(4), 405–409.

Wahlström, N. (2010). Do we need to talk to each other? How the concept of experience can contribute to an understanding of Bildung and democracy. *Educational Philosophy and Theory, 42*(3), 293–309.

Weber, S. (2008). Visual images in research. In G. Knowles & A. Cole (Eds.), *Handbook of the arts in qualitative research* (pp. 41–53). Thousand Oaks, CA: Sage.

Webster, L., & Mertova, P. (2007). *Using narrative inquiry as a research method: An introduction to using critical event narrative analysis in research on learning and teaching.* New York, NY: Routledge.

Weiler, K. (1988). *Women teaching for change: Gender, class, and power.* South Hadley, MA: Bergin & Garvey.

Weiler, K. (2001). Introduction. In K. Weiler (Ed.), *Feminist engagements: Reading, resisting, and revisioning male theorists in education and cultural studies* (pp. 1–12). New York, NY: Routledge.

Weis, L., & Fine, M. (2000). *Speed bumps: A student-friendly guide to qualitative research.* New York, NY: Teachers College Press.

Willox, A. C., Harper, S. L., & Edge, V. L. (2012). Storytelling in a digital age: Digital storytelling as an emerging narrative method for preserving and promoting indigenous oral wisdom. *Qualitative Research, 13*(2), 127–147.

Winant, H. (2000). Race and race theory. *Annual Review of Sociology, 26,* 169–185.

Winant, H. (2007). The dark side of The Force: One hundred years of the sociology of race. In C. Calhoun (Ed.), *Sociology in America: A history* (pp. 535–571). Chicago, IL: University of Chicago Press.

Winter, S. (1989). The cognitive dimension of the *Agon* between legal power and narrative meaning. *Michigan Law Review, 87*(8), 2225–2279.

Wolcott, H. (1994). *Transforming qualitative research: Description, analysis and interpretation.* Thousand Oaks, CA: Sage.

Wolcott, H. (2002). *Sneaky kid and its aftermath: Ethics and intimacy in fieldwork.* Walnut Creek, CA: AltaMira Press.

Woodson, C. G. (1990). *The mis-education of the Negro*. Trenton, NJ: Africa World Press. (Original work published 1933)

Wragg, E. C. (2012). *An introduction to classroom observation*. New York, NY: Routledge.

Xu, S., & Connelly, F. M. (2010). Narrative inquiry for school-based research. *Narrative Inquiry, 20*(2), 349–370.

Yates, L. (2010). The story they want to tell, and the visual story as evidence: Young people, research authority and research purposes in the education and health domains. *Visual Studies, 25*(3), 280–291.

Yenawine, P., & Miller, A. (2014). Visual thinking, images, and learning in college. *About Campus, 19*(4), 2–8.

Yosso, T. (2005). Whose culture has capital? A critical race theory discussion of community cultural wealth. *Race Ethnicity and Education, 8*(1), 69–91.

Yow, V. (1997). "Do I like them too much?" Effects of the oral history interview on the interviewer and vice-versa. *Oral History Review, 24*(1), 55–79.

Zaner, R. M. (2004). *Conversations on the edge: Narratives of ethics and illness*. Washington, DC: Georgetown University Press.

Žižek, S. (2000). Class struggle or postmodernism? Yes please! In J. Butler & E. Laclau (Eds.), *Contingency, hegemony, universality—Contemporary dialogues on the left* (pp. 90–135). London, NY: Verso.

Zylinska, J. (2005). *The ethics of cultural studies*. New York, NY: Continuum.

Index